THE MORAL DEMANDS OF AFFLUENCE

The Moral Demands of Affluence

GARRETT CULLITY

CLARENDON PRESS · OXFORD

OXFORD
UNIVERSITY PRESS

Great Clarendon Street, Oxford OX2 6DP

Oxford University Press is a department of the University of Oxford.
It furthers the University's objective of excellence in research, scholarship,
and education by publishing worldwide in

Oxford New York

Auckland Bangkok Buenos Aires Cape Town Chennai
Dar es Salaam Delhi Hong Kong Istanbul Karachi Kolkata
Kuala Lumpur Madrid Melbourne Mexico City Mumbai Nairobi
São Paulo Shanghai Taipei Tokyo Toronto

Oxford is a registered trade mark of Oxford University Press
in the UK and in certain other countries

Published in the United States
by Oxford University Press Inc., New York

First published 2004

British Library Cataloguing in Publication Data
Data available

Library of Congress Cataloging in Publication Data
Data available

ISBN 0-19-925811-2

1 3 5 7 9 10 8 6 4 2

Typeset by Newgen Imaging Systems (P) Ltd., Chennai, India
Printed in Great Britain
on acid-free paper by
Biddles Ltd., King's Lynn, Norfolk

For Adrienne,
life-enhancer

Preface

THIS book has been a long time in the writing—longer, no doubt, than the results justify. I have been working on it, on and off, since my doctoral studies, and many institutions and people have helped me in that time.

Various institutions have supported my work throughout the gestation of the ideas presented here. My doctoral studies were financed through scholarship support from the Shell International Petroleum Company and the Rank Xerox Corporation. St Andrews University supported two periods of research leave during my time as a member of its Moral Philosophy Department. The Carnegie Trust for the Universities of Scotland funded my travel during one of those periods, when I was generously hosted by the Philosophy Department at Monash University. More recently I have been helped by a University Research Grant at the University of Adelaide. And my work on the final draft was made possible by a Discovery—Projects Grant from the Australian Research Council.

A few sentences in the book have appeared in previously published work. I thank the publishers of the following pieces for reprinting permission:

'Asking Too Much', *The Monist*, 86 (2003), 402–18.

'Beneficence, Rights and Citizenship', *Australian Journal of Human Rights*, 9 (2003), 85–105.

'Pooled Beneficence', in Michael J. Almeida (ed.), *Imperceptible Harms* (Dordrecht: Kluwer, 2000), 9–42.

Thanking everyone who has helped me to think about the various topics that contribute to this book would be impossible (if only for the unsatisfactory reason that my memory isn't good enough). But I will, perhaps invidiously, single some people out for special thanks. First of all, my doctoral thesis was supervised with great acuity and helpfulness by Jonathan Glover, Derek Parfit, and James Griffin. I have been fortunate enough to receive further comments on entire drafts of the book from Derek Parfit since then: like very many other moral philosophers, I owe a lot to the generosity with which he has shared his intellectual gifts. The searching criticism of my doctoral examiners, Onora O'Neill and the late Bernard Williams, also had a big influence on my subsequent thinking about this topic. And the same goes for many other people at various times since then: among them, I am especially grateful to Will Aiken, David Archard, Marcia Baron, John Broome, Tim Chappell, Tony Coady, Ramon Das, Berys Gaut, Paul Gomberg, John Haldane, Virginia Held, Brad Hooker, Keith Horton, Ian Hunt, Frank Jackson, Jennifer Jackson, Susan Khin Zaw, James Lenman, Thad Metz, Tim

Mulgan, Alex Neill, Basil O'Neill, Philip Pettit, Alan Ryan, Daniel Shapiro, Peter Singer, John Skorupski, Howard Sobel, Janna Thompson, Peter Unger, and Suzanne Uniacke. Several anonymous readers provided very insightful comments on an earlier draft. One whose anonymity I managed to unravel was Larry Temkin, whom I thank for an extraordinarily detailed and stimulating set of comments. Peter Mayer kindly shared his expertise in the politics of development work. And for research assistance during my work on the final draft, I am grateful to Peter Quigley, Nicole Vincent, and Chris Walsh.

I doubt whether any of these people will agree with the following pages. I don't know: none of them has seen the final draft. However, they have all helped to convince me that I had to throw out previous, less satisfactory ones. Many, just as importantly, have encouraged me to continue thinking that the project is worthwhile. And a few have pressed on me what, for someone with my temperament, is perhaps the most important advice of all: 'It will never be perfect—just finish it!'

This is a book about aid to the world's poorest people, and how much you and I ought to be doing to support it. I have spent some periods of my life working, in a modest way, for the kinds of aid agencies I write about here. In doing so, I suppose I displayed some competence, if not much initiative or talent. (Nothing, at any rate, like the qualities of my former boss at Community Aid Abroad in Perth, Jeremy Hobbs, who is now the Director of Oxfam International.) These days, I do give money to Oxfam and Amnesty International, but I do not spend any of my time working for them. Instead, I spend it writing about why it is morally justifiable for me not to be doing so, teaching philosophy, and playing with my children. No doubt part of the grip of this topic for me comes from a need to justify to myself why I am not doing more than this. But I should not convey the impression that I spend a lot of time worrying about whether this is right—and I think that is as it should be. This book attempts to justify that attitude. But as is often the case—both in philosophy and in practical decision-making—I have fewer doubts about my conclusions than I have about whether I have succeeded in accurately articulating the reasons for them.

There is something undeniably odd about describing a major part of your life's work as writing a book that attempts to justify the activity of writing that book. However, if the question addressed in these pages is real, we need an answer to it. And the question is real. Is this book the answer to it? It would be too much to hope that I will succeed in convincing many readers of that. No one writing primarily for an audience of philosophers should delude himself on that score. The view for which I argue—a view intermediate between two more commonly argued extremes—runs the risk of pleasing no one. It will seem over-earnest and moralistic to some readers; a complacent whitewash to others. However, I do hold out the hope that some will concede that I am half right; and others, that I am instructively wrong. That would still be progress, of a sort.

Contents

Introduction 1

Part I Demands

1. The Life-Saving Analogy 7
2. An Argument from Beneficence 16
3. Objections to Aid 34
4. Saving Lives 54
5. The Extreme Demand 70
6. Problems of Demandingness 90

Part II Limits

7. Impartiality, Fairness, and Beneficence 111
8. The Rejection of the Extreme Demand 128
9. Permission 147
10. Requirement 167

11. Overview 189

Appendix 1. Poverty and Aid 205
Appendix 2. The Cost of Saving a Life 215

Notes 221
References 259
Index 279

Introduction

ANYONE who makes some effort to acquaint him- or herself with what the world is like will soon appreciate that, for many millions of people who live outside the cocoon of security and comfort that we enjoy, it is horrible: a wasteland of suffering, deprivation, and injustice. This raises two obvious and urgent questions: Why? And what needs to be done in order to change this? In my view, the core of a cogent answer is this. Poverty is disempowerment, and fighting it means establishing structures of political accountability that can afford protection against the extremes of human vulnerability.

However, defending that view is not the focus of this book. I shall say something about it in what follows—but nothing original: the chapter in which I discuss these first two questions will draw entirely on the opinions of other writers who are much better qualified to answer them. Instead, the focus of this book is on a third, different question: How much ought you and I to be doing about other people's desperate need? We are part of the minority of the world's population able to command enough resources to enjoy a life of ease, comfort, and privilege. How much of those resources ought we to be using to help the many people who suffer from extreme material want? The book is arranged in two parts. Part I argues that this is a real and insistent moral question that needs to be answered by any affluent person. Part II then defends an answer. (In doing so, it also spells out how affluent you have to be for the question to apply.)

To say that my question is different from those first two is not to say any more than that. It is not to say that it can substitute for those questions, nor that it can be answered independently. In particular, I want to disclaim emphatically the idea that exhorting people to individual philanthropy could in itself be seen as an appropriate solution to the problems of world poverty; or that, for individuals, the question of how best to help people who need it can be answered in a politically neutral way. However, I do think that, for anyone who is not a fatalist about human misery, the question I am asking does arise, and calls for answer. If there are effective things that can be done, how much ought I to be doing to support them?

The book does not discuss all of the reasons that might be given for thinking that I ought to use my resources to help the destitute. Rather, it concentrates on an argument from *beneficence*: that is, an argument that simply grounds the moral case for helping the poor directly in their pressing need for assistance. This is not the only reason for thinking that affluent individuals morally ought to help the poor, but it is the simplest and most forceful: I shall explain this in the first two chapters.

The starting point for my argument is simple and familiar: it is a 'life-saving analogy' between helping people at a distance, through aid agencies, and saving a person's life directly, with your own hands. This analogy, familiar from Peter Singer's comparison of giving money to aid agencies with pulling a drowning child from a pond, is by now well known to philosophers—perhaps even hackneyed. However, I think its widespread use says something about its force: a force that it has independently of the utilitarianism with which it is associated in Singer's thought. So, at least, I shall argue in Chapters 1 and 2.

The simplicity of this analogy does help to make a forceful moral point. However, there are good grounds for thinking that it is not only simple, but simplistic. Some critics have complained that it is misleading, even demeaning, to compare destitute Africans to drowning children. They have a point. In some humanitarian crises, a closer analogy would be with domestic abuse. And in all cases, the situation is more complicated than a case of simple rescue. As Sadako Ogata (UN High Commissioner for Refugees, 1991–2000) has said, 'there are no humanitarian solutions to humanitarian problems'.[1] Humanitarian action may palliate, but it does not cure. It is important to recognize this. However, there remains an important truth in the simple analogy. It is that we are morally required to help. There is help that we can give, and there is no excuse for not giving it. The many disanalogies do not affect *this* fact.

Part I defends these claims, and then asks how far this moral requirement extends. In Chapter 5 I present the case for thinking that this leads towards an extremely demanding view: the view that each of us is morally required to renounce spending on practically all of the things from which we currently get enjoyment and fulfilment, in order to do as much as possible to help people who have nothing. Some philosophers accept this. Many others find it absurd, myself included. Indeed, the absurdity of the extremely demanding view is sometimes used as a premiss in arguments on this topic. By contrast, I think it is a conclusion that stands in need of justification, and I aim to supply that justification in Part II.

In discussing this topic, guilt-inducing metaphors are easy to produce. Moreover, there is a good deal of truth in them. We do inhabit a bubble of privilege, floating on a deep pool of human misery. But such metaphors can be misleading. We should not suggest that there is a radical separation in the human experiences and fulfilments of rich and poor. We do not inhabit separate worlds. 'The poor' are people like us, in horrible circumstances. That, of course, is part of what raises so acutely the question I am discussing.

But it is also, I shall argue, part of the answer to that question. I call the argument presented in Part II an argument from the presuppositions of beneficence. Its strategy is to draw attention to the range of goods—above and beyond the basic good of being alive—that ground requirements on us to help each other. And it shows how these requirements only make sense on the assumption that a life of a certain kind—a life that is not restricted in the extremely demanding way—is one that it is not wrong for us to live.

The conclusion I defend does still demand more of us than many of us find comfortable, but it is moderately rather than extremely demanding. My aim in this book is not to preach. (What could be more counter-productive, in writing for an audience of philosophers?) But I think it is important not to duck the challenge of spelling out the practical implications of my argument, and I do that in Chapter 10.

I have made an effort to be careful, but I hope not excruciatingly so: to take an important topic and make it dull would be unforgivable. There is a quick way to read the book, to see whether the rest of it is worth the trouble. Chapters 1, 2, and 5 contain the essence of the challenge presented by Part I; Chapters 8, 9, and 10 give the main structure of my reply to that challenge. Even if you are reading all of the chapters, do not bother with the endnotes, unless you are interested in my references to other literature and asides.

Part I

DEMANDS

I

The Life-Saving Analogy

WE inhabit a world in which the lives of many millions of people are impaired and shortened by extreme material poverty.[1] How much ought affluent people—people like you and me—to be doing to help them? There are different ways of reading this question. One of them furnishes the subject of this book.

One way to take the question is to see it as asking what we collectively ought to be doing.[2] Many people are prepared to agree that the answer to *this* is: much more than we actually are. (The people of the world's richer countries currently give about 0.26 per cent of their gross national income in government and non-government 'aid' of one kind or another to the poorer ones.)[3] But you can agree with this while believing that you are not personally open to moral criticism. After all, there is nothing you can personally do that would itself make the difference between our collectively doing or failing to do what we ought.

The other way of reading the question, though, addresses it to each of us individually rather than all of us collectively. Arguably, every taxpayer is already doing something for the very poor, in contributing through tax to government-funded aid programmes. But what ought you to be doing in addition to this? Let us sharpen the question further. Asking what you *ought* to do can be taken as an invitation to say what would be best—what it would be good to aspire to as an ideal. Or it can be taken as a question about what it would be wrong not to do. We can think that a certain standard of conduct is best—is especially admirable—and still feel comfortable about not meeting that standard ourselves. However, let us look at the tougher question: What standard of conduct towards the poor should we feel morally *un*comfortable with? What is the amount which it would be *wrong* not to give to help them?

It is this question, addressed to each of us individually, that I shall try to answer in this book. That is not because I think that the individual question takes precedence over the collective one. There is a clear sense in which the first, collective question is more important. The only way ultimately to end the scandal of world poverty will be by large-scale collective action—and this will not simply be a matter of raising levels of material 'aid' from rich to poor, either, but requires transforming the political, economic, and social structures that produce these patterns of deprivation.[4] I emphasize this point at the outset, because I do not want to create the impression that I think individual philanthropy is the answer to world poverty.[5] However, the importance of asking what should be done on a global scale about the forces that create and sustain poverty—a question that applies to us all collectively—should not lead us to ignore the further question that applies to each of us individually. How much should *I* be doing to help the poor? I do not want to suggest that this is *the* moral question about world poverty. But it is a question each of us needs to answer, and it is the question I am going to try to answer here.

The first part of my answer is supplied in Part I. It argues that affluent individuals are acting morally wrongly if they do not privately contribute their time and money to voluntary humanitarian or other aid agencies, over and above the contributions they may be making as taxpayers to the aid programmes supported by their governments.[6] In itself, perhaps, this is not a very contentious conclusion. Of course, there are those who disagree with it, and that alone makes it worth trying to show fully why we ought to believe it. But there are many people who believe it already. It is at least as much to them, however, that this first part of the book is addressed. For what anyone who accepts this claim wants to know is, Where does it leave us? If giving up nothing is wrong, how much must I give up before I have done enough? We can only answer this by carefully examining the argument for thinking it wrong to do nothing: we need to see how much further that argument extends. And when we do, we shall find that it threatens to extend a very long way indeed. So far, in fact, that Part I will leave us with the challenge of seeing how to avoid saying that we must give up so much that we jeopardize practically all the sources of personal fulfilment in our lives.

In Part II, however, I shall argue that this challenge can be met.

One particular question has just been picked out concerning what the affluent should do for the poor. Now let us narrow our attention further. There are different ways of arguing for the conclusion that it is wrong for affluent individuals not to contribute privately to helping the poor. I shall be focusing on one of them in particular.

Arguments for this conclusion can be divided into two broad classes.[7] In the first, there are what we can call *collectively based* arguments: these yield conclusions about what each affluent individual ought to be doing for the poor, but derive those conclusions from claims about what we ought to be doing collectively. The most familiar collectively based arguments are arguments from *justice*. For example, there is the following argument from rectificatory justice: we are collectively responsible for the injustice done in creating and sustaining other people's poverty, this puts us under a duty to redress that injustice, and I must discharge my share of that duty.[8] Each of us ought to help them because we together are responsible for their needing help. Another possibility is an argument from distributive rather than rectificatory justice. This holds that it is simply the fact that the world's resources are inequitably distributed, rather than the explanation of how that distribution came about, that gives us a duty to change it, and makes it wrong for me not to discharge my share of this collective duty.[9] A third, distinct possibility is an argument from regulative justice, objecting to the rules that currently govern international trade and financial accountability—to the rules themselves, rather than the distributions resulting from their application. These rules, it might well be argued, unfairly enforce others' poverty for our advantage; we are collectively responsible for reforming them; and I ought to play my part in doing so.[10]

In this book I shall be concentrating on an argument that is different from these. It is not an argument from justice. And the initial version of it that I shall set out shortly is individually rather than collectively based: it does not derive its conclusions from claims about what we ought to be doing collectively. It is not that arguments from justice of the kinds just mentioned are implausible. It is just that, given the complexity of the issues that need to be resolved in order to develop them convincingly, I could not hope to discuss them thoroughly alongside the argument I do discuss. A convincing argument from rectificatory justice, for example, would need to settle the complicated economic and other historical questions required in order to identify the causes of the current stark disparities in global standards of living. But that would only be a first step. It would need to defend a principle for the transmission of responsibility over time, in order to support the claim that we now bear responsibility for injustices committed by past members of groups to which we belong; and it would need to defend a principle of derivation that generates demands on individuals out of such collective responsibilities. I could not hope to do all of that adequately in a book that discussed anything else.

The argument I focus on in this book is simpler and more direct, but at least as familiar and influential. It avoids these complexities, and I think this makes it more forceful. Furthermore, it threatens to support a much stronger and more troubling conclusion. The conclusion that it is most natural to draw from a collectively based argument is that the amount I must give up in order not to be doing wrong—as I shall put it, the amount that can be morally 'demanded' or 'required' of me—is my own fair share of what we ought collectively to be doing.[11] It is not obvious straight off what that 'fair share' is: there is plenty of scope for debating how shares of a collective responsibility should be divided among the members of the group that bears it. However, it is at least arguable that, if the costs of eliminating poverty were appropriately divided among the world's affluent, giving up my share would still leave me plenty to spend on myself. Certainly, it is standardly claimed to be one of the virtues of a 'fair share' view of the moral demands of affluence that it avoids an extremely demanding conclusion.[12] The argument that I develop here, by contrast, does threaten to support a conclusion that is extremely demanding. My concern in Part I will be to develop this line of argument into what I hold to be its strongest form. In Part II the aim will be to respond to it.

1.1 THE LIFE-SAVING ANALOGY

The argument I am going to develop will be assembled carefully over the course of four chapters. But let me start with a simple initial statement of the central idea. (We shall find out in the following chapters that this initial statement is *too* simple; but we'll come to the need for complications and qualifications as we go along.)

The initial thought that is at the heart of my argument is one that many people have had. The life of one of the world's poorest people could be transformed by an amount of money that would mean very little to me, and I could easily give that money to an aid agency to help it to have that effect. Even if I have nothing to do with creating the poverty that afflicts much of the world's population, there remains a serious moral question what I am prepared to do in response to it. And it is hard to see how doing nothing could be right. After all, if I were confronted directly by the great need of someone whom I could help at negligible cost to myself, it would certainly be wrong not to help.[13] So unless being confronted directly makes a difference—and why should it?—the same should be said about giving money to aid agencies. Moreover, since volunteering my time to work for such agencies would help them to achieve more, the argument applies to contributions of time as well as money.

Stated in this way, the argument is individually based: it does not derive its conclusion concerning what I ought to do from claims about what we all ought to be doing. The strategy is the simple one of maintaining that not contributing time and money to aid agencies is morally analogous to failing to help needy people directly. Attempts to formulate this argument carefully have often concentrated on comparing contributions to aid agencies with the direct saving of life, as this puts the case in its starkest and clearest form.[14] I shall do the same here. The analogy I shall examine and defend is a life-saving analogy.[15]

Pressing this analogy runs the risk of suggesting that threats to life exhaust what is bad about extreme poverty. That is far from true. Indeed, it is arguable that threats to life are not even the worst thing about destitution: what matters more is the way it diminishes the quality, rather than merely the duration, of people's lives.[16] However, we can acknowledge this and still sensibly point out that at least one consequence of extreme poverty is threats to people's lives. And that is all that is needed for a powerful statement of the life-saving analogy. If I could easily save someone's life right in front of me, and there are no mitigating circumstances, then it seems obvious to most of us that not doing so would be wrong—whether or not I have done anything to cause the threat in the first place. This would be a fundamental failure to take other people's interests seriously, and that makes it morally wrong. But if aid agencies save lives that would otherwise be lost through the diseases, accidents, and starvation caused by poverty, then how is the failure to make a small but life-saving donation to such agencies relevantly different? There *are* differences, of course. My relationship with the needy people is direct or immediate in the one case, indirect or mediated in the other. This is true in two separate ways: their need is presented to me immediately when it is right in front of me, and any help I give to people at a distance is given indirectly, since it is mediated by the agency through which I give it. But what needs to be shown is why these differences should be thought relevant to whether not helping is wrong. And it is hard to see what good grounds could be given for thinking that they should.[17]

I said above that this is a familiar and influential argument. Of course, many people find it implausible to suggest that not giving money to aid agencies is as bad as letting people die right in front of you. I find that implausible too, and I explain why in the next chapter.[a] But advocating the life-saving analogy—the claim that there is a morally relevant analogy between saving lives directly and contributing to aid agencies—need not involve going that far. The claim I shall be defending is that the analogy shows why not giving to aid agencies is wrong: it is wrong for the same reason that it is wrong not to save a life when you could easily have done so. But I shall not be arguing that it is *as* wrong.

One radical way to resist this line of argument would be to deny that there is actually anything wrong with letting people die right in front of you.[18] This sort of view is not something I am going to attempt to answer here. It is not that I think there is simply nothing to be said in reply to it. But the differences of moral outlook between someone who holds this view and those of us who do not are so great that we need to know a good deal more about the rest of his moral opinions before knowing where to start. In explaining what is wrong with letting someone die when you could easily have helped, it makes sense to point out that this involves a failure to take adequate account of other people's interests. But this is not much good as a reply to someone who is just as likely to be denying *that*. The difference of moral opinion is obviously a deep one: we need to know which moral claims are accepted by such a radical opponent before knowing what kind of argument it makes sense to respond with. I shall not try to survey the

[a] Sect. 2.4.

possibilities here. Instead, I shall assume a readership that agrees at least with this starting point, and offer what follows to them.

There are different ways of developing an argument in defence of the life-saving analogy. However, all of them have a broad common structure. They begin by offering an account of *why* it is wrong to let someone die directly, when you could easily have helped. They then aim to show that those reasons equally support the view that it is wrong not to give to aid agencies. Read one way, the question why it is wrong to let a person die directly is the one I have just declined to answer—the question how to refute the view of someone who disagrees. However, there is a less ambitious way to take it. Those of us who already agree with the judgement can ask what there is to be said in its favour. Different ways of answering this question offer us different ways of defending the life-saving analogy. Let me say a little now to indicate what is distinctive about the argument that follows.

1.2 SUBSUMPTIVE AND NON-SUBSUMPTIVE VERSIONS

I do not claim to have invented what I am calling the 'life-saving analogy'. Peter Singer did that, in 1972, when he compared the failure to donate money towards relief of the then-recent Bengal famine with the failure to stop to pull a drowning child from a shallow pond.[19] Since then his example, and the analogy he drew with emergency relief aid at a distance, have been cited, discussed, and reused in many different places.[20]

Singer's own presentations of the life-saving analogy differ slightly, but they share a common structure. Their form is subsumptive: they treat the task of justifying moral judgements about particular actions as the task of identifying general moral principles under which those judgements can be subsumed as instances.[21] According to Singer, we can explain what is wrong about failing to pull the child from the pond by invoking the principle that the failure to avert great harm to someone else at a comparatively insignificant cost to yourself is wrong (other things equal).[22] The argument for the life-saving analogy then continues by pointing out that this principle covers the failure to contribute to aid agencies as well; therefore that must be wrong too.

The version of the life-saving analogy that I shall defend in this book is different from Singer's. In part, this is because I share with others some general worries about the subsumptive picture of moral justification.[23] One obvious worry concerns how the justifying principles appealed to in this style of argument are themselves justified. Another concerns the status of the 'other things equal' clause, and whether it can ever be fully eliminated. However, I do not propose to develop these lines of criticism: the emphasis will be on pursuing a positive alternative argument of my own. There is a second reason for wanting to do this. It is that there is a deeper methodological challenge that needs to be addressed not only by arguments for the life-saving analogy but by many other arguments for revisionary moral conclusions too. I shall describe this challenge shortly. My main reason for wanting to formulate a different argument for the life-saving analogy will be to show how this challenge can be met.

What are we complaining about when we say that your failure to provide life-saving help was wrong? Rather than looking for a principle under which to subsume this judgement, I propose instead to characterize the attitudes towards other people that you are being criticized for lacking. The most natural way to explain what is wrong with egregious failures to help other people is to make two simple points. Other people's interests in receiving our help give us a clear reason to help them; and the failure to respond to this reason by going ahead and helping them can be morally wrong. When it is wrong, this is because it is a failure to display an adequate practical concern for other people's interests—a failure of *beneficence*.[24] This, I think, is the most natural and straightforward way to develop the life-saving analogy. If what is wrong about failing to make a small effort to save a life directly is that it displays a failure of beneficence, then there is a strong case for thinking that the same failure is displayed by non-contribution to aid agencies.[25]

This non-subsumptive way of developing the life-saving analogy is not complicated. It can plausibly claim to capture the straightforward force of the analogy. It is the plain fact of the acute need of the world's poorest people that makes it wrong to do nothing about it—independently of any questions about your responsibility for creating it—in the same way that people's acute need makes it wrong not to help them when they are right in front of you. However, it also faces a straightforward challenge, which will have to be met if this argument is to be taken seriously.

1.3 THE METHODOLOGICAL CHALLENGE

To see this problem, let us return for a moment to Singer's subsumptive version of the argument for the life-saving analogy.

That argument has a three-stage structure. At stage 1 it begins with some confidently endorsed moral judgements—judgements about the refusal to make a small sacrifice to save someone's life directly. From these, at stage 2, a general principle is abstracted: the principle that failing to avert great harm to someone else at a comparatively insignificant cost to oneself is wrong (other things equal). This principle is then invoked to support, at stage 3, another moral judgement: that contributing nothing to aid agencies is wrong. In this way, it is argued that the stage 3 judgement is justified, and that if our ethical outlook does not include this judgement, it ought to be revised.

An argument with this structure invites the following dilemma. It looks as though what we begin with at stage 1 will always underdetermine the content of the stage 2 principle, unless it simply begs the question outright. We can hardly include among the stage 1 judgements the one we are aiming to justify: that would beg the question. But if we do not, we face the problem that there will be many possible ways to generalize at stage 2 from the judgements we do begin with. In particular, there will always—as long as we have not simply begged the question—be a way of generalizing from them that yields very different conclusions at stage 3. In the case that concerns us, a rival principle to consider is this: failing to help another person *directly*, *in an immediately presented emergency*, at a comparatively insignificant cost to oneself is wrong (other things equal). *This* more restricted principle is consistent with the same set of stage 1 judgements about saving lives directly. But it is also consistent with the judgement that, where my relation to a harm I could avert is not direct and immediate, doing nothing about it is *not* wrong.

Indeed, what makes this methodological challenge especially awkward is that, to almost everyone, it is about as obvious that there is a moral difference between your relation to someone whose life is threatened right in front of you and someone starving in another country as it is that failing to help in the former case is wrong.[26] The need in the former case is presented to you directly and urgently, as demanding an immediate response, and this fact is clearly taken by most of us to be morally important. If we are beginning, at stage 1, with confidently endorsed moral judgements, then one of these may be the judgement that it is wrong not to help someone whose life you could save directly at small cost; but another is that this is morally different from not contributing to helping people at a distance.[27]

It might seem tempting to locate the problem here in the subsumptive picture of moral justification. However, the methodological challenge is general enough to mean that *any* argument for the life-saving analogy will confront it. After all, any argument for the life-saving analogy proceeds by taking an initial group of judgements (about the direct saving of life), and deriving from them a test for good ethical judgements; it then applies that test to a second group of judgements (about giving to aid agencies). Prescind from the question of whether the test should properly be conceived as a principle under which correct moral judgements are to be subsumed. The form of the problem remains: if the test itself is supposed to gain its authority from a group of confidently endorsed initial judgements, what prevents someone from invoking further judgements as a ground for revising the test?

My aim in the next chapter is to formulate an argument for the life-saving analogy that meets this challenge. I think the methodological challenge can be met by an argument with the three-stage structure, as long as it works from the judgements endorsed at stage 1 by plausibly identifying the *reasons* for making them. As I have indicated, the version of the argument I shall be developing explains the wrongness of not helping other people as a failure with respect to a form of morally important concern—namely, beneficence.

The concern to identify what is 'morally required' and (later) 'morally permitted' will seem to some readers to carry with it a suspect picture of the nature of ethical enquiry. On that picture, morality is viewed as a system of prohibitions and permissions, and the business of normative moral enquiry is to establish the extent of the prohibitions: then, as long as we avoid what is forbidden, our action is morally impeccable. But this, it can be complained, is a narrow-mindedly legalistic approach to ethical thought. The kind of ethical reflection that ought to matter to us is reflection on how to live well, not what to avoid.[28]

Actually, I agree that it is a serious distortion of ethical thought to reduce it to a concern with avoiding what is wrong. But I am not doing that. All I need you to agree with is that *one* important part of our ethical thought concerns which ways of acting and living there is decisive reason to reject. It is not just that there is a lot to be said for saving a person's life when you could easily do so: not doing so can be *wrong*. This ought to engage us because it concerns one of the most basic forms of consideration for other people.[29] Any ethical outlook worthy of respect will be one according to which others' interests are taken seriously—seriously enough to count threats to others' lives for more than inconveniences to oneself. And if so, why not when they are distant? This is enough to generate the challenge that this book has set out to address. I shall continue to discuss this challenge by talking about moral requirement and permission. However, for someone to whom this is uncongenial, everything I say could be rephrased instead as a discussion of the ways of living that could deserve our respect or emulation, all things considered.

2

An Argument from Beneficence

ACCORDING to the life-saving analogy, it is wrong not to donate your time and money to humanitarian aid agencies, because refusing to do this is, in a morally relevant way, like failing to save someone's life right in front of you. There are different ways of arguing for this view, and in this chapter I am going to develop my own in some detail.

The central idea I shall pursue is that these two sorts of inaction are morally analogous because both amount to a failure of practical concern for others' interests. In line with current philosophical usage, I shall refer to this practical concern as 'beneficence'.[1] Admittedly, this departs from the broader usage that the etymology of this word suggests: as I shall be using it, it will not refer to doing good generally, but only to the morally appropriate furthering of other people's interests.[2] In this chapter I start by describing beneficence and its application to the life-saving analogy. Then I consider the main forms that a methodological challenge to this version of the life-saving analogy can take, and show why they fail.

2.1 BENEFICENCE

Beneficence, as I understand it, is a practical concern for other people's interests.[3] In calling it a *practical* concern, I mean that it is a concern expressed in action. Beneficence is more than simply wishing someone well: it involves acting appropriately to help other people when they will benefit from it or, more strongly, when they need it.[4] And in calling it a practical *concern*, I mean that there is a distinctive class of considerations that a beneficent person characteristically regards as good reasons for action.[5] I shall call these considerations 'a beneficent person's reasons for action'.[6] The core of beneficence is this: it involves helping other people, and doing so because you regard the fact that it will be good for them as a good reason for helping them.

This simple description of the core of beneficence must be qualified in two important ways, however. First, we need to be careful not to misrepresent the content of a beneficent person's reasons—that is, the object of her concern. A concern for *other people's interests*, under that description, would be strangely abstract and impersonal. However, it does seem right to say that this description picks out the extension of the class of particular things that beneficent people are characteristically concerned about. Beneficence involves treating as reasons for an action facts that belong to the class *ways in which the action is in someone else's interests*. Thus, when we describe beneficence as a concern for other people's interests, we must make it clear that this description is to be read as identifying a feature that the objects of that concern characteristically possess in common, rather than as specifying the object of that concern itself. I shall call this 'reading the description extensionally'.

The second qualification is that, if 'beneficence' is really the name of a quality that we should be criticized for lacking, then it must name a practical concern that is *discriminating*.[7] According to most of us, acting from a concern to further someone else's interests might be improvident (for example, if I gave all my savings to the Queen), irresponsible (if I attended to the needs of strangers rather than the equal needs of my children), unjust (if I stole to help my friends), or crassly insensitive (if I helped you carry out a malicious plan).[8] The quality of beneficence we should aspire to have involves more than simply a practical concern to further other people's interests: it includes a sensitivity to when and how it is right to further other people's interests. A discerningly beneficent person will recognize the ways in which various other considerations can *countervail* against the force of others' interests as reasons on which it is appropriate to act. The interests in question may not be ones I ought to further (as when they are malicious), the available means of promoting them might be wrong (as in stealing to help my friends), or there might be something more important that I ought to be doing instead (like looking after my own children). A discerningly beneficent person is someone who characteristically acts to further others' interests, for that reason, when that reason is not countervailed against by considerations of these various kinds.

Notice that there is a distinction to be made between two different ways in which we can treat considerations as countervailing. The most obvious way is given by the following sort of case. Suppose someone needs my help, but the only way I could help him is by stealing or neglecting my children: many of us think that, in at least some such cases, it would be wrong to help. This is not because of the absence of a good reason for helping, though: his needs do still provide me with a good *pro tanto* reason to help him. Rather, there is a stronger reason to do something else. In this sort of case, the reason to help him is outweighed. However, some countervailing considerations seem to work in a different way. Suppose you need my help to carry out a malicious plan. Again, many of us think that helping under these circumstances would be wrong. Malicious interests are not interests of the kind a beneficent person ought to be concerned to further: the maliciousness of your interests clearly countervails against the force of those interests as a beneficent person's reason for helping you. However, it does not seem right to say that it countervails in the same way as before, by outweighing. For it is not as if I have one good reason for helping you—that it is in your interests—and another for doing something else instead. Rather, the maliciousness of your interests shows why *these* interests fail to provide me with a good reason for helping you at all. Thus, maliciousness countervails by *undermining* the status of your interests as a reason for helping.[9]

To illustrate the points I am making, I have reported some common opinions about particular cases. Maybe our opinions about these cases are wrong: my argument does not rely on them. The only important points are the general ones they illustrate. We need to be aware of the possibility that considerations can countervail against the force of others' interests as reasons on which it is appropriate to act; and that they can countervail in different ways—by either outweighing or undermining.

2.2 FAILURES OF BENEFICENCE, AND THE LIFE-SAVING ANALOGY

Beneficence is a discriminating practical concern for other people's interests. The relevant form of concern involves treating other people's interests as a good reason for helping them, and the relevant form of discrimination is a sensitivity to the considerations that can countervail against this reason. But what about failures of beneficence—those actions that are wrong because they are not beneficent? What general description of these can we give, and which actions are included?

If, by a failure of beneficence, we mean an action that is *wrong*, then this cannot simply be conceptually identified with not doing something that would have been beneficent. To see this, consider instances of kindness and unkindness—that is, beneficence and the failure of beneficence on a small and everyday scale. When we accuse someone of acting unkindly, the *meaning* of our utterance is not preserved by saying simply that there is something she did not do that would have been kind. For, at least in popular belief, while making great efforts on behalf of others is certainly kind, not making such efforts is not unkind. According to popular opinion, had I spent this afternoon keeping old people company at a home for the aged, it would have been kind; but my not having done so was not unkind. Perhaps popular opinion is mistaken. However, if there is an error here, it is not an error about meaning: 'acting unkindly' does not simply mean 'not doing something which would have been kind'.

Unkindness is not merely conduct that is *not* kind, but conduct that is *insufficiently* kind: on this, all competent users of the word can agree. The same point, for the same reasons, holds true of beneficence more generally, covering large- as well as small-scale help. Here we do not seem to have a word to cover all those failures of beneficence that are wrong, in the way that 'unkindness' covers all those failures of kindness that are wrong.[10] I propose to get round this by stipulatively reserving talk of 'failures of beneficence' for conduct that is wrong. Failures of beneficence, then, amount to conduct that is insufficiently beneficent, rather than simply not doing something that would have been beneficent. When not performing a certain action would be a failure of beneficence, I shall say that that action is 'required by beneficence'.

How much beneficence is sufficient, and how little is insufficient? At the moment, it is an open question how far we shall be able to go towards giving a general answer to this question. (I shall start tackling it in earnest in Chapter 7.) However, the description of beneficence just given does at least tell us what would make a person's conduct less beneficent, and hence what we should be thinking about in determining whether it is *insufficiently* beneficent. Situations in which questions of beneficence arise are situations in which someone can be helped. How beneficent my response to such a situation is depends on two things: the strength of the reason for helping, and the significance of any considerations that countervail against that reason. The stronger the reason for helping, and the less significant the countervailing considerations, the less beneficent it is not to help. And when someone's interests will be very seriously compromised if I do not help him, but there is no seriously countervailing consideration, then not helping is a *failure* of beneficence—it is insufficiently beneficent, and therefore morally wrong.

How serious is 'serious'? We are not yet in any position to give a general account of this. But we do not need that. It is enough that we can identify one kind of case that clearly does fit this description. If I could save someone's life directly, the cost to me would simply be short-term exertion or inconvenience, and there is no other countervailing consideration, then not helping him is wrong. When the reason for helping is that it would save someone's life, then that is serious enough, and when the countervailing consideration is only that it would involve a short-term exertion or inconvenience, that is slight enough, to mean that this counts as a *failure* of beneficence. We do not yet have a general way of drawing the line between failures of beneficence and other actions of not helping; but we do at least know that this case falls on the failure side of the line.

But if so, we have all we need in order to formulate a forceful version of the life-saving analogy. Suppose I could easily save someone's life when it is threatened right in front of me, and there is no further countervailing consideration, beyond the small effort it would cost me to help. Not helping in these circumstances is, obviously, a failure of beneficence—it is morally wrong. But if so, how can we properly avoid saying the same about the failure to make life-saving donations to aid agencies? If my doing so would save other people's lives, then that is the sort of consideration that beneficence requires us to treat as a sufficient reason to help, in the absence of countervailing considerations. If there are no countervailing considerations, the failure to act on this is a failure of beneficence, and that makes it morally wrong. But what new considerations are present in the case of donating to aid agencies which could appropriately countervail against a beneficent person's reason to act? If there are none, then we have exactly the same case for calling this failure morally wrong as we had for saying that about letting someone die in front of me.[11]

2.3 THE METHODOLOGICAL CHALLENGE REVISITED

In Chapter 1, I described the broad three-part structure that is common to arguments for the life-saving analogy. The argument just presented is no exception. At stage 1 we begin with the thought that refusing to save a life at small cost is wrong, all else equal. We then ask why. The answer is proposed: this involves failing to treat as a decisive reason to act the fact that you could greatly benefit someone else, when there are no relevantly countervailing considerations; so its wrongness consists in a failure of beneficence. This gives us, at stage 2, a general test for failures of beneficence. We then apply this, at stage 3, to the case of non-contribution to aid agencies, to draw the conclusion that this is wrong in the same way.

However, if it has this structure, the argument is going to confront Chapter 1's methodological challenge. If our test for failures of beneficence is being drawn from initial judgements about what seems to be obvious, why not adopt a different test—one favouring the view that it is only when a person's needs are presented to me immediately and could be addressed by me directly that not helping him involves any failure of beneficence? There are two main ways to press this challenge, and they correspond to the two points emphasized in my description of beneficence. Both the claim about the content of a beneficent person's reason and the treatment of the considerations that can properly be treated as countervailing against it can seem tendentious. I claim that the content of a beneficent person's reason for helping is the simple fact that it would benefit the person who is helped. But why not say instead that a beneficent person's reason for helping is the fact *that it would benefit someone whose need is presented to me immediately*, or the fact *that it would benefit someone directly*? Suppose this first challenge can be met: there is a second. For suppose it can be shown that the content of a beneficent person's reason for helping must simply be that it would benefit the person helped. Why not then treat the non-immediacy of my relation to someone's need, or the indirectness of the help I could give, as a countervailing consideration? The claim, to be sure, will not be that this shows that it is actually wrong to provide help of a non-immediate kind. But it will be that when someone else's need is not immediately presented to me, that shows why my not helping involves no failure of beneficence.[12]

Non-immediacy and indirectness seem to be the considerations that someone pressing this challenge should concentrate on. I take it that the challenge to be addressed is that what makes the difference between letting someone die right in front of you and not saving someone's life overseas is simply the way in which the first situation *engages* any normal person in an inescapable way in which the second does not. Moreover, it should not be thought that this challenge can be rebutted by isolating the various components that may contribute to immediacy or directness—physical proximity, the number of potential victims, the independence of my help from others', and so on—and arguing that none of *them* is morally significant.[13] A moral category like that of 'immediate emergency', it might be objected, is *itself* morally significant, and it may have a significance beyond that of any of the components that a reductive analysis of it might identify. One might as well argue that torture is not morally wrong on the grounds that neither the deliberate infliction of pain, nor acting to secure one's own ends, nor any of the other particular features which cases of torture may have in common, is by itself morally significant.[14]

What I now need to show is that both forms of challenge can be met. I begin with the first, concerning the content of a beneficent person's reasons, and then return to the question about countervailing considerations.

In Chapter 1, I distinguished two different ways in which my relationship to someone else's need might be direct or immediate: if he is right in front of me, his need is immediately presented to me, and if my help will not be mediated by some further agency, I can help him directly.[a] The following discussion covers both. I shall talk simply about 'immediacy', since it would be tedious to keep making this distinction; but the points I make apply equally to immediacy or directness in both of these forms.

Immediacy and the Content of a Beneficent Person's Reason

I have been claiming that a beneficent person's reason for helping other people is this: *it is in their interests to be helped*. But why not think that the content of a beneficent person's reason is more restricted than that—that it includes a further condition of immediacy or directness? There are various possibilities to consider here, given the different ways of spelling out this further condition. However, the problem with all of them is fundamentally

[a] Sect. 1.1.

the same. They make the reason to help other people too self-regarding for action motivated in this way to be sensibly thought of as beneficence.

To see this problem, we can start with a different suggestion—one that does not mention immediacy at all. It is sometimes suggested that, if I help someone out of sympathy, I am taking the fact *that I feel like helping* as a good reason for doing so.[15] I myself think this is a caricature of sympathetically motivated action.[16] However, it does seem right to think that, against any actions that *were* motivated in this way, there would be a forceful criticism: this motivation would be unduly self-regarding.[17] A good reason for action is a consideration that counts in its favour—shows why it is worth performing.[18] But there is a big difference between thinking that what speaks in favour of the action is what it gets *him*, and thinking that what favours it is a fact about *me*: the agreement between the action and my feelings. This is not to say that sympathetic agents, on this picture, ought to be accused of having the selfish aim of helping other people only for the sake of their own enjoyment: these agents, unlike selfish ones, would still have helping other people as the ultimate aim of their action. But their *reason* for performing an action with this ultimate aim would be self-regarding, in a way that makes it sharply different from someone who sees the benefit to the other person as what counts in favour of acting.[19]

Now turn back to the proposals for making immediacy part of the content of a beneficent person's reason for helping. Why not say that a beneficent person's reason for helping is *that someone's need is immediately presented to me*? The problem is again that this offers a fact about *me* as the reason for helping, rather than the good it would do for *him*. But there is surely a sharp difference between people who see the first and those who see the second of these two different facts as what makes the action worth performing. And given the difference between the two, we surely ought to think of beneficence proper as taking the other-regarding consideration as its reason, rather than the self-regarding one. As before, the objection is not that action motivated in the self-regarding way would be simple selfishness: it would still be action the ultimate aim of which is to help others rather than yourself. But there does seem to be a big difference between taking as your reason for this aim the benefit to them, and taking as your reason the relation between them and you.

The complaint about this proposal is that it replaces a fact about what the action does for the needy person with a fact about me. Other proposals in the same spirit might seem to avoid this objection. Why not suggest that a beneficent person's reason is *both that he needs it and also that his need is immediately presented to me*? This does not replace a fact about him with a fact about me: it makes the reason into the conjunction of the two. Or why not say that the reason for helping is *that this will address his immediately presented need*? Here, the thought is that the immediate presentation qualifies the content of the reason; not that it *replaces* the other person's need as a reason altogether.

These proposals will make it inappropriate to express the objection as a complaint about replacement. But the underlying objection applies to them as well. To identify the content of a reason for a given action is to specify what it is about the action that makes it worth performing. But if I could save someone's life in front of me, what makes the action worth performing is the good it does to him. It is not as if the action only becomes worth performing if we conjoin or qualify this fact about him with some further fact about *me*. If it is right for me to respond with help, what I ought to be responding to—what I ought to see as recommending the action—is his need; not his need together with some further facts about myself. So although the form of these further proposals is different, the objection to them is the same. They make a beneficent person's reason too self-regarding.

I am not claiming that *no* morally important reason can contain a reference to the agent. The claim is simply that *some* such reasons—the ones it is characteristic of a beneficent person to recognize—do not. Thus, consider a situation in which you have to choose between saving a stranger and saving your own child. The fact that this is your child may give you reasons over and above the facts about his need. At least, nothing that has been said so far prevents us from accepting this. And if this is true, it could explain why it would be wrong not to save your own child in such a situation. Accepting this is quite compatible with my argument. The content of some of my reasons to help other people may make reference to me. What I have been denying is that the *only* reasons there are to help other people are ones that make reference to me. The facts about other people's need do provide reasons independently of facts about me—whether or not there are also facts about me that provide additional reasons to help some people.

Non-Immediacy as a Countervailing Consideration

We should not treat immediacy as part of the content of a beneficent person's reason. The content of a beneficent person's reason for helping other people is simply *that it is in their interests to be helped*. However, we have seen that declining to help someone who needs it does not always amount to a failure of beneficence. For other considerations may countervail against the force of others' interests as reasons on which it is appropriate to act. If so, we need to consider the suggestion that non-immediacy or indirectness is a countervailing consideration. Someone who says this could agree with my claims about the content of a beneficent person's reason, while still insisting that it can only be wrong not to help someone when your relationship to his need is immediate or direct. What is the problem with that?

Someone who proposes to treat non-immediacy as a countervailing consideration will have to be treating it as an underminer, not an outweigher. An outweigher is a stronger reason that favours an alternative action. But non-immediacy does not count as a reason *for* doing anything. The thought has to be that it lessens the extent to which others' interests provide me with a reason—that is, that it undermines their status as a reason for helping.

My earlier example of a consideration that works as an underminer in relation to beneficence was maliciousness. If your interests are malicious, that undermines their status as a beneficent person's reason for helping you, because it shows why these are the wrong sorts of interests to further. In that case, the underminer works to show that helping would itself be morally objectionable. However, if non-immediacy is proposed as an underminer, it will have to work in a different way. No one thinks that when someone's need is not immediately presented to me that actually makes it morally wrong to help him. Rather, the suggestion must be that the reason to help him is weakened—not that it is actually transformed into a reason against helping him.[20] Notice that there are other underminers that appear to work this way—by weakening the reasons they undermine, rather than 'reversing their polarity' altogether.[21] One example is the consideration that a person has brought his misfortune on himself. This does not seem to make it wrong to help someone, but does seem to lessen the reason there is to help. If I have to choose between helping two equally needy people, only one of whom has brought his misfortune on himself, that can make it the case that I have more reason to help the other.[22] This is not the place to attempt a full justification for this view. But it is easy to see, in a general way, how bringing your misfortune on yourself makes your interests less morally important ones to further, given the moral significance of questions about whether you are morally responsible for, or deserving of, your predicament. Why not say something similar about non-immediacy?

A reason to help someone is a consideration that shows why helping him is worthwhile—what there is that counts in favour of helping him, makes helping appropriate or right. The fact that it is in his interests will do this, unless there are features of his interests that lessen the extent to which they are worth furthering—the extent to which they count in favour of helping him. If his interests are malicious, or if they are interests in avoiding a misfortune he has brought on himself, then that might help to lessen the extent to which we should think of those interests as worth furthering. But the problem is to see how the fact that his interests are not immediately presented to me could do this. How does this fact about my relationship to them show that they are interests belonging to a kind that it is less morally appropriate to respond to? It does not seem to be a feature of those interests that lessens their worthiness to be furthered. It situates me in relation to those interests; but it is not a feature of those interests themselves that affects their moral quality. It does not show that those interests are bad, or morally questionable; nor does it identify some further feature of them that reflects on their worthiness to be furthered. So it is hard to see how it could affect the extent to which those interests really do count as a reason for helping him.[23]

This line of attack invites the following reply. Of course, the non-immediacy of my relationship to your interests does not constitute some non-relational feature of those interests that diminishes their force as reasons for other people to help you. But what it shows is why there is less reason for *me* to help you.

I have two responses to this. The first is to challenge someone who thinks this to say *why* we should agree. We can say why the fact that your interests are malicious, or the fact that you have brought your misfortunes on yourself, should be treated as an underminer. But it is hard to see what further explanation can be given for why non-immediacy should be treated as an underminer. I accept that saying this is not a refutation of this view. For it remains open to claim that the status of non-immediacy as an underminer is simply a primitive normative fact, for which no *further* justification can be given. However, having accepted the possibility, I still want to know why we should agree to say this.

The second response, however, is that there is a justification for *not* treating non-immediacy as an underminer in relation to beneficence. That justification is, again, that it would make the attitudes of a beneficent person too self-regarding. Earlier, this objection was raised against the suggestion that the immediacy with which others' need is presented to me is part of the content of my reason for helping them. The current suggestion is different. It is that, although the *content* of a beneficent person's reason for helping other people is simply *that it is in their interests to be helped*, this reason is undermined when their need is not immediately presented to me. This amounts to claiming that facts about immediacy, although not part of the content of a beneficent person's reason, are conditions governing the strength of that reason.[24] But although the suggestion is different, it is met by a similar objection. For it still amounts to saying that the extent to which facts about other people's interests provide reasons to help them is conditional upon facts about me. However, the force of the reason for me to help someone who needs it comes from a fact about him, not a fact about me. At least, this is true of the reasons distinctive of beneficence. There may be further facts about me that provide extra reasons to help other people—facts about the special relationships in which I may stand to them. But what is distinctive of beneficence is an attitude of recognizing facts about other people, and not facts about me, as presenting me with reason to help them.

I conclude that non-immediacy should not be treated as countervailing against the force of others' interests as a reason for helping them. There is no justification for treating non-immediacy as a countervailing consideration; and furthermore, there is a positive case *against* doing so.

You might accept this but think that it overlooks something important. True, it is hard to see how the non-immediacy of my relationship to someone who needs help can affect the status of the reasons for helping him, and that makes it hard to see how it could be a consideration that countervails against those reasons. On the other hand, it is very easy to see how this consideration affects my *relationship* to the reasons for helping him. And isn't *that* morally significant?

Actually, I think it is. I shall come back to this shortly.

Particularity and Beneficence

It might be thought that an attack on the life-saving analogy should focus not on immediacy or directness, but on some other factor that differentiates the direct saving of life from giving money to aid agencies. The next two chapters will consider various possibilities. But there is one thought that we ought to deal with straight away. This is that what makes the two cases relevantly different is not the immediacy with which the need is presented, but the particularity of the person to be helped.[25]

When we described beneficence by saying that it involves taking others' interests as a reason for helping them, we saw that this must be read extensionally. A beneficent person is not someone whose concern is for *other people's interests*, under that description. Rather, she is someone whose concern, given some particular person who needs help, will be for *his* interests. However, when I think about helping some of the world's needy people by giving money to an aid agency, it is not as if there is any particular individual to whom I am responding. And *this*, it might be thought, is what explains why not giving the money does not amount to a failure of beneficence. Beneficence involves responding to the needs of particular individuals; it is different from the kind of generalized philanthropy that reacts to other people's need in general. When I am aware of the need of some particular person, and fail to help although it would have been easy to do so, that can be a failure of beneficence, and be wrong. But when I merely refrain from responding to other people's need in general, this is just refraining from philanthropy, and it is not wrong.[26]

However, the reply to this can be shorter. Think of what we should say about immediately presented emergencies where no particular beneficiary of my help can be identified. Suppose I confront a disaster in which many lives are threatened. A rescue team is organized; if I join it, several more lives will be saved, but even if I join, not all will be. In joining, I may have no idea which particular individuals will benefit from my help; if I refuse, it may be impossible to say *which* of the threatened lives were lost as a result.

However, if contributing to the rescue would not be a large sacrifice, then refusing to join it seems no less wrong than refusing to save a single life. To put the point at its strongest, think of an earthquake, where help is needed to dig through the rubble of a collapsed building. Nothing is known about the identity of the people in the building; there might even be no one to save. But if my assistance with the rescue effort is needed, and it is not a big sacrifice to ask of me, it may still be wrong to refuse. Notice here, though, that a beneficent person's reason for helping in this case is simply this: there is something I can easily do that *might* help someone else greatly. Failing to treat this reason as decisive would be wrong, in the absence of countervailing considerations. It is simply a mistake to think that a beneficent person's reason must pick out particular beneficiaries, and that when you cannot do this, refusing to help can involve no failure of beneficence.

There is a further point that we shall need to return to. In the circumstances just described, it is not possible to *identify* a particular beneficiary of my help. I do think this is enough to deal with the objection that beneficence requires an awareness of the needs of particular individuals to whom I am responding. However, there is a different but similar thought that has not yet been addressed. This is that, in cases of the kind just described, if I act there is a likelihood that some particular individuals will be better off as a result (whether I am aware of their identities in advance or not). But if I give money to an aid agency, there are no particular individuals who will be better off as a result of my adding to the agency's overall pool of funds. I discuss this objection in Chapter 4.

2.4 THE MORAL SIGNIFICANCE OF IMMEDIACY

In defending the life-saving analogy, I have argued that the reasons we have for thinking that it can be wrong to let someone die right in front of you are equally reasons for thinking that it is wrong to contribute nothing to aid agencies in order to address the life-threatening need of people far away. However, I have already mentioned my doubts about whether not helping at a distance is as bad as failing to help someone right in front of you.[b] I now want to say some more about this. It is consistent with what I have been arguing to accept that the immediacy of my relationship to someone else's need does make a moral difference, in two ways.

The first of these is a point I alluded to a short while ago. Although the fact that someone's need is not immediately presented to me does not undermine the extent to which his interests provide a reason for helping him, it certainly affects my relationship to that reason. This is psychologically

[b] Sect. 1.1.

important. Clearly, it is a matter of psychological fact that our motivation to act on threats to other people's lives is triggered far more easily when they are right in front of us.[27] It is not at all surprising that we respond more readily to threats to people's lives when they are presented to us immediately, and we can help them directly. The reason may not be different when it is presented to me immediately, but it is more salient, and that makes it more motivationally engaging.[28] And this may be not only psychologically important, but morally important too. For the salience of a reason may affect how reasonable it is to expect us to attend to it, and how reasonable it is to criticize us for not doing something about it.[29]

For an illustration of this point, consider what we should say about past practices which were once commonplace, but which have now rightly been abandoned: slavery is the obvious example. Racial and religious slavery seemed normal to people growing up and receiving their moral education in circumstances in which it had become part of the accepted social fabric.[30] And this fact seems morally significant. Where it is unquestioningly taken for granted that outsiders' interests are morally less important than those of one's own group, they may simply not have the same salience as appropriate objects of concern. This does nothing to weaken the argument for thinking that slavery is wrong, for it does nothing to weaken the reasons for respecting people's liberty, irrespective of their race or religion. But it may affect our judgement of how bad the people who acquiesced in such practices were, and our judgement of how blameworthy they were for upholding them.

There are different ways of expressing this point. It seems to me that the most satisfactory is to say that the actions of some slaveholders in the past were less *blameworthy* than my actions would be if I enslaved someone, but that they were no less *wrong*. Saying that they were no less wrong expresses the fact that the reason against doing what they did was just as strong—for it was the same—as the reason there is for me not to enslave anyone today. The facts about slavery that count as reasons against it were no weaker in the past than they are now; but it may be less reasonable to have expected some past slaveholders who lived then to attend to these reasons than it is to expect me to attend to them today. Another way to put the same point is to employ a distinction between objective and subjective wrongness, and say that the actions of ancient slaveholders were no less objectively wrong but were less subjectively wrong.[31] Or one might just sidestep these verbal issues, and say simply that the reason not to enslave people was no weaker, but that it is reasonable to level less criticism against them than against me.

However we describe it, this distinction seems important. How reasonable it is to criticize someone for acting on a reason is one thing; but the strength of the reason itself is another. This gives us the first respect in which immediacy makes a moral difference. The failure to respond to an emergency that confronts you directly exhibits a depth of indifference to the interests of other people that makes moral criticism more appropriate than it is in relation to the failure to act in response to more distant need. If the considerations one ought to be acting on are more vividly inescapable, the failure to respond to them is more blameworthy.

Of course, if this opened the way to arguing that not helping at a distance is not blameworthy at all, that would take much of the sting out of my conclusion that it is wrong. If this were a case of 'blameless wrongdoing' then, although we should accept that there is a moral case against doing nothing, we should not think ill of anyone—including ourselves—for doing nothing.[32] However, I cannot see any plausibility in going *that* far. The non-immediacy of the needs of distant strangers shows that it is not reasonable to criticize us for being less engaged by them than by the needs of someone right in front of us. But it does not explain why we should not be criticized if we ignore them altogether.

There is a second way in which immediacy might still make a moral difference, compatibly with my argument. Notice that, for all I have said, immediacy might still make a difference not just to the blameworthiness of our actions, but to their *wrongness* too. I have argued that the non-immediacy of my relationship to someone's need does not lessen the reason there is to help him, and I am not about to retract that claim. But this still leaves open the possibility that relationships of immediacy create *further* reasons for helping people. Remember: I have not been making a blanket claim that no morally significant reason contains a reference to the agent who has it. Rather, the claim is that certain morally significant reasons—reasons of beneficence—do not. As I noted earlier, this leaves open the possibility that family relationships create reasons to help people. In a similar vein, there is no obstacle to the claim that relationships of immediacy provide further reasons to help people. Of course, nothing has been said here to support this view.[33] But equally, nothing has been said to refute it. It has been argued that, since reasons of *beneficence* for me to help needy people are independent of facts about me, the failure to respond to life-threatening need at a distance is a failure of beneficence, and is morally wrong. However, it is consistent with this to think that facts about my immediate relationship to a needy person can provide further reasons to help. And if there are further reasons to help, that would lend support to the view that it is *more* wrong not to.

2.5 WHAT KIND OF ARGUMENT IS THIS?

That completes the substantive argument of this chapter. A natural question to ask about it concerns its theoretical presuppositions. You might think that, as an argument in applied ethics, it must be assuming some general moral theory—a version of consequentialism, perhaps, or some kind of 'virtue theory'—and applying that to the particular case under discussion. However, I do not present the argument this way, because I do not think it relies on any such theory. It may be helpful if I briefly explain why not before we continue.

I have already described the argument's three-stage structure. This does involve a kind of normative theorizing. After all, it generalizes about our reasons, and draws conclusions from this about the normative commitments we are justified in holding. However, if this is a form of theorizing, it is only a preliminary one. It is preliminary in two different dimensions, which we might think of as its depth and its scope. It lacks depth, because it only seeks to generalize about what we *take* to be good reasons; a deeper theory would be one that aims to vindicate conclusions about what really are good reasons. It is true that I have been assuming that the convictions I am working from can ultimately be vindicated. But I have not taken sides on the more controversial question *how* our convictions about reasons are to be vindicated. In addition to this, theorizing of the three-stage kind is preliminary in scope, since it takes only some of our judgements, and restricts itself to identifying our justifications for them. The fullest kind of theory would be one that aims to cover moral judgements, and the reasons for and against them, quite generally. At its most ambitious, a normative moral theory will aim to be complete in both of these dimensions, giving us a fully vindicated, completely general description of good moral reasons. Equipped with this, we would then be able to invoke it to resolve any moral controversy definitively.

What has emerged from this discussion is much more modest: it is a rudimentary theory of beneficence. This theory contains two components: a general characterization of the kind of concern distinctive of beneficence, and a description of what is common to the kinds of consideration that can properly countervail in relation to this concern. It amounts only to a rudimentary theory: an outline to be filled in. Filling it in would mean giving a substantive account of just which considerations do countervail in relation to this form of concern, and that is not something I have attempted. I have sought to explain what a consideration would have to be like in order to be intelligibly treated as countervailing in relation to beneficence, but not to give incontrovertible examples of considerations that do countervail.[34]

Ignoring my argument's restriction in scope might lead you to see it as involving a commitment to a welfarist version of consequentialism: a normative theory that links right action to the production of the highest level of welfare.[35] However, my discussion of beneficence assumes only that other people's welfare is morally important. It is not committed to the much stronger claim that *everything* that is morally important is important because of its contribution to people's welfare.[36]

The other main temptation will be to see this argument as involving a commitment to a distinctively 'virtue-ethical' approach to normative moral theory. However, I do not think that is right either. True, the argument does concern beneficence, which is a quality both of character and of action. However, I cannot see that it contains any commitment to claiming a priority of the assessment of character over that of action.[37] And true, my preferred usage of a virtue-term like 'beneficence' makes the virtues interdependent: in requiring beneficence to be discriminating, I am claiming that if injustice, dishonesty, or capriciousness makes an action wrong, it cannot count as beneficent.[38] However, the argument does not rely on this way of speaking. In the present context, the discrepancy between my own usage and the rival one allowing that beneficent actions are sometimes wrong can be treated as merely verbal. What I have been calling 'beneficence' should simply be spoken of by someone who dislikes this usage as 'those forms of beneficence that it is wrong for us not to pursue'. My arguments could be rewritten substituting for 'beneficence' this more awkward phrase without affecting anything of substance. These forms of beneficence do require an appropriate sensitivity to countervailing considerations, and from the fact that an agent fails to help someone when such considerations are absent, the wrongness of her action will be inferrable as before. But if it can be reformulated this way, the argument cannot be relying on an inference from failure of virtue to wrongness. Indeed—and this is the clinching point as far as suspicions about 'virtue ethics' are concerned—the whole argument could be phrased without using virtue-terminology at all. The claim on which the argument is grounded is that what we criticize someone for, when he fails easily to save someone's life, is an insufficient concern for others' interests. The question that that invites is how much concern for others' interests is sufficient or insufficient; and the discussion of countervailing considerations that responds to this question could have been presented without mentioning beneficence at all.

I emphasize this not because I think it is a mistake to try to construct a more general theory, but because the theoretical modesty of my argument seems to me one of its strengths. The argument here is not presuppositionless, and it is not immune to challenges of various sorts. Its presuppositions are clear, and clearly undefended. They are the judgements about the wrongness of not saving lives directly at small cost from which we started, and the assumption that the considerations we regard as good reasons for these judgements are indeed good reasons for them. However, the argument I have presented is not presupposing an undeclared moral theory. This adds to the force of the challenge it presents; for it means that it needs to be seriously engaged with, whatever your theoretical orientation.

2.6 CONCLUSION

Not contributing to aid agencies is like failing to avert threats to life directly: it exhibits a failure of beneficence, and that makes it morally wrong.

The primary focus of my argument for this conclusion has been on answering the methodological challenge set out in Chapter 1—the challenge of saying why, if we begin from a set of commonplace judgements, we should generalize from them in a way that supports a contentious conclusion. I have sought to do this by giving a plausible account of the reason supporting those commonplace judgements—judgements about the wrongness of failing to save a life directly. The reason why failing to save a life directly is wrong is that it displays an inadequate concern for other people's interests, and this is equally a reason for faulting non-contribution to aid agencies.

I think this is a good answer to the methodological challenge, but it is not a proof of my conclusion. It makes a case for one coherent account of the reason for the commonplace judgements from which we started; but no moral judgement *entails* the reason why it is true. An argument of this form will never completely refute the methodological challenge by showing that no alternative generalization from our initial judgements is possible. But that is not a sensible aim. What is important is whether any alternative generalization gives a more plausible account of the reason why the initial judgements are true; and I have been making a case for thinking not.

The argument I have developed is an attractive one, for three main reasons. First, it captures the intuitive force of one of the main lines of thought that leads many people to the same conclusion: non-contribution to aid agencies is wrong simply because it is a failure of those who have more than enough to respond to others' desperate need. And it does so while meeting the methodological challenge invited by other attempts to develop this line of thought carefully. Secondly, the style of argument I have used has a kind of theoretical neutrality that means it is free of more general theoretical commitments, and needs to be taken seriously by proponents of any plausible moral theory. And thirdly, it generates a plausibly qualified conclusion, that although non-contribution to aid agencies is wrong, it is not as blameworthy as letting someone die in front of you, and perhaps not as wrong either.

However, in order to arrive at this conclusion, two assumptions are required. One is that contributions to aid agencies will indeed avert threats to people's lives. And the other is that there is no *other* countervailing consideration, beyond non-immediacy or indirectness, that supplies a morally relevant difference between helping a person directly and giving money to an aid agency. Both of these assumptions, though, are frequently challenged. It is objected that by feeding the world's surplus population now, we are simply contributing to worse problems in the future, that responsibility for the relief of poverty belongs to governments rather than to individuals, that the absence of proper birth control practices in poor countries makes them responsible for their own plight, and that charity degrades people as objects of our pity. Aid agencies are accused of doing economic damage, colluding with corruption within the countries they are supposed to be helping, and of being driven by the business imperative of feeding their own growth rather than producing any long-term benefits for the world's poor. Moreover, even if you accept that aid agencies' activity as a whole averts threats to people's lives, you might still doubt whether any one individual's contribution to those agencies does that.

The next two chapters discuss these two assumptions in the light of objections such as the ones just mentioned. The second assumption, I shall argue, is right, and the objections to it fail. The first, on the other hand, may be wrong—but even if it is, that does not spoil the argument. If you are already disposed to believe these things, you can turn directly to Chapter 5. There I take up the question that arises next: How demanding a moral outlook does this argument leave us with?

3

Objections to Aid

> Aid is not bad . . . because it is sometimes misused, corrupt, or crass; rather, it is *inherently* bad, bad to the bone, and utterly beyond reform. . . . it is possibly the most formidable obstacle to the productive endeavours of the poor. It is also a denial of their potential, and a patronising insult to their unique, unrecognised abilities.
>
> (Graham Hancock, *Lords of Poverty*, 183)

> The violent events that occurred [in Somalia] in 1993 were not an aberration; they were, in fact, foreign aid carried out to its logical extreme. Foreign aid run amok. The desire to help had—as it almost always does—become the desire to control.
>
> (Michael Maren, *The Road to Hell*, 218)

> . . . most current humanitarian activity in Africa is useless or damaging and should be abandoned. Humanitarian action is too noble an enterprise to become debased and discredited in this manner.
>
> (Alex de Waal, *Famine Crimes*, p. xvi)

> . . . majorities in rich countries ritually affirm their wish to see misery curbed, especially at moments of catastrophe. Such attitudes rest on shifting and culture-bound mixes of guilt, duty, despair, fear and the wish to be seen to belong to respectable society. They can hardly rest on solid convictions about aid effectiveness, or much knowledge of it.
>
> (David Sogge, *Give and Take*, 196)

I SAID in Chapter 1 that Peter Singer invented the life-saving analogy. That is a bit misleading. For he was simply spelling out an idea that has always been implicit in the way that aid agencies have presented themselves to us. 'Through us', they say, 'you can reach out and transform the lives of people in desperate need. They are innocent victims of poverty and you are their potential rescuer. It only takes a few dollars—an amount of money that will make little difference to you. But your small act of compassion can make a huge difference to them. The choice is yours: will you ignore our request and let those people go uncared for, or will you allow us to save them?'

Does this idea—the idea that, by giving money to an aid agency, I am reaching out to transform someone's life—stand up to careful examination?[1] Or is this way of thinking about humanitarian aid a misleading fantasy? In this chapter and the next I examine this question.

One ground on which this way of thinking about aid might be challenged is that it overrates the effect of my contribution. Even if, overall, an aid agency's activities have a transforming effect on people's lives, my donation to those agencies does not. That challenge is discussed in Chapter 4.

In the current chapter, however, I discuss the prior question: Are the activities of aid agencies actually good? Are they trying to do the right things, and do they succeed? We need to consider the case that can be made for thinking that the activities of aid agencies are ineffectual or even positively damaging. The aid agencies tell us they are doing good: are they?

The case against the aid agencies needs to be taken seriously. After all, their most eloquent and forceful critics are not armchair commentators, but people like the authors quoted above, whose opinions come from lengthy personal experience of aid agencies and the countries in which they operate.[2] According to them, the idea behind the life-saving analogy *is* a misleading fantasy. Moreover, the fantasy involved is not just the relatively harmless one of misrepresenting the effects of a single donor's actions. It is the much more damaging fantasy that comes from simplistically conceiving of the problems of the poor as a need for rescue—a need to be plucked away from a situation of threat by a single beneficent action, like the plucking of a child from a pond. One of the more sympathetic critics, David Rieff, puts it this way: 'the first and greatest humanitarian trap is this need to simplify, if not actually lie about, the way things are in the crisis zones, in order to make the story more morally and psychologically palatable—in short, to sugarcoat the horror of the world, which includes the horror of the cost of a good deed'.[3] Our moral concern, according to Rieff, is not sophisticated enough to respond to anything other than a fairytale about the rescue of innocent victims—a fairytale that humanitarian workers need to tell themselves.

Other critics press the objection further. This way of thinking, they complain, is not just politically and economically naive: it is pernicious. It infantilizes the poor, treating them as victims to be acted upon. It treats poverty-related need and suffering as an act of god, rather than a political problem which needs to be met by political action. It creates patterns of short-term interference and manipulation without long-term commitment. Above all, institutionalizing this style of thinking in an international aid industry perpetuates the problem it is supposed to be addressing. It acts as an alibi for the failure to support genuine political reform, and it simply feeds resources into the structures of manipulation and injustice that enforce the subjugation and disempowerment of the poor.

Some philosophers, reflecting this line of criticism, present it as a refutation of the life-saving analogy.[4] In this chapter I want to face up squarely to this objection. I think the critics' arguments are forceful, and have great practical importance. However, I shall explain why they do not undermine an argument of the form I have given for thinking that, as individuals, we are morally required to act to help the poor.

3.1 'AID IS COUNTER-PRODUCTIVE'

The activities of aid agencies do have good effects: no one seriously disputes that. However, they have bad effects too. And a claim that deserves a serious response is that the bad effects outweigh the good ones: the efforts of any given aid agency, taken overall, are at best ineffectual and at worst actually counter-productive. This view is often expressed, and I need to respond to it.

If aid agencies are ineffectual or counter-productive, then it is obvious how that undermines the argument developed in the last two chapters. If, in helping one person, I would only harm others, then that clearly *would* be a countervailing consideration in relation to beneficence—it would clearly show how not helping is consistent with being sufficiently beneficent. Beneficence is a concern for other people's interests, and that means not only the interests of the one who will be helped, but also the interests of the others who will be harmed.

I shall structure my discussion around the three major reasons that are often given for thinking that aid agencies are counter-productive: that aid worsens the root problem of overpopulation, that it inflicts economic damage, and that it impedes political progress.

Aid and Population

According to the demographic theory of Thomas Malthus (1766–1834), there is a natural tendency for population growth to outstrip growth in food production: whereas the first, if left unchecked, increases exponentially, the second increases only arithmetically. Accordingly, if population growth remains unchecked, we should expect a population eventually to stabilize at the miserable point at which it is only just sustained by the available food resources: any further population growth will be checked by starvation, while any further growth in food production will simply allow an expansion in population until a similar point is reached.[5]

Neo-Malthusians see starvation and malnutrition today as evidence that, in the regions where they occur, this point has already been reached. They are caused by the overpopulation of regions that are insufficiently fertile to sustain the food requirements of their inhabitants. This view leads quickly to a first argument for the counter-productivity of international aid: feeding the hungry now ensures only that their populations will continue to grow, while the rate of growth in food production is unlikely even to keep up with the rate of population growth, let alone surpass it. Unfortunately, in a world no longer capable of sustaining its human population, the best policy is to let nature restore it to sustainable levels, rather than ensuring the same fate for greater numbers of people in the future. Moreover, it is added, the ultimate consequence of responding with aid can only be to bleed the resources of the relatively affluent until we reach the same miserable level ourselves. The earth, according to the metaphor favoured by proponents of this argument, is an overcrowded lifeboat.[6] This neo-Malthusian view, much advocated in the 1970s, still dominates some people's thinking about world poverty.[7]

Aid and Economics

The neo-Malthusian view of world hunger can sound like simple common sense: starvation occurs when there are too many people and not enough food. But we must be careful. What common sense tells us is that starving people themselves do not have enough food. It is a further claim that their not having enough food is caused by a scarcity of food relative to the size of the population to which they belong. And, on investigation, that further claim turns out to be false. To begin with, raw statistics tell against it. Global food production, if distributed across the world's population, would currently be more than sufficient to meet everyone's nutritional needs, and in the second half of the twentieth century its rate of increase comfortably outstripped that of global population.[8] Even the countries of sub-Saharan Africa, where food production per person is declining, have been net exporters of food throughout periods of drought, despite the use of only a small proportion of cultivable farmland.[9]

More significantly, the economic analyses of famine and malnutrition conducted by Amartya Sen and others tell strongly against the view that hunger is caused by declining food availability relative to population size.[10] As Sen has shown, the worst Indian famine in the last century—the Bengal catastrophe of 1943 in which 3 million people are estimated to have died—appears actually to have been a 'boom famine', the central feature of which was the inflationary economic pressure produced by the contemporary war. (The most telling statistic Sen produces against explaining the Bengal famine in terms of a declining availability of food is that the 'current supply' of rice 'for 1943 was only about 5 per cent lower than the average of the preceding five years. It was, in fact, 13 per cent *higher* than in 1941, and there was, of course, no famine in 1941.')[11] Likewise, the famous

Bangladesh famine of 1974 occurred during a peak year for per capita rice production in the country: what the floods contributed to reducing was not the availability of food but employment opportunities, leading to a fall in wages relative to the price of rice.[12] Conversely, and more optimistically, cases are cited of sharp declines in food availability which have not resulted in famine, the Maharashtra drought of 1970–3 being a particularly spectacular example. 'By any criterion, the severity of agricultural decline in Maharashtra before the early 1970s, and the extent of crop failures during the drought, dwarf the food crises which led to dramatic famines in the Sahel over the same period . . . '.[13] And in general, 'the period during which the frequency of famines started to decline in India (the first half of this century) was actually one of steadily *declining* food production per head'.[14]

But if food scarcity is neither a necessary nor a sufficient condition for the existence of famines, then what is the causal explanation of them? The main explanatory strategy employed by Sen, and following him, by many others, is the investigation within a famine-affected population of the 'exchange entitlements' of its members—the set of alternative bundles of commodities that they can acquire in exchange for what they own.[15] 'A person will be exposed to starvation if, for the ownership that he actually has, the exchange entitlement set does not contain any feasible bundle including enough food.'[16] The possibility of boom famines is explained by the way in which inflation in food prices can dissolve the food entitlements of those whose labour produces goods the relative value of which has drastically declined; and the possibility of famineless food shortages by publicly sponsored programmes of 'entitlement protection', through, for example, mass employment on public works.[17]

The general form of such explanations is clear, and in breaking the assumed connection between starvation and food scarcity, they puncture the apocalyptic neo-Malthusian view. However, in order to identify mechanisms of famine prevention, detailed studies are needed of the way in which specific economic and social structures work to preserve or compromise such entitlements. (What we want to know, for instance, is why inflation in food prices led to widespread hoarding and speculation in the Bengal famine of 1943; whereas the same inflationary phenomenon during the Sahelian famine of 1973 encouraged grain stock owners to capitalize on their profits—without, moreover, averting mass starvation.)[18] Much work is currently being done to supply such detailed explanations, and draw conclusions concerning how future famines can be prevented.[19]

What form do these conclusions take? The direction in which they suggest we should look for the means of preventing famine is primarily a political one.[20] According to Sen and others, the common theme of the successful attempts to prevent food shortages from producing famines is a governmental commitment to measured intervention for the sake of entitlement protection, and freedom of criticism and dissent has played a crucial role in securing that commitment.[21] The most effective form of development in preventing famine, it seems, is the fostering of political responsibility and freedom. To encapsulate this school of thought in a slogan, the best form of famine prevention is democracy.[22]

This line of argument does effectively refute the first, neo-Malthusian objection concerning the pointlessness of international aid. But it seems that it has done so only by opening up a second line of objection. What is needed to prevent starvation in famine-prone countries, it suggests, is a politically driven social and economic restructuring. But surely the kinds of non-governmental aid organizations to which I could contribute do not have the power to produce such structural changes on anything but the smallest scale.

Moreover, the problem does not simply concern the modest scale of our aid. The problem with 'aid', it is often argued, is not that there is too little of it. It is that it is the wrong kind of intervention to make the changes that are needed. If simple resource-transfer were the answer to global poverty, it would have been eliminated by now. But it has not; and this is not simply because pouring resources into an unsound economy is ineffectual: it actually makes things worse.

The natural dynamic of large-scale international aid programmes, it is frequently complained, is simply to damage the local economy and pauperize the 'target population'. Development programmes that concentrate on food aid, in particular, are often criticized for doing this. Inserting free food into an economy means undercutting local commodity prices.[23] Distributing food aid means competing with local produce for scarce administrative and infrastructural resources, especially those of storage and transport.[24] International food aid diverts trade away from developing-country food exporters, particularly where (as is standardly the case) it is an offshoot of donor-country agricultural protectionism.[25] And a factor to which some writers attach more importance than any of these is the ignorance and complacency which food aid programmes can encourage concerning indigenous agricultural mismanagement.[26] The effect is to create aid-dependent economies in which the task of developing economic self-sufficiency has been made much harder than it was before.[27]

These criticisms are often applied primarily to food aid development programmes. However, aid workers admit that disaster relief food distribution is afflicted with similar problems. Emergency food aid is commonly oversupplied, or simply arrives late, and when this happens, all the forms of economic damage just described can result. The economic distortions produced by the availability of large amounts of free food have the effect of jeopardizing the recovery of the local economy when the immediate crisis has passed; and this is compounded by damaging social effects: the motivation to work is undermined, community structures disrupted, and corruption encouraged.[28]

Not all international aid is food aid, of course. But in relation to aid of other sorts the criticisms are if anything stronger. The large capital- and technology-intensive agricultural development projects of the last forty years, far from benefiting the poor, are frequently criticized for impoverishing them further;[29] and there is widespread scepticism concerning whether the effect of loans released for Third World development is to 'trickle down' for the benefit of the poorest sections of the recipient countries' populations.[30] The underlying reason for these failures seems clear. If poverty is caused not by scarcity but by powerlessness—if people are poor because a country's resources are controlled in a way that excludes them—supplying more resources from outside without more fundamental structural change is not going to help. It only impedes that structural change by supporting those who already have power.

Aid and Politics

It is now widely agreed that eliminating poverty is not simply a matter of resource transfer or technological innovation.[31] It requires structural change—a change that is fundamentally political.[32] It is only where governments are genuinely accountable to all of their citizens that the institutions of government will function to protect the entitlements of their least well-off citizens.

As we have already seen, this already leads to a pair of objections. Private philanthropy will not produce political change, and in its absence can be economically damaging. But a further point can be added to these. Even if our philanthropy could produce political change, it is not obvious what form that change should take. What is widely agreed is that protecting the entitlements of the worst-off members of a society requires us to institute structures that ensure that government is accountable to them. However, there is very wide disagreement about just which structures will do this. This disagreement exhausts the whole political spectrum from the endorsement of communist land reform,[33] through the recommendation of market distribution of a publicly held food supply,[34] to the view that the thrust of international aid policy should be the stimulation of private enterprise in developing countries and the counteracting of 'public sector bias'.[35] The advocates of each of these competing political programmes will claim that support for a rival damages the development of the right alternative. Moreover, it is far from clear, even if there were an obvious course of political reform that was needed to eliminate poverty, that it would be right to impose it from outside. For these reasons, it can seem doubtful whether, even if our aid were capable of producing political change, this could be morally required of us.

So it is not obvious how aid can do political good. However, on the other hand, it *is* clearly capable of doing political harm—this in addition to the economic damage we have already noticed. Aid encourages reprehensible political regimes, in two ways: it camouflages their irresponsibility; and much of it, if not given to them directly, is appropriated or controlled by them, thus materially supporting those responsible for the plight of the poor in the first place.[36] The larger the volume of aid, the greater the incentive there is to control it.[37] Moreover, Western aid activity is itself widely criticized as an instrument of political domination over the developing world, effected through the structural adjustment programmes forced on aid-dependent governments by the World Bank and International Monetary Fund, and the dismantling of tariff protections secured by the World Trade Organization.[38] The real function of international aid, according to its most vocal critics on the left, is to open up developing countries for Western businesses, and to supervise the transfer of resources from poor to rich.[39] Our 'aid', according to these critics, is simply imperialism dressed in new clothes.[40] The aid business is propelled by the same mixture of naivety, racist condescension, and callous or hypocritical self-interest that governed the Third World's colonial past, and created its current problems.[41]

Aid and NGOs

To what extent do these objections apply to the aid activities of non-government organizations (NGOs)?[42] Clearly, NGOs cannot be accused of the damage done by structural adjustment programmes. (On the contrary, some NGOs have been among the loudest advocates of the cause of debt relief and other international institutional reform.) And the strongest critics of international aid usually make it clear that it is the Official Development Assistance administered through government aid programmes or multilateral institutions that are their targets. Thus Graham Hancock, whom I quoted at the start of this chapter, explicitly excludes NGOs from his criticisms. NGOs, he writes, 'are funded on a voluntary basis by contributions from the general public and thus are under considerable pressure to use properly the money they receive. They rarely do significant harm; sometimes they do great good.'[43]

Other critics of aid, however, do not let NGOs off so lightly. The major African disasters of the 1990s, in Somalia and Rwanda, have given rise to a genre of books by disillusioned former aid workers laying bare the deficiencies of the private charity industry.[44] Partly, their criticism stems from the use of NGOs as subcontractors to deliver government aid: this implicates the private charities in the kinds of economic damage and political collusion that government aid is routinely accused of. However, the indictment produced by the most strident critics, such as Maren, is much more sweeping. He depicts an industry organized around the commercialization of pity. In being driven by pity, it is fundamentally demeaning.[45] This comes out in the 'disaster pornography' through which the agencies sell their product, and in the lack of consultation or real engagement with the people who are supposedly being helped, with an implicit assumption that the problems of the poor are caused by their own incompetence and recalcitrance. The assumption that a Western college graduate can teach Ogadeen nomads how to provide for their children is insulting. This condescension is one half of the ideology of the NGOs; the commercial imperative is the other. They are driven by the imperative to raise and spend more money than their rivals, competing for media attention, but without being disciplined by any serious attempt to assess the results of their programmes.[46] And if Third World governments can be criticized for their lack of accountability to the poor, so can the aid agencies.[47] Their customers are the donors, who are buying the illusion of help. Aid agencies invent figures to make the problems sound worse and their efforts to address them sound better.[48] And meanwhile, aid workers themselves inhabit a first-world bubble within the Third World countries they operate in, renting headquarters at inflated rates from the oppressors of the people they are supposed to be helping.[49] Aid almost always involves working with (or at least, with the consent of) the oppressors of the poor, over their heads. And in some cases, it has provided the main economic tool to feed and equip armies, buy the loyalty of refugees, and amass personal fortunes.[50]

Alternative Conclusions

What conclusion should be drawn from the various related objections we have just surveyed? Do they provide good grounds for thinking that the aid industry should be disbanded, and that we should not support it?[51] Different claims concerning the political and economic effects of aid might be and have been made on the strength of these objections. Let me distinguish the main ones, and examine the extent to which they challenge the argument I have presented in the first two chapters. I shall work towards the claim that poses the most serious challenge; in the next section I answer it.

A first conclusion is this:

(1) NGO aid is politically and economically useless.

Poverty needs to be tackled by addressing its underlying causes, and not merely its symptoms. NGOs cannot make the kind of large-scale impact that will do this.

To reply, we should distinguish aid that aims to give personal help from aid that aims to achieve systemic reform. Effective aid of the first kind will make some individuals significantly better off than they otherwise would have been. Effective aid of the second kind will usually do that too; but its primary aim is to change the institutional and social relationships that create and sustain poverty, need, and disadvantage. Support for a programme of land reform, or a charter to establish press freedom, would be examples of the second kind of aid. The first covers emergency relief aid, but also inoculation programmes, nutrition clinics, financing and training staff for schools and hospitals, farmer field schools to disseminate good agricultural practice, and lending initiatives like the Grameen Bank in Bangladesh.[52]

Are NGOs powerless to do valuable work towards effecting systemic change? There is little reason to believe that this general claim is true. The work that the best agencies do in education, facilitating communication between disadvantaged groups, administering revolving loan funds, publicizing good and bad practice, and lobbying for international institutional change is widely acknowledged to be valuable in this way.[53] What is true is that these projects are on a relatively small scale. But small-scale experiments—experiments like the Grameen Bank, when it was first launched—can make important advances that can then be applied on a wider scale.[54]

However, suppose that is wrong. Suppose that private aid agencies are powerless to contribute towards systemic reform. That still leaves the possibility of giving personal help to people who desperately need it. Giving that help may not address the root causes of poverty. But to see why *that* is not a sensible objection to it, we need only return to the life-saving analogy. Suppose I can easily save someone's life right in front of me, but if I do so, that will not do anything to address the underlying causes of the threat, so that it will remain as likely as before that others will face similar threats in future. It remains obvious what I should do. I should save the life, and it would be wrong not to do so. Even if the best way to dramatize the general problem, and get something done about it, would be to let this person die, doing so would obviously be wrong.[55] Once this life is saved, questions will then arise about averting the future threats that would be likely without further action. But the fact that these further questions remain to be addressed is not a good reason for me to do nothing for the person who needs it now.

This point is one that has long been embodied in the practice of humanitarian aid agencies. They talk of 'the humanitarian imperative' of helping people in desperate need, where this is distinguished from the political and economic task of preventing the need for humanitarian assistance in future.[56] My point here is slightly broader: the personal help I have in mind encompasses more than humanitarian relief. But the core point is essentially the one they have always made. Confronted with other people's need, there are two questions to ask: 'What can we do to stop this from happening again?' and 'What can we do to help these people now?' Recognizing that humanitarian aid will not answer the first question does not detract from its importance in addressing the second.

This is a good reply to the objection that aid is politically and economically useless. However, some critics of aid want to draw a stronger, more troubling conclusion:

(2) NGO aid is politically and economically regressive.

According to critics such as Maren and de Waal, it is not just that appealing to 'the humanitarian imperative' does not solve the underlying problems of poverty. An approach driven by the thought 'We ought to intervene to save lives now, and it is for others to fix up the underlying problems later' is itself an important part of the *problem*.[57] The humanitarian industry has become so large and so powerful in relation to the governments of the poorest countries, that it has itself become one of the central political and economic forces in the affairs of those countries. It is a force that stands in the way of moving those countries towards self-sufficiency. Flooding poor countries with goods and services at below market cost kills off a healthy local economy and replaces it with an artificial aid economy. Working with unaccountable political structures (or attempting to bypass them and establish a foreign-run aid delivery administration) counteracts the attempt to establish genuine 'political contracts' between vulnerable people and the holders of political power.[58] And, all too often, it is used as an alibi for the absence of concerted international political action.[59]

Invoking 'the humanitarian imperative', therefore, is not a satisfactory reply to (2). However, it does at least suggest that the case for (2) will need to be a compelling one if it is to countervail against the reasons there are for giving humanitarian aid. If people desperately need help now, and they can be helped, then there had better be a very strong case for thinking that the overall effects of doing so would be bad in order to justify withholding it.

Broadly speaking, there are two forms that a defence of (2) can take. The first involves defending (2) by arguing for a claim about the effects of any particular aid intervention:

(2*a*) Given the record of past NGO aid, any particular aid intervention is likely to do political and economic damage that outweighs the benefits that it produces.

An argument for (2*a*) will need to begin from assessments of particular aid interventions, and an examination of their overall consequences, good and bad. It will then need to maintain that the record is such that, if I am considering some new aid intervention, the likelihood is that it will be counter-productive.

We should not overstate what would be required for a convincing argument of this form. It would not need to survey all aid interventions. (It couldn't: the data does not exist.)[60] Rather, it would need to look carefully at a representative sample. And it need not be claiming that *all* aid interventions have bad overall consequences. Rather, it must (if it is to amount to a case for not giving aid at all) make a convincing case for thinking two things: that the overall consequences of aid interventions are more often bad than good; and that there is no feature of aid interventions that is a reliable predictor of the ones whose overall consequences are good.

However, this is still asking a lot. Notice that carrying it through fully would involve the contentious philosophical work of defending claims about the relative importance of the benefits and harms produced by aid, and of saying to whose agency they should be attributed. That is on top of the large prior task of showing convincingly that one's sample of aid interventions is representative, and saying what their long-term consequences are.

Some critics of aid do suggest an argument of this form: Maren is one. But no one has done so convincingly. Maren in particular has been widely criticized for overstating his case.[61] Certainly, you need to extrapolate a long way from Somalia and Rwanda, which most observers point to as the two recent situations where the performance of the humanitarian agencies has been worst, to get to the extreme conclusion that humanitarian aid should be abandoned altogether. (And even in the case of Somalia, Maren himself accepts that 100,000 lives were saved by the aid agencies.)[62] More importantly, those analysts who can claim to have conducted a broad survey of the record of NGO aid draw the opposite conclusion: that, although some aid fails, there are reliable indicators of success, and the record is improving.[63]

There does not seem to be convincing evidence for (2*a*). Might it nonetheless be right? And if so, would that undermine my argument? I shall return to this question in the next section.

First, though, we should notice that an argument for claim (2) can take a different form. When a writer like de Waal advances claim (2), he is making a claim, not about the likely costs and benefits of any particular aid intervention, but about the overall effect of the aid industry:

(2*b*) The aid industry is an obstacle, not a stimulus, to political and economic progress towards eradicating poverty.

Notice that (2*b*) could be true even if (2*a*) is false. This could be true if the kind of 'coordination problem' that can arise in relation to actions of other kinds applies to humanitarian action. Perhaps, if each aid agency takes the action that does the most good out of the alternatives open to it, they still might collectively be making things worse.[64] Even if, given the overall political context, a particular aid intervention may do more good than harm, it may be the case that the aid industry as a whole does more harm than good. For, as de Waal argues, the aid industry may itself be an important part of the overall political context, and a part that reinforces features of that context that are the prime causes of poverty and deprivation.

To support (2*b*), you do not need to produce the kind of argument that (2*a*) requires. What is necessary is not to survey aid interventions generally, and to establish that there is no source or category of aid that tends to do more good than harm. Rather, the argument here will proceed, as de Waal's does, by giving a theoretical explanation of the political factors underlying severe deprivation, coupled to plausible examples of progress and deterioration that are explained by those factors, and an explanation of how the aid industry reinforces those factors.

Finally, notice that (2*b*) comes in different strengths. Someone who advocates it might be making the strong claim:

(2*b*—strong) Removing rich-country NGOs from poor countries would itself, given the other prevailing factors, produce political and economic progress.

However, this claim is implausibly strong.[65] It is hard to see any grounds for thinking that the severe political and economic problems of Africa (or anywhere else) will solve themselves if they are simply left alone, and critics such as de Waal are careful to disclaim this idea.[66] What they are advancing, then, is a second, weaker claim:

(2*b*—weak) The operations of rich-country NGOs in poor countries give further support to the politically and economically regressive forces that produce poverty and deprivation.

Someone advancing this weaker claim is arguing for the abandonment of aid not on the grounds that this would by itself make the situation significantly better, but on the grounds that it is an obstacle to the kinds of action and policy that, if introduced, would be able to make the situation significantly better.

3.2 REPLY

The claim that needs to be taken most seriously as a challenge to my argument is (2*b*—weak). I now set out three replies to it.

First, notice the form that this claim must take in order to support a challenge to the argument I have been making. It would need to be claimed not just that NGO aid, taken as a whole, works to strengthen the causes of poverty and destitution, but that there is no form or source of NGO aid that succeeds in being economically and politically sensitive enough to avoid doing this. The studies of aid effectiveness that have been done do not seem to bear out that global claim. There *are* ways of designing aid projects and relief operations that minimize damage to local economies and structures of political accountability.[67] Given the emphasis that the better agencies such as Oxfam place on this issue, this is not surprising. And indeed, it is hard to find any careful critics who make it. (In the passage I quoted at the start of this chapter, for example, de Waal does not claim that *all* humanitarian activity in Africa ought to be abandoned.)

Secondly, even if the global form of (2*b*—weak) is right, there is still a gap between this and the conclusion that all aid should be withdrawn now. After all, needy people now rely on it to palliate the most severe hardship. Even if we should be aiming to withdraw aid as part of a strategy for achieving economic self-sufficiency and political accountability, it is obvious that we should not withdraw it in a way that avoidably causes massive suffering.[68] Any argument based on (2*b*—weak) for the disengagement of aid in favour of new local political and economic strategies would have to be an argument for phasing it out, and not for stopping it altogether now.

However, suppose all of this is wrong. I have asserted that the weight of expert opinion rejects the versions of claim (2) that I have been discussing. However, some people with knowledge and experience of the effects of international aid disagree. My third point is that, even if *that* is right, there still remains a forceful argument from the life-saving analogy for a moral requirement on us to act to help the poor.

The most that could be shown by the objections I have been considering is that we are not helping them by supporting humanitarian aid agencies. But that still does not mean that the most helpful thing we can do is *nothing*. It does not undermine the case for thinking that we ought to be supporting other efforts: efforts to expose the causes of destitution, efforts to publicize and encourage the structures of political accountability that can counteract its worst effects, efforts to protest against oppression and abuses of basic human freedoms, and efforts to reform those principles of international trade and finance that are obstacles to fighting poverty.

It is not just that no objection has been supported against the idea that doing these things would be good. A moral *requirement* to do them is still supported by the life-saving analogy set out in the previous two chapters. Suppose you encounter someone whose life is threatened, but you know that your efforts to save him will be counter-productive: they will be exploited, perhaps, by another person who is responsible for the threat. But suppose you can help in another way: by publicizing the threat, say. If that would be difficult or dangerous—if it would expose you to a similar threat yourself, for example—then there would begin to be a case to excuse your not taking that further action. But otherwise, there would not. If it would be *easy* for you to help in this further way, then doing so is not simply something it would be morally good to do. It would be morally wrong not to do it. The important question is whether you can easily do something to help. If you can, there remains an argument from beneficence for doing so. This argument remains in place even if the help you can give is not a matter of saving a life, but amounts to helping in some other important way.[69]

Thus, even if we ought to think some version of claim (2) is right, that still does not undermine an argument from beneficence for imposing moral requirements on us to help the poor. The most it could show is that the help we should be giving does not take the form of humanitarian aid. It would mean that we should not be supporting agencies like Oxfam or Médecins Sans Frontières. Instead, we should be supporting groups that concentrate on the other areas I identified above: groups like Food First (which seeks to research and publicize the causes of poverty), Justice Africa (which works to identify and encourage structures of political accountability), Amnesty International (which aims to expose oppression and abuses of basic human freedoms), and Jubilee 2000 (which campaigns for international financial reform).[70] You would need to have grounds for thinking that none of *these* activities were helpful to the poor before you could claim to have an argument undermining the case I have been presenting.

Moreover, as I have said, the evidence for drawing a conclusion as strong as (2) appears to be flimsy. There does not appear to be a serious case for believing that the most widely respected and reflective aid agencies, such as Oxfam—agencies with a long-term commitment to partnership with the countries in which they work, and a commitment to empowering the poor rather than treating them as charity objects—do more harm than good.[71] Such agencies, moreover, engage in a range of advocacy and publicity work of the kinds just mentioned, in addition to humanitarian relief work and development projects.[72]

What is Right about the Case against Aid

The view that aid is harmful enough to undermine the case for thinking that the rich are morally required to help the poor is unwarranted. This is so for two simple reasons: at least some forms of aid are helpful, and help need not take the form of humanitarian aid. However, that is not to say that the complaints about aid should be ignored. The problems created by the provision of some aid are real; and a relationship of aid-dependency can hardly itself be thought of as a solution to the problems of the poor.

There *is* a compelling case for withdrawing all aid—eventually—and for not giving some kinds of 'aid' at all. The aim has to be to arrive at a state of affairs in which people's most basic needs are secured without relying on humanitarian intervention. Part of the force of the criticisms of aid surveyed here has been to emphasize the ways in which aid tends to become self-perpetuating, creating vested interests in its continuation, and undermining the alternatives. For these reasons, as well as the reasons creating poverty in the first place, a transition to self-sufficiency will always meet resistance.

However, that has to be the goal to aim for. My point is the simple one that, although the withdrawal of aid should be our ultimate aim, we should avoid withdrawing it in a way that results in massive suffering. We could only be justified in withdrawing it in a way that *does* result in massive suffering if we were sure there was no alternative. But there are alternatives. They are not easy to implement. But we need to persevere in implementing them rather than abandoning the poor altogether.

The failures surveyed above are important. They do constitute a strong case for the regulatory proposal urged by several of the critics I have mentioned: that aid agencies should be overseen by an independent watchdog.[73] And those failures also make it important that we should support only the agencies that are serious about avoiding them. It is our responsibility to find out which agencies are the good ones (just as, if I am confronted directly with someone needing help, I ought to make a proper effort to find out the best way to help). But nothing has yet been said to defeat the case for thinking that it is also our responsibility to contribute to those agencies. We ought to support the aid agencies, *and* support efforts to scrutinize and improve them. And certainly, we ought not to be doing nothing.

3.3 THE BELIEF THAT AID IS COUNTER-PRODUCTIVE

I have argued against the view that aid should be abandoned because it does at least as much harm as good. However, there is a further thought to consider. It might seem that, whether or not aid agencies are actually counter-productive, it is enough to create a problem for my argument that a lot of people *believe* they are. After all, if we return once more to situations in which I can save someone's life directly, my beliefs about what I am capable of doing will be important to the moral assessment of what I do. Suppose someone's life needs to be saved, and I can do so: there is a life-buoy nearby. However, I do not know it: the life-buoy is concealed from me. Surely I cannot be blamed for not saving the life under *these* circumstances. Even when I could have saved a life, it can seem that the fact that I believed I could not is enough to show that I have acted blamelessly. Likewise, it may seem that if someone *believes* that aid agencies are counter-productive—as many people do—that is enough to show that she cannot reasonably be blamed giving nothing to them.

This is easy to answer, though. Ignorance does not produce immunity from blame. It does not silence moral criticism of me if I say that I did not know I could have helped. Maybe I should have known. And this might be because I should have made a greater effort to find out whether I could have helped. If I couldn't see the life-buoy, but didn't make a proper effort to look for one, then I could certainly be blameworthy for that. It is debatable whether this kind of negligence is properly called a failure of beneficence. But if not, it is a moral failure of a closely related kind. If someone is in desperate need right in front of me, then part of what a proper concern for his interests requires of me is to exert myself to see whether I can help him. If his life is at stake, I owe it to him to make a sincere and sustained effort before concluding there is nothing I can helpfully do. If I do not make this effort, then the lack of concern for his interests that this displays is obviously wrong, and I am blameworthy for it.

If so, then the life-saving analogy gives us a corresponding conclusion about the belief that aid agencies are counter-productive. This belief ought to be scrutinized with as much effort as you ought to make in looking for a way to save someone's life: it would be wrong for you not to do this, and you are blameworthy if you do not.[74] I doubt whether many of those who believe that aid is counter-productive have given their belief *this* much sincere and sustained scrutiny. Some people have, though.[75] The appropriate thing to say about them is that their failure to give to aid agencies is blameless. However, we should still say that they act wrongly.[76] For, as I have argued, we ought not to believe that aid is counter-productive, and there remains a forceful moral case for requiring us to give it.

3.4 'WHY SINGLE OUT OVERSEAS AID?'

Before concluding this chapter, let me briefly deal with one other objection that my discussion invites as it stands. Are there not many other valuable ends that are just as worthy of support as the relief of distant poverty? If so, it cannot be right to single out this one cause as the one that it is wrong not to support. When I am confronted with someone who needs to be saved by me there and then, I have no reasonable choice what to do; when I am offered the opportunity to give money to an international aid agency, that is different.[77]

In response to this, I want to concede some ground. I have not shown that there is no other cause that it would be equally good to support. And if there is, it is a mistake to assert without qualification, as I have been doing so far, that it is wrong not to contribute to international aid agencies. You could be supporting some other equally good cause instead, without acting wrongly. (For one thing, it is an obvious mistake to think that poverty and material need only exist overseas.) However, this does not show that the life-saving analogy defended in Chapters 1 and 2 should be rejected. Rather, it broadens the conclusion we should draw from it. My argument for the life-saving analogy is based upon attending to what beneficence requires of us in responding to the extreme needs of other people. But people overseas are not the only ones with extreme needs. And there may be other causes of comparable importance to addressing people's extreme needs. This is not an argument for requiring us to help everyone, and to do everything else that is comparably important. We can't. But it is an argument for the wrongness of doing nothing. So the right response to this objection is simply to broaden the conclusion drawn from the life-saving analogy. If you are contributing neither to international aid agencies nor to some other equally good cause, then that is wrong. More accurately still: if you are not making a serious effort to find an effective way to help the poor, or contributing to some other comparably important cause, then you are acting wrongly. Broadening the conclusion in this way makes it more accurate. But, since it will not affect any of my subsequent arguments, I shall continue to state the conclusion of the life-saving analogy in the simpler and less accurate form, for convenience.

3.5 CONCLUSION

Other people's chronic need provides us with a strong reason to help them. Beneficence requires us to act on this reason when a needy person is right in front of us and we can help him easily. So unless there is a relevantly countervailing consideration, we should say the same about giving indirect help to needy people who are not right in front of us. *Is* there a relevantly countervailing difference between the two kinds of case? I have now rejected what I think are the most important attempts to find one.

These attempts have been met, in this chapter and the previous one, by five different kinds of reply. The first was the strategy used in Chapter 2 to discuss non-immediacy and indirectness. Claims about the non-immediacy and indirectness of my relationship to the beneficiaries of aid agencies are true, and these considerations do distinguish contributions to aid agencies from helping someone right in front of you. The problem is that they cannot sensibly be treated as countervailing. These considerations cannot explain why not contributing to a life-saving aid agency does not amount to a failure of beneficence, when not saving a life directly does.

The attempt to identify a countervailing consideration can fail in a second obvious way, which is the converse of the first. We saw this in discussing the proposal that aid agencies do as much harm as good, which has occupied most of this chapter. This proposal would give us a relevantly countervailing consideration if it were true, but it is false.

A third kind of failure will occur when the fact that is proposed as a countervailing consideration, although it is true enough, does not succeed in distinguishing non-contribution to aid agencies from refusals to help people directly that seem obviously wrong. Several of the claims we have considered were shown to fail in this third way: that emergency relief aid does not address the long-term causes of poverty, that the impact of NGO development aid on the overall problems of poverty is only small, and that non-contributors to aid agencies do not believe that there is an appropriate way of helping. The reply to these proposals involved simply modifying the starting point of the life-saving analogy, and then showing that the argument of the first two chapters remains intact. When we look at cases of saving a life directly that have analogous features, it is still obvious that not helping would be wrong. Therefore, the life-saving analogy will still support the conclusion that I am morally required to contribute to aid agencies when these various claims are true.[78]

A fourth kind of reply involved showing that a proposed countervailing consideration works against some forms of aid but not others, so that all it tells us is that we should be discriminating about the agencies we choose to support. And finally, there was the strategy of conceding that there *are* considerations that give us effective objections to the conclusion that Chapters 1 and 2 were drawing from the life-saving analogy—but adding that this shows only that that conclusion needs to be broadened, and not that it should be rejected outright. One ground for doing this came from thinking about people who *believe* that aid is counter-productive; another from the thought that international aid should not be singled out above all other causes that are worthy of our support. These points suggested that it is too strong simply to conclude that you are morally required to contribute to international aid agencies. But it remains the case that you are acting wrongly if you are not making a serious effort to find an effective way to help the poor, or contributing to some other comparably important cause. Likewise, I argued that even if there were a convincing case for thinking that humanitarian aid does more harm than good, that would only show that we should be helping through avenues other than humanitarian aid.

It would have been tedious to try to cover every possible candidate disanalogy, or even to treat those I have mentioned in full detail; so I have done neither of these things. A full list would have included the objections that responsibility for the welfare of the destitute belongs to themselves,[79] their own governments, or to global institutions,[80] that the beneficiaries of aid agencies belong to different communities from ours,[81] that we have a right to use our own property as we wish,[82] that charity is motivated by guilt rather than genuine concern, and several others. To have worked through this list would simply have meant further repetitions of these five simple kinds of reply. And I think enough has now been said to show that, if there is anything wrong with the life-saving analogy, it will not be found in some further, undiscussed countervailing consideration.

To appreciate this, think about the challenge that someone proposing a further countervailing consideration is trying to meet. Our question is why refusing to give money to aid agencies is not wrong, given that letting someone die right in front of you would be. Chapter 2 argued that the most natural candidate answer—citing differences in immediacy or directness—should be rejected. If this is right, then a further countervailing consideration will have to meet the following test: it must be a fact which, if incorporated in a case of letting someone die directly, should lead us to deny that doing so would be wrong. What we have seen is that, once you accept this test, it looks difficult to meet. The most plausible considerations for an opponent to mention turn out either to fail it, to be false when asserted of aid agencies, or to leave open ways of responding to other people's need that are still morally required of us. However, what an opponent of the life-saving analogy should really be doing is not to search for another consideration that meets this test, but to reject the test. After all, accepting it means accepting that not giving money to aid agencies *is* to be treated like letting someone die directly, but then trying to show that it resembles a kind of letting die that is not wrong. The crucial issue for someone who opposes the life-saving analogy to focus on should really be whether non-contribution is comparable to any sort of direct letting die. Once it is conceded that it *is*, the opponent takes on the onus of showing the moral relevance of some supposedly distinguishing feature of the help that is given through aid agencies. I think enough attempts to do this have now been discussed to display the difficulties in making a convincing case of this kind. The main line of opposition should come, instead, by rejecting the comparison in the first place, and hence the need to defend some countervailing difference.

We have already seen one way of pressing this more radical attack, rejecting the life-saving analogy outright. If the analogy is applied too crudely, it can be criticized for offering a naive and even harmful way of thinking about international assistance. However, applied less crudely—that is, once the important points made by the critics of aid are taken into account—an argument from the life-saving analogy still generates a powerful case for a moral requirement to help the poor.

I think there remain two plausible grounds on which the life-saving analogy might be challenged. I discuss them next.

4

Saving Lives

WILL my contributions to aid agencies save people's lives? The argument for the life-saving analogy presented in the first two chapters assumes so. However, this assumption faces two important challenges that we have not yet considered—challenges that are independent of any of the objections to aid we have just been discussing. Even if aid agencies do achieve their aim of helping people, there remain grounds for doubting whether my contributions to those agencies can be said to save anyone's life. Often, the good that those agencies do is not a matter of saving people's lives. And even when it is, there is still room to doubt whether *my contributions* to the agency save people's lives.

In the previous two chapters I have been discussing attempts to refute the life-saving analogy by identifying countervailing considerations. Those attempts tried to show that, although there is the same reason of beneficence for helping people at a distance as there is for saving a life directly, there is a further feature of the former case that stops it from generating a requirement of beneficence. The two challenges I am now going to consider are different: they attack my argument in a more fundamental way. They provide grounds for thinking that there is not the same reason of beneficence in the two cases: my contribution to an aid agency is not an action of saving anyone's life.

The first challenge develops out of a point that was made in the previous chapter. To defend the efficacy of aid agencies, I appealed in part to the contribution their development work makes towards improving poor people's lives. If aid agencies' work does that, few people would want to say it is bad. Some people would want to say that it is as good as saving lives. But whether or not that is true, this work is not itself the saving of lives. It is (among other things) the preventing of threats to life. But that is different; and it affects the form that a compelling argument for contributing to aid agencies must take. We need to replace the life-saving analogy with a threat-preventing analogy. But when we do, it is not so obvious that this will generate a compelling argument. It may be obvious enough as a starting point for moral discussion that we can be morally required to save lives. But is it so obvious that we are acting wrongly if we do not work to prevent threats to life?

The other challenge I consider in this chapter is independent of the first. Even if we confine our attention to aid agencies that concentrate exclusively on saving lives, it can be doubted whether the effect of any contribution I make to those agencies will be the saving of a person's life. Even if aid agencies rescue people, the idea that *I* am reaching out to rescue someone when I give money to an aid agency may still be a myth. I think this line of objection has a good deal of force. Indeed, I shall concede that it might well be right. If so, the assumption we have been making will have to be rejected. However, the aim of this chapter is to show that this does not actually matter. It turns out that the argument for the life-saving analogy does not depend on this assumption after all.

4.1 PREVENTING THREATS

Since the 1960s there has been a growing emphasis among aid agencies on tackling the causes of deprivation rather than simply responding to its distressing effects. Merely giving goods to people who are already destitute, and leaving in place the underlying causes of that destitution, only guarantees that the same effects will be regularly produced again in the future.

The most obvious practical applications of this thought involve work in basic preventive health care: improving sanitation, especially through securing clean water supplies; setting up vaccination programmes; and giving dietary advice to help people make the best nutritional use of limited incomes. At a deeper level, the aim that has been widely embraced, and is becoming increasingly dominant in the work of some non-government aid agencies, is to contribute towards the social change that is needed to reduce people's vulnerability to chronic deprivation. In Chapter 3 I mentioned the kinds of work that non-government organizations do towards this larger goal, in education, supporting local economic and political self-reliance, and lobbying for structural change.[a]

This reorientation of aid agencies, away from an exclusive concern with administering emergency relief operations and towards taking practical steps to prevent the need for life-saving aid, is surely sensible. However, it does undermine the case for thinking that the good that aid agencies do is a matter of saving lives: it often amounts not to this, but to preventing threats to life.

To the extent that aid agencies work on long-term help or development rather than on the relief of present crises, it becomes inappropriate to think of contributions to those agencies in terms of a life-saving analogy. A threat-preventing analogy is more appropriate. Contributing to an agency

[a] Sect. 3.1, 'Alternative Conclusions'.

that is working to avert crises rather than to alleviate them is more like funding a fire safety programme than saving someone from a fire. But changing the analogy in this way makes the argument much less compelling. The argument presented in Chapters 1 and 2 began from the claim that the failure to save a life directly, when you could easily have done so, is obviously wrong. This is uncontroversial enough to be a good starting point for moral argument. But surely, although it is uncontroversial that your funding a fire safety programme would be good, it is much less obvious that your not doing so is wrong. If anything, this is *less* obvious than the conclusion for which I am arguing—that not contributing to aid agencies is wrong. If our argument needs to be restructured around a threat-preventing rather than a life-saving analogy, that makes it much weaker.

Of course, while the long-term preventive work goes on, current emergencies also call to be addressed. Some voluntary aid agencies do devote themselves entirely to emergency relief work, and many others do so in part. And it seems that the original analogy will still apply to the contributions you could make to this sort of work. However, an opponent might reason as follows. Surely, it is better for us to tackle the causes of poverty and work towards its eradication, rather than merely addressing its life-threatening effects, for the reasons that have been given. So, if anything, we ought to support long-term development work rather than relief work. But supporting long-term development work, although it might be a good thing to do, is not morally required: it is like funding a fire safety programme rather than rescuing someone from a fire. And if supporting development work is preferable to supporting relief work but is not morally required, then supporting relief work cannot be morally required either. Thus, although it might be good for me to contribute to aid agencies, it is not wrong not to.

4.2 AN INITIAL REPLY

The argument just described is unconvincing. It makes two basic moves. First, it argues that supporting long-term development work is analogous not to saving a life but to preventing a threat, and maintains on the strength of this analogy that supporting long-term development work is not morally required. Secondly, it attempts to infer that, since development work is better than relief work, supporting the latter cannot be morally required either. But the problem is that this has done nothing to undermine the claim that supporting relief work is analogous to saving a life directly. And until *that* claim is challenged, we should reject the second move.

To see this, consider your actual situation. You have two non-exclusive options: you can support development work or relief work. So suppose we accept the suggestion that supporting development work is analogous to funding a fire safety programme. No objection has yet been raised against the idea that supporting relief work is analogous to rescuing someone from a fire. Thus, the most this suggests is that your actual situation is analogous to one in which you can either easily rescue someone from a fire or fund a fire safety programme. And in *that* situation, it is just as obvious as ever that doing nothing would be wrong. Maybe there could be a case for thinking that it would be morally acceptable to fund the fire safety programme instead of rescuing the person—although that is surely hard to believe. But what is much harder to believe is that adding the option of funding the fire safety programme now makes it morally acceptable to do nothing at all. If so, the argument just described must fail. Unless there are grounds for doubting whether supporting relief work is analogous to a case of direct rescue, this will be the right analogy to draw. And it will support the conclusion that it is wrong not to contribute to aid agencies, just as strongly as before.

Moreover, and more importantly, the conclusion supported by this analogy is backed up by an argument from beneficence, along the lines set out in Chapter 2. It is not as though all we can say is that not contributing to aid agencies is analogous to an example of conduct which intuitively seems wrong. We can give a simple and convincing explanation of why it is wrong. If your alternatives are either to provide someone with life-saving help at little cost or to do nothing, then the reason doing nothing would be wrong is that it would be a failure of beneficence—it would be a glaring failure to respond to another person's urgent needs, in the absence of any countervailing reasons to excuse it. And adding a third alternative—the alternative of preventing future threats—does nothing to change this. It does not help to explain how doing nothing escapes the same criticism, of being a glaring failure to respond to others' needs.

So far, then, it looks as though this first attempt to challenge the life-saving analogy can be quickly dismissed. The life-saving analogy itself remains intact, and gives us a strong reply.

However, this reply has revealed an apparent anomaly. If you could either easily rescue someone from a fire or fund a fire safety programme, then obviously it would be wrong to do nothing. But, more than that, surely a stronger claim is obvious: it would be wrong not to rescue the person. It would be perverse in such a situation to let the person die and fund a safety programme instead. But then, if direct rescue is analogous to supporting a relief agency and funding the safety programme is analogous to supporting a development agency, does this not lead to the conclusion that it is wrong to support development agencies in preference to relief agencies? And won't this apply to *every* well-off individual? But surely that is difficult to believe. For surely we *should*, as was suggested above, be doing what we can to eradicate poverty rather than just confining ourselves to addressing its effects.

This suggests one of two uncomfortable conclusions. Either there is something wrong with the analogies I have been making, or we should accept those analogies and draw the hard-to-believe conclusion that we are morally required to support relief work to the exclusion of development work.

I shall come back to this problem later in the chapter. It will be easier to see the answer to it after I have dealt with this chapter's second challenge, to which I now turn.

4.3 THE EFFECT OF MY CONTRIBUTION

The first challenge to the life-saving analogy has concerned the kind of help produced by aid agencies. The second challenge instead concerns the effects of my own actions in furthering that help. In discussing the effectiveness of aid, Chapter 3 has discussed whether we collectively make a positive difference through aid agencies. But the question this book has set out to address concerns the moral requirements that apply to each of us individually. And arguably, even if our collective support of aid agencies has a significant positive effect, *my* actions do not. Any donation that I give will be pooled along with others, and used by the agency as part of a larger fund. It obviously makes sense for donations to be handled this way: pooling them is more efficient, which is to say that it allows more help to be given. But just what difference will it make whether or not I contribute to the pool?

For simplicity, let us concentrate on a case of famine relief. If I give a donation to a famine relief agency, it will be added to a fund which the agency will use to buy a large quantity of food, to equip and staff a distribution camp, and to transport the food there. A first, natural thought is that, to calculate the effect of my donation, we should take the total amount of food distributed and the total cost of distributing it, and then work out the proportion of the cost I have met. Suppose, when we do this, the proportion of the cost attributed to me corresponds to enough food to feed one person for the duration of the crisis. It still seems wrong to say that the effect of my action has been the saving of one life. For suppose I had not made my donation. The effect of this would not have been that one of the people who was actually fed would have gone without any food. It is tempting to think instead that the effect would be to lessen the agency's total stock of food, causing the available food to be spread a little more thinly around all the hungry people. But, on reflection, even this seems to exaggerate the effects of my donation. If I make a donation corresponding to enough food to feed one person, this will not mean that that amount of food goes to the camp. Relief agencies do not buy food in such small amounts. Instead, they make a large-scale calculation of the size of the overall need, the amount of money they are likely to be able to raise from various sources to pay for it, and the extent to which it makes sense to draw on contingency funds in the light of other likely calls on them. Guided by these large-scale considerations, they then arrange the shipment of a large quantity of food. The agency's deliberations will thus be conducted on a scale that is simply not sensitive to the difference I would make by donating enough to help one person. My decision to donate, therefore, will not even produce an effect which is dispersed among the fund's many beneficiaries; rather, it will have no effect at all on them.

This invites a reply.[1] Perhaps it is true that my donation will *probably* have no effect on whether another food consignment is sent. But what is important is not the actual but the expected benefit that I produce. And if there is a small chance that my action will produce a large benefit, then the expected benefit may still be significant. After all, if an agency's appeal fund continues to grow as individual contributions are made to it, then eventually it will send another consignment. And for each consignment sent by an efficiently run agency, reliable expectations can be formed of the number of lives that will be saved by it. My donation will probably not be the one that triggers the threshold that causes the agency to send another consignment, but there is some chance that it will be. If my donation is, say, one thousandth of the amount needed to make a consignment that can be expected to save a thousand lives, then on average my donating that amount would trigger that threshold once in every thousand times I made it. This gives me a one in a thousand chance that my donation will be the one that makes the difference between saving and not saving a thousand lives. So the expected benefit is the saving of one life.

However, this reply does not seem decisive. For it can plausibly be denied that any such threshold is triggered by a single donation. Granted, aid agency decisions about whether to send another food consignment are certainly sensitive to the size of their appeal fund; and donors to that fund will collectively affect the decision over whether to send more food. But those decisions will not be so sensitive to the exact size of the fund that any single donation will have such an effect; and if not, there is not even a small chance that my donation will be the one to have that effect.[2] Given the agency's assessment of the amount of food it is desirable to buy, any small shortfall that results from my not making a donation will be covered—indeed, much larger shortfalls will be covered—by extra fundraising efforts, or absorbed in administrative savings.[3]

Given these thoughts, there are different ways in which an objection against the life-saving analogy might be formulated. It might simply be objected that my donation confers no benefit at all on anyone; or, more cautiously, that it confers no perceptible benefit; or that needy people ought to be indifferent to whether or not I give the donation. In general, the objection will be that my donation does not produce a benefit significant enough to be morally required of me. Just what feature a benefit has to have in order to give it this significance would be a matter for further debate. But the objection will be that my donation does not produce a benefit with this feature. Far from saving anyone's life, my action of donating money has no significant impact at all: it would not be missed by any of the people for whose sake it is performed.[4] The problem for the life-saving analogy is obvious. If we are looking for a case of direct help which is analogous to donating to an aid agency, we need a case where I can join a collective effort to save a number of lives directly, but I know that my own contribution will not make the difference between anyone's living and dying. Perhaps there is something wrong with refusing to do this; but it hardly seems satisfactory to begin an argument for the wrongness of non-contribution to aid agencies by simply claiming that that would *obviously* be wrong.

4.4 REPLY: A COLLECTIVE MORAL REQUIREMENT

When many of us find that we share an aim, we tend to cooperate in pursuing it. This makes sense; for, by cooperating, we will often collectively be able to achieve that aim more effectively than if we had each pursued it independently. When we do this, we turn our common aim into a collective aim—the aim of a collective action that we perform together.

There are some aims that each of us is morally required to have. One of them is the aim characteristic of beneficence: the aim of furthering other people's interests. Each of us is morally required to have this aim, and to act on it in the absence of countervailing considerations. And this is certainly an aim that can often be more effectively pursued if we cooperate in pursuing it collectively. When there is a large-scale need for assistance, the most effective response is often one that involves pooling individual contributions and then organizing the distribution of resources from the pool. If more people can be helped to a greater extent than by uncoordinated acts of beneficence, then this seems to provide us with a very clear case for cooperation. Indeed, the possibility of collectively organized, large-scale beneficent activity can create opportunities for beneficence that would not otherwise exist. Where people who need help are distant from us, and a threshold of resources needs to be surpassed before the help can be effective, there may be little any of us could usefully do alone, whereas by combining our efforts we may be able to achieve a lot.

When we ought to cooperate in collectively pursuing an aim that each of us is morally required to have, a new moral requirement is created: a *collective* moral requirement—a moral requirement of which *we* together are the subject. A collective requirement of beneficence can exist when it is possible for us to help someone together, even if none of us could have helped on her own. This is shown clearly by examples, and is a straightforward implication of the account of beneficence I have given in Chapter 2. If someone is drowning in front of you and me, and can be rescued only by using a winch mechanism that requires two people to operate, then it is obvious that we are morally required to help him, even if neither of us could do so single-handedly. Why? Because he desperately needs this help, and we could provide it at small cost to ourselves. The explanation of the requirement of beneficence is the same as before: the only difference is that the subject of the requirement is the two of us collectively, rather than one person individually. The reasons for imposing requirements of beneficence on individuals clearly apply equally to groups.

This is not yet a reply to someone who emphasizes the insignificant effect of my contributions to aid agencies. But it is a claim that someone with this view cannot sensibly oppose. Clearly, our collective actions can have a significant effect in helping other people; and this is the basis of collective requirements on us to do so. This must be accepted even by someone who thinks that only benefits that make a difference worth caring about can be morally required. Collectively produced benefits clearly can make a difference worth caring about.

Given this, the objection will have to take the following form. The wrongness of a collective action does not entail the wrongness of the actions of any member of the group that is collectively acting wrongly. Suppose, for example, that we ought collectively to make a gesture of reconciliation to an unjustly treated group. If we do not collectively do so, we are collectively acting wrongly. But it may not be in the power of any member of the group to offer that gesture on his own: what is required is a gesture from the group. And, plausibly, it might be supererogatory for any individual to undertake the political leadership necessary to getting the group to make the gesture. Thus, there is no straightforward inference from the existence of a collective moral requirement to the existence of a corresponding moral requirement on individuals. Not all collective moral requirements distribute onto individuals in this way. So why not hold that there are collective requirements of beneficence that fail to distribute onto individuals? Since we could collectively make a significant difference to poor people at a distance, we are collectively required to do so: if we do nothing, we are collectively acting wrongly. But since none of us could individually make a significant difference, no individual acts wrongly if she does nothing.

I accept that collective moral requirements do not always distribute onto individuals. However, I shall now show that in this case there are good grounds, given the collective moral requirement we have established, for thinking that individuals are morally required to contribute to meeting it.

Fairness and Collective Imperatives

How, if my contribution to a collective effort makes no difference worth caring about, can it be wrong not to make it? There is now an interesting literature on this problem; but it is not going to help us here.[5] Most prominent writers on this topic simply take it that the issue I am raising here is settled by counter-example.[6] They take it as obviously false that only actions that do make a difference worth caring about can be morally required: their interest is in saying whether this requires us to accept the existence of imperceptible harms and benefits, and which imperatives of beneficence we should endorse as a result.[7] But what should we say to someone for whom this is not obvious?

What we should say is that failing to contribute towards meeting the collective moral requirement is *unfair*. If you leave it to others to contribute, you are arrogating a special privilege to yourself: the privilege of freeing yourself of the costs that must be borne if we are to do what we ought. You are relying on others to contribute, without being prepared to do so yourself, and without any justification for treating yourself differently from them. And if this is what is wrong with your conduct, then pointing out that your contribution would not itself make a difference is irrelevant. For of course that is true of everyone else as well. The point is that the collective requirement is only going to be met if individuals make a contribution to meeting it, despite the ineffectiveness of any one contribution by itself. *This* is what provides a fair-minded person with sufficient reason to contribute. And when we are collectively required to do something, and we are doing so because of some people's willingness to contribute, my own unwillingness to do so will involve relying on others to do what must be done while exempting myself from doing so, but without having any good reason for the special exemption.

Now, for someone who thinks that an action can only be morally required if it makes a difference worth caring about, there might seem to be this reply: 'Whether or not any individual contributes to the pool makes no difference to whether the collective action is performed—the collective imperative is no better met if I contribute than if I do not. In fact, no individual act of participation in the pool is contributing to meeting the collective imperative; so I cannot be relying on anyone's doing this when I refuse to participate in the pool, and I cannot be doing anything wrong in refusing.' However, this involves a mistake. Let us concede that no single contribution will itself have the effect that the collective imperative is better met. It is a mistake to infer from this that individual acts of participation in the pool are not contributions to meeting the collective imperative. The *contribution* is perceptible—I put a perceptible amount into the pool—even if it does not have a perceptible effect on what is achieved by the group.

Thus there is no good objection to saying that the collective imperative is only being met because others are prepared to make contributions to meeting it: we should simply add that what they are prepared to do is to make those contributions even when each has no perceptible effect on what is achieved by the group. Therefore, if I am not myself prepared to make a contribution of this kind, I am relying on others to do what must be done if the collective imperative is to be fulfilled, without being prepared to do so myself. And that is unfair.

This can be supported by noticing the way in which the same explanation is needed for other kinds of obviously unfair conduct. For example, consider paradigm cases of free riding: helping yourself to a collectively produced good without being prepared to pay towards its production. If you do this—you abuse an 'honour' system for public transport fares by riding without paying, let's say—then you are acting unfairly. You are arrogating to yourself a privilege of not paying for benefits for which you rely on others' willingness to pay. Here, too, the unfairness of what you are doing has nothing to do with any adverse effects on anyone else: you can point out correctly that no one else is made any worse off by your actions. (To use the economists' term, the good you are enjoying may be 'non-rival'.)[8] But again, that is irrelevant. Your conduct is unfair because of the way you are taking a special privilege for yourself—a privilege that other, fairminded people have renounced. If everyone thought like you, the good would not be produced at all. It is only produced, that is to say, if individuals think collectively, in the following sense. We need the individual members of the group to take the fact that we ought collectively to be producing a good as a sufficient reason to make an individual contribution, meeting the (fairly distributed) share of the cost that has to be met by each in order to produce the good for the benefit of everyone. And we need people to think like that even if it is true that whether or not any one individual meets her share of the cost will itself make no significant difference to everyone else. If the good is being produced, people *are* thinking like that. You are relying on this in order to have an opportunity to enjoy the good at all. And yet you are arrogating to yourself the privilege of not contributing your own share.

A free rider could try replying as follows: 'I am not arrogating any special privileges to myself. I think that each other person ought to be doing what I do. Of course, if everyone did so, then there would be no benefits for anyone. And, speaking *collectively*, it is more sensible for us to produce the benefits than to go without them. But that does not show that anyone ought individually to contribute to our collectively doing so.'

However, this does not answer the complaint of unfairness. The way in which the free rider is arrogating privileges to herself is not that she makes a claim of permission for herself which she is not prepared to make for other individuals. Rather, it is this: she relies on others to contribute to what we ought collectively to be doing, without contributing herself. As she can see, the group to which she belongs ought to be acting to produce the benefit she is enjoying, because the benefit is worth its cost. There is, in this sense, a collective imperative: something we ought collectively to be doing. That collective imperative is being met, but she is leaving the work of meeting it to others. Thus, when she protests that she can accept the collective imperative while consistently denying that this gives rise to any individual imperatives, the response to her is that this is irrelevant. The complaint against her is not that she is being inconsistent, but that she is violating a requirement of fairness. Fairness is what tells us to derive the individual imperative from the collective one.[9]

I am not saying that failing to contribute to collective acts of beneficence is itself free riding. My description of the two cases makes it clear that they are different. The paradigm cases of free riding are those in which we ought to be collectively producing a good, but not because we are *morally required* to do so. Rather, we ought to be producing the good because it is worth the cost: in the purest case, having it would be good for each of us, and if we cooperate to produce it, the cost to each of us will be less than the benefit to each of us.[10] The collective imperative is an imperative of self-interest, rather than a moral requirement. However, what cases of free riding do illustrate is the way in which fairness compels us to derive individual imperatives from collective imperatives—and how it is irrelevant to this derivation whether any individual contribution itself has a significant effect.

I am not claiming, either, that fairness *always* compels deriving individual imperatives from collective ones. No doubt, there are very many things that we all ought to be doing, but are not. That does not mean that I ought to launch unilaterally into making some active contribution towards each of the goals we ought collectively to be pursuing. If my city ought to be developing its water reservoir capacity, that does not mean that I ought to start digging a hole in the ground. However, that is consistent with the claims I have been making about fairness. It is unfair to rely on others to contribute to meeting a collective imperative, without being prepared to contribute myself. Obviously, where no one is yet meeting that imperative, I am not unfairly relying on other people in this way.[11] Often, what fairness requires of me is a preparedness to cooperate in an agreed method for reaching a collective goal. Where no agreed method has yet been settled upon, the fact that I do not unilaterally start acting towards that collective goal will not be unfair.[12]

It is not part of my aim here to defend a full account of fairness. My point here is more modest. The fact that my contribution to a pool supporting beneficent action, when considered on its own, does not have a significant impact on the intended beneficiaries is no defence against an argument from *fairness* for requiring us to make them. And that there is such an argument is illustrated by the parallel explanation of what is wrong with free riding.

Fairness or Beneficence?

It might appear that this has changed my argument in a fundamental way. In Chapters 1 and 2 the case for requiring us to contribute to aid agencies was presented as an argument from beneficence. It now turns out that it is actually an argument from fairness.

However, putting it that way is misleading. I have not replaced an argument from beneficence with an argument from fairness. Rather, I have maintained that we stand under a collective moral requirement of beneficence to help needy people through aid agencies, and there is an individual moral requirement of fairness upon each of us to contribute towards meeting that collective requirement. Chapters 1, 2, and 3 are still needed to make the case for the requirement of beneficence. What the current chapter has done is not to supplant that argument with a different argument from fairness. Rather, it has pointed out that, given the way that contributions to aid agencies are cooperatively pooled, the requirement of beneficence that is established by Chapters 1–3 is a collective requirement. And it has supplemented this with a further argument from fairness to derive individual moral requirements from this collective one.

This does still leave us with a serious question to answer, though. In Chapter 1, I introduced my argument for the wrongness of failing to contribute to aid agencies by saying that the initial version of it would be 'individually based', in contrast to those collectively based arguments—such as arguments from rectificatory or distributive justice—that derive conclusions about what an affluent individual ought to be doing for the poor from claims about what we are collectively required to do. However, it now turns out that, in its more considered version, the argument I am advocating is a collectively based argument after all. And it looks as though that will make an important difference to the conclusions that the argument generates. Rather than leading towards the kind of extremely demanding conclusion endorsed by advocates of individually based arguments, it seems to be leading to the conclusion that what is morally required of me is that I discharge my fair share of what we all ought collectively to be doing. And that seems to promise a more moderate conclusion.[13]

However, I think that this 'fair share' view is wrong. I explain why in the next chapter.

4.5 COLLECTIVE REQUIREMENTS OF BENEFICENCE, AND PREVENTING THREATS

The aim characteristic of beneficence is furthering other people's interests. We are morally required to act in pursuit of this aim, in the absence of countervailing considerations. This is a requirement that applies to us both individually and collectively. This means saving people's lives when we could easily do so. But it also means preventing threats to them when we could easily do so. If I am aware of a threat to someone else's life, and could easily avert it, then my failure to do so (in the absence of any further countervailing consideration) is wrong, in the same way that other failures of beneficence are wrong. And if we could collectively avert a threat, then we might be collectively acting wrongly if we fail to do so.

However, what is the right thing to say about situations in which there is a choice between either saving a life or averting a threat? As we noticed at the end of Section 4.2, this question produces an apparent anomaly. Saving life seems to take precedence in individual action, but not in collective action. For surely, if I could either rescue you from a fire or fund a fire safety programme, I ought to rescue you. But it seems equally clear that it would be a bad policy for us collectively to privilege saving lives over preventing threats. Devoting all our resources to saving lives would be a mistake, if we could allocate at least some of them to preventing threats, and thereby not need to save as many lives in the future. That is why it makes sense for aid agencies to work towards long-term development and the protection of rights, and not just to concentrate on emergency relief.

This gives us two problems. One is to explain why saving life takes precedence in the first case but not the second. The second is to explain how this could be consistent with my use of the life-saving analogy. If, when I could save a life directly, I am required to do that in preference to helping to prevent future threats, then the life-saving analogy seems to suggest that I should contribute to life-saving agencies rather than preventive agencies. And so should everyone else. But, as we have seen, that seems wrong. Surely we ought to support development work as well as relief work.

We are now in a position to address these problems. To do so, we need to begin by looking more carefully at the choices being described. When I could either rescue you from a fire or fund a fire safety programme, the choice is between an individual action of saving a life on the one hand, and a contribution to the collective action of preventing threats on the other. The choice in the second case, by contrast, is a choice between two collective actions: our concentrating exclusively on saving lives, and our working to prevent threats too.

In the first case, a simple explanation can be given for why I should rescue you. By doing this, I would do much more good to other people than if I contributed to fire safety. For, as we have seen, it is questionable whether *my* contribution to fire safety will itself make a significant difference to anyone at all. This does not mean that there is no reason to make this contribution. There is a reason (based in considerations of fairness) that supports my doing so, despite the insignificant effects of my action. However, it is plausible to think that, given the difference I will make to you by helping you, the direct reason of beneficence for rescuing you in this case overrides the reason of fairness for contributing to the collective action. Turning to the second case, there is an equally simple explanation why we should collectively prevent threats, rather than concentrating on saving lives. It is the same explanation. It would do more good to other people. If our action is an expression of concern for other people's interests, a more effective way to help them is to obviate the need for rescue, addressing the causes of people's need and not merely its effects. Here, the reason for us collectively to save lives and the reason for us collectively to prevent threats are both reasons of beneficence. There is a stronger reason of beneficence to do what does more good to other people. That means preventing threats as well as saving lives.

I am not appealing here to the 'welfarist' view that we should *always* do whatever does the most good to other people. Rather, I am simply pointing out that there is a clear, consistent explanation of why saving life takes precedence in the first case but not the second.[14] I have not *shown* that the reason of beneficence prevails over the reason of fairness in the first case. My claim is simply that this is a plausible thing to say. And if so, there is nothing anomalous about thinking that saving life takes precedence in one case but not the other.

We are also now in a position to see how this is consistent with my use of the life-saving analogy. We have seen in this chapter that, if the effects of my contributions to aid agencies are themselves insignificant, the life-saving analogy will not directly apply to individual contributions to aid agencies. However, we have also seen that it applies to our collective action of helping the needy through aid agencies. And given this, fairness requires me individually to contribute to what we ought collectively to be doing. Thus, it is not an implication of my use of the life-saving analogy that if we say that I am required to rescue you from a fire rather than funding a fire safety programme, we must say that aid agencies should concentrate on relief to the exclusion of development. They should do both, because there is a stronger reason of beneficence for us to do both.

Notice that this does not mean that *I* am required to contribute to relief, rights-protection, *and* development agencies. The collective activity to which I am required to contribute ought to contain relief and prevention. I am required to support that collective effort. But that is not to say that I am required to contribute to all parts of that collective effort.

A Corollary: Other Evils

As I said in Chapter 1, it seems wrong to reduce issues about world poverty to the mere preservation of life. What is bad about poverty is arguably more a matter of the kind of life it forces on people than merely of the shortening of life. This is reflected in the activities of the aid agencies worth supporting. They are concerned to combat the evils that poverty introduces into people's lives, and not merely to prolong those lives. We should not overdraw the contrast: you cannot help people to improve their lives unless they have the means of subsistence. However, there is an obvious truth in this line of thought. Aid programmes that aim to make people's lives better should be preferred to those that aim merely to prolong them.

Notice, then, that our argument about preventing threats to life has an important corollary. According to that argument, we ought to be contributing to some aid agencies from among the available range rather than doing nothing. The best ones to contribute to may be ones that concentrate more on improving people's lives than merely on saving them and preventing threats to them. But this just means that the case for giving money to them is, if anything, stronger than the case for giving to life-saving agencies, while doing neither remains wrong.

4.6 CONCLUSION

The first two chapters of this book presented an argument for the life-saving analogy: the claim that contributing to an aid agency is morally analogous to saving a life directly, and is consequently morally required. At the end of Chapter 2 I pointed to two assumptions that this argument requires. The first was that contributions to aid agencies will indeed avert threats to people's lives. The second was that the objections commonly raised against the activities of aid agencies do not establish a relevantly countervailing difference between giving money to those agencies and helping a person directly.

Chapter 3 defended the second assumption. Chapter 4 has examined the first. What we have found is that, read one way, this assumption is dubious. There are grounds for doubting that contributions to aid agencies, considered individually, do save people's lives. And if so, then that casts doubt on the life-saving analogy, read as a claim about individual contributions: the claim that any individual contribution of mine to an aid agency is morally analogous to saving a life directly.

However, the main aim of the current chapter has been to show that this does not matter. For, read another way—as a claim about contributions to aid agencies taken collectively—the assumption is correct. These contributions, taken collectively, do avert threats to people's lives. And this means that the life-saving analogy will still remain defensible as a claim about our collective action of contributing to aid agencies: *this* is morally analogous to the direct saving of life. If so, the argument set out in the first three chapters still shows that our collectively contributing to aid agencies is morally required. And given this, I have argued that there are reasons of fairness for thinking that each of us is morally required to contribute to that collective action.

This completes my defence of the first claim I set out to establish in this book: the claim that not contributing to aid agencies is wrong. More carefully stated, the conclusion I have reached is that you are acting wrongly if you are not making a serious effort to find an effective way to help the poor, or contributing to some other comparably important cause. The rest of the book is concerned with the question that arises next. Suppose that I have started contributing to aid agencies, because I find this argument convincing. When is it morally acceptable to stop?

5

The Extreme Demand

THE conclusion we have reached so far is this: morality demands that each affluent person devotes time and money to helping the very poor. The next question is obvious: How much? How far do the moral demands of affluence extend?

According to one line of thought, those demands are *extreme*, in the following clear sense: morality demands of each of us that we renounce spending on practically all sources of personal fulfilment. To say this does not mean holding that there is something morally wrong about the pursuit of personal fulfilment as such. But it does mean holding that, as things now stand, it is wrong to spend a significant amount on your own personal fulfilment, given what you could be doing to help other people instead. There is a straightforward case for thinking that the moral outlook that is generated by the life-saving analogy is extremely demanding, in this sense. The aim of this chapter is to set out that case.

5.1 THE SEVERE DEMAND

A first approach to the life-saving analogy—one that is encouraged by its best-known advocates—involves thinking about its implications as follows.[1] By giving a small amount of money to an aid agency, I could save the life of a desperately needy person. If that were the cost of saving someone's life directly, I would be morally required to do so. So, given the moral analogy between the two cases, I am morally required to donate this amount to an aid agency. Suppose I have done so. Now I could stop contributing. But a second donation would save a second life. And the life-saving analogy tells me to think about this in the same way as a situation in which, having directly saved a first person's life, I come across a second person whom I could save at the same cost. Surely, I cannot excuse myself from helping the second by appealing to what I have already done for the first. If the cost of saving the second person is very small too, failing to do so is morally wrong, for the same reason that failing to save the first person would have been wrong. Given this, the failure to follow a first life-saving donation to an aid agency with a second must also be wrong, in the same way. It will still only be a small sacrifice for me to make, and it will save another person's life.

Approached in this way, the case for requiring me to donate to aid agencies is iterative. For any given endangered life, it is the disparity between what this person loses if I do not help and what it costs me if I do that makes it wrong for me not to help. No matter how many lives I may have saved already, the wrongness of not saving the next one is to be determined by iterating the same comparison. So, for each further life-saving donation I could make, I am required to make it as long as the cost of that donation itself is small—irrespective of any donations I have previously made.

Even on this approach to the life-saving analogy, there is one way in which my previous contributions to aid agencies may affect the wrongness of not making further ones. If I continue to give away money to aid agencies, I'll become poorer; as this happens, the sacrifice to me in making another life-saving donation will become greater. The monetary cost will be the same each time, but its effect on my interests will increase. Eventually, that sacrifice might become so great that, if that were the cost of saving someone's life directly, it would not be wrong to refuse. Once I reach *this* point, I can justifiably refuse to make another donation. Of course, the other way in which the analogy could cease to hold would be if there ceased to be people in chronic poverty. But this does not look like happening any time soon.[a]

Thus, on this approach to the life-saving analogy, the conclusion to be drawn is this:[2]

> *The Severe Demand*. I am morally required to keep contributing to aid agencies increments of time and money each of which is large enough to save a life, until either:
>
> (*a*) there are no longer any lives to be saved by those agencies, or
> (*b*) contributing another increment would itself be a large enough sacrifice to excuse my refusing to save a person's life directly at that cost.

How severe is the Severe Demand? That depends on the answers to two further questions. How much does it cost aid agencies to save a life? And how great must a sacrifice of mine be in order to excuse the failure to save a life?

For answers to the first question, we can turn to the aid agencies for their estimates. It would be unreasonable to expect them to be able to produce a figure that exactly reflects the cost of saving one life, given the difficulty of taking into account the various resources that need to be harnessed to the task, and of answering the counterfactual question whether the beneficiaries of a given programme would have survived without it. Further, the economics of responding to life-threatening need varies from one situation to another

[a] See App. 1.

depending on the availability of transport and other infrastructure, the prevailing political conditions, current prices for food and medicine, different economies of scale, and so forth. However, having said this, aid agencies do produce figures that indicate their costings for providing the kind of help that can save a person's life. These figures relate to two main kinds of life-saving aid work: supplying emergency relief, and working with the health system of poor countries to reduce mortality from easily treatable diseases. In the past decade Oxfam's estimates for providing emergency supplies of food and other basic necessities (shelter, sanitation, and basic medical care) for one person for six months have varied between about £50 and £150 (at today's prices).[3] And when we ask about the costs of treating the diseases that routinely kill many of the world's poorest people, some are reported to be very small indeed. The most dramatic example of this is probably oral rehydration therapy (ORT): as a treatment for the dehydration caused by diarrhoea (which currently kills 1.6 million children annually), this is estimated to be effective in 90 per cent of cases, and the 'total cost (including staff salaries and other overhead) for treating a child with ORT at a health facility is about $US1'.[4] According to the World Health Organization, the cost of the drugs required for an effective course of treatment of tuberculosis (which kills 2 million people annually) can be as low as $10.[5] And, turning from the treatment of disease to its prevention through vaccination programmes, UNICEF currently estimates the cost of protection against many of the major causes of global child mortality at $20–30 per child.[6]

The second question—how great must a sacrifice be before the harm it would do me excuses letting someone die?—is a substantial moral question, and thoroughly defending an answer would involve a lot of work. However, the argument for the life-saving analogy sidesteps this question. It simply takes as its starting point our ordinary 'common-sense' understanding of what is required of us to save another person's life. It is not controversial that sacrifices of money and time that are merely inconvenient can be demanded of us to save someone's life directly. Moreover, as Unger and others have emphasized, it seems to most of us that very substantial financial sacrifices could be morally required of us. To take Unger's example, if the only way for Bob to save someone's life is to crash the uninsured Bugatti in which he has invested his life savings, he seems to be morally required to do that.[7] What does ordinary thought have to say about when a sacrifice becomes too much to demand? Nothing very precise, no doubt. But it does at least seem common to think that risking death, permanent injury, or the impairment of your life prospects is more than can be morally demanded of you, even to save a life directly: risking these would be heroic, but refusing to do so would not be wrong.

Equipped with these broad answers to the two questions raised above, it is easy enough to see that the Severe Demand is very severe indeed. Surely, I would have to be extremely poor myself before I could credibly claim that giving away £150, or the other smaller figures just cited, would be a sacrifice comparable to a long-term injury.[8]

The Objection to the Severe Demand

You might be sceptical about the figures I have just quoted—and with some reason. One complaint they invite is that, at best, they can only claim to tell us the cost of 'providing the kind of help that can save a person's life', and that is not the same as the cost of saving someone's life: the people to whom this help is given might have survived without it.[9] However, it is not clear that *this* point matters to the success of the argument. For a 'desperate need analogy' will be just as effective as a life-saving analogy. If I can see that you are in desperate need of something because it *might* be required to save your life, and I could easily provide it, then it can be wrong for me not to do so. (If you are a weak swimmer in difficulty, it can be wrong for me not to rescue you, even if you might have saved yourself without me.)

There are other questions to be raised about these figures: but I leave a discussion of them for Appendix 2. For the main point to be made in response to the Severe Demand is independent of such questions. We should surely doubt whether my giving $1 to a charity will save the life of a dehydrated child. But we should also doubt whether my giving a much larger amount will have the effect of saving someone's life. As Chapter 4 acknowledged, aid agencies don't work that way. And if so, the argument that leads to the Severe Demand fails. My first contribution to an aid agency will not save anyone's life; nor will any subsequent contribution of mine.

The Severe Demand, then, is not the right conclusion to draw from the life-saving analogy. What should we say instead? The alternative conclusion argued for in Chapter 4 was this. Although, arguably, no individual contribution to an aid agency will save anyone's life, it remains true that by contributing to aid agencies we can collectively save many lives, and help needy people in other important ways. The life-saving analogy shows that this is something we are collectively required to do. What is morally demanded of me is that I contribute as much as fairness requires of me towards doing what we collectively ought to be doing.

5.2 FAIR SHARE VIEWS

It turns out that there is more than one way to fill out this thought. Let me begin with the most natural and obvious way. Then I shall explain why it is wrong.

The most natural way to interpret the implications of Chapter 4 is this. To work out what each affluent individual is morally required to contribute to the collective action of helping the poor, we should divide the overall burden among all those on whom it falls. Thus, to work out what is morally required of me, it is necessary to estimate the total cost of alleviating chronic poverty worldwide, and then, given all those affluent people whose help can be morally demanded, to calculate what proportion of that cost it would be fair to allocate to me, if every affluent person were actually contributing towards it. That is then the amount I am morally required to contribute; after I have contributed that much, it is not morally wrong for me to stop. I shall call views with this structure Fair Share Views of the moral demands of affluence.

In order to specify exactly how much I am required to give, a view of this kind will need to do three things: define chronic poverty in material terms, specify a threshold beyond which a person counts as affluent enough to be required to help, and supply a principle for fairly distributing the cost of helping among those above that threshold.[10] In advance of doing these three things, we cannot say exactly how much a Fair Share View requires each of us to give up. However, it does seem plausible for advocates of this view to deny that it is extremely demanding: anyone satisfying its requirements would still have plenty of opportunity to pursue her own personal fulfilment. After all, even on the strongest reading of the World Bank's figures, there are just as many people above its poverty lines as below them, and the amount required to take someone who has nothing to a level above those poverty lines is only a matter of a few hundred dollars or pounds per year.[11]

Murphy's Fair Share View

My argument in Chapter 4 does derive individual requirements to contribute to aid agencies from collective requirements of beneficence, and this suggests that its conclusion will be a version of the Fair Share View. Shortly, I shall question this natural thought. First, however, let me point out how the route that my argument suggests to a Fair Share View differs from the one advocated by Liam Murphy, who has given the most thoroughly argued presentation of a Fair Share View to date.[12]

Murphy gives a general, theoretical reason for thinking that all individual requirements of beneficence are derived from collective ones.[13] The moral requirement to act beneficently can be contrasted with other moral requirements, such as the requirement to keep promises, in the following respect. The latter requirement is agent-relative: it requires me to keep my promises and you to keep yours. In contrast, the requirement of beneficence is agent-neutral, giving each agent the same aim: to promote others' interests. (The aim can be specified without referring to the agent who has it.)[14] And when several of us share the same aim, it makes sense to pursue that aim collectively.

So the agent-neutrality of beneficence explains why we should think of it primarily as generating collective moral requirements on us—requirements from which we should derive individual requirements to do one's fair share.

I find this unconvincing. True, there is a level of description at which all beneficent agents share the same aim. Speaking extensionally, beneficence involves taking other people's interests as good reasons for action. What this means is that it involves treating as reasons for an action facts which belong to the class: *ways in which the action is in other people's interests*. However, this does not specify the object of a beneficent person's concern on a particular occasion. If you need help, then my concern should be to help *you*. And if there is no one else around, then there may be no one else who does, or should, share this aim. If you are needy enough, and there are no countervailing considerations, then I might be required to help you. But this requirement will not derive from some more fundamental collective requirement. For the aim of helping *you* is not one I will, or should, share with anyone else.

Notice a second problem that is awkward for Murphy's view.[15] This concerns its implications for cases of direct rescue. In general, I cannot properly invoke the moral failings of others as an excuse for my own; and in particular, this seems clearly to apply to the saving of lives. If I and another bystander come across two people whose lives need to be saved, and he walks off without helping, I cannot justify saving only one life on the ground that this is my fair share. The other person may have acted wrongly, but this is irrelevant to whether *I* act wrongly in refusing to save the second life. Moreover, it is easy to explain why. True, the other person ought to have done his share, and left me with only my own share to do. But if he has not, and it would be easy for me to save the second person's life, then the grounds for thinking that beneficence requires me to do it are plain. They are just the same as they would be in a situation in which I alone could easily rescue one person: he desperately needs it, and I could easily help.[16]

On Murphy's view, all requirements of beneficence derive from a basic collective requirement to help other people. So, if I am already contributing my fair share of what we all ought to be doing to help others and I then come across people who need to be rescued, I will not be morally required to help *any* of them, no matter how easy it would be to do so. Although this sounds wrong, Murphy accepts this consequence of his view. He believes that it is less difficult to accept once he says that, although my action would not be wrong, it would display a bad character. And he correctly points out that, even if this consequence of his view sounds implausible, that cannot by itself be a decisive objection, since the overall plausibility of his view might still be higher than that of any rival.[17] However, the difficulty here is not simply that it is counter-intuitive to think that I am not morally required to rescue anyone in these circumstances. It is that the reason why we think this seems to tell so clearly against his treatment of requirements of beneficence. When I am required to rescue someone, the reason comes from what *I* could do for *him*, and not from what we can all do for other people collectively.

However, the route to a Fair Share View that is suggested by my argument avoids this problem. For that argument distinguishes between requirements of beneficence that are collectively based and ones that are not. If I am now the sole bystander who could rescue you directly, the requirement on me to help does not derive from a collective requirement. When I could contribute to an aid agency, on the other hand, it does. So, if this argument leads to a Fair Share View about the moral requirement to contribute to aid agencies, it does so without carrying the implausible implications about cases of rescue.

Objection: New Collective Requirements

Thus, my argument appears to lead to a version of the Fair Share View, and it is a relatively plausible one. However, this appearance is misleading. The Fair Share View is not, after all, the right conclusion to draw from the life-saving analogy, and it should be rejected. True, I have argued that the requirement on individuals to contribute to aid agencies derives from a requirement of fairness to join in a collective action of beneficence. But, although we should accept this, we should still reject Fair Share Views.

To see why, we should return to the problem that Fair Share Views have with cases of direct rescue. Consider the following variant of an earlier example.[b] There are three people drowning, and three bystanders, including me. We can rescue them, but only by using a winch mechanism that can be operated by a minimum of two people or, more easily, by three. Two things seem obvious here. First, we should winch them out. Thus, there is a collective requirement in this case: we should cooperate in saving the lives. And from the collective requirement an individual one is derivable: I should join in the cooperative effort. Even if the other two bystanders could operate the winch and save all the drowning people by working harder without me, I should not simply leave the job to them. Now suppose one of the other bystanders walks off. This does not mean that the two of us who are left have done enough if we winch out only two people. Each of us should be prepared to save all three, given that the effort involved is small. And if we can only do so by cooperating, we should cooperate. The two of us now constitute a new group upon which a collective requirement falls—to help

[b] Sect. 4.4.

the people who still need it—and I should fully contribute to fulfilling this further requirement.

This example suggests something important. In situations where several of us have done our fair share but people still need help, a new *collective* requirement can apply to us. This does not replace the original collective requirement. It is still the case that *everyone* with the ability to help should together be helping. But some of them have dropped out. The question for the rest of us has become, What are *we* now prepared to do? If, by cooperating, we could easily save lives at little cost to ourselves, then we are morally required to do so. In other words, more than one collective requirement applies to groups of people to which I belong. First, there is what *all* of those who are able to help ought to be doing by way of helping the people who need it. But, because there are plenty of non-compliers with this first requirement, there is a second. This is what those of us who have already helped ought to be doing to help those who are still vulnerable, thanks to the non-compliers. Furthermore, once others have started complying with this second requirement, it would be wrong for me to leave it to them rather than joining in. Once I have done my fair share in discharging the first collective requirement, the second still makes it wrong for me to stop giving.

The point is not just that this seems an intuitive thing to say about the imaginary example just described. What is significant is the way in which the account of beneficence given here supports it. When some of us have done our fair share of what everyone ought to have done, it can still be the case that, because some people are not doing their fair share, there remain many people needing help. We know that other people who should be helping them are not. But that does not affect the powerful reason that there is for us to go further, and help the remaining people: they need it desperately. If we could help them at little cost, the original case for requiring us to do so remains in force, as strongly as ever. There are people desperately needing our help, and no seriously countervailing consideration, so not helping is a *failure* of beneficence. A proponent of a Fair Share View might be tempted to say that *the fact that we have already done our fair share* is a countervailing consideration. However, that would be very unconvincing as a defence of leaving the third person in the example to drown. And it is easy to explain why: this fails to bear on the case for helping *him*, which is that he desperately needs it and we could easily do so.

This is not an objection to the claim that what is morally demanded of me is that I contribute as much as fairness requires of me towards doing what we collectively ought to be doing. It is an objection to interpreting this claim in line with a Fair Share View. What we collectively ought to be doing includes continuing to help people who desperately need it, when others are not helping them and we could easily address their need. Fair Share Views fail to allow for this; that is why they should be rejected.

5.3 THE EXTREME DEMAND

We have now rejected two attempts to identify the conclusion that should be drawn from the life-saving analogy. The Severe Demand fails to recognize the way in which individual requirements to contribute to aid agencies derive from collective ones. And Fair Share Views fail to recognize the way in which new collective requirements will be generated as long as there remain people who could be easily helped. If we avoid these two mistakes, what alternative conclusion are we led to? Let us follow through the lessons learned so far, and see where they take us.

The requirement on me to contribute to aid agencies derives from our collective ability to help desperately needy people. This is something we can do easily, so beneficence requires us to do it; and fairness requires me to join in. As long as there remain desperately needy people, and there is a group of people for whom the cost of helping would still be small, there will be a collective requirement of beneficence to provide that help. As long as the cost to *me* of contributing a one-person share towards that collective action would still be small, I will count as a member of the group to which the collective requirement applies. And as long as the collective action is actually taking place, and the cost to me of contributing my share would still be small, I am morally required to contribute it.

When does this requirement disappear? What determines whether the cost to me of continuing to contribute is small enough to mean that it is morally required, or has become large enough to mean that I can justifiably stop?

Here is one way to approach this question. It might seem to be the only way: later in the chapter, I shall argue that it is not. But let us examine this approach first.

This first approach has the same iterative form as the argument that led to the Severe Demand. For each person whom we could easily help, we are collectively required to do so. As long as there remains one person in chronic need, and there is a group of us who could easily help him, we are collectively morally required to do so. And as long as a collective effort is being made to help him, I have to ask myself whether I am prepared to join in that collective effort. If the cost to me of joining in—that is, my share of the collective cost of helping one further person—is large enough, it could justify me in refusing. But as long as the cost to me of contributing towards our helping one further person remains small, I am required to keep contributing.

The conclusion generated by this iterative approach is not the same as the Severe Demand; but it is similar. I shall call it

> *The Extreme Demand.* I am morally required to keep contributing my time and money to aid agencies (or to some other comparably important

cause), until either:

(*a*) there are no longer any lives to be saved (or comparably important goals achieved) by those agencies, or

(*b*) contributing my share of the cost of our collectively saving one further life (or doing something comparably important) would itself be a large enough sacrifice to excuse my refusing to contribute.

How extreme is the Extreme Demand? This depends on the answers to two questions, corresponding to the two questions raised by the Severe Demand earlier. How much would it cost us collectively to provide a person with life-saving help (or do something comparably important)? And when is the cost to me of contributing to providing that help great enough to excuse refusing?

When we discussed the Severe Demand, we saw some of the figures that aid agencies suggest we can think of as the cost of providing the kind of help that can save a person's life. The problem for the Severe Demand is that it is dubious to think that my contributing this amount to an aid agency will result in the provision of help to a person who would otherwise have gone without it: aid agencies don't work like that. However, aid agencies do provide people with life-saving help, even if individual contributions to them do not; and these figures report the average cost. So the aid agencies' figures do answer our first question: it does make sense to think of them as reporting the cost of our collectively providing a person with life-saving help.[18]

Our second question is different from the one that was asked in relation to the Severe Demand. There, the question was how great a sacrifice of mine must be before it will excuse my letting someone die. The 'common-sense' answer appears to be that large financial sacrifices can be demanded of me, but that risking death, permanent injury, or the impairment of my life prospects cannot. But now the question is what can be demanded of me as a contribution towards a collective action of saving someone's life. And it is not obvious that this question has the same answer. Unger suggests that I could be required to give up my life savings to save someone's life. However, if saving a life requires a collective action in which a large number of us each lose our life savings, then it is not as obvious that each of us is required to make this sacrifice—especially if it is also true that no one individual's making this sacrifice will itself make any difference to whether the life is saved.

No doubt, 'common sense' is even less precise in answering this question than it was in telling us how much I can be required to give up to save a life on my own. But I do not think that matters. Here is why. The Extreme Demand requires me to keep contributing until my share of the cost of our collectively providing life-saving help is too much to require of me. But my share of that cost is minuscule, given the number of people contributing to aid agencies. If the cost of providing life-saving help is £150, my share of that cost is a very small fraction of a penny. (Indeed, even if the cost of our saving a life ran into millions of pounds, my share would only be a few pennies.) Thus suppose we make the most lenient possible assumption about the amount I can be required to sacrifice in contributing to a collective action of saving a life. Arguably, as we have seen, this is smaller than the amount I can be required to sacrifice to save a life myself. It is not true that it is nothing at all: it is obvious that we are required to make *some* sacrifice in contributing to collective life-saving actions. But suppose we only accept that. Suppose that, as soon as my contribution towards saving a life involves a cost which makes the smallest noticeable difference to my well-being, I am no longer required to make it. Even on *this* assumption, the Extreme Demand is immensely demanding. For giving up a fraction of a penny would only have this effect on me if I possessed practically nothing.

Remember that the argument applies to donations of time as well as money. The Extreme Demand requires me to keep volunteering time to aid agencies until I reach the point at which a single further contribution, representing my share of the collective cost of saving a life, would be too much to ask of me. And again, the size of that contribution will be tiny. Of course, visiting the office of an aid agency to volunteer two minutes of one's time is not much help: with time, unlike money, a certain minimum amount is required to achieve anything productive, even from many increments. However, if I am already spending sessions of that minimum length to support the work of an aid agency, then it is plausible that by adding small increments to these sessions I could, over months or years, add to the agency's revenue or effectiveness.

If this is what it requires of me, then the Extreme Demand does indeed seem to allow me to spend practically no time or money on my own personal fulfilment. The amount of my resources which represents my share of the collective action of saving a life will be truly minuscule. And only someone near a mere subsistence level of spending on herself could credibly hold that sacrifices *this* small are burdensome enough to excuse the failure to contribute to saving a life. The Extreme Demand appears to be so demanding that it looks doubtful whether anyone, no matter how altruistic their life's work, has ever counted as meeting it. It tells us that Albert Schweitzer's Bach scholarship was morally wrong.[19]

This is a striking conclusion. Earlier, I rejected the Severe Demand. Contributions to aid agencies do not themselves save lives; they are contributions to collective actions of saving lives. However, we now find that, even on the most lenient possible assumption about the amount that individuals are required to contribute to collective actions of saving a life, we have ended up at a conclusion—the Extreme Demand—that is even more severe than the Severe Demand.

Motivational Limits

As just stated, the Extreme Demand faces an objection that has some force. Most of us, it might be objected, are simply incapable of being this self-denying: this surpasses the natural limits of the human will. But morality cannot require us to do what we are incapable of doing: 'ought' implies 'can'.[20] Furthermore, perhaps, even if we *are* capable of meeting the Extreme Demand, we will be able to do more for the needy if we do not meet it. There are surely very few people who could remain fully productive if they tried to spend practically no time on anything but the most highly paid available job and volunteer work for aid agencies, and to give away practically all of their money. And if, by being less self-denying, you were able to do more to help the needy, then an argument from the life-saving analogy should allow this—indeed, it should require it. Once it becomes true that further self-sacrifice ceases to help the poor, it ceases to be morally required.[21]

This does suggest that, for most of us, it would be a mistake to try to meet the Extreme Demand in one dramatic step, even if we could. However, the success of this objection is limited. For this line of objection has done nothing to attack either the life-saving analogy itself, or the kind of iterative approach to it that leads in the direction of the Extreme Demand. Rather, it shows that our first statement of the conclusion of that argument was too simple. The right conclusion to draw is not that it is wrong not to meet the Extreme Demand; but rather, that it is wrong not to get as close to meeting the Extreme Demand as you productively can.

After all, according to the life-saving analogy, someone who is motivationally incapable, beyond a certain point, of making further donations to aid agencies should be compared to someone who is motivationally incapable of helping to save lives. Suppose I am so squeamish that I will be no use to anyone in an accident: I freeze or faint at the sight of blood. Then perhaps when an accident happens in front of me, it does not make sense to criticize me for not helping. However, if I know that people are likely to need my help, and I have done nothing to try to make myself less squeamish, then I can be criticized for *that*. And unless there is something wrong with an iterative approach to the life-saving analogy, we must say the same thing about the failure of motivation to give money to aid agencies. If your motivation to do this gives out beyond a certain point, then perhaps you cannot be criticized for not doing it; but you can be criticized for not doing everything you can to change your motivation.[22]

How could you go about making yourself more self-sacrificing? A more and a less radical option will be open to you. The less radical option is to achieve progressively greater levels of self-sacrifice through a gradual process of habituation. After you get used to a new, lower level of spending on yourself, it is likely that there will be scope for reducing it further without impairing your own productivity. And if this does not work, there is the more radical option: externally imposed mental conditioning. There is evidence that for almost all of us, there are techniques of psychological manipulation which could be employed to weaken our personal attachments and make us more impartial, inducing the political or religious convert's conviction that 'service is perfect freedom'.[23]

A more precise conclusion about the limits of human beings' capacity for altruistic self-sacrifice would need to be based on a proper survey of the historical and psychological research.[24] However, that is not necessary in order to appreciate the reply to the objection from motivational limits. This objection does not stand in the way of the conclusion that I am required to get as close as I productively can—as gradually as necessary (but no more so)—to meeting the Extreme Demand. And doing this would be very uncomfortable. Indeed, it *has* to be very uncomfortable: if I am comfortable with my current level of spending on myself, I should be working to reduce it.

Of course, the sort of self-manipulation I have just described sounds not just uncomfortable, but thoroughly repellent. However, we have yet to see why *that* is a good objection. After all, someone advocating an iterative approach to the life-saving analogy has a clear rejoinder. It is of course undesirable *for me* to end up with such an unfulfilling and possibly self-manipulative life, but this is what results from a series of personal sacrifices each of which is very small compared to the harms I could avert in the lives of *other* people.[25]

5.4 AGGREGATIVE APPROACHES

An iterative approach to the life-saving analogy leads to the conclusion that you are required to get as close as you productively can to meeting the Extreme Demand. However, we should now notice that another kind of approach is possible.

This does not question the idea that there is a succession of collective requirements of beneficence; nor does it question the idea that I am morally required to keep contributing until the cost to me is excessive. What it does is to offer a different approach to the question when the cost to me is excessive. The iterative approach treats this as the question when the cost to me of contributing to helping the *next* needy person is excessive. The alternative, though, is to ask instead when the *aggregate* cost to me of my successive contributions to helping needy people has become great enough to excuse refusing to go further. Once my aggregate sacrifice has reached this threshold, it is not wrong for me to stop contributing, even if the cost to me of contributing towards helping one further person would still itself be small.[26]

A thought that seems compelling is this: if I have contributed to saving one person's life but then find that I could contribute to saving another at small cost, I cannot justify refusing to join in helping the second person by appealing to what I have already done for the first. This seems right, and at first glance, it seems to lead to an iterative approach to the life-saving analogy. However, notice that the alternative approach just mentioned is consistent with the same compelling thought. If the cost of contributing towards saving the second life is still small, that means the overall sacrifice I would need to make to save *both* lives is small. And perhaps *that* is why refusing to join in helping the second person cannot be justified by appealing to what I have done for the first. The same will apply to any small number of lives. But as the overall number of lives to be saved grows larger, there will start to be a more serious case for thinking that my overall sacrifice in contributing towards helping them is large enough to justify me in stopping.

Notice that this second, aggregative kind of approach covers many different possibilities. What aggregative approaches have in common is that they deny what an iterative approach asserts: namely, that the overall sacrifice that can be required of me to contribute towards helping several people is arrived at by summing the separate sacrifices that could be required of me to help them one after the other, until the cost of contributing towards helping the next person would be excessive if he were the only person needing help. But denying this leaves open many different ways of specifying that overall sacrifice. One source of variation concerns the goods in terms of which it is measured—are these time and money themselves, or some group of goods which they can help secure? The overall sacrifice might then be specified either in terms of an amount of those goods which is given up (either in absolute terms, or as a proportion of one's original holdings), or an amount retained. Each of the different possibilities this gives us will then yield as many different aggregative views as there are different magnitudes of the goods in question.

But beyond this, there are two further ways in which aggregative approaches can differ from each other. On one kind of aggregative view, the claim will be that there is a single maximum sacrifice which can be demanded of me in contributing to helping other people, whatever the number. As much can be demanded of me to contribute towards saving one life as to contribute towards saving a thousand; no more can be demanded of me to contribute towards saving a thousand than to contribute towards saving one. Taking an aggregative approach does not entail saying this, though. For another possibility, consider the following view: a small sacrifice can be demanded of me in relation to each of the lives I could contribute towards saving, and when the sum of a series of such sacrifices reaches a certain threshold amount, I may permissibly refuse to do any more. Or—a further alternative—it might be allowed that the sacrifice required of me varies in proportion to the number of people I could contribute towards helping. Perhaps a greater overall sacrifice can be demanded of me to contribute towards helping a million people than to contribute towards helping a thousand. But, as long as the amount that is demanded of me overall is not arrived at by iterating the demand that would be made of me in relation to each individual taken separately, we shall have an aggregative rather than an iterative view.

The other source of variation concerns whether aggregation is understood diachronically or synchronically. One view would be that to each agent is attached a sort of lifelong moral account, recording the cumulative sacrifice you have made on behalf of the need of other people: when your accumulated credit builds up to a certain point, you are released henceforth from having to do anything to contribute towards helping others. However, an aggregative view need not involve this odd-sounding idea. An alternative is to consider the aggregate sacrifice that a person is actually making at the time at which a further opportunity to contribute towards helping someone else presents itself. On this alternative, the claim is that there is a maximum aggregate sacrifice that can be demanded of you at a particular time:[27] if your past actions do not affect the size of the sacrifice you are now being called on to make, then they cannot help to show that it is too much to ask of you.

Practically all aggregative approaches to the life-saving analogy will yield less severe demands than an iterative approach.[28] Just how much less demanding they are will depend on their treatment of the issues just mentioned. And notice that the kinds of 'common-sense' claims we have been invoking so far are not going to give us much guidance in thinking about this. If we ask how much I can be required to give up in order to save one life directly by myself, a broad 'common-sense' consensus can be found: large financial sacrifices can be required, but not serious long-term injury. However, it is harder to see any such consensus about the amount I can be required to give up in contributing to a collective life-saving effort. This did not matter much in interpreting the Extreme Demand: even if this amount is very small, the Extreme Demand is still extreme. But it will make a big difference to the strength of the demands to be drawn from an aggregative approach.

Spelling out just how demanding the most plausible aggregative approach turns out to be will be one of the main aims of Part II.

5.5 WHICH APPROACH IS BETTER?

We have two possible approaches to the life-saving analogy: an iterative approach, which leads to the Extreme Demand, and an aggregative approach, which suggests a less demanding conclusion. Which is better?

Let us first consider the case in favour of an aggregative approach. Then we can turn to the argument that can be offered in reply.

The Intuitive Case for an Aggregative Approach

I have explained the difference between iterative and aggregative approaches to the life-saving analogy by describing the different ways in which they tell us to think about the cost a person is required to bear in contributing towards collective actions of helping others. But notice that they are equally available as alternative ways of thinking about individual actions of helping people directly. And thinking about cases of direct helping, it might be suggested, provides us with an intuitive case in favour of the aggregative approach.

Suppose I faced the nightmare scenario in which everywhere I went I directly encountered people needing my life-saving help, in practically unlimited numbers, and each of whom I could save at small cost.[29] Approaching this iteratively would mean continuing to save lives until the sacrifice involved in saving one further life would itself be so great that, if that were the cost of saving a single life in isolation, I could justifiably refuse. On the 'common-sense' assumption that only a permanently life-impairing harm would justify refusing to save one person's life, an iterative approach would therefore be extremely demanding: it would require me to give up practically everything, and devote myself to saving lives. An aggregative approach, by contrast, would tell me to keep helping until my *overall* contribution involved a cost great enough to justify me in stopping. And is it not plausible to think that my overall sacrifice would become this large well before I reached the point at which I was devoting my whole life to saving other people's lives? No doubt, saving no one would be wrong. But suppose I made a substantial and ongoing commitment to helping, while retaining part of my life for other things: I spent my mornings saving people's lives, perhaps, and my afternoons having a life of my own. Surely the claim that this is morally acceptable gives us a more intuitively attractive view.

It would be a mistake to place much emphasis on this: intuitive responses to a sketchily described thought experiment like this one, so remote from our experience, cannot carry much argumentative weight.[30] However, it does at least seem clearly a mistake to think that the iterative approach can be supported over the aggregative one by appealing to conformity with intuitive verdicts about possible situations. And, more importantly, it invites us to pass from thinking about this imagined situation to our actual one. An iterative approach to the life-saving analogy, when applied to our actual situation, calls for the wholesale abandonment of almost all of our everyday lives. This conclusion is extremely unintuitive: to most of us, it seems obvious that, in not reducing myself to a subsistence level of spending on myself, I am not acting wrongly. Indeed, it would not seem to be an exaggeration to say that, to most of us, this judgement is about as obvious as the judgement that failing easily to save someone's life right in front of me *would* be wrong.

What this gives us is a renewed version of Chapter 1's methodological challenge—directed this time against the iterative approach to the life-saving analogy.[c] Given that the argument takes intuitive ethical convictions as its starting point, how can it be right to prefer the iterative approach, which requires us to revise strongly held ethical convictions, when an alternative is available—the aggregative approach—which can agree with them? At the very least, the onus seems to lie with a proponent of the iterative interpretation to explain why it should be preferred in spite of its conflict with these convictions.

Reply: The Case for an Iterative Approach

When we first encountered a challenge of this form, against the life-saving analogy itself, we found that it failed. There is equally a response to it this time.

The force of the iterative approach to saving lives can be brought out plainly by putting it like this. Why should my failure to contribute towards helping the hundred-and-first, or the thousand-and-first person be any more excusable than my failure to contribute towards helping the first, if the cost to me remains insignificant in comparison with what he stands to lose? Pointing out that I have already contributed towards helping a thousand people, and drawing attention to what that has cost me, do nothing to alter the fact that I could contribute towards helping the next person at an insignificant cost. The aggregative approach is suggesting, in effect, that we should lump together all of the people I could contribute to helping, and ask what I should be prepared to do for this collective entity; but does this not ignore the reality of the individual need of each of the people conglomerated in this way? If I refuse to contribute a small amount towards saving someone's life, how does what I have done for others countervail against the strength of the reason there is for helping? It says something in my favour that I have been prepared to do something for others. But how can that help me to rebut the complaint that taking proper account of the interests of the next person will require me to contribute towards helping *him*?[31]

This question becomes especially awkward when we recall once more the earlier account of beneficence. Beneficence can be described as a concern for others' interests, but only if this description is read extensionally.[d] In a situation where someone's life could be saved, a beneficent person's reason

[c] Sect. 1.3.
[d] Sect. 2.1.

to help him will be that *he needs help*, and not that *this action furthers the interests of other people*. What considerations can sensibly be treated as countervailing against this reason? A countervailing consideration is one that shows why, if you refuse to help, you should not be faulted for being insufficiently concerned to act on this reason. But it is hard to see how what you have done for others in the past can help to show this. If a beneficent person's reason to help is *his* need, how can considerations about what you have done for others be relevant to whether your concern to act on *this* reason is sufficient for beneficence?

It might seem tempting to object that the cost to the agent of helping *is* surely a potentially countervailing consideration in relation to beneficence. I can exhibit a sufficient concern for others' interests while displaying a greater concern for my own. So why not say that, when my overall sacrifice becomes significant, I am justified in refusing to contribute towards saving any more lives? Refusing to contribute towards helping the next person does not show that I am insufficiently concerned for his interests: it shows that I am more concerned not to impoverish myself, and that is compatible with being sufficiently beneficent. Had I refused to give up a small amount to contribute towards helping the *first* person, that would have been wrong: the concern I would be showing for my own interests in comparison with his would be excessive. But when I draw the line at contributing towards helping the thousand-and-first, on the grounds that my overall sacrifice is now significant, then that is different: once the sacrifice I am making is substantial, refusing to go further involves no *failure* of beneficence.

However, this begs the question against the iterative approach. The issue is not whether the cost to the agent of helping is an appropriately countervailing consideration in relation to beneficence. It is whether we should think of the cost to the agent iteratively or aggregatively. And we have just been given an argument for preferring the iterative approach. A beneficent person's reason to help the next person is that *he* needs help. The question, then, is how appealing to my own interests can countervail against this reason. As long as helping *him* would not itself impoverish me, I still face the question of whether I am prepared to give up a small amount to help him. Suppose it is right that I can legitimately give a preference to my own interests over those of another person, and that this means that I can only be required to make a small sacrifice to contribute towards saving someone else's life. This does not help to explain why I should not be required to make that small sacrifice for the thousand-and-first person, just as I was required to make it for the first. The case remains for saying that, if I am not prepared to give up a small amount to contribute towards helping *him*, my concern for myself is excessive: I am failing in relation to beneficence.

This defence of the iterative approach meets the methodological challenge in the same way that it was originally met on behalf of the life-saving analogy, in Chapter 2. The case for the iterative approach goes beyond simply presenting some initial intuitive judgements and generalizing from them. Instead, it gets its force from concentrating on the *reasons* for these intuitive judgements. Given our reasons for the judgements we make about the failure of beneficence involved in refusing to save a person's life—that it is *his* needs which call to be addressed—we have a powerful case for taking an iterative rather than an aggregative approach to what is required of us to help other people, or contribute towards helping them.

5.6 CONCLUSION

There appears to be a strong case for the iterative approach to the saving of life, and a strong case also (supplied in Chapters 1–4) for the life-saving analogy. Together, they generate the conclusion that we are required to get as close as possible to meeting the Extreme Demand.

This conclusion is very hard to believe. We have seen how demanding a standard of requirement this is, and the lengths to which a person attempting to meet it would have to go. If *this* is what morality requires of the affluent in relation to the poor, there can be very few people who are attempting to meet it, or who have ever even considered doing so. However, this is not because we are all morally weak. It is because we do not think the Extreme Demand is true. It is not hard to believe the conclusion for which I initially argued: that it is wrong to contribute nothing to helping people who are desperately needy. But it is very hard to believe that we are morally required to get as close as we can to meeting the Extreme Demand—hard enough to mean that it surely makes sense to question the argument that leads to this conclusion.[32]

One approach to criticizing that argument would be to attack the life-saving analogy itself, or the account of beneficence that I have offered in conjunction with it, going back over the ground of the previous four chapters and finding fault with them. (Indeed, it might be argued that the intolerable nature of the Extreme Demand is *itself* a justification for treating the immediacy of others' need as having the kind of moral significance I have denied.)[33] However, I am not going to do that: it seems to me that what was said there was correct. What I shall do instead is to spend the rest of this book developing the case for thinking that, even if Chapters 1–4 are right, the correct conclusion to draw is a more moderate one. The argument we have just seen for taking an iterative approach to the life-saving analogy can be refuted, and a certain aggregative approach defended instead. However, it will require the whole of Part II to vindicate this view.[34]

Before I do that, it makes sense to place this discussion in the context of others. The idea that a moral outlook might be severely demanding has been the subject of prominent recent discussion and criticism by several other contemporary philosophers. Before setting out my own response to this idea, I should explain why it does not make sense to turn to their work for help with the version of the problem that has been uncovered here. If you are inclined to think that other philosophers have already answered this problem, you will find in Chapter 6 an explanation of why I disagree. If not, you should skip Chapter 6 and turn directly to Part II.

6

Problems of Demandingness

THE argument so far has led to a moral outlook that is extremely demanding, and this leaves us with a problem. Just what kind of problem it gives us is open to debate, however. There are three different 'problems of demandingness' which the Extreme Demand might be held to involve: in Part II we shall need to decide between them.[1]

First, it might be held that the demandingness of this outlook is a problem because it shows that this outlook must be rejected. It is absurd to think that morality could require me to live such a self-denying life. Any argument generating this conclusion must be wrong. By contrast, a second view is that the problem here is a problem for morality itself, rather than an objection to a claim about its content. According to the argument for the Extreme Demand, morality requires me to renounce practically every source of personal fulfilment: so much the worse for morality. If *this* is what morality demands of me, morality and practical reason part company. Whatever I have reason to do, I do not have most reason to strip my life of personal fulfilment. If morality is extremely demanding, reason permits me to disregard it and guide myself by a non-moral standard instead.[2]

These first two lines of response can be seen as sharing a common thought: any moral outlook that I have reason to pursue cannot be extremely demanding. The third response denies this. For perhaps the argument that has been given cannot be dismissed in either of these ways. Perhaps morality does place extreme demands on me, and reason does not permit me to disregard morality. The problem of demandingness which then arises is not a problem for morality, or for the claim concerning its content. It is a problem for me. The life I ought to lead may be much more difficult than I would like it to be.[3]

There is no question, then, that the argument for the Extreme Demand presents us with a problem of demandingness: the question is which one. The right procedure for settling that question seems to be this. First, we should see whether there is a good case for rejecting the demanding conclusion about the content of morality. If so, the problem belongs to the first kind. If not, we should ask whether this means that reason permits me to abandon morality—giving us the second kind of problem. If that is not true either, we are left with a problem of the third kind. In fact, in this book

I shall stop at the first of these stages. For in Part II I shall argue that there is indeed a good objection to the Extreme Demand.

This is bound to be a common reaction to the argument I have presented for the Extreme Demand. Extremely demanding moral outlooks have been widely discussed by contemporary moral philosophers, and it is often argued that they must be rejected. Morality must leave us room to lead a fulfilling life, rather than a life emptied of fulfilment in the service of others. And if leading a fulfilling life is justifiable, then we are justified in rejecting the iterative accumulation of small demands into large ones, since it is incompatible with having such a life.

In the first two chapters of Part II I shall argue that, roughly speaking, that is correct. (Only roughly, though: the claim that 'morality must leave us room to lead a fulfilling life' is too sweeping to be true without qualification.) This might seem unnecessary. It might seem that, for a refutation of the Extreme Demand, we can simply turn to those other discussions of what is wrong with an extremely demanding moral outlook.

In this chapter I need to explain why we cannot simply do that. I begin by examining the relationship between the problems of demandingness most widely discussed in the literature and the problem posed by the Extreme Demand. Most of the existing discussion centres around two general ways of theorizing about morality that threaten to generate extreme demands. The first aim of this chapter will be to point out how those familiar routes to a problem of demandingness differ from the one that has been set out here.

The rest of the chapter gives a short survey of the range of objections to demanding moral outlooks in the existing literature. A broad, four-category taxonomy of these objections will be set out, and I shall introduce the kind of argument to be presented in Part II. I shall explain why I think this is the most promising avenue to explore in looking for an explanation of what is wrong with the Extreme Demand, and I shall identify various problems faced by the other responses to demanding moral outlooks. The aim will not be to show that the argument I go on to develop is the only one that could succeed. Rather, it will be to locate that argument in relation to others, and to compile a list of the difficulties and problems that this argument will have to overcome if it is to be convincing.

6.1 TWO THEORETICAL SOURCES

Broadly speaking, we can trace the problems of demandingness that have been the focus of contemporary discussion to two general theoretical sources. A thought the two share in common is that the moral point of view is an impartial point of view: the point of view I take when

I recognize that, morally speaking, I am no more important than anyone else. From this general thought, it is easy to see how an extremely demanding conception of morality might result.[4] However, there is a significant difference between the two main ways in which this thought has been developed. One characterizes moral agency as impartiality in relation to what is valuable; the second characterizes it as impartiality in one's response to reasons.

The first line of thought runs as follows. The goods through which I attain personal fulfilment are genuinely valuable, as is that fulfilment itself. But if these goods are valuable, then more of them is more valuable. And if so, then whenever I could be promoting others' fulfilment more effectively than my own I ought to do so. This cannot be resisted by appealing to the value of personal fulfilment: I can promote that value better by restricting my own fulfilment in favour of others'.

This line of thought makes two assumptions. It draws conclusions about what I ought to do from claims about the value of the outcomes promoted by my actions. So the first assumption is that the rightness of an action is determined by the value, or at least the expected value, of its outcome. The second is that the evaluation of outcomes that is relevant to the rightness of actions is agent-neutral: it contains no essential reference to the evaluator.[5] For it is being assumed that promoting more of *my own* fulfilment cannot be what makes my action right. These two assumptions are often now thought of as definitive of consequentialism.[6]

However, making the consequentialist assumptions is not the only way in which philosophers have been attracted to identifying the moral point of view with the impartial point of view. Another prominent line of thought has been this. The recognition of reasons to pursue and avoid certain objects for myself commits me to recognizing reasons to pursue and avoid the corresponding objects in the lives of others. From the moral point of view, then, I must recognize others' distress as giving me a reason to prevent it, just as I recognize my own distress as giving me a reason to prevent it. Holding this does not mean embracing consequentialism—for it can be added that I have a stronger, agent-relative reason not to produce others' distress myself than I have to prevent it. However, provided only that the reason-giving force of others' distress is strong enough to ground claims of wrongness, the extent of our opportunities for relieving distress means that the resulting moral outlook would appear to be an extremely demanding one.[7]

My aim here is not to add to the literature discussing these two lines of thought. Instead, I want to emphasize the following simple point. The problem of demandingness that has been generated by iterating the life-saving analogy is independent of these two sources. The reason these two ways of characterizing morality as impartiality seem demanding is that they seem to deny the following 'common-sense' claim:

> It may be wrong for me to be prepared to do nothing to help another person, but it is not wrong to be prepared to do significantly less for him than I would do for myself.

However, the argument for the Extreme Demand has *accepted* this claim. Even if we assume this claim to be true, iterating the life-saving analogy will still lead us to an extremely demanding moral outlook. Provided only that there is *some* small amount that can be demanded of me to save a life, the amount that can be demanded when there are very many lives to be saved can still be great, on an iterative approach.[8] And this is quite compatible with thinking that there is nothing wrong with giving the interests of another person very little weight in comparison with my own. To generate the Extreme Demand, we need not suppose that morality requires complete impartiality of us—only that it requires less than complete partiality. Thus, iterating the life-saving analogy gives us a third source of an extremely demanding moral outlook, which does not require identifying morality with impartiality in either of the two ways just described.

This gives us reason to be dubious about how much there is for us to learn from existing attempts to show what is wrong with extremely demanding moral outlooks. The dominant concern in these discussions is to reply to arguments from the two theoretical sources just mentioned; and their aim is to defend the 'common-sense' claim set out above. What we are looking to answer is a problem of demandingness that arises even if we take that claim for granted.

Nevertheless, it does make sense for us to survey the range of objections to demanding moral outlooks that are available. For demanding outlooks that arise from different sources might share the same faults. We ought to consider whether the existing kinds of objection to demanding moral outlooks might tell us what is wrong with the Extreme Demand; and if not, what are the problems that a better line of objection must overcome.

6.2 THE COST OF MEETING EXTREME MORAL DEMANDS

At a very general level of description, it is clear enough what form a refutation of an extremely demanding morality must take. It must:

(*a*) characterize what would be lost in meeting an extremely demanding standard of moral requirement; and
(*b*) explain why it is legitimate for us to refuse to give that up.

This covers many different possible arguments. First, we should notice the variety of different ways of approaching task (*a*). The following sections will survey the various possibilities covered by (*b*).

So far in this book I have been writing of the 'sacrifice' or 'cost' that must be borne in order to act beneficently towards another person. In the kinds of simple examples from which the life-saving analogy begins, that cost is simply a matter of inconvenience, monetary loss, physical discomfort, or injury. However, in explaining what would be lost in living up (or down?) to a standard of moral requirement as demanding as the Extreme Demand, it is natural to emphasize losses of other, deeper kinds. The most significant losses that would be borne by someone attempting to meet that standard of requirement would not simply be material cost, discomfort, or forgone enjoyment. It is argued by various writers that such a life would be stunted in more serious ways: it would involve compromising your personal relationships,[9] your fulfilment from and commitment to personal projects;[10] perhaps also your integrity and self-respect,[11] your agency and identity,[12] your autonomy,[13] or your standing as a bearer of rights.[14] It would mean going to war against your own humanity: setting yourself against the kinds of good that shape a human life at its best.[15]

Explaining this loss as a cost to the self-denying agent, though, runs the risk of excluding two ways of looking at this issue that deserve to be mentioned. Following Scanlon, one might doubt whether the right way for me to think about what would be lost in living the hyper-altruistic life is by asking *how much worse off I would be*. For arguably, among the reasons I have for pursuing and valuing various goods, their effect on how well off I am plays (and should play) only a minor role. Granted, it *is* better for me if I am absorbed in worthwhile relationships and activities; but that is not my reason for pursuing them: it is the character of the people and projects themselves that gives me a reason to shape my life around them. A *loss* would certainly be sustained if I devoted my life to helping others, but on this way of looking at it, that loss is better characterized as a failure to respond to the goods I have reason to respond to, rather than a reduction in how well off I am.[16]

The other point to notice is that an objection to extremely demanding moral standards might focus not on what would be lost by me personally if I met those standards, but rather the social costs that would be entailed by our doing so collectively: the way of life that would be lost.[17]

Having seen the range of possibilities covered by (*a*), we are in a position to appreciate the general form that an objection to the Extreme Demand will take. The Extreme Demand results from iterating the requirement that I make a small sacrifice to contribute towards helping someone who desperately needs it. Each of the sacrifices in the sequence may itself be insignificant. But if I make them all, then that might involve a different kind of loss—one that is much more important. And if I can legitimately refuse to sustain that more important loss, then that might itself justify me in refusing to think in the iterative way.[18]

This is an important first step towards seeing how to respond to the Extreme Demand. However, it is no more than that. After all, altruism is only altruistic if it involves a loss or cost of some sort; and why cannot many small morally required losses add up to a large morally required loss? What has to be shown is why it is legitimate for us to refuse to give up what would be lost in meeting the Extreme Demand: that is, task (*b*) must be carried through. Again, there are various possibilities to consider. In the following sections I divide them into four main categories. The argument to be developed in Part II belongs to the fourth.

As we go through these categories, I shall accumulate a list of problems that will have to be solved if a convincing argument is to be given. Let me mention one general problem at the outset. Suppose that (*b*) can indeed be carried through convincingly: there is a good argument for thinking that losses of fulfilment, integrity, or some other good are losses I can legitimately refuse to bear. We still face the following problem. Fulfilment and integrity, important as they are, obviously do not excuse a complete refusal to contribute to helping other people. Cases of direct rescue are sufficient to show us this. It would be ridiculous to cite the loss of such goods as a justification for refusing to rescue a person directly: partly because it is so implausible that this could impinge on your fulfilment or integrity, but also because if it *did* impinge on them, that would only suffice to show that your fulfilment or integrity were focused in an objectionably self-centred way. If your fulfilment and integrity come from living in a way that involves refusing to make any effort to rescue another person, then you can be criticized for *that*. For there are lives of equal fulfilment and integrity that do not involve refusing to do this, and you should be living one of those lives instead. However, once we say this, we invite the following question. Could not an *altruistically* focused life be a life of just as much fulfilment and integrity? And if so, how does invoking the importance of these goods help to show that I cannot be required to live an altruistically focused life?

Answering this question will be a major preoccupation in Part II. For now, let us turn to the four categories of argument I just mentioned.

6.3 APPEALING TO A THEORY OF MORALITY

The first kind of argument is the most ambitious: it involves defending a general theory of morality that is not extremely demanding.

By 'a general theory of morality', I mean to cover two different things. One is a normative moral theory: a theory spelling out which ways of living are morally right and wrong, good and bad. If a theory of this kind can be defended, and it is not extremely demanding, then we have a defence of the claim that morality is not extremely demanding. This might be claimed for a Kantian, consequentialist, Aristotelian, or contractualist theory, a further 'virtue theory', a religiously based moral outlook, any of the various possible kinds of pluralist theory, or any other general normative ethical view.[19] A proponent of any such general theory might argue as follows. 'A demanding claim about the content of morality will only be credible to the extent that it can be integrated into a convincing overall account of what we morally ought to do, think, feel, and be. But the best overall account of this kind is Theory T. And Theory T is not extremely demanding. So the claim that we are morally required to forgo almost all personal fulfilment must be rejected.'

I also include in the category of 'general theories of morality' various general claims about the point or distinctive nature of morality which might be invoked to try to show what is wrong with an extremely demanding moral outlook. Let me offer four prominent examples of what I have in mind.

First, we can consider the Hobbesian claim that morality has a practical function: the function of allowing us to manage conflicts of interest to everyone's advantage. Left to interact with each other solely on the basis of self-interest, we would face a situation in which the lack of restraint in pursuing conflicting interests would be to everyone's disadvantage. Morality is the device we have collectively instituted as the solution to this collective problem. Its point is to protect us from a social dynamic that would be mutually disastrous, by motivating us to cooperate.[20] But, it might be argued, if the function of morality is to protect the interests of each of us, it cannot make sense for it to require any of us to compromise our interests any further than we all must to secure the advantages of society that result from mutual respect. If protecting our interests is the point of morality, it cannot be extremely demanding.[21]

A second kind of claim is meta-ethical. On metaphysical and epistemological grounds, it is often held that we should see morality as invented by us, not discovered. This claim may be combined with the previous one, concerning the conflict-managing point of morality—as it is famously by Mackie.[22] But it might also be thought on its own to undermine the view that the demands of morality might be extreme. If moral facts are ingredients of the world fixed independently of us, then there seems little reason to think that when we discover them we should find them to be congenial. But if we ourselves are the authors of morality, then it is harder to believe that the standards we should set for ourselves should be inimical to the living of a fulfilling life.[23]

A third claim makes this more than hard to believe—it rules it out of consideration altogether. On an approach to ethical thought which is broadly Aristotelian in inspiration, the essential ethical question is what is the best life to lead. Certainly, it is to be hoped that the answer will include a respect for other people and a concern for their interests. However, it might be complained, it is only by a distortion of reasoning that we could be led to think that having an adequate concern for other people's interests means living a personally stunted and unfulfilling life ourselves. Helping other people so much that you make your own life worse cannot be part of the best life for you, and if not, it cannot be recommended to you as part of the life you ought to lead.[24]

A fourth claim characterizes the point of morality as being to reconcile the demands of two competing perspectives we are capable of occupying in thinking about what is important. One is the perspective internal to those commitments that have special importance for me—my own personal, and partial, perspective. However, I can also see that, from an impartial perspective, my own commitments are no more important than anyone else's. One direct route to a demanding moral outlook involves simply identifying the moral point of view with this impartial point of view. But the thought that some philosophers have is that the distinction between these two perspectives might be used to describe the nature of morality in a different way. For perhaps we should think of moral norms as themselves norms for balancing the competing demands of the partial and impartial perspectives.[25] And if *this* is the fundamental task of morality, then we can see why its requirements cannot be extremely demanding. It must allow us a substantial degree of personal partiality if it is to take adequate account of one of the perspectives that we occupy.

Problems

I am not about to argue that none of these competing theoretical claims could succeed in defending a moderately demanding moral outlook. However, there are two general reasons to look elsewhere for an explanation of what is wrong with the Extreme Demand.

First, notice that the starting point of the argument for the Extreme Demand is a claim that is not in dispute between any of these theories. Any plausible theory of morality is going to recognize that I am morally required to save lives directly at small personal cost. What is in question is the cogency of the iterative reasoning that takes us from this starting point to the Extreme Demand. Perhaps one or more theories of the kinds just mentioned contains the resources for saying what is wrong with the iterative argument. However, on the face of it, it looks as though the claims about beneficence from which the argument has started are common to every plausible theory, and that if there is a problem with the argument from those claims to the Extreme Demand, it should be possible to point it out without having to appeal to one of those theories over others. I think that this can be done, and aim to show how in Part II.

So the first reason for not going down this route is that it seems to me unnecessary. The second is this. The rejection of the Extreme Demand is not itself a controversial view. That is not to say that it is easy to say what is wrong with it, that it does not deserve a careful argument, or that we can dismiss out of hand the possibility that it should be accepted after all. But it does mean that rejecting the Extreme Demand is a lot less controversial than defending any of the general theories just mentioned. Any argument against the Extreme Demand that took this theoretical route would have to give an elaborate defence of contentious premisses, in support of a less contentious conclusion. If so, it makes sense to look elsewhere for a more convincing argument.

6.4 APPEALING TO PARTICULAR MORAL FACTS

A less ambitious strategy of argument for showing that the demands of morality cannot be extreme appeals not to a general theory of morality, but to particular moral facts, in order to ground its case.

The most straightforward argument of this kind is one that simply invokes a basic moral principle that we are not morally required to make great sacrifices in responding to others' interests. This need not involve claiming this principle to be simply self-evident: saying that it is 'basic' need only mean that it is not derived by inferring it from other normative claims. The work that would have to be done in order to mount a serious argument of this kind would be to vindicate this principle by appealing to a plausible moral epistemology that explains how we can be warranted in believing it.

Other arguments in this category are possible, though: these involve appealing to substantive moral norms which can themselves be used to state conditions for the acceptability of moral requirements. Fair Share Views illustrate this form of argument. They appeal to a norm that is presented as part of the substance of morality: it is unreasonable to require me to bear other people's share of the burden in a collective project. But beneficence itself, it continues, should be seen as a collective project. Therefore, the claim that beneficence requires me to make great sacrifices when others make none should itself be rejected by the application of this moral norm.

Another example is the appeal to the bad consequences of a demanding morality. For most people, the fact that some practice has bad consequences provides at least *a* morally good reason against it; so this gives us a moral norm that might be used to argue against an extremely demanding moral outlook. Different versions of this argument have been mentioned already. It might be argued, in this vein, that we collectively do more good by having full personal commitments of our own; that this is true of me personally;[26] or that people will tend to do less good if extreme demands are advocated to them.[27]

A third example is the simple generalization argument: it is worse for everyone if each of us is required to be extremely self-sacrificing; therefore, this cannot be required of any of us.[28] This involves an appeal to the claimed moral norm: if everyone's doing a certain thing would be better for everyone, then my doing it must be morally acceptable. This norm is then applied to the action of *refusing to meet a requirement of extreme self-sacrifice* to justify the conclusion that this must be morally acceptable.

Problems

My main reason for not looking to an argument in this second category for a refutation of the Extreme Demand is simply that I cannot see a convincing one. We have already seen the limitations of Fair Share Views[a] and of appeals to the bad consequences of a demanding morality.[b] And it is also hard to see how the generalization argument just sketched is going to help. After all, the Extreme Demand is only extreme under circumstances of partial compliance. It only requires that I give up a lot when others are not doing enough. Under such conditions of partial compliance, it does make an extreme demand of each of us. But it does not demand that all of us together make a great self-sacrifice.[29]

I also mentioned the possibility of appealing to a basic moral principle that we are not morally required to make great sacrifices in responding to others' interests. This shares one of the problems I identified for the first, theoretical category of argument: the problem of arguing from the controversial to the relatively uncontroversial. The major task that arguments of this kind must complete is to defend a favoured moral epistemology that will vindicate claims about basic normative facts. But this would mean having to develop a very widely ramified argument for a controversial claim in order to secure the premisses of an argument for a less controversial one.

Moreover, notice the following further problem. The conclusion that morality cannot be extremely demanding looks implausibly blunt.[30] A blanket claim of this kind would mean drastically revising the moral opinions held by most of us. For although few people accept the Extreme Demand in relation to humanitarian aid, many of us still think that there can be some situations in which it *would* be wrong not to make great personal sacrifices. Meeting my debts might mean reducing myself to penury; and if another person were convicted of a capital crime I had committed, or if I were required to fight in a self-defensive war, it might be wrong not to give up my life. Of course, the mere fact that many of us believe these things does not mean we are right. But it is at least going to require a substantial argument to show convincingly that we are mistaken.

[a] Sect. 5.2. [b] Sect. 5.3, 'Motivational Limits'.

6.5 OBJECTIONS FROM PRACTICAL REASON

The two categories of objections to demanding moral outlooks that have been considered so far aim to show that the content of morality could not be extremely demanding. The third category to consider contains arguments whose direct target is different: their aim is to show that if the content of morality is extremely demanding then reason permits me to disregard it.

This covers two different kinds of view about the relationship between morality and practical reason. One is the view of those who are happy to accept that morality is extremely demanding, but who conjoin this with (and often, take it as evidence for) a thesis about the disunity of practical reason. On this view, I can identify the reasons for doing what is morally right, and I can identify the reasons for doing what is best for me; but it is a mistake for me then to ask what, taking all of these reasons into account, there is most reason for me to do. There is simply no fully unified normative perspective from which to make such global judgements. The life that is morally right is, trivially, *morally* better than the life that is personally best, but I have no decisive reason to be swayed by that fact rather than the fact that the latter is *personally* better. If I live the life that is best for me, there is a moral cost, but I do not have more reason to be concerned about that than about the personal cost to me of adhering to the demands of morality.[31]

The second view takes a tougher line. An extremely demanding morality is one that I have most reason to disregard. There are two directions in which this might be taken. Does it make sense to say that although a certain action is morally wrong I have most reason to perform it? If not, then showing that I have most reason not to lead a life of extreme self-denial will establish that such a life cannot be what morality requires of me.[32] The content of morality cannot be extremely demanding after all. On the other hand, if that does make sense, we are led in a different direction. Morality may be extremely demanding, but so much the worse for morality. Perhaps, morally speaking, we ought to live a life of minimal personal fulfilment: that simply means that we have most reason to ignore what morality tells us to do.

Thus, the claim that reason permits me to disregard an extremely demanding moral outlook comes in different forms, and can be taken in different directions. How might you seek to support this claim? Broadly speaking, in one of two ways, which are analogues of the first two categories of argument I have already surveyed. You might seek to support it via a more general theory of practical reason, or to argue for its plausibility independently of any such theory

We have already met two of the main strategies for theorizing about practical reason that are sometimes invoked to argue against demanding moral outlooks. A first, 'Aristotelian' kind of argument seeks to derive conclusions about reasons from claims about value. What there is reason to pursue and what is good are conceptually connected. From the fact that something is good, it follows that I have a reason to pursue it; from the fact that it is bad, it follows that I have a reason to avoid it. But an extremely demanding morality would require me to give myself a life that is bad for me. If so, I cannot have most reason to follow it.[33] A second, 'Humean' kind of argument draws its conclusions about our reasons from facts about our motivation.[34] The usual strategy is to invoke the following 'internalism' requirement. A consideration will only qualify as a reason for me to perform a given action if my awareness of that consideration would motivate me to perform it, if I were thinking about it fully rationally and with full knowledge.[35] But if I am not motivated to meet an extreme set of moral demands, that does not involve any failure of rationality. There is no way to integrate such demands into a unified practical outlook along with my deepest commitments. And if not, I cannot have a compelling reason to adopt such a life.[36]

What other strategies for theorizing about practical reason are there? A third, broadly 'Kantian' kind of argument concerns the preconditions of recognizing a consideration as a practical reason. It attempts to pass from considering the formal conditions that a consideration must satisfy in order to have the status of a reason to an account of which considerations have that status.[37] We shall meet some examples of this strategy in the next section.

Instead of trying to defend an entire normative theory of practical reason, you might instead appeal to general claims about the point or function of practical reason. One such claim, which has attracted philosophers whose views about practical reason are otherwise very different, is that the role of practical reason is to shape an agent's ends in a way that brings them into harmony with each other. And given the way in which personal attachments and commitments provide some of our most fundamental ends, a life that is shaped by reason in this way is not going to be one that excludes them.[38]

Alternatively, you might seek to reject extreme moral demands on the strength of an appeal to basic normative facts. These might be facts about reasons: one version of this strategy simply argues that when we appreciate correctly the various substantive reasons that we have, and their respective strengths, we find that there is not most reason for us to meet an extreme standard of demand. Or they might be facts about reasonableness: when we are properly appreciative of the requirements it is reasonable for us to apply to each other in order to live together, we see that it is unreasonable to require a person to give away practically everything to help others.[39]

Problems

We saw that arguments in the first of our categories faced one group of problems, and arguments in the second faced another. The arguments we have just met in the third category face problems from both of the earlier groups.

The problem that these arguments share with the second category (appeals to particular moral facts) concerns the strength of their conclusion. Again, they invite a worry about how, if they succeed against the Extreme Demand, they can avoid the implausible-looking conclusion that significant self-sacrifice can *never* be required of us. Indeed, it looks as though it is going to be awkward to explain how this could even be *permitted*. How can these arguments for thinking that practical reason does not require extremes of self-sacrifice avoid the conclusion that practical reason requires me *not* to go to extremes of self-sacrifice—and thus to rule out most apparently 'supererogatory' actions? It certainly seems that there can be situations in which if I greatly compromise my own fulfilment on others' behalf, not out of self-hatred but from concern for them, it will not be wrong to do so: on the contrary, it might be morally outstanding, going beyond what I am morally required to do. That this is widely believed does not show that it is true. But a convincing argument against it will require a lot of work.[40]

Worse, the practical reason arguments face a challenge not simply to explain how they can accommodate supererogation: they need to explain how they avoid egoism.[41] They had better not give us the conclusion that reason permits, or even requires, me to do what is best for me. Our problem has arisen by assuming that this egoistic view is false, and developing the life-saving analogy from this starting point: it is no surprise to be reminded that if we reject the assumption, an extremely demanding outlook is avoided. The sensible thing to say is that my own interests are only one source of good reasons to act. The problem is to show why admitting this does not supply enough materials for an iterative argument to the Extreme Demand.

This brings us to the worry that these arguments concerning the nature of practical reason provoke in common with arguments from a theory of morality. How far will these controversial and ambitious arguments actually get us towards explaining what is wrong with the argument for the Extreme Demand? Suppose they can avoid the over-strong conclusion that reason permits me to refuse to make small sacrifices to confer large benefits on others. What then blocks the iterative thought that, since I can be required to make such sacrifices, I can be required to make *many* such sacrifices to help many others?

6.6 THE PRESUPPOSITIONS OF BENEFICENCE

I have offered a quick survey of three different categories of arguments against an extremely demanding moral outlook, and some of the problems that they face. I have not shown that those problems cannot be resolved, and that there is no argument from these various categories that succeeds. But what I am going to do is to develop an argument of a different kind, which has certain advantages over the ones considered so far.

This fourth and final category of argument concerns what we can call the presuppositions of beneficence. A beneficent person takes others' interests to provide her with good reasons to help them. The argument for the Extreme Demand begins by assuming that we are right to take others' interests to provide us with reasons, and that we can be criticized for failing to act appropriately on those reasons. If we could show that accepting this assumption involves presuppositions that themselves compel the rejection of the Extreme Demand, that would give us a powerful argument against it.

What might such an argument look like? Let me give two examples. These will help us to see the form that such an argument might take, but also some of the problems that it, too, needs to overcome.

One example of this strategy is given, famously, by Kant's discussion of benevolence in *The Metaphysics of Morals*, where he argues that benevolence to myself must be permissible if benevolence to others is to be required.[42] Kant's thought is that our duties in regard to the welfare of others are duties primarily of benevolence—*willing* the good of others—rather than beneficence—*doing* good to them. My duty is to treat others' interests as an end of mine, and this makes it an 'imperfect' duty: on just which occasions I should act to further this end, given all the other ends that I properly have, is a matter for the exercise of occasion-by-occasion judgement.[43] We might worry that there can be circumstances—such as when you could easily save someone's life—in which the failure to act beneficently *on this occasion* will be wrong. It is not as if I could properly choose not to save someone's life in a direct emergency, opting to exercise my benevolence some other time instead. However, it is not obvious that Kant must deny this. Although he is not explicit about this, nothing seems to prevent him from saying, sensibly enough, that anyone who fails to save someone's life at small cost (where there are no mitigating circumstances) cannot be genuinely treating others' interests as an end. But given this treatment of benevolence in my relations to others, Kant then reasons that this will carry implications too for my relations to myself. Given the universalizability of moral reasons, benevolence to myself must at least be permissible if benevolence towards others is required. If others' interests are to make a claim on me, my own must legitimately do so too. The claims that others' interests make on me cannot be so strong that I must give up practically everything of my own to satisfy them: '. . . a maxim of promoting others' happiness at the sacrifice of one's own happiness, one's true needs, would conflict with itself if it were made a universal law.'[44]

A second way of pursuing this strategy is more general. This involves asking: What are the presuppositions of supposing that—not just others' interests, but—*any* consideration provides me with a good reason for acting? This concerns the presuppositions of beneficence because it concerns the presuppositions of reason-recognition as such. Thus, it also belongs to the previous category of arguments, from the nature of practical reason: it is an instance of the 'broadly Kantian' strategy of argument I mentioned there.[45]

Bernard Williams's well-known argument in 'Persons, Character and Morality' has this form. According to him, recognizing that I have reason to pursue sources of personal fulfilment (or 'projects', to use Williams's term) is a precondition of recognizing reasons to do anything. As Williams puts it, 'my present projects are the condition of my existence, in the sense that unless I am propelled forward by the conatus of desire, project and interest, it is unclear why I should go on at all'.[46] And if so, he argues, then there is an objection to extremely demanding, impartialist conceptions of morality: 'Life has to have substance if anything is to have sense, including adherence to the impartial system; but if it has substance, then it cannot grant supreme importance to the impartial system, and that system's hold on it will be, at the limit, insecure.'[47] Recognizing a reason to pursue anything requires recognizing my own life as worth living, but doing this requires recognizing compelling reasons to pursue sources of personal fulfilment. I can only take myself to have a reason to do anything (such as further other people's interests) to the extent that I am committed to the personal projects and relationships that give my life its significance to me. If these commitments are a precondition of my recognizing a reason to do anything, I cannot sensibly accept that I have good reason to abandon them. A view that gives me no greater reason to pursue my own fulfilment than anyone else's is simply unlivable: for if I recognize practical reasons at all, I cannot adopt this view of them.[48]

Advantages and Problems

Arguments of this form, from the presuppositions of beneficence, avoid several of the problems we found with the other arguments we have surveyed. What several of them require is a global argument about morality that is going to be more controversial than the conclusion it is being used to support. But that is not the case here. The starting point of this argument will simply be the claim that we do stand under requirements of beneficence. And *that* is not a matter of controversy between supporters and opponents of the Extreme Demand. Moreover, arguing in this way does not seem to run the risk of leading to a conclusion that is too strong. It clearly promises to avoid egoism: its starting point is the supposition that egoism is false. And because its emphasis is on examining the presuppositions of *beneficence*, rather than on making global claims about morality as a whole, it will not offer resistance to moral requirements of substantial self-sacrifice that arise from sources other than beneficence.

This makes it attractive to look in this direction for an explanation of what is wrong with the Extreme Demand, and that is what I shall do in Part II. However, this is not to say that arguments of this kind do not face problems of their own. In particular, they provoke a worry that they have avoided producing a conclusion that is too strong only at the cost of producing one that is too weak.

Take the argument from Williams first. This offers a suggestive response to those demanding moral outlooks that derive from impartialist conceptions of morality—conceptions such as those arising from the two theoretical sources considered earlier.[49] However, it is harder to see how it can amount to an adequate reply to the Extreme Demand; for this, as we have seen, does not amount to a requirement of complete impartiality. Perhaps we should agree with Williams that granting supreme importance to the impartial system may deprive one's life of substance, without which nothing has sense; but a life meeting the Extreme Demand is still a life with *some* substance. It does allow us to remain committed to personal projects and relationships: it is just that it instructs us to restrict our pursuit of these commitments as much as we bearably can.[50]

Moreover, Kant's argument looks vulnerable to the same point. As I have represented his reasoning, it is that my own interests must legitimately make a claim on me, given that others' interests do so. However, the Extreme Demand is consistent with accepting this. The Extreme Demand is compatible with accepting that my own interests can properly be allowed a much greater claim on me than other people's. I can legitimately refuse to make a large sacrifice for another person, even to save his life. But provided only that I can be required to make a small one, this requirement will be iterated when there are many people who stand in need of my help. It is hard to see how the Extreme Demand could fail any universalization test a Kantian might set for it. It is not, absurdly, instructing everyone simultaneously to compromise their most fundamental interests in order to promote other people's. Rather, to each of us it addresses the following requirement: when someone else's most fundamental interests—interests in survival—are at stake, and a much less important sacrifice in your own interests would help them, you must do so. There is a sense in which this requires promoting others' happiness at the sacrifice of one's own happiness—but it is only that I am required to make small sacrifices in my interests to provide much more important benefits to others. And if everyone were following this requirement, the amount each of us would have to give up would not be great. So it is hard to see how *this* requirement could conflict with itself if it were made a universal law.

Thus, it is hard to see how these two arguments from the presuppositions of beneficence can succeed in showing that a more-than-minimal level of personal spending is defensible.[51] If we are going to make any progress in opposing the Extreme Demand with an argument of this kind, we need to do better.

6.7 CONCLUSION

In this chapter I have done two things. The first is to emphasize that the problem of demandingness raised by the arguments so far in this book cannot be brushed aside by responding that it only arises for someone committed to substantial theoretical assumptions about the connection between morality and impartiality. What makes the problem troubling is that it can be generated without making such assumptions. It is a problem that anyone ought to be disturbed by, and that we all need to find a response to.

As I suggested in Chapter 2, this has significant implications for what a satisfactory response to the problem must be like.[c] The theoretically uncommitted nature of the argument for the Extreme Demand adds substantially to the challenge we have to meet in Part II. For if the problem of demandingness that it sets us is generated without relying on a particular theoretical orientation, a fully effective reply ought to avoid this as well. Anyone needs a reply to the problem, whatever theoretical (or anti-theoretical) view they accept. If so, the impact of a reply to it will be significantly weakened if it requires us first to suppose that some particular theory of morality is correct.

The other thing the chapter has done is to offer a broad classification of arguments against demanding moral outlooks, including the kind of argument I am going on to develop. No doubt, this classification is incomplete. There must be other ways of arguing against extremely demanding moral outlooks.[52] Maybe some of them are successful. Indeed, this may well be true for some of the arguments I have described. I have not been trying to establish that these arguments all fail. But I think enough has been said to show why it makes sense to be looking in the direction I do for a good argument, and why there is not a response to the Extreme Demand which is obvious enough to make the next two chapters, which set out a detailed argument against it, unnecessary.

Although I do not claim to have produced a decisive refutation of any of the arguments I have described, I have sought to spell out some of the main problems that a successful argument will have to address. First, and most obviously, it will have to respond to the iterative argument for the Extreme Demand, rather than simply overcoming the difficulties apparently produced by identifying the moral point of view with the impartial point of

[c] Sect. 2.5.

view. The iterative argument takes as its starting point the position that is reached once those difficulties have been overcome. Our own response had better not itself be vulnerable to an iterative argument. In responding to this iterative argument, we shall need to defend a more-than-minimal level of personal spending, going beyond the apparent limitations of the arguments from Kant and Williams. And our argument should preferably show what mistake in reasoning is made by the iterative argument, rather than simply supporting a different conclusion. At the same time, care will need to be taken over the strength of the conclusion that this argument produces. It must allow for (or, more surprisingly, deny the existence of) cases where extremes of self-sacrifice *are* morally required, and cases of supererogation. And it must avoid egoism, given that the problem we are trying to address only arises once egoism has been rejected. Finally, it should preferably do all this without appealing to claims that are markedly more controversial than its conclusion.

This gives us a list of seven requirements that a convincing refutation of the Extreme Demand must meet. The first aim in Part II will be to give an argument that meets these requirements. The second, more important aim will be to develop out of this a better account of the moral demands of affluence.

Part II

LIMITS

7

Impartiality, Fairness, and Beneficence

PART I has presented us with a problem of demandingness. I have tried to show that this problem is genuine, and troubling. At times the argument has had to be detailed, in order to show how various avenues which might seem to allow us to avoid its conclusion are in fact closed off. But its force comes from the fact that its two central ingredients are so simple. The first of these is the life-saving analogy between contributions to aid agencies and the direct saving of life. The second is the iteration of that analogy in respect of each successive contribution I might make. Together, they generate the conclusion that we are required to get as close as we can to meeting the Extreme Demand.

This line of thought is unsettling. I think it does correspond to one of the main grounds on which many of us feel uneasy about enjoying plenty in a world in which many people are in desperate poverty. But despite all this—despite the detailed articulation of the argument, and the power of its central thoughts—the conclusion it leads to is surely very difficult to accept. We may be unsettled if we do not find it obvious what was wrong with the argument of Part I. But surely, there are few people who will ever be led by this argument to give their considered endorsement either to the Extreme Demand itself, or to the view that we are required to get as close as we can to meeting this demand.

An uncompromising response to this is that it is just a sign of our moral frailty.[1] It should not be surprising if we find ourselves reluctant to accept such an extremely demanding view of how we ought to live. Given how uncomfortable this would be, it is unsurprising that hardly anyone attempts to live this way. And few of us are willing to think so ill of ourselves that we can be easily brought to accept that the way we routinely act is morally wrong.

However, before adopting this dismissive response to the 'common-sense' view of the Extreme Demand, we ought to do our best to see what can be said for a less dismissive one. After all, our resistance to accepting this demand does not simply amount to the thought that attempting to live up to it would be uncomfortable. The Extreme Demand seems wrong. One way in which it is natural to express what seems wrong about it is by talking about what is reasonable. We might protest: whether or not it is reasonable for us to be living exactly as we do, surely it is reasonable for us not to be constricting our lives as drastically as the Extreme Demand requires. We ought to be concerned for others, and to respond to their needs, but it cannot be unreasonable for us to have lives of our own, containing personal fulfilments that go beyond the extreme restrictions involved in trying to meet the Extreme Demand.[2] This thought surely has some resonance for most of us: it is worth seeing what can be said in its defence. That is what I am going to do in the rest of this book.

Of course, on their own, these thoughts about reasonableness do not make a very impressive objection to the argument of Part I: its aim was precisely to undermine thoughts such as these. It begins by pointing out that it is reasonable to demand an insignificant sacrifice of me to save someone's life, but then shows that the iteration of this, given the life-saving analogy, will lead to the reasonableness of the Extreme Demand. If our thoughts about the reasonableness of not trying to meet the Extreme Demand are to stand up in the face of this argument, they will need to be given a substantial further defence.

The strategy to be pursued here will be to provide that defence by showing that the Extreme Demand can be rejected from an appropriately impartial point of view.

The first thing I need to do is to explain this claim, and to show why, if it could be justified, it would amount to a good objection to the Extreme Demand. What is an 'appropriately' impartial point of view? Exactly what is being asked when I ask whether a proposed moral requirement such as the Extreme Demand can be rejected from this point of view? And how is this going to be relevant to undermining the case we have seen in favour of the Extreme Demand? These are the questions I shall be answering in this chapter. The next task will be to *justify* the claim that the Extreme Demand can be rejected from an appropriately impartial point of view. That will occupy us in Chapter 8.

This can only be carried through if there is, after all, something wrong with the argument of Part I. I have already said where I think the error lies: not with the life-saving analogy itself, but with the iterative approach to it. But if the argument for the iterative approach was mistaken, why not simply go back to that argument, identify the error in the reasoning, and—having refuted the attempt to argue for the Extreme Demand—stop there? There are two reasons why the task ahead of us cannot be this simple. The first is that we do not yet have the materials we need in order to show what is wrong with the iterative approach. An extended further argument will be needed to supply those materials: that is what the discussion that follows is going to give us.

There is a second reason why there is more to be done than merely pointing out an error in the argument of Part I. This is that, although the immediate aim of the discussion that follows is to show that the Extreme Demand should be rejected, its ultimate aim is more ambitious. Showing what is wrong with the argument for the Extreme Demand is certainly worthwhile, if the argument for that demand does, as I think, crystallize a line of thought that is genuinely troubling to many of us. However, what we are ultimately interested in is not simply the rejection of one view about the moral demands of affluence that most of us find implausibly extreme. Rather, we want to find the right view. We want to know what the moral demands of affluence *are*. Chapters 9 and 10 turn to that further question.

The final chapter—Chapter 11—gives an overview of the book, discussing the structure and scope of its arguments, and how the two parts of the book fit together. Our destination will be a demanding view: it asks more of us than most of us find comfortable. However, it is much more moderate than the Extreme Demand. I think that makes it more difficult to ignore.

7.1 IMPARTIALITY AND THE REJECTION OF THE EXTREME DEMAND

How can we show that a proposed standard of moral requirement should be rejected? What kind of argument will work to show that such a standard goes beyond what morality really does require of us? Perhaps there is a correct, general theory of morality that generates a global test for justified moral requirements, and that will answer our question for us. But if there is, I shall not be trying to identify it. It seems that there are many different grounds on which putative moral demands might be faulted, and that the one it makes sense to emphasize will depend on what kind of moral demand is being proposed. Our interest here is in one particular kind of moral requirement: a moral requirement in relation to how much we contribute to helping other people. I shall be arguing that it is reasonable to reject a proposed standard of requirement of *this* kind if it can be rejected from an appropriately impartial point of view. I do not propose this as part of a general theory of the justification of moral judgements. But I do think that if this can be shown, it undermines the case for the Extreme Demand.

It is not hard to see, in a general way, why showing that the Extreme Demand can be impartially rejected should be thought to undermine the case in its favour. That case, after all, is in essence an accusation of selfishness. According to the argument of Part I, failing to aim at meeting the Extreme Demand involves an excessive concern for my own interests in comparison to other people's. However, suppose it could be shown that this demand can be rejected from a point of view that is appropriately impartial between the interests of everyone affected by it—in particular, between my interests and those who stand to gain from my help. If so, I would be in a strong position to deny that, when I refuse to meet the Extreme Demand, there is anything objectionably selfish about the amount of consideration I give to others' interests. For I would be able to point out that the kind of partiality I am displaying towards myself is acceptable from a point of view that is impartially disengaged from my own—that gives no special weight to my own position or anyone else's. My self-concern is only the kind of self-concern that must be agreed to be acceptable in everyone, from a point of view that privileges no one.

What we are doing if we argue in this way is to say that a certain amount of personal partiality is impartially acceptable—an amount that exceeds what the Extreme Demand would allow us.[3] At first glance, this may look incoherent. How could it make sense to say that partiality is impartially acceptable? Here is one suggestion. Perhaps there are certain fundamentally important goods that are only accessible to us if we act from attitudes of personal partiality—perhaps because they are *constituted* by such attitudes. If so, it might make sense from a point of view that favoured no one to recommend that we foster the attitudes that make those goods available to anyone.

This is not the only possible way of trying to show that personal partiality is impartially acceptable.[4] However, it is the one that will occupy us here. This line of argument—from the importance of partiality-constituted goods to the impartial acceptability of personal partiality—will be developed, and its implications explored, in the following chapters.

I have just given a general indication of why, if we can show that the Extreme Demand is impartially rejectable, that should be thought to undermine the case in its favour. But this needs to be explained in greater detail and with more care. After all, all that seems necessary for talk of 'impartiality' to make sense is the absence of an intention to favour any particular affected party.[5] And that makes it hard to see what stops outright egoism—indeed, universal malevolence—from counting as impartially acceptable. Clearly, then, not every respect in which a standard of conduct counts as impartially acceptable will be sufficient to show that it is free of selfishness.[6] Even the demand that we do not kill people for personal advantage could be rejected from a point of view that favours no one. Thus, in order to have a good argument against the Extreme Demand, it is not enough to show that it could be rejected from an impartial point of view. What needs to be shown is that this could be done from a point of view that involves an *appropriate* kind of impartiality—that is, a kind of impartiality appropriate to drawing conclusions about the adequacy of a level of concern for other people's interests.

We need, then, to look more carefully at the case for the Extreme Demand and examine more closely which claims about impartial rejection will undermine it. The case for the Extreme Demand invoked two different sources of moral requirements. First, there was an argument from beneficence for the conclusion that we are collectively required to help desperately needy people at small cost. To this, an argument from fairness was then added, drawing the conclusion that each of us is individually required to contribute to discharging that collective requirement of beneficence. An iterative approach to this pair of requirements generates the Extreme Demand.

In the rest of this chapter I shall show that, if the Extreme Demand can be rejected from an appropriately impartial point of view, then the case in its favour is undermined in two different ways. If a proposed standard of moral requirement can be rejected from such a point of view, then it cannot be a requirement of fairness. And if it can be rejected from such a point of view, then it cannot be a requirement of beneficence either. Showing one of these things would be sufficient to supply a telling objection to the Extreme Demand. However, both are true.

I shall take these points in turn, discussing fairness first, and then beneficence. Then I shall sum up what this tells us about the kind of impartiality that is 'appropriate' in evaluating the Extreme Demand.

7.2 IMPARTIALITY AND FAIRNESS

The Extreme Demand relies on claims about what fairness requires me to contribute towards collective actions of furthering others' interests. However, if the Extreme Demand can be rejected from an appropriately impartial point of view, that would be a decisive objection to those claims. The reason for this is the close conceptual connection between fairness and impartiality. Kinds of fairness *are* kinds of appropriate impartiality. Let me illustrate this by looking briefly at some contexts in which we talk of fairness and unfairness.

Consider first those contexts in which there is a good to be distributed. The action of distributing the good can be fair or unfair, and so can the resulting distribution.[7] What is distributively fair depends, obviously enough, on the aim it is appropriate to have in distributing the good in question. It can be fair to distribute sporting or musical bursaries to those who are already better off in terms of musical or sporting ability; but it will be unfair to give state welfare handouts to the better-off in preference to the worse-off; and unfair to take either ability or need into account when awarding the prize for winning a race. If the aims governing the distribution of these goods changed, the criteria for fairness would change too. If the only good produced by athletics were the athlete's own enjoyment, maybe it would be unfair to fund elite athletes more than mediocre ones; if the point of awarding prizes was to acknowledge effort rather than achievement, then obviously it would be fair to give them to the hardest triers rather than the highest achievers.

If we are looking for a general account of distributive fairness, then perhaps the best one is this. Distributive fairness requires responding to claims to a good in a way that is appropriately proportional to the strength of each person's claim to that good.[8] In different circumstances, it is appropriate to recognize different kinds of claim: this reflects the way in which the fairness of a distribution depends on its point. My claim to a bursary is a function of the musical or sporting ability that can be reasonably attributed to me; but my claim to a welfare handout depends on my need; and the only relevant claim to the prize for winning a race is that I am the first competitor, running within the rules of the race, to cross the line.

Fairness is not restricted to questions of distribution.[9] A second class of cases to consider concerns procedural fairness. A trial might be unfair, either because judicial rules are being broken, or because the rules governing it are themselves unfair. For non-judicial examples of procedural unfairness, consider jumping a queue, or insurance fraud. In these cases, the unfairness is not that of a distributor of a good among people with various claims to it.[10] Rather, procedural unfairness involves either the breach of fairly established rules for regulating recurring situations where interests conflict, or the unfair imposition of such rules. In the most obvious examples, procedural unfairness involves bias, as when I make or break a rule for the advantage of myself or someone with a special connection to me—or when there is more than one equally fair rule for decision about certain cases of conflict and I decide which one to apply in a given situation by working out which is best for me. Notice, however, that involving bias in these ways seems to be neither sufficient nor necessary for unfairness. Jumping a queue to save my child in an emergency is not unfair; conversely, the unfairness of decimation as a punishment is not that it involves bias against any of the people who have been arbitrarily picked out.

There are other kinds of judgement of fairness and unfairness besides the distributive and procedural—kinds that do not reduce to these first two. If a father selfishly leaves his partner to bring up their children on her own, it is natural to complain that he is being unfair to her and the children. But here, the unfairness is neither distributive nor procedural. It is a matter of the losses produced by an abuse of trust: 'unfairness-as-betrayal', we might call it. What is important in this case is that the other members of the family have been left badly off because of their reliance on him to fulfil the legitimate normative expectations they have of him. In this case, those normative expectations relate to the duties created by becoming a parent. Other cases of unfairness-as-betrayal will involve normative expectations of different sorts. Thus, if I induce you to cooperate with me by getting you to believe that I will reciprocate, but then let you down when the time comes to deliver, the complaint against me is again naturally phrased in terms of unfairness, and this is again a case of unfairness-as-betrayal. Actually, if

I swindle you, and go on to flourish while you suffer badly from the loss, then unfairness will be involved in several different ways. The initial betrayal has violated one kind of requirement of fairness. But my ongoing failure to restore your loss violates another, and the fact that I have gone unpunished violates a further one. This suggests that two further kinds of fairness—restorative fairness and retributive fairness—need to be added to our list.

The list might be extended, no doubt; but let us stop it there. There is a natural way to describe what is common to the various kinds of unfairness we have just surveyed. Unfairness, in each of these cases, involves a failure of appropriate impartiality. Ways of being impartial are ways of abstracting from the interests and points of view of the different individuals involved in a situation. There are various different ways of doing this, and different ones are appropriate in different situations. When we criticize someone for unfairness, what we are complaining about is that something ought to be done, and there is an appropriate form of impartiality that is required if it is to be done, yet he fails to exhibit that kind of impartiality.[11] Thus, distributive unfairness is a failure to be impartial between those among whom a good is distributed, in a way that is appropriate to the point of the distribution. Procedural unfairness is a failure to frame, follow, or apply a rule for regulating conflicts of interest with the kind of impartiality that is appropriate to regulating such conflicts. Unfairness-as-betrayal involves arrogating to yourself the privilege of abusing the trust of others when it is to your advantage. And restorative and retributive unfairness are failures to implement what can be seen to be required from a point of view that abstracts from the identities of the victim and the perpetrator of an offence.

I do not propose to amplify these remarks into a full-blown theory of fairness. What I have said leaves open the possibility that there are failures of appropriate impartiality that are not failures of fairness. It would be interesting to know whether this is true; and, if it *is* true, what is the characteristic that distinguishes the requirements of appropriate impartiality that are requirements of fairness from the ones that are not. However, that would be a digression. What is important here is that requirements of fairness are requirements of appropriate impartiality. Given this, it is easy to see why, if the Extreme Demand can be rejected from an appropriately impartial point of view, it cannot be claimed to correspond to a requirement of fairness.

The Extreme Demand is a claim about how far we are required to go in contributing towards furthering others' interests. Could it be a requirement of fairness? To read it this way would be to read it as a claim about appropriate impartiality—about the impartiality appropriate in contributing towards our collective action of helping other people. But suppose we could show that the Extreme Demand can be rejected from a point of view of appropriately impartial concern for others' interests. This would mean that it could be rejected compatibly with a fair concern for others' interests. But if so, it could not be a requirement of fairness.

Thus, showing that the Extreme Demand can be rejected from an appropriately impartial point of view would indeed undermine the case in its favour. It would undermine the claim that fairness could require us to go this far in contributing to collective actions of helping other people.

In explaining this, I have said one thing about what 'appropriate' impartiality will need to amount to in this argument: it is an impartial concern for everyone's interests. However, there are two further questions that need to be addressed. First, there are various rival conceptions of what a properly impartial concern for others' interests requires. One obvious suggestion is that it requires weighting everyone's interests equally. But there are others, as we shall see later in the chapter. My strategy will be to produce an argument that ranges across *all* of these conceptions of an appropriately impartial concern for others' interests. If I can show that the Extreme Demand can be rejected on all such conceptions, it will follow that it can be rejected on any one of them, whichever is correct. The second question is this. Given a kind of impartiality which is appropriate to evaluating a proposed moral requirement of fairness, *how much* impartiality of that kind is appropriate? But again, I shall sidestep this issue by arguing for an ambitious claim. Even from a point of view of *complete* impartiality, the Extreme Demand can be rejected. If so, then it can be rejected from any less impartial point of view as well. *However* much impartiality an appropriately impartial concern for others' interests involves, the Extreme Demand can be rejected from an appropriately impartial point of view. And we have just seen how that undermines the case for it, by undermining the claim that fairness could require this of me.

7.3 IMPARTIALITY AND BENEFICENCE

The case for the Extreme Demand relies on two thoughts: the thought that beneficence requires us collectively to help the desperately needy at small cost, and the thought that fairness requires me individually to contribute to fulfilling that collective requirement. I have just explained how the second of those two thoughts would be undermined if the Extreme Demand can be rejected from an appropriately impartial point of view (where that means: a point of view of impartial concern for other people's interests). That would suffice to show that the Extreme Demand cannot be the product of a requirement of fairness. Now let me explain how, if the Extreme Demand can be rejected from this point of view, the first thought is undermined as well: it cannot be the product of a requirement of beneficence either.

The general form of the argument for thinking this has already been given: I cannot properly be accused of being too self-centred if the amount of self-centredness I display is acceptable from a completely unself-centred point of view. Let me now develop this argument a bit more rigorously.

Beneficence involves a practical concern for other people's interests, rather than solely for your own. It involves observing limits on your pursuit of your own interests, in responding to the needs of other people. What we want to know is how strict those limits are. How much self-sacrifice is *required* by beneficence? If we consider the schema

> Beneficence requires us to make an overall compromise in pursuit of our own interests, in responding to the interests of others, of degree D,

how should we fill out D?

A range of different answers to this question can be considered. Near one end of the range is the extreme answer that identifies D with complete impartiality. As we have seen, not even the Extreme Demand makes this claim.[a] Notice that an even more extreme answer is possible: the self-abnegating view that you should give your own interests *less* consideration than those of any other person. (Is this proposal, which requires *more* than complete impartiality of us, one that we need to take seriously? I'll return to it in a moment.) Every less demanding answer should be thought of as belonging to this range—including the Extreme Demand.

We have been offered an argument for thinking that the Extreme Demand is the right way to fill out D. As long as some small sacrifice is required of us to help a single needy person, iterating this requirement many times over will lead to the requirement that our overall sacrifice is large. However, let us ask whether there is an independent way of evaluating the stringency of different proposed overall standards of requirement for beneficence. I suggest that there is.

I suggest that we approach the question how to fill out D from the point of view of beneficence itself. That is, we should consider the range of different conceivable standards of requirement for beneficence, extending from the weakest to the strongest, and then evaluate these standards from the point of view of a properly discriminating practical concern for other people's interests. If we can show that, from *this* point of view, there is one proposed standard of requirement that it makes sense to favour, then that will give us a very forceful argument. After all, it is only to someone who has the concerns distinctive of beneficence that the question what sort of conduct counts as a failure in relation to beneficence matters. If this question can be answered for someone with these concerns, then it can be answered for the only person who needs an answer. I shall call this the 'internal approach' to settling the standard of requirement for beneficence.

At first glance, this 'internal approach' may look hopelessly circular. Suppose you and I disagree, say, over whether refusing to give money to

[a] Sect. 6.1.

beggars amounts to a failure of beneficence. Let's say we disagree about whether the social implications of a practice of helping people are relevant to whether it is required by beneficence. I think beneficence requires me to give money to beggars even though, if people act the way I do, that encourages begging and sleeping rough; you disagree. It hardly helps us to suggest that we settle our disagreement by asking what standard of requirement for beneficence there is most reason to accept from the point of view of beneficence. For our dispute *is* a dispute about what is involved in the point of view of beneficence: what kind of concern to further other people's interests this involves. We are disagreeing about whether not helping would be a failure of beneficence because we disagree about whether helping would be beneficent.[12]

In that case, applying the internal approach would indeed be hopeless. The internal approach to settling a disagreement about the requirements of beneficence will be viciously circular if, when it appeals to what there is most reason to accept from 'the point of view of beneficence', it takes sides on the issue of disagreement. However, at least sometimes, this circularity can be avoided, and then the internal approach works. Consider again the self-abnegating view that you are required to give your own interests less consideration than those of any other person. I am not aware that this proposal has ever been seriously endorsed.[13] But notice that one way to express what seems untenable about it is to use an internal argument: *this* standard of requirement for beneficence is one that there is most reason to reject from the point of view of beneficence itself. From a point of view of concern for others' interests it makes no sense to require one person to damage her own interests for the sake of conferring a lesser benefit on someone else. This simple argument avoids any problem of circularity. All it asks us to suppose about the point of view of beneficence is that it involves a discriminating practical concern for others' interests. And *this* claim does not beg the question against the self-abnegating view. If the argument relied on assumptions about how much self-sacrifice beneficence *requires*—how much self-sacrifice is needed to avoid a *failure* of beneficence—then it would be circular; but it need not rely on such assumptions.

The internal approach, then, gives us a first conclusion about the requirements of beneficence. Recalling the schema for such requirements:

> Beneficence requires us to make an overall compromise in pursuit of our own interests, in responding to the interests of others, of degree D,

we have just learnt that a self-abnegating view about the value of D should be rejected. By itself, that is a rather modest conclusion. However, generalizing the point, we can draw the following broader lesson. For *any* proposed requirement of beneficence, an internal approach to evaluating it—an approach that evaluates it from the point of view of beneficence itself—will make sense provided that, in invoking 'the point of view of beneficence', we remain neutral about how far the requirements of beneficence extend. How can we remain neutral about that? In the same way as we just did in rejecting the self-abnegating proposal. The beneficent point of view is a point of view of concern for others' interests. The question we want to settle is how much self-sacrifice one is required to make—how far one is required to restrict one's personal partiality—in expressing this concern. So that is what we need to remain neutral about.

This is possible: after all, the disagreement about how much self-sacrifice is required by beneficence is not grounded in any disagreement about whether being extremely self-sacrificing would be beneficent. It is agreed on all sides that it would be. All sides of the disagreement can share a common conception of the point of view of beneficence, and agree that an extremely self-sacrificing person is beneficent, to a high degree. What they disagree about is how high a degree of beneficence is *required* of us, and how much can be criticized as insufficient. This is what gives us the scope for an internal argument.

A good argument of this form will need to make a convincing case for thinking that certain proposals concerning the requirements of beneficence can be rejected from the point of view of beneficence itself, without making any question-begging assumptions about how much self-sacrifice—how much restriction in personal partiality—this point of view requires of us. Doing this means showing that, *whatever* the amount of impartiality we were to think of as required by the point of view of beneficence, certain proposed standards of requirement should be rejected from that point of view. How could we show this? Here is one way. We could do this by showing that there is most reason to reject certain proposed standards of requirement as excessively demanding, even from a point of view of *completely* impartial beneficence. After all, if this is true even of a point of view of *complete* impartiality, then it will be true of any lesser degree of impartiality as well. It will be true whatever the amount of impartiality we associate with the point of view of beneficence. (In rejecting the self-abnegating view, we have ruled out the idea that beneficence could require *more* than complete impartiality.) If so, we would have a good, non-circular internal argument for rejecting those proposed standards of requirement for beneficence.

Thus, by applying the internal approach, we find that there will be a good objection to a proposed requirement of beneficence if it can be rejected from an appropriately impartial point of view. For these purposes, an appropriately impartial point of view is a point of view of completely impartial beneficence. That is to say, it is a point of view of completely impartial concern for each person's interests.

Notice that this is the same as the impartial point of view that is appropriate to evaluating the proposed requirements of fairness discussed in the previous section. It was pointed out then that there are different rival conceptions of what a properly impartial concern for everyone's interests should involve. It is time to say some more about this.

7.4 APPROPRIATE IMPARTIALITY

I have explained how, if the Extreme Demand can be rejected from an appropriately impartial point of view, that would undermine the case in its favour, in two different ways: it would undermine the claims about both beneficence and fairness upon which that case relies. Having said this, we have not yet identified errors in the reasoning leading to the Extreme Demand: for this, we must wait until the argument against it has been fully spelled out. But we have seen why an argument of this kind will be a forceful one.

An 'appropriately' impartial point of view, for the purposes of this argument, is a point of view of impartial concern for other people's interests. This is true whether we are evaluating standards of requirement for either fairness or beneficence. In relation to fairness, we get this conclusion from the simple thought that fairness in a context simply is whatever form of impartiality is appropriate to the context, and here the context is evaluating standards of concern for other people's interests. In relation to beneficence, we get the same conclusion from the internal approach.

Saying that appropriate impartiality here amounts to an impartial concern for each person's interests does rule out several kinds of impartiality. As we saw earlier, universal egoism or malevolence could give us kinds of impartiality; but these involve a concern for no one else's interests. The same is true of various forms of impartiality that are appropriate in other contexts: the impartiality appropriate to judging a prize competition will not take into account the interests of candidates in being awarded it. Other forms of impartiality take into account some people's interests, but not everyone's: the impartiality that a parent ought to have between her children, for example.

Another view that is ruled out in this way is what we can call the Proceduralist View of impartiality. According to this view, when an action or policy affects people's interests, impartially assessing it should involve assessing the procedure that generates those effects, and not the effects themselves. Provided there are no particular individuals whom that procedure is designed to favour, it is impartially acceptable: so are actions in accordance with that procedure, and the effects they generate. This view seems uncontroversially to supply the kind of impartiality appropriate to some contexts (such as the prize-awarding context just mentioned); much more controversially, it has to be considered as one proposal about what impartiality requires in relation to distributive justice.[14] Where it has no plausibility, however, is as a view about what an impartial concern for other people's interests should involve: it is a view of impartiality that is not concerned for others' interests at all.[15] After all, on a Proceduralist View, the requirement that I do *anything* to help other people, simply because of how badly off they are, can be impartially rejected. And if so, it cannot give us a view that it makes sense for us to take seriously as a view about the kind of impartiality appropriate to assessing standards of requirement for concern for other people's interests. We implicitly rejected this view at the outset, in taking it for granted that some failures to help other people are wrong.

Thus, when we say that appropriate impartiality in the current context amounts to an impartial concern for each person's interests, we do rule out several kinds of impartiality. However, as I have already suggested, this still leaves open various rival conceptions of what a properly impartial concern for each person's interests should involve. In calling them rival conceptions of impartiality, I do not mean to suggest that they are rival analyses of the concept *impartiality*. Rather, they are rival normative claims about what ought to be involved in an impartial concern for the interests of each member of a group.

The most immediately obvious of these conceptions we can call the Equal Weighting View. According to this view, impartially evaluating an action or policy requires us to evaluate its effects, giving equal weight to all those interests that qualify for impartial consideration.[16] However, several prominent moral philosophers have recently argued against this. They maintain that, although the effects of an action or policy are relevant to its impartial evaluation, the interests of those affected should not be equally weighted: rather, priority should be given to the interests of the worse-off.[17] Again, we should allow ourselves a qualification in stating this Priority View: it deals with those interests which qualify for impartial consideration. As I shall understand them, neither the Equal Weighting View nor the Priority View is committed to giving as much weight to the interests of someone who is badly off through his own fault as to those of someone who is just as badly off through no fault of his own.

The Equal Weighting View and the Priority View each come in many different versions. Clearly, a particular version of the Priority View will have to specify what kind of priority is to be given to the worse-off: there are therefore as many different versions of this view as there are answers to this question. But notice also the scope for different ways of thinking of the equal weighting of interests: these will equally generate different versions of the Equal Weighting View. One way of thinking about this is by asking what you would choose for yourself if you were given an equal chance of being in anyone's position: this uses equal chances to represent equal weighting.[18] Another is to use the device of a veil of ignorance to represent equal weighting, but without turning this into a calculation based on an assumption about equal chances.[19] Other versions will deny that we should compare the interests of different individuals in a situation by reference to the preferences of a single individual considering the possibility of being in their different positions. And beyond this, there remain various different ways of relating interests to desires, preferences, or objective goods.[20]

Other ways of conceiving of an appropriately impartial concern for everyone's interests are possible. Some kinds of Perfectionist View will claim that priority ought to be given to the better-off (or, slightly less implausibly, to those with the capacity to reach the highest levels of well-being).[21] The debate over which of these various rival conceptions is right is extensive, and important. If resolving this were necessary to completing my argument, we would be in for a very long discussion. Instead, my approach will be to sidestep this debate, as follows. I shall argue that on *any* plausible conception of the kind of impartiality appropriate to assessing standards of consideration for others' interests, the Extreme Demand can be impartially rejected. Showing *this* will surely give us a powerful case for the conclusion that the Extreme Demand should be rejected from an appropriately impartial point of view. And we have seen why that is a forceful objection to it.

Our discussion leaves open two questions about appropriate impartiality. One, as we have just seen, is the question which of the rival conceptions of properly impartial concern for others' interests is the right one. The other question, which we noticed earlier, is this: *How much* of this impartial concern is appropriate to evaluating standards of requirement for concern for others' interests? Again, my strategy will not be to offer a direct answer to this question. Instead, I shall argue that the Extreme Demand can be rejected even from a point of view of *complete* impartiality. If this can be established then, whatever is the right answer to the second question, the Extreme Demand should be rejected.

7.5 TWO CLARIFICATIONS

This is an ambitious claim. However, before I start to argue for it, let me first correct two possible misunderstandings about what I am trying to do.

Distributive versus Post-Distributive Questions

The various conceptions of impartiality I have named and distinguished—the Proceduralist, Equal Weighting, Priority, and Perfectionist Views—will be familiar as conceptions of distributive impartiality, and that may encourage a mistake. The question being discussed here is *not* 'By what distributive principles ought we collectively to regulate the allocation of resources?' Our question does not concern which publicly regulated distributive practice to adopt, but rather what each of us should do with those private resources left after such a practice has been adopted. Because the form of impartiality appropriate to answering this question is an impartial concern for everyone's interests, the conceptions of impartiality to consider belong to the same range as those governing distributive impartiality. But that does not mean that the question is the same.

This is not to deny that the answer to the distributive question may carry implications for what I should do with my private resources. When the distributive practice that has been publicly adopted takes less from me than the distributive practice that *ought* to have been adopted, am I morally required to give away voluntarily what ought to have been taken from me? There is a plausible (if contested) case for thinking this; I shall discuss it briefly later.[b] However, the argument for the Extreme Demand has arisen independently of this and goes beyond it. Whether or not I am voluntarily contributing my part of the collective redistribution we ought to be making, the claim is that I ought to be going much further.

It might seem tempting to think that settling the distributive question will also settle my post-distributive one as a corollary. 'If it is impartially best that we collectively adopt a certain practice of publicly enforced redistribution, then that means it is impartially best if each of us is allowed to possess the private resources which that distribution would leave us with. And if an impartially acceptable distribution would leave me with certain private resources, it must be impartially acceptable for me to dispose of those resources in whatever way I wish.' However, this is a non sequitur: the impartial rejection of the Extreme Demand is not as simple as this. To say that the possession of private resources is impartially acceptable is only to say that it is impartially acceptable for the private use of those resources to be protected from coercive interference: it is not to say that it is impartially acceptable to spend those resources on ourselves, in whatever way we choose. And after all, a compelling reason to deny this comes from the cases of easy rescue we began with. If it would be easy for you to save a life directly, you can be morally required to give up personal resources to do so. It may be wrong for others to take these resources away from you, but it can also be wrong for you not to use them to help other people.

The question which standards of moral requirement should govern the use of our personal resources is separate from the question which distributions of personal resources there should be. As a result, the impartial evaluation of these standards of requirement is separate from the impartial evaluation of candidate distributive principles. Confusing our question with the distributive one would make answering it too easy.

[b] Sect. 11.3, 'Arguments from Justice'.

Questions about Full versus Partial Compliance

The other misunderstanding to correct is this. In asking whether the Extreme Demand can be impartially rejected, I am not asking a question about the effects of general compliance with or advocacy of the Extreme Demand. If that were the right question to ask, then it would certainly be hard to see how the view I am going to argue for could be correct. For it would be telling us to ask whether the consequences of everyone's simultaneously complying with the Extreme Demand would be impartially preferable to the consequences of no one's complying. But what the Extreme Demand would require each of us to give away if everyone were complying is relatively moderate; and what the badly-off would stand to gain, if everyone complied, would be very great. So there are surely plausible conceptions of impartiality on which everyone's complying with the Extreme Demand is impartially preferable.

The problem with this approach, though, is that our interest in the Extreme Demand is in the costs that it would impose on any complier in circumstances in which hardly anyone is complying with it. What we are asking is whether or not the demands that it makes of each of us in *these* circumstances are impartially rejectable; not whether this is true of the more moderate demands it would make of us under conditions of widespread compliance.

7.6 CONCLUSION

In this chapter I have argued that if the Extreme Demand can be rejected from an appropriately impartial point of view then we have a decisive objection to it.

The scope of this claim is limited. This chapter is not a contribution to the debate over whether there is a general test of impartial acceptability for determining what morality requires of us.[22] I have not been making the general claim that if a standard of moral requirement is impartially best, then that justifies it. Nor have I been making the general claim that if any proposed standard of moral requirement is impartially rejectable, then that rules it out.

What I have been seeking to do is to show the relevance of thoughts about impartial rejectability to one particular kind of moral requirement: a requirement concerning the extent of our practical concern for other people's interests. Part I has set out a case for thinking that someone who is not trying to meet the Extreme Demand is inadequately concerned for other people's interests. The question what standard of requirement we should accept for concern for others' interests is the question where to draw the line between adequate and inadequate concern. I have now argued that, if a proposed standard of requirement is rejectable from a point of view of completely impartial concern for everyone's interests, then that undermines its claim to provide us with a requirement of either fairness or beneficence. Perhaps there are grounds on which a test of impartial acceptability can be seen to be relevant to determining other standards of moral requirement as well: to determining when telling the truth, say, or keeping your promises is morally required. But if so, we would need another argument to show it.

My aim in the next chapter will be to provide a good argument of this form against the Extreme Demand. It may appear difficult to see how there could be such an argument. For the Extreme Demand does not itself require complete impartiality of us. So how can it be rejected as excessively demanding from a point of view that *is* completely impartial? Earlier in the current chapter I sketched one way in which this might be argued: by claiming that certain fundamentally important goods presuppose forms of personal partiality. This is the line of thought I shall now develop.

8

The Rejection of the Extreme Demand

THERE cannot be many people who actually believe either the Extreme Demand, or the claim that each of us is required to get as close as possible to meeting it. Nevertheless, it is still important to show what is wrong with these claims. One reason for this, of course, is that we need to be able to show that the denial of these claims is not simply a self-serving falsehood, as a minority of philosophers claims it to be. But more importantly, we need to know what view about the moral demands of affluence we should hold instead. There is a natural temptation to think that, given the implausibility of the Extreme Demand, there must be something wrong with the life-saving analogy we met at the start of the book. I shall argue that that is a mistake. The objection to the Extreme Demand lies elsewhere: I shall spell it out in this chapter. (For convenience, I shall phrase my discussion as an argument against the Extreme Demand itself. However, it will be equally effective against the claim that each of us is required to get as close as possible to meeting the Extreme Demand.)

The general form of my argument has been described already. I am going to show that the Extreme Demand can be rejected from an appropriately impartial point of view—and that this holds true for *any* plausible conception of appropriate impartiality. Certain forms of personal partiality are themselves impartially acceptable; and they include forms of personal partiality that the Extreme Demand cannot allow for. My argument has affinities with the arguments from Kant and Williams that we met earlier.[a] Like them, it is an argument from the presuppositions of beneficence. Beneficence requires us to accept that other people's interests give us compelling moral reasons for acting in their favour; but in accepting this, we are making presuppositions from which it follows that acting out of partiality towards our own interests is not wrong.

The emphasis here, however, will be on overcoming a serious limitation that Kant's and Williams's arguments seem to have. What is wrong with a standard of requirement, such as the Extreme Demand, that would allow us *some* personal partiality but would restrict it very tightly? If all that an appeal to the presuppositions of beneficence will establish is that *some*

[a] Sect. 6.6.

personal partiality is impartially acceptable, that is not enough to refute the Extreme Demand, which does not require us to be completely impartial. The aim of this chapter will be to show that there is an argument of the same broad kind that succeeds in answering this question, and refutes the Extreme Demand.

My strategy is to begin by describing certain personal goods—friendships and commitments to personal projects will be my leading examples—that are in an important sense constituted by attitudes of personal partiality. Focusing on these goods involves no bias towards the well-off: they are goods that have fundamental importance to people's lives, irrespective of the material standard of living of those who possess them. Next, I shall point out the way in which your pursuit of these goods would be fundamentally compromised if you were attempting to follow the Extreme Demand. Your life would have to be altruistically focused, in a distinctive way that I shall describe. The rest of the chapter then demonstrates that this is not just a tough consequence of the Extreme Demand: it is a reason for rejecting it. If other people's interests in life are to ground a requirement on us to save them—as surely they do—then, I shall argue, it must be impartially acceptable to pursue the kinds of good that give people such interests. An ethical outlook will be impartially rejectable if it does not properly accommodate the pursuit of these goods—on any plausible conception of appropriate impartiality.

8.1 GOODS OF PARTIALITY

Let us begin by asking this: Why is a life valuable to its possessor? An answer to this question will naturally cite the various constituent goods that a life can contain, the presence or absence of which can make it better or worse for the person whose life it is—'intrinsically life-enhancing' goods, as we can call them.[1] I shall refer to these often in what follows: usually, for convenience, simply as 'life-enhancing goods'. However, in doing so, I still mean to focus on those goods that intrinsically make a person's life better, rather than those that do so instrumentally, like money or good health. The things that intrinsically make your life good for you include the friendships, the achievements, the enjoyments it contains; and its value to you as a source of these goods gives me a reason to help you if your life is endangered.

Just *which* goods it is reasonable to think of as intrinsically life-enhancing? I shall say some more about that important question in Chapter 9. For now, I shall make a plausible-looking assumption: these include goods like friendship, achievements in the pursuit of worthwhile personal projects, and involvement in the life of one's community—goods the possession of which essentially involves attitudes of personal partiality.

The point that such goods essentially involve personal partiality will be of central importance to my argument; so let us examine it with some care. In order to have friends, or to have the kinds of ongoing project that provide the ground of personal achievements, I cannot take others' friends and projects as having an equal claim on me to my own: to do this would make such goods unavailable to me.[2] This is not a point about psychological contingency—that we are in fact likelier to achieve these goods to the extent that we possess an attitude of personal partiality. Rather, to lack partiality in one's relation to the appropriate objects is to fail to possess these goods. Attitudes of partiality are constitutive of possessing them. If your life contains the good of friendship, then part of what that friendship *is* is an attitude of personal partiality towards your friend.[3]

What do I mean by personal partiality? Not—as the example of friendship makes clear—an attitude of partiality towards myself, in any straightforward sense.[4] We can begin simply by saying this: it involves an attitude of special practical concern for the friends and projects to which I bear a personal relationship. The object of my concern is not myself, nor is it the relationship between me and my friends and projects: it is the friends and the contents of the projects themselves. To say that it is a practical concern is to say that it is a concern that distinctively issues in action. The attitude of personal partiality I bear towards my friends and projects is a matter of taking them to justify my acting a certain way, out of proportion to the impartial value of acting that way.

In saying this, I am not claiming that having friendships or pursuing personal projects is a matter of giving a greater weight in my practical deliberations to the interests of my friends, or to my own interests in achieving worthwhile things, than I give to other people's.[5] That claim looks wrong. There are many things I could do to further my friends' interests, but which are not required by friendship. No doubt, there are many expensive gifts that it would be in my friends' interests to receive. But it is not as if my not giving those gifts—indeed, my not even thinking of giving them—amounts to a limitation on the relationship of friendship which I bear towards them.[6] The relationship of friendship between two people is a relationship of mutual concern and involvement in each other's lives. But there are many ways of furthering a friend's interests which are irrelevant or even antithetical to this. This is not to say that I shouldn't care whether my friends get what is in their interests; it is just that, often, my friendship with them does not call for me to do what would satisfy their interests myself.

Moreover, even when my friendship with someone does mean giving special attention to him, it is still often wrong to think of this as giving greater weight to his interests. The special claims of friendship are often claims of companionship, solace, and solidarity in hard times. And although I am certainly responding to my friend's interests if I provide these things, the interests I am responding to are precisely *interests in the expression of friendship*. The best solace our friends can provide us with is often the assurance that we have friends. And while it is true that many people have an interest in receiving this—and there will always be those whose need for it is much more acute than my own friends'—this is a good that only friends can provide. It is only to people who are already my friends that I can provide a needed assurance of friendship. When I do so, I should accept that there are almost always going to be more impartially valuable things I could be doing instead. So acting as a friend does mean choosing to act in a way that is out of proportion to the impartial value of that action. However, it is wrong to represent my action as giving greater weighting to my friends' interests than I give to others' interests in receiving the same good. I cannot satisfy others' interests in receiving *this* good.[7]

There are similar problems with the corresponding claim about commitments to personal projects. Our commitment to the projects that yield worthwhile personal achievements is not a matter of giving a determinately greater weighting to our own achievement-related interests. It is a matter of dedication to the projects themselves.[8] If I have this attitude, it involves taking a project to provide me with reasons for acting, out of proportion to the impartial value of those actions. But that does not mean that I am giving a certain greater weight to my own interests in pursuing my projects than I give to other people's in pursuing theirs.

If there are any life-enhancing goods at all, it is hard to see how it could sensibly be doubted whether goods such as friendships and achievements in the pursuit of worthwhile personal projects are among them.[9] But these goods, we have seen, are themselves constituted by attitudes of personal partiality. If you lacked that partiality, you would not have friends or commitments to personal projects: you would not be attached to *these* people or projects any more than any others. Moreover, in acknowledging this we are not favouring the point of view of any one individual or group. Although a person's material resources may affect how much of these goods he is able to enjoy, they do not affect whether they are good for that person. Poverty is bad, surely, because it deprives people of goods such as *these*. Thus, the view that these attitudes of personal partiality are genuinely valuable is surely itself impartially acceptable.

The conclusion so far is a conclusion about the things that have value. I have not yet defended any conclusions about rightness. I have yet to say anything about when we really *ought* to pursue our friendships or personal projects. The question so far has been, What are the attitudes in relation to friendship and the pursuit of personal projects that it makes sense for us to value? The question when I *ought* to help a friend rather than a stranger, or when I am justified in pursuing personally significant projects, is a separate one. For that we need to move from questions of value to questions of rightness and moral permissibility—as we shall be doing shortly.

8.2 THE COST OF THE EXTREME DEMAND

Attitudes of personal partiality are important, we have just seen, because they are constitutive of the possession of certain important goods. Now we ought to consider what the Extreme Demand says about these goods.

In Chapter 5 we saw that the costs of compliance with the Extreme Demand—or with the claim that each of us is required to get as close as possible to meeting the Extreme Demand—are very great.[b] Given the way the world is, trying to meet this demand would mean having to give away practically everything and reduce yourself close to a level of mere subsistence. The point to emphasize now is that the sacrifice involved would amount to more than just forgoing the extra enjoyments you could have in spending more money on yourself. More seriously and significantly, it would mean compromising the goods we think of as being the most important components of our lives. For it would mean compromising such goods of personal partiality as our friendships, participation in the life of our community and culture, our dedication to projects of understanding and personal achievement, and our development of personal excellences and skills beyond those that are instrumental to the service of others' interests.

True, it is not as though meeting the Extreme Demand would deprive you of these goods altogether. It tells you to give up so much that contributing your share of the cost of saving one further life would itself be bad enough for you to justify refusing to do so. Once you have reached that point, it tells you that you can defensibly refuse to go any further. However, the series of incremental sacrifices you would have to make before you could claim to have reached this point would have the cumulative effect of confining your possession of these goods to a very tightly restricted extent. If any further restriction of the time and money you spend on participating in the life of your community or enjoying the company of your family and friends could be used to contribute towards a collective life-saving action instead, without *itself* compromising your friendships or community bonds badly enough to justify refusing to help save someone's life, then the Extreme Demand tells you to do that.

Now we must be careful not to confuse the restriction of spending on friends with the restriction of friendship itself; for as we have seen, not every way of spending money on a friend is an enhancement of a friendship. However, if my expenditure of time and money on friends is restricted far enough, then eventually the relationship of friendship itself will be restricted—for eventually, my opportunity to engage and interact with my friends will be compromised. And the Extreme Demand does require this. For it requires that I continue restricting my personal spending until my

[b] Sect. 5.3.

share of the cost of saving one further life would itself be a substantial enough loss to me to excuse refusing to do so. This will apply not just to sacrifices in spending on my friends, but to sacrifices in friendship itself. When another incremental sacrifice would itself impair my friendships so badly that I could justifiably refuse to help save someone's life rather than meet that cost, the Extreme Demand will allow me to refuse. But I must continue to restrict my friendships—my friendships themselves, and not just my spending on friends—until I reach that point.

Following the Extreme Demand would not require me to go without friendships altogether. But it would require me to govern my friendships in a closely constrained way. Although I could allow myself to exhibit partiality towards my friends, I would have to be vigilant for opportunities to restrict these relationships. After all, any small restriction I could make, that would not by itself compromise these relationships substantially enough to excuse refusing to help save a life, is one that is required of me, according to the Extreme Demand.

The kind of self-constraint that would have to characterize the life of anyone who was aiming to comply with the Extreme Demand (or to get as close as possible to complying with it) would give it a distinctive kind of structure. I shall refer to such lives as 'altruistically focused'. An altruistically focused life is not one that precludes personal satisfactions and fulfilments altogether: the Extreme Demand doesn't require that. But it is more than simply one in which personal commitments are constrained by overriding other-regarding goals. All minimally decent lives are constrained in that way: allowing that respect for other people imposes some constraints on how we can properly pursue our own fulfilment is not enough to make a life altruistically focused. Rather, I have an altruistically focused life if I am constricting my pursuit of my own fulfilment as much as I bearably and usefully can, for the purpose of contributing to helping others.[10] Lives that are not like this we can call 'non-altruistically-focused'. They will include those lives that have an overall non-altruistic focus, and those that lack a single overall focus (as most lives do).

For most of us, an altruistically focused life would be less fulfilling than the lives we actually lead. Governing your relationships with others in this altruistically focused way will certainly look unattractive to most people. After all, a friendship, as we have seen, is more than simply a preferential attitude towards the interests of another person. It is a relationship of mutual openness and engagement—a reciprocal involvement that people can have in each other's lives.[11] This means that, for most of us, the best kind of friendship is governed by an attitude of seeking opportunities to amplify and expand this mutual involvement. But this is the opposite of the attitude of self-constraint that a follower of the Extreme Demand would be committing herself to.

This point extends to other important sources of personal fulfilment, such as commitments to personal projects. It is one thing to have pastimes that are enjoyable: as such, they will qualify as life-enhancing goods, as long as forms of enjoyment do count as such. But there can also be commitments to projects which are life-enhancing in a different and fuller way: their life-enhancing value comes from the way they fill up and define a person's life. And again, the attitudes that characterize a person who possesses goods of this further sort involve an aspiration to expand her contact with them, rather than to contract it to the limit of what is bearable, as the Extreme Demand requires. This would not mean that someone complying with the Extreme Demand would be unable to live a life of personal endeavour at all. But it would deprive her of a kind of relationship to her endeavours that many of us think of as the one most worth having.

In this way, the fulfilment of most of us would be lessened by living the altruistically focused life which is required of us by the Extreme Demand. However, I doubt whether that is true of everyone. There are some people whose lives are orchestrated around projects of aid, public welfare, and community service to such an extent that their lives are altruistically focused already. And as far as I can see, there is nothing preventing such a life from containing goods of all of the life-enhancing kinds identified so far, focused around the core project of improving the lot of the worst-off. This project can obviously be a source of enjoyment, understanding, and community involvement. But it can also be a focus for friendship. Some friendships have as their core a common endeavour: central to these friendships is a mutually appreciative cooperation in pursuing the same goal. Making that goal the welfare of other people surely allows for friendships that are as deep and valuable as any.[12]

Moreover, even for the majority of us for whom living an altruistically focused life would mean sacrificing our own fulfilment, *that* will not by itself be an objection to the Extreme Demand. After all, surely we *are* required to make sacrifices in response to others' life-threatening need. Of course, the sacrifices that a follower of the Extreme Demand would have to make are very great. But we knew that already: according to the Extreme Demand, morality is tough. So we have not yet produced an objection to the Extreme Demand. However, we now have the materials to produce it.

8.3 REASONS FOR HELPING PEOPLE

Saving other people's lives can be morally required of us. As Part I showed, the case for the Extreme Demand is based on this uncontroversial claim. Why is this required of us? What is it about other people's lives that makes them worth saving, and makes it appropriate to demand that we should be concerned to save them? The argument for the Extreme Demand relies on a straightforward and obvious answer to this question. It is in other people's interests to have their lives saved. That should give me sufficient reason to do so, if the cost to me is small; and if I do not, that is a serious failure of beneficence. According to this first answer, what makes others' lives worth saving is their value to those whose lives they are.

Of course, giving this first answer to the question what makes people's lives worth saving does not preclude offering others as well. According to a second kind of answer, life should be respected and preserved, independently of the benefits it brings to its possessors.[13] This second answer is compatible with the first: so although the argument for the Extreme Demand is committed to the first answer, it is not opposing this second one.

In giving the first answer, the Extreme Demand is relying on the thought that there are moral requirements of beneficence. We can be morally required to help other people because it is in their interests to be helped. Other people's interests can provide reasons for helping them which we ought to act on—indeed, that it would be morally wrong not to act on. Let us put this point by saying that they can provide *morally compelling* reasons.

Just which of a person's interests provide us with morally compelling reasons to help him? Clearly, his interest in life can do so. Any plausible view of the requirements of beneficence is going to accept that. But let us ask this: What gives a person an interest in life? Here again, various answers are possible. The simplest is that life is non-instrumentally good for its bearer: life itself is something it is good for a person to have, for its own sake. However, this is not the only answer, nor, for most of us, the most important one. What is more important, for most of us, is that our lives are vehicles for the fulfilments that a well-lived life can contain. These fulfilments are the ones that a person gains through possessing what I have been calling life-enhancing goods: those goods the possession of which makes a life better for the person who lives it.

Moreover, it is clear that people's interests in these fulfilments give us reasons to help them independently of whether their lives are threatened. This is something we noticed at the start of Chapter 1, in introducing the life-saving analogy. The fact that poverty threatens to kill some people is a powerful reason to help them. But it is not obviously more powerful than the fact that poverty stunts people's lives, rather than merely shortening them. At least *part* of the morally compelling reason we have for responding to poverty is the way in which it damages the relationships, accomplishments, self-expression, and other fulfilments that life offers.[14] Indeed, if we were confronted with a choice between responding to one person's non-instrumental interest in life itself, or making a great contribution to another person's fulfilment, the latter might be what we ought to do. If you had to choose between prolonging the life of someone whose life had ceased to be fulfilling, and reuniting a long-parted family, is it obvious that it would always be wrong to do the latter?

Whatever our answer to that last question—a question about the relative importance of interests in life itself and interests in the fulfilments a life can contain—we should surely accept that the latter do provide us with morally compelling reasons. Perhaps you should not let someone die—even someone whose life has ceased to be fulfilling—to reunite a long-parted family. However, suppose that, by making some small effort—passing on a piece of information, say—you could reunite the family, and there was nothing to be said morally against doing so. Or suppose some small effort of yours would determine whether a gifted student is able to pursue a musical career, and there was nothing to be said morally against doing so. It would clearly be wrong not to do these things. Clearly, the moral requirements of beneficence extend not just to saving people's lives, but to responding to their interests in the fulfilments that life can contain.

But let us extend this line of thought one step further. Interests in the fulfilments of a well-lived life can provide us with morally compelling reasons to help other people. Now ask this: Which fulfilments? Which kind of life? In particular, do people's interests in the fulfilments of a *non-altruistically-focused* life provide us with morally compelling reasons to help them? The answer has to be Yes. If you think that the interests of the people around you in the fulfilments that their lives contain ever do provide you with morally compelling reasons to help them, then you are committed to thinking that their interests in the fulfilments of a non-altruistically-focused life provide such reasons. For the lives of the people around you *are* non-altruistically-focused lives.[15] The morally compelling reason I have for helping does not disappear if I know that the lives of the family members, or the music student, are not (as almost all people's are not) altruistically focused: that the family members' engagement with each other, or the musician's with her music, is not constrained in the way that the Extreme Demand would require. Indeed, on a view according to which only the fulfilments of a non-altruistically-focused life give compelling reasons for us to help others, very few of the actual projects, aspirations, and relationships of other people qualify as appropriate grounds for beneficent action. An interest in life itself will do so, but interests in most of the goods around which our lives are actually structured will not. And that is very hard to accept.

People's interests in life provide morally compelling reasons to help them when their lives are threatened. The case for the Extreme Demand begins from that claim, and that claim is surely right. Another claim that is surely right is that people's interests in the fulfilments a well-lived life can contain provide morally compelling reasons to help them too. After all, this is the most obvious reason why people have interests in life itself. And by itself, this second claim is not a problem for the Extreme Demand either: it is natural to invoke it in supporting the judgements about helping other people from which the case for the Extreme Demand begins. However, a third claim also seems right: people's interests in the fulfilments of a non-altruistically-focused life provide morally compelling reasons to help them. And this claim *is* a serious problem for the Extreme Demand, as I shall now explain.

8.4 THE EXTREME DEMAND AND NON-ALTRUISTICALLY-FOCUSED LIVES

Other people's interests in the fulfilments of a non-altruistically-focused life clearly provide us with morally compelling reasons to help them. But according to the Extreme Demand, it is *wrong* to lead a non-altruistically-focused life, at least in our current circumstances. And that means it faces the following serious objection. Someone else's interests in getting what it is *wrong* for her to have cannot be a good reason for requiring me to help her. So the Extreme Demand would commit us to denying that the fulfilments of a non-altruistically-focused life can provide us with morally compelling reasons. But that is absurd.

As we noticed when beneficence was described in Chapter 2, not every interest is of the right kind to ground requirements of beneficence.[c] The most obvious class of exceptions is the class of interests in getting what it is morally wrong to have: *these* are not the sorts of interests we are morally required to help other people to satisfy. But if not, then the Extreme Demand cannot make sense of the requirements of beneficence that arise from the ordinary lives of other people around us. For those lives are non-altruistically-focused. However, as we have just seen, such requirements of beneficence are obvious. Indeed, it seems no less obvious that it would be wrong to refuse to make a small effort to reunite a long-parted family than that it would be wrong to refuse to make a small effort to save someone's life.[16] If these are moral requirements of beneficence, but there cannot be requirements of beneficence to help people get what it is wrong to have, then having the fulfilments of a non-altruistically-focused life cannot be wrong. The Extreme Demand says that this *is* wrong. So the Extreme Demand should be rejected.

This argument contains three main claims. The first is that helping people is obviously morally required in response to their interests in the fulfilments of a non-altruistically-focused life. Secondly, I claim that the Extreme Demand implies that the interests to which we are responding in

[c] Sect. 2.1.

such cases are interests in having what it is wrong to have, since the Extreme Demand requires us to lead altruistically focused lives. And the third claim is the following principle:

> When your interest in having (or doing) a certain thing is an interest in having (or doing) what it would be wrong for you to have (or do), that interest cannot be a good reason for morally requiring me to help you to get (or do) it.

I now defend these three claims, taking them in reverse order.

Interests in What it is Wrong to Have

The principle I have just set out is certainly widely recognized. It underlies the thought, for example, that sadistic or malicious enjoyments, although they might be things it is in the interests of a sadistic or malicious person to have, are not goods that I ought morally to take into account in helping other people.[17] Likewise, it is a staple of the literature on sympathetically motivated action that indiscriminately promoting the interests of other people is morally problematic: proper discernment involves appreciating that not all interests are ones that I ought to be helping other people to further.[18] If a gangster's gun jams, I ought not to help him fix it. Appealing to thoughts such as these gives us one form of justification that can be offered for the principle: a range of considered judgements is unified and explained by it. However, we ought also to be able to give a more direct justification. Why should it be right to make this range of judgements?

We can get further by asking two questions. The first is this: Which of your interests provide you with reasons that it is morally acceptable for you to act on? Obviously, no interests in having what it is *wrong* for you to have can do so. After all, to say that something is wrong is to say that it is morally unacceptable. So interests in having what it is wrong to have are interests in having what it is morally unacceptable to have. And your interests in having what it is morally unacceptable for you to have cannot be morally acceptable reasons for you to act on. Now consider a second question. Which of *your* interests provide *me* with reasons that make it morally acceptable for me to help you? The answer to the first question shows what we must also say in response to the second. If your interests in having what it is wrong to have cannot provide you with reasons that it is morally acceptable to act on, they cannot provide me with reasons that it is morally acceptable to act on either. *These* interests—interests in having what it is morally unacceptable for you to have—are of the wrong kind to provide me with morally acceptable reasons for action. They are the wrong kind of interests to count morally in favour of the actions that promote them. From here, we can add that, obviously, any interests of yours that do not provide me with morally acceptable reasons to help you cannot be reasons for the moral acceptability of my helping. If not, they cannot be reasons for the unacceptability of my not helping. But that is to say that they cannot be reasons for the wrongness of my not helping. And that in turn means that they cannot be reasons for my being morally required to help. The conclusion we reach is the principle just set out: your interest in obtaining what it is *wrong* to have cannot be a good reason for my being morally required to help you.

A second, complementary argument for this principle appeals to the implications of impartiality. We have been asking which standards of requirement for concern for other people's interests are impartially acceptable. So let us ask which of your interests will provide me with impartially acceptable grounds for requiring me to act in your favour. What should we say about any interests you may have in getting what it is wrong for you to have? One thing that impartiality clearly requires us to say is that if your getting something is wrong, and my circumstances are relevantly similar, then my getting the same thing must also be wrong. But anything that it is wrong for me to have is something I am morally required not to get for myself. If so, requiring me to help you to further your interests in getting what it is wrong for you to have would amount to requiring me to further your interests in getting something I am required not to get for myself (unless there is a relevant difference between us). But then, if there is no relevant difference between us, that cannot be acceptable from an impartial point of view. In the absence of any relevant difference between two people, it cannot be impartially acceptable to forbid one person to pursue for himself what he is required to help others to pursue. So again, we reach the conclusion that your interest in having what it would be wrong for you to have cannot be a good reason for morally requiring me to help you get it.

The Extreme Demand and Interests in What it is Wrong to Have

The second of the three main claims I am making is this. Since the Extreme Demand requires us to lead altruistically focused lives, it implies that most of the interests to which we are responding in helping people who lead ordinary, non-altruistically-focused lives are interests in having what it is wrong to have.

This claim may look wrong. When we respond to the interests of other people by helping them, as in the family reunion example, we are responding to the interests of people who are leading non-altruistically-focused lives. But the Extreme Demand does not imply that, in such cases, we are responding to others' interests in having what it is wrong to have. For it is not an implication of the Extreme Demand that *having your family reunited* is itself morally wrong. It may be true that, once your family is reunited, you will go on to pursue your family relationships in a non-altruistically-focused way.

And it may also be true that, according to the Extreme Demand, going on to live that way would be wrong. But surely *that* is not a serious problem. After all, on any plausible view, anyone whom I help will go on to lead a life that is in some respects morally wrong. What is important is whether the interest that provides me with a morally compelling reason to help is itself an interest in having what it is wrong to have. But in this case, that interest is simply an interest in being reunited, and this is clearly not itself morally wrong. So there is no difficulty for a proponent of the Extreme Demand in accepting that we are morally required to help people whose lives are non-altruistically-focused, while also accepting the principle that interests in obtaining what it is morally wrong to have cannot provide morally compelling reasons for helping people.

However, a simple example shows what is wrong with this line of thought. In itself, there is nothing wrong with having your gun unjammed, and in itself, there is nothing wrong with my unjamming it for you. But if your interest in unjamming it is in order to murder someone, it is the wrong sort of interest to provide me with a morally compelling reason to help you. The general point should be clear. When you have an interest in getting something that is innocuous in itself, but your interest in getting it is as part of an activity that is wrong, this is not an interest that will ground requirements on me to help you. And this means that the problem for the Extreme Demand remains. According to the Extreme Demand, developing family relationships that are not themselves constrained in an altruistically focused way, or developing a musical talent as fully as possible, is morally wrong, given our current circumstances. So an interest in getting something as a part of these activities must be counted as an interest in getting it as part of an activity that is morally wrong. Therefore, the Extreme Demand *is* committed to holding that such interests do not provide morally compelling reasons for helping people. And that is absurd.

The principle I defended above is best read in a way that includes this point. It says:

> When your interest in having (or doing) a certain thing is an interest in having (or doing) what it would be wrong for you to have (or do), that interest cannot be a good reason for morally requiring me to help you to get (or do) it.

Where you need your gun unjammed to commit a murder, it seems right to say that your interest in unjamming your gun is an interest in doing something wrong. There may be nothing in itself wrong about having an unjammed gun, but your *interest* in getting it unjammed is in order to commit a murder. Perhaps this description will be disputed. Someone might insist on saying that you have an interest in getting the gun unjammed, which is not wrong, and an interest in committing murder, which is. To someone who wants to say this, the best response is not to debate the point, but to reformulate the principle, as follows:

> When your interest in having (or doing) a certain thing is an interest in having (or doing) what it would be wrong for you to have (or do), or your interest in having (or doing) it is an interest in having (or doing) it as part of a purpose that is morally wrong, that interest cannot be a good reason for morally requiring me to help you to get (or do) it.

This broadened principle is defensible in the same way as before. When your interest in having something is as part of an immoral purpose, that cannot provide a morally acceptable reason for you to be acting on; and it therefore cannot provide a morally acceptable reason for me to act to help you either.

Helping People with Non-Altruistically-Focused Lives

Now to the third claim on which my case against the Extreme Demand relies. This is that other people's interests in the fulfilments of a non-altruistically-focused life obviously do provide us with morally compelling reasons to help them. It would obviously be wrong not to reunite the family, or to help the music student in our earlier examples; and if the Extreme Demand is committed to denying this, that is absurd.

However, why not respond to the argument by simply accepting the judgements that I am claiming are absurd? The Extreme Demand is not being offered as an intuitively attractive view. Indeed, it may well itself look absurd, from the standpoint of moral 'common sense'. But the case for the Extreme Demand is intended as a case for thinking that moral 'common sense' is itself flawed. If the argument of this chapter is right, then the Extreme Demand leads to two counter-intuitive conclusions, and not just one. It implies, as we saw in Part I, that the requirements of beneficence in respect of people who are far away are much greater than we ordinarily accept. But it also implies, we now find, that the requirements of beneficence in respect of the people we routinely encounter—people leading non-altruistically-focused lives—are much *less* than we ordinarily accept. That might be hard to believe. But maybe the truth is hard to believe.

In response to this, let me explain what I take to be the force of the complaint of absurdity that I am making. I am not claiming to have identified a moral axiom from which a neat disproof of the Extreme Demand can be derived. Simply calling a view absurd is not an end to moral argument: after all, if it were, we could have dismissed the Extreme Demand much more quickly. However, the more drastically we are being asked to revise our firm conception of what is morally important, the greater is the burden of justification that must be met in arguing for the revision. In making the claim

I am calling absurd, a proponent of the Extreme Demand would be overturning our conception of beneficence altogether. This vastly complicates the task of arguing for the Extreme Demand—to such a degree that it is reasonable for us to reject it, until we are given a convincing case for this drastic revision. Let me explain why I think this.

To begin with it looked as though the Extreme Demand simply seeks to add to the requirements of beneficence that we already accept. The strategy of argument set out in Part I looked at the conception of beneficence that underlies the judgements we make about what beneficence does require, and argued from this that there is a further range of requirements that we fail to recognize. Our failure to recognize these requirements, it suggests, can be attributed to wishful thinking.

However, in the current chapter we find that the Extreme Demand requires a far more drastic revision to our conception of beneficence. It is not just asking us to reject commonly held views about what beneficence does *not* require. Most of our judgements about what beneficence *does* require will have to be rejected too. And this is deeply problematic in two ways. First, it is no longer simply being claimed that we have overlooked something morally important. The claim is now that many of the things that we think *are* morally important are *not*. The interests of other people in the fulfilments of a non-altruistically-focused life—and that means practically *all* of their interests—do not provide us with morally compelling reasons to help them. What we need is a convincing explanation of how we could be so fundamentally misguided about the moral significance of other people's interests. And now the wishful-thinking explanation is obviously not available.

The second and more acute problem is that the objection here does not concern the conclusion to be drawn from the Extreme Demand, so much as the starting point that it turns out to require. The strategy of argument can no longer be to start from the conception of beneficence embodied in the judgements we already make about what beneficence requires. Instead, its starting point is one that accepts only some of the judgements we already make about requirements of beneficence—judgements about some cases of rescue—while rejecting the equally obvious-seeming judgements we make about almost all of the further everyday requirements of beneficence that we recognize. What needs to be given is some justification, independent of the Extreme Demand itself, for thinking that the first set of judgements is more credible than the second. Without that justification, the case for the Extreme Demand collapses: its privileging the initial judgements it does would be arbitrary. But producing that justification amounts to arguing for a radically revised conception of beneficence—one that drastically restricts the range of interests that can ground requirements of beneficence. That is where the main task in a defence of the Extreme Demand would have to lie. Until we are presented with that justification, we should not take the Extreme Demand seriously.

(I say that the Extreme Demand starts by accepting judgements about requirements of beneficence in *some* cases of rescue. Here is why. If your interest in having your life saved is simply that life is in itself good for you, or is that life is a means to altruistically focused fulfilments, then the Extreme Demand can allow that there is a morally compelling reason to save you. But otherwise it cannot. For anyone whose life is good for her only as a vehicle for the non-altruistically-focused fulfilments it contains—and I cannot see why we should believe that there is no one like this—the Extreme Demand entails that her interests do not provide a morally acceptable reason to save her life. The restriction that the Extreme Demand would impose on the range of interests that can ground requirements of beneficence is so drastic that it seems to exclude some cases of saving a person's life.)

Having said this, I do accept that my argument against the Extreme Demand will only carry conviction to the extent that I can do better myself. The complaint against the Extreme Demand is ultimately that it cannot be reasonable to accept it without a very substantial independent argument for overturning our conception of beneficence completely. But that is only a convincing objection to the extent that I can defend a more satisfactory alternative account of the demands of beneficence—one that does not require such a drastic overturning of our conception of beneficence. Doing that will be my goal in the remaining chapters.

8.5 HELPING OTHERS TO GET WHAT IT IS WRONG FOR THEM TO HAVE

My argument against the Extreme Demand relies on the principle that we cannot be morally required to help people on the strength of their interests in having what it is wrong for them to have. Given this principle, the Extreme Demand carries the implication that people's interests in the fulfilments contained in the lives they actually lead—non-altruistically-focused lives—cannot provide morally compelling reasons for us to help them. That is absurd. So the Extreme Demand should be rejected.

The principle I am advocating should be carefully distinguished from various other similar-sounding but implausible claims. For a start, I am not saying that there can never be morally compelling reasons for saving the lives of evildoers. I might be required to save the life of someone whose projects are uniformly evil, if I could easily do so. But this is not because of his interest in evil sources of fulfilment. It is because of his interest in life, as such. Being alive is not wrong. So there is no obstacle to the thought that this person's interest in being alive can ground a requirement on me to save his life. But his interest in evil projects cannot ground such a requirement. Only interests in goods that it is not morally wrong to have can do that.

Therefore, if we allow (as surely we should) that a person's interests in the fulfilments of a non-altruistically-focused life *can* ground a moral requirement on me to save his life, we are committing ourselves to the moral defensibility of living a non-altruistically-focused life.

Here are four other claims which should be distinguished from the one I am making:

(1) The reason for holding that it is wrong for me to pursue a certain good cannot be other people's interests in getting that same good.

(2) If others' interests in a certain good are to be a good reason for me to help them, then it must be defensible for me to act to pursue that good for myself.

(3) If it would be wrong for you to take for yourself something that it is in your interests to have, your interest in having that thing cannot be a good reason for morally requiring me to help you to get it.

(4) If it would be wrong for you to do something, then I cannot be required to assist you to do it.

To see the problem with (1) and (2), consider a situation in which I am entrusted with the responsibility to distribute a given good fairly among the members of a group. Or suppose I have assumed obligations as a trustee with responsibility for promoting the interests of a particular person. In circumstances such as these, it would be fallacious for me to reason that, since I am morally required to treat other people's interests in getting a certain good as a good reason for helping them to get it, it must be defensible for me to take that good for myself. For I may have an obligation in such circumstances to give no more weight to my own interests in obtaining the good than to anyone else's, or to give weight *only* to someone else's interests in obtaining it. But while this shows that (1) and (2) should be rejected, it is not an objection to the claim I am advancing. My claim is that your interests in getting something it would be wrong for you to get cannot be a good reason for requiring me to forgo that good myself. If, in either of these scenarios, it would be *wrong* for you to get a certain good, then your interests in getting it cannot sensibly be the sorts of interests I am morally required to further, either as a fair distributor of that good, or as a trustee for your interests.

Claim (3), although closer to the claim I am making, should be rejected too. If you are hungry, it might be wrong for you to take my food, but wrong for me not to give it to you. Your interest in getting what it would be wrong for you to take for yourself is in this case a morally compelling reason for me to give it to you. However, the point here is that, although it may be wrong for you to take the good in question, it is not wrong for you to *have* it. My claim is that when it is wrong for you to have a certain good, I cannot be morally required to give it to you.

To illustrate the problem with (4), suppose that you want to humiliate someone by disclosing a certain piece of information that I hold. You might have a right to its disclosure, and I might stand under a correlative duty to respect that right—say, if I have promised to do so. I might not like it, but I ought to assist you, even though you are doing something wrong. But notice that, again, this is compatible with the principle set out above. According to that principle, your interest in doing what is wrong cannot provide me with a morally compelling reason to help you. And that remains true here. What provides the morally compelling reason is not that you have an interest in humiliating someone: *that* is not a consideration I am morally required to act on. It is that I have made the promise.

In objecting to the Extreme Demand, I am complaining that there are forms of help that we obviously should give to other people, but which the Extreme Demand cannot allow for, since it implies that the interests to which I would be responding are interests in wrongdoing. And such interests cannot supply a good reason for morally requiring me to help a person. I can be morally required to help people who are engaged in doing things that are wrong. I can even be morally required to help people to get the things they need in order to do what is wrong. But your interests in doing something that is wrong are not the right kind of interests to provide me with morally compelling reasons to help you.

8.6 CONCLUSION

We ought to reject the Extreme Demand. The Extreme Demand appeals—quite rightly—to other people's interests in life in order to ground requirements on us to save their lives. But it seeks to draw from this the conclusion that it is wrong to lead a non-altruistically-focused life. And that cannot be the right conclusion to draw. Only interests in obtaining goods that it is not *wrong* to have can properly ground claims on our help. So, if the Extreme Demand were right, others' interests in the fulfilments of a non-altruistically-focused life could not properly be appealed to as good reasons for helping them. But such interests surely *are* good reasons for helping them. The result is a dilemma. Proponents of the Extreme Demand cannot sensibly deny that non-altruistically-focused fulfilments provide morally compelling reasons for helping people: denying this would mean rejecting almost all of the actual requirements of beneficence we recognize. But they cannot sensibly accept this either: as we have seen, that would mean violating the principle that another person's interest in obtaining what it is wrong to have cannot be a good reason for morally requiring me to act in that person's favour. So, either way, the Extreme Demand must be rejected.

It should be evident that this objection applies equally to the claim that each of us is required to get as close as possible to meeting the Extreme

Demand. That claim implies the wrongness of leading a non-altruistically-focused life; it must therefore be rejected too, for the same reasons. If it is absurd to deny that your pursuing or having something can ground requirements on others to help you, then your pursuing or having that thing must be morally permissible.

The argument that has been given for this conclusion does not rely on a particular conception of appropriate impartiality: it goes through even on a conception of impartiality that gives priority to the worse-off. The argument relies on appealing to goods of personal partiality; but on any plausible conception of impartiality, the value of these goods must be recognized: they are as important for the badly-off as for the well-off. And it relies on the thought that people's interests in attaining these goods ground requirements on us to help them. But that thought, too, must be accepted on any plausible conception of impartiality. Indeed, that thought is at the heart of the initial case for thinking that the well-off are morally required to help the badly-off. It is, at least in part, because of the way poverty impairs friendships, the pursuit of fulfilling projects, and the ability of people to participate in the life of their communities, that there are morally compelling reasons for us to help the people who suffer it. So the argument that has been given here against the Extreme Demand is an argument for thinking that it can be rejected from an appropriately impartial point of view—on any plausible conception of appropriate impartiality. And Chapter 7 showed us why that gives us a strong objection to it.

This tells us something worth knowing: we have found one statement of the moral demands of affluence that ought to be rejected. But what we set out to find is the view that ought to be accepted. It might seem that we have a lot of work still to do. However, many of the materials we need in order to state this view have now been provided. In the next two chapters I use these materials to identify the set of demands we ought to endorse instead. So far, I have argued that living a non-altruistically-focused life is morally defensible. I now need to say what *kind* of non-altruistically-focused life is defensible. We have seen what the moral demands of affluence are not. Now we need to find out what they are.

9

Permission

To give an account of the moral demands of affluence is to spell out how much anyone who is materially well off is morally required to do to help the badly-off. Defending such an account means doing two things:

(1) Showing that a certain degree of sacrifice is morally required of the well-off in helping the badly-off.

(2) Showing that going further is not morally required.

Doing the first of these things amounts to giving an argument for requirement; doing the second is giving an argument for permission.[1]

So far, we have gone some way towards addressing (2)—but only a very small part of the way. We have found that the Extreme Demand should be rejected. So we do at least know that the degree of sacrifice that is morally required of us is not as extreme as the Extreme Demand claims. However, as I have acknowledged, that is by itself an unsurprising conclusion. The real usefulness of the argument we have just seen against the Extreme Demand will be in showing us how to justify saying more than that.

In this chapter I aim to show how far an argument for permission of the form that was used against the Extreme Demand can be extended. We can imagine possible standards of requirement arranged on a scale from the most to the least demanding. What has been shown so far is that a standard towards the most demanding end of that scale can be impartially rejected. It will not be surprising to discover that, against any standard that is only marginally less demanding than the Extreme Demand, there will be an argument of the same kind for rejecting it too. But what we can now ask is, What is the *least* demanding standard that can be rejected on the same grounds? How far can the earlier argument reach?

9.1 TWO QUESTIONS ABOUT PERMISSION

I shall approach this question by asking two subsidiary ones. Which kinds of life can be shown, by means of an argument of the form used against the Extreme Demand, to be ones that it is morally permissible to live? And within those lives, which goods is it morally permissible to pursue, according to an argument of this form?

This is a convenient way of expressing the questions I shall be trying to resolve; but it is potentially a bit misleading. We ought to bear in mind that the scope of this discussion is governed by an important restriction. The concern in this book is to say what can and cannot be morally required of us in responding to other people's interests in getting our help: what is and is not required by *beneficence*. If the argument succeeds, it shows that there are limits to how far I can be required to compromise my own interests in responding to other people's. However, concern for the interests of other people, although important, is not the only source of moral requirements on our conduct. Far from it: moral requirements come from many other sources—justice, honesty, loyalty, gratitude, and so on—which are not limited by the arguments given here. (I shall discuss some examples in Chapter 11.) Phrased more carefully, then, the two questions I am setting out to answer can be put like this:

> Which kinds of life are the ones such that living those lives violates no requirement of beneficence?
>
> Which goods are the ones such that pursuing those goods violates no requirement of beneficence?

This is cumbersome, and I shall often revert to the simpler talk of moral permissibility, for convenience. But when I do so, I intend the scope of my discussion to be understood in this more restricted way, as concerning the limits on requirements of *beneficence*.

Chapter 8 used a distinctive strategy of argument to establish such limits. This involved making a connection between how much I can be required to do in responding to other people's interests, and the requirements on other people to respond to *my* interests. My interests in getting what it would be wrong for me to have, it was argued, cannot ground a requirement on others to help me to get it. That is (contraposing), if others *are* required to help me to get something, it cannot be wrong for me to get it for myself. From here it was argued that, if we consider the wide range of interests people have in non-altruistically-focused fulfilments, it is absurd to deny that these can ground requirements on others to help them.[2] Denying this would be absurd, in the following way: it would involve radically departing from our ordinary judgements about the range of interests that can ground requirements of beneficence. And that is a serious problem for an argument which purports to begin from those ordinary judgements: such an argument must fail if it leads to a view which is committed to rejecting those same judgements.

In Chapter 8 a specific conclusion was drawn from this: pursuing the fulfilments of a non-altruistically-focused life violates no requirement of beneficence, so the Extreme Demand should be rejected. However, we should notice that this conclusion is being drawn from a more general principle:

> If it is absurd to deny that your pursuing or having x can ground requirements on others to help you, then your pursuing or having x violates no requirement of beneficence.

What I am going to do in this chapter and the next is to ask what further conclusions can be established by invoking this principle, and to show how far such conclusions extend.

In the current chapter I shall look at four main ways of applying this principle. First, and most obviously, we can substitute for x particular goods, or perhaps classes of goods, and argue for the conclusion that it is morally permissible to pursue those goods. We saw this kind of argument in Chapter 8, where the examples of pursuing a musical training and achieving a family reunion were discussed, as instances of the more general class of non-altruistically-focused fulfilments. It would be absurd to deny that these goods can ground requirements on others to help you; so pursuing them yourself must be permissible.

A second strategy is to apply the principle directly to the pursuit of certain goods, and then use that to draw conclusions concerning the kinds of life it is morally permissible to live. It might be argued that the permissibility of pursuing certain goods presupposes the permissibility of living a certain kind of life that contains them. Chapter 8 also illustrated this. Given the absurdity of denying that we can be morally required to help someone pursue a musical training or achieve a family reunion, it must be permissible to lead the kind of non-altruistically-focused life within which such goods are pursued. The permissibility of living this kind of life is a presupposition of the permissibility of pursuing those goods. In this way, an answer to our question concerning lives may be derived from an answer to the question concerning goods.

A third application of the principle involves substituting for x a kind of *life* rather than a kind of good. Thus, suppose I faced a choice between different lives, one of which would clearly be better for me than the alternatives. But suppose my being able to live that life depended on your making some trivial effort to help me, and that you knew this. If that would give me a much better life, it might be absurd to deny that you are required to help me. And if so, then the principle just stated could be invoked to show that my living this life is morally permissible.

We should also examine a fourth possibility: this involves arguing in the reverse direction. Conclusions about the goods it is morally permissible to pursue might be derived from conclusions about morally permissible lives. If we can show (by means of the third kind of argument, applying our principle directly to lives) that a certain kind of life is morally permissible, we might then infer the permissibility of pursuing the goods contained within that life.

This gives us four kinds of argument using the above principle to establish conclusions about the permissibility of goods and lives: a direct argument concerning goods; an argument from goods to lives; a direct argument concerning lives; and an argument from lives to goods. In the rest of the chapter I shall take each kind of argument in turn, and ask how extensive are the conclusions about permissibility that they support.

9.2 DIRECT ARGUMENTS CONCERNING GOODS

In Chapter 8 I gave examples of some large-scale and important goods for which there is a good argument of the first of these four forms. Given the importance of goods such as developing a musical talent or reuniting your family, it would be absurd to deny that your interests in having such goods can provide morally compelling reasons for others to help you when it would be easy to do so. But if so then, according to the principle set out above, it must be morally permissible for you to pursue these goods.

Notice, however, that the goods to which this principle applies need not be so important. After all, think of the various opportunities for beneficent action and occasions for failures of beneficence that actually present themselves to us. Most of the beneficent actions that anyone ever performs confer benefits on a much smaller scale (at least when taken separately). And these smaller-scale goods surely do ground *requirements* of beneficence. If I can see that you have dropped your car keys, or left your umbrella behind, or you're standing at the wrong bus stop, but I do not take the trouble to tell you, then that would be mean-spirited (unless there is some further explanation).[3] It is not just that it would be nice to help you out in these small ways: not to do so is something for which I am open to criticism—it is a *failure* of beneficence. Of course, the failure of beneficence is less serious than in the earlier examples; but it is a failure of beneficence all the same. For I still face the question 'Why am I not prepared to help you?' And I ought to have something to say in reply to this—some good reason for not helping—in order to meet the case for helping you. To be sure, in these examples that reason need not itself be very substantial (as far as I can see, the fact that I am in a hurry will do); but if there is none, then I have acted wrongly.

These large- and small-scale goods share a common feature: people's interests in these goods provide reasons for helping them which it would be morally wrong not to act on. This point can be expressed in different ways. We can say that people's interests in pursuing these goods provide 'morally compelling' reasons to help them; or, as I have also been saying, they ground moral requirements to help people. More strongly, it would be absurd to deny this. When it would be absurd to deny that your interest in pursuing a good can ground requirements on me to help you, let us say that

that good is 'requirement-grounding' (or, equivalently, that losing it would be a 'requirement-grounding loss'). For any requirement-grounding good, there will be an argument, invoking the principle stated above, for the permissibility of pursuing it.

At this point it is natural to want to ask for a further substantive account of what makes a good requirement-grounding. Clearly, that is connected to how important the good is for the person whose interests in that good ground the requirement. If a stranger's life is threatened, I am morally required to help him; if he prefers one drink to another, I am not. Can a general substantive account be given of just how large a good must be in order to qualify as requirement-grounding? I am not sure. It would surely be a mistake to expect that we shall ever be able to give a completely precise account—an exact specification of the size that a prospective loss must have in order for there to be a requirement on me to help to avert it. That seems no more reasonable than looking for an exact amount of money that a person can be morally required to give up to save another person's life. Having said that, I am not ruling out the possibility of a general account of the sorts of loss that are requirement-grounding and what makes them so. My reason for not attempting such an account here is simply that I do not see how to derive it from the other things I have said in this book. Any attempt to develop an account of requirement-grounding losses would amount to a further, independent project. If that further project were carried through, that would serve to supplement what is said here.

Is the absence of a further substantive account of this kind a problem? I don't think so. Most of us have tolerably clear opinions about the sorts of loss to other people that are significant enough to ground requirements on us to help them—albeit opinions that do not amount to a precise demarcation of the boundary between those that are and those that are not. It looks as though there is a graduated spectrum of cases, and that fits naturally with what has been said here. The smaller a benefit to me, the less absurd it is to deny that you can be morally required to help me to secure it; and consequently, the weaker an argument of the form just described will be if it is used to maintain that securing that benefit for myself must be morally permissible. I think that this is enough to offer us some clear practical guidance in thinking about how much we can and cannot be morally required to give up to help other people: I shall spell that out in Chapter 10.

What it is Absurd to Deny

My argument depends on appealing to claims about requirements of beneficence which 'it is absurd to deny'. At first glance, this might seem highly unsatisfactory. It might look as though the argument reduces to the inference: certain claims about the requirements of beneficence would take us too far away from conventionally accepted opinions about the requirements of beneficence, so they cannot be right. However, that would be a very feeble and frustrating response to the argument of Part I. It would be frustrating, because of course we knew all along that an extremely demanding moral outlook is at odds with conventional moral opinion: a book of this length is hardly needed to make *this* response to the extremely demanding proposal. And it would be feeble, because the argument of Part I provides us with a case for thinking that conventional opinion requires a substantial defence. The aim has been to show to what extent there is anything to be said in *favour* of the moral permissibility of a life of personal fulfilment—not just that conventional opinions about the requirements of beneficence happen to protect it.

It is important to emphasize, then, that my argument does not work that way at all. What it is doing is to respond to the case (presented in Part I) for thinking that, once we accept the life-saving analogy, ordinary claims about what beneficence requires lead to an extremely demanding conclusion. My response to this is not the obvious but unimpressive point that this conclusion is at odds with conventional opinion. Rather it is a point about the ordinary conception of what beneficence requires (what it *does* require, and not how those requirements are limited) in which the argument for the demanding conclusion is supposedly grounded.[a] Our ordinary conception of what beneficence requires, while it certainly includes saving lives in dramatic circumstances, also includes benefiting people in a range of less dramatic, everyday ways when it is easy to do so. I am not making a question-begging appeal to conventional views about the limits on requirements of beneficence. Rather, I am pointing out the way in which obvious claims about what beneficence *does* require cause the argument for a demanding conclusion to collapse.

In the final chapter I shall discuss another way in which my appeal to claims about requirements of beneficence which 'it is absurd to deny' might seem question-begging.[b] But for now, let me carry on with setting out my argument.

Choices between Goods

It may seem that we are heading towards a strikingly permissive conclusion. For if it is permissible to pursue requirement-grounding goods, it seems that some of those goods can be very expensive. The projects around which some people structure their lives can include amassing a great private art collection, travelling the world exhaustively, developing 'an exquisite sense

[a] See Sect. 8.4, 'Helping People with Non-Altruistically-Focused Lives'.

[b] Sect. 11.2.

of the luxurious',[4] or simply amplifying the family fortune. Of course, it is not as if the mere fact that a project is pursued makes it good for a person. Some projects, many of us want to say, are themselves worthless; and if so, then people who devote their lives to pursuing them are mistaken in thinking that this makes them better off. However, it is hard to see why this should be thought to apply to very expensive pursuits as a class. Platitudinously, some people are spoiled by their wealth. But unless that is *always* true, we have no case for thinking that the things that are genuinely good for a person cannot be hugely expensive, at least in some cases.

Once we accept *this*, it is hard to see what stops such goods from being requirement-grounding. One might wonder whether I could be morally required to spend any money of my own to help someone who already has much more than me; but if the cost of helping you is only to expend some trivial effort, then it is hard to see what good reason there could be for not helping you. If, by passing on a simple warning, I can prevent your art collection from being destroyed, then surely it would be mean-spirited of me not to do *that*.[5] Moreover, notice that what is at stake does not have to be a loss of life-changing significance. If I notice that one of your valuable paintings is about to be damaged, and I could easily prevent this, I ought to do that too. If not bothering to tell you that you have dropped your car keys is a failure of beneficence, then surely not bothering to warn you about your painting is a failure of beneficence too. So it may seem that the argument I have developed supports the moral permissibility of having and pursuing luxuries—including luxuries that are beyond the reach of all but the richest people in the world. It could be wrong for me not to alert you to the fact that one of your antique champagne glasses is about to fall off the side of your yacht. Indeed, it looks as though practically *any* good is requirement-grounding, and therefore (according to my argument) morally permissible.

There is a sense in which this is true. However, it is a limited sense, and the impression of a permissive conclusion is misleading. To see why, we need to make an important distinction. There is a difference between helping you to retain or gain a good, and helping you to pursue one good instead of a possible alternative.[6] So far, we have been talking about the first kind of case, in which, by giving you a warning, I can help you to avoid losing a good—here, the alternatives at stake are simply your having that good or lacking it. However, turn to the second kind of case. Suppose you have a choice between pursuing one genuine good and pursuing another. Choices of this kind are very common. Often, there are two different goods either of which you could pursue fully, but you cannot pursue both of them fully. If pursuing one of them is substantially better for you, then the argument set out above will offer a defence of pursuing it in preference to the other one. If it is better by a requirement-grounding margin—that is, a margin big enough to make it absurd to deny that others can be morally required to help you to pursue it—then the principle set out above can be used to argue that it is morally permissible to pursue it, rather than pursuing the alternative. But otherwise it cannot.

This makes it hard to see how our argument could supply a defence of the kinds of expensive pursuit mentioned above. If they were much better for the people who pursue them than the cheaper alternatives, then there would be a ground for thinking this. But it is hard to see why we should believe that. Choosing a career as the curator of a public art collection over a life as a private collector would rarely be substantially worse for a person. True, if you have already structured your life around some expensive project, there is likely to be a genuine cost to you in abandoning it in favour of a cheaper alternative. However, it is only when that cost is great enough to be requirement-grounding—that is, great enough for it to be absurd to deny that I can be required to help you to avoid it—that there will be a case for the permissibility of refusing to make it. And if the cheaper alternative involves similar skills, aptitudes, and fulfilments, then the case for thinking this looks unconvincing. This point applies to both achievements in the pursuit of expensive projects, and enjoyments. Indeed, it is more far-reaching in relation to enjoyments, since it seems that, for any enjoyment that costs something, there are always alternative enjoyments that are free.

This is consistent with thinking that I can be required to help you to avoid damage to one of your precious paintings, or the loss of your champagne glass overboard. It is just that we need to be careful about what is implied by those judgements. Combining them with the principle I have defended, what follows is that it is permissible for you to avoid that damage or loss yourself. If you can see that one of your paintings is about to be damaged, there is nothing morally wrong with your acting to prevent it. But accepting *this* does not mean accepting that it is morally defensible for you to structure your life around collecting expensive paintings in the first place, rather than living in an alternative way that is not substantially worse for you and using the money you would otherwise have spent on yourself to help other people.

Notice that the important point here is whether you *could* pursue a cheaper alternative that would not be substantially worse for you. This is not a matter of whether you *think* it would be substantially worse. But nor is it simply a matter of whether it is likely that, if you were restricted to the cheaper alternative, your life would actually be worse. After all, if you falsely think that a cheaper alternative is much worse, that is likely to mean that you would be less wholehearted in pursuing it. However, if the only reason you would do less well in pursuing an alternative project is your false evaluative attitudes about it, *that* will not show that there is no equally good alternative that you could pursue instead. All it will show is that you are not receptive to that alternative. Compare the corresponding point about enjoyments. Suppose I have become so habituated to spending a lot of money on myself that I'll become seriously miserable if I stop. I can now credibly assert that my life will be substantially worse if I give up this spending. However, that will not be enough to show that it is morally defensible for me to carry on as before. For perhaps it is only my *attitude* towards spending on myself that would make the alternatives worse. There may be many cheaper sources of enjoyment that remain open to me, if I bring myself to be receptive to them. The fact that I *could* pursue cheaper alternatives that would not be substantially worse for me is enough to undermine the case for the permissibility of taking the expensive alternative.[7]

'Commitment Goods'

The point I have just been making needs to be qualified. For most achievements and all enjoyments, there will be no defence of pursuing an expensive alternative when I could instead pursue a cheaper alternative that would not be substantially worse for me. I think this is also true of many goods of understanding. But it is not true of all goods.

In particular, it is implausible as a claim about friendship. A willingness to replace your friendships with cheaper ones that are just as good for you would involve a very unappealing detachment from your friends. Indeed, the fullest kind of friendship is a good which this sort of willingness would prevent me from possessing.[8] And if so, this sort of attitude towards my friends cannot be required of me.

To see why, ask yourself what would be involved in a willingness to replace your friendships with cheaper ones that are not substantially worse for you. A relationship covered by this attitude could involve a reciprocal partiality and affection towards particular people that would furnish goods of enjoyment. But what it would lack is the dimension of mutual *commitment* that characterizes the kind of relationship that constitutes a distinctive, further kind of life-enhancing good. A friendship of this fuller kind centrally includes a reciprocal recognition of norms of mutual concern—an understanding that we can properly expect certain forms of engagement, interest, support, and help from each other. A willingness to replace my relationship to a person with another relationship that is just as good would deprive me of this dimension of commitment.[9] Why is that important? It is important because of the importance of relationships of this fuller kind. These relationships are central to people's lives: they figure among the most important of their non-altruistically-focused interests. And if so, there is an argument for the moral defensibility of such relationships, of the form set out above. Relationships of this kind ground requirements on us. If I could easily reunite two people who stand in this kind of relationship to each other, then it could certainly be wrong not to do so. But I cannot be required to further people's interests in what is wrong. So pursuing such relationships cannot be wrong.

Thus, it may well be true that there are many people with whom it would be cheaper and no worse for me to have friendships than it is with my actual friends. (Indeed, no doubt there are plenty of people whose friendship would be *better* for me than my actual friends.) If so, the replacement of my friends would not itself be worse for me. But having a *willingness* to replace them would deprive me of a certain kind of friendship altogether, and that cannot be morally required of me, because of the requirement-grounding status of this good.

A similar point applies to the good of integrity: living in conformity with one's convictions. It may be the case that if I had different convictions, it would be cheaper to live in conformity with them. But in relation to many convictions, to regard myself as having the choice of replacing them with cheaper ones would be to lack those convictions altogether. I do not want to suggest that a person of integrity cannot reconsider her convictions. However, integrity is a kind of steadfastness in standing by one's convictions that precludes treating considerations of cost as grounds for reconsidering them.[10]

Moreover, there seem to be some forms of achievement in the pursuit of personal projects that call to be thought of in the same way. For an advocate of an important cause, or a custodian of something of great value, a proper devotion to these projects may preclude questions about how expensive they are.[11] I said above that abandoning a private art collection in favour of a career as the curator of a public one would rarely be substantially worse for a person. But this suggests one way in which it might be. If, say, you have inherited a significant collection from your artist parents, abandoning it might not simply be a change of career that employs your skills in an alternative way, but a betrayal of their legacy.

I shall call goods of these various kinds 'commitment goods'.[12] Commitment goods have two features. First, they are life-enhancing goods that are unavailable to someone who is willing to replace them with cheaper alternatives that are no worse for him. Secondly, they are requirement-grounding: it is absurd to deny that someone who could easily help another person to avoid or restore the loss of such goods can be morally required to do so. And since they are requirement-grounding, a person's pursuit of commitment goods will be morally permissible, even when cheaper alternatives would be no worse for him.

Let me repeat, though, that most achievements in the pursuit of personal projects and all enjoyments are not commitment goods. Achievements, of course, do usually require a kind of steadfastness too: a steady determination to accomplish a goal. But many do not require the special kind of steadfastness that is distinctive of integrity or friendship, where a willingess to take cheaper alternatives that are no worse for you precludes you from possessing a requirement-grounding good altogether.[13]

9.3 ARGUMENTS FROM GOODS TO LIVES

It might now seem that, far from defending a life full of expensive luxuries, our argument will not defend anything beyond a very ascetic one. I can justify pursuing a good when either there is no cheaper alternative that would not be substantially worse for me, or it is a commitment good. But how often is *that* true? It was acknowledged back in Chapter 8 that it is possible to have fulfilling friendships, achievements, enjoyments, and community involvement while focusing these fulfilments around the core project of helping other people.[c] Admittedly, Chapter 8 also argued that leading a non-altruistically-focused life is morally defensible. If so, we cannot be required to abandon *all* of the goods that are components of a non-altruistically-focused life. But that remains compatible with thinking that our pursuit of these goods should be drastically curtailed. Is it true that doing that would necessarily be substantially worse for me? If not, what is wrong with thinking that I ought to be doing the most I possibly can to help the needy, consistently with spending *something* on the fulfilments of a non-altruistically-focused life? So far we seem to have defended only those personal pursuits that are the very cheapest—or at least, those that allow you to do the most for other people.

That is because, so far, we have only considered a first kind of argument. This has involved taking the principle:

> If it is absurd to deny that your pursuing or having *x* can ground requirements on others to help you, then your pursuing or having *x* violates no requirement of beneficence,

and substituting for *x* particular goods or classes of goods, in order to derive conclusions concerning the permissibility of pursuing those goods. A second strategy is to apply the principle directly to the pursuit of certain goods, and then use that to draw conclusions concerning lives, arguing that the permissibility of pursuing those goods presupposes the permissibility of living a certain kind of life that contains them. This second strategy of argument can show us what is wrong with the ascetic view.

This second strategy was used in Chapter 8 to argue that it is permissible to live a non-altruistically-focused life. The permissibility of living this kind of life is a presupposition of the permissibility of pursuing goods such as a musical career or a family reunion. Given the absurdity of denying that I can be required to help you to pursue those goods, it must be permissible to lead the kind of life within which those goods are pursued.

The ascetic view we are now considering concedes this point. Perhaps I cannot be required to live an altruistically focused life—that is, one in which I constrict my pursuit of my own fulfilment as much as I bearably

[c] Sect. 8.2.

can, for the purpose of benefiting others. But what is wrong with requiring me to do as much as possible to help other people, compatibly with having *some* non-altruistic focus? We can call this a 'minimally non-altruistic' life: it does include non-altruistically-focused fulfilments, but it involves benefiting others as much as possible, compatibly with that fact.

A life of this kind would not count as altruistically focused. However, it would be very similar. It would involve a similar self-constraint—a vigilance in seeking to constrict the non-altruistic part of one's life as tightly as possible (without extinguishing it altogether) for the sake of benefiting others, rather than seeking to amplify and expand one's non-altruistic commitments and relationships. Furthermore, and crucially, it cannot sensibly be denied that fulfilments that are not constrained in this way provide morally compelling reasons for helping people. Denying this is about as absurd as denying that non-altruistically-focused fulfilments provide morally compelling reasons for helping people. It would mean rejecting almost all of the actual requirements we recognize to respond to others' interests. But on the other hand, if interests in such fulfilments do provide morally compelling reasons to help other people, then pursuing those fulfilments (according to the principle I have defended) cannot be wrong. Therefore, the proposal that we are required to lead minimally non-altruistic lives must be rejected, along with (and for the same reason as) the Extreme Demand. If I am morally required to act out of consideration for the interests of others in acting from more-than-minimally non-altruistic attitudes, then it must be defensible for me to act from such attitudes myself.

We should therefore reject the ascetic view that beneficence could require us to lead minimally non-altruistic lives. Moreover, the same will go for the suggestion that we are required to lead lives that are only marginally less altruistically governed than *that*. The same objection will apply. Any life that is governed by attitudes of constraint that are incompatible with the possession of goods that obviously do ground requirements of beneficence is one that I can justifiably refuse to live. We can put the general conclusion like this. If a life is governed by attitudes of constraint that are incompatible with the possession of requirement-grounding goods, let us say that it is an 'altruistically directed' life. Then what we have found is that it is morally permissible to lead a life that is not only non-altruistically-focused, but also non-altruistically-*directed*.

9.4 DIRECT ARGUMENTS CONCERNING LIVES

Which kind of life is it morally defensible to live? We have a first, general answer to this question. It is morally defensible to structure my life in a non-altruistically-directed way. But now let us ask for a more specific answer.

There are many different non-altruistically-directed lives I could lead: many different careers, for example, I could pursue. Is it morally defensible for me to be leading *this* one? Can I morally justify spending my life as a philosophy teacher?[14]

We have looked so far at two ways in which the principle derived from Chapter 8 can be used to derive conclusions about permissibility. To answer this question, we should turn to a third. This involves taking that principle:

> If it is absurd to deny that your pursuing or having x can ground requirements on others to help you, then your pursuing or having x violates no requirement of beneficence,

and substituting for x a particular kind of life. If my leading a certain kind of life is requirement-grounding, then it must be morally permissible for me to live that kind of life.

When asking whether a certain kind of life is requirement-grounding, there are two importantly different questions to distinguish. They correspond to the different questions we asked earlier about requirement-grounding goods.[d] The first is whether it is absurd to deny that others can be required to help me in leading the life I am living. The second, more important question is whether it is absurd to deny that others can be required to help me to attain one kind of life rather than another, alternative kind of life. To show that it is morally permissible for me to live in this way rather than in some other way, I need to be able to defend answers to the second question rather than the first.

Of course, such life-choices are not common. But that is beside the point. The question is not whether the difference between how good various alternative lives would be for me *does* ground requirements on others to help me. It is whether this difference *could* ground requirements on others to help me. If it is absurd to deny that it is the sort of difference that could do this, then the better life must be morally permissible.

An argument of this form can justify a specific kind of non-altruistically-directed life, provided it is markedly better than the alternatives. If it is better than the alternatives by a large enough margin, then it can be absurd to deny that someone who knew this, and could easily act to ensure that I had this life but failed to do so, would be displaying a failure of beneficence. But if denying this is absurd, then (invoking our principle) it is morally permissible for me to live that life.

This is not to say that a life's being markedly better for me than the alternatives is *sufficient* to generate a good argument of this kind. Nothing has been said here to rule out the possibility that, for some people, their lives go best for them when they are full of opportunities to exploit, harm,

[d] Sect. 9.2. 'Choices between Goods'.

and dominate other people. It is not absurd to deny that you can be required to help me to lead a life of this kind, because of the way in which it is directed towards immoral ends. However, it is absurd to deny that substantially improving your life, when it is not directed towards immoral ends, can ground requirements on me to help you: denying this would overturn our conception of beneficence altogether. And if so, there will be a good argument for thinking that your living the better life violates no requirement of beneficence.[15]

9.5 ARGUMENTS FROM LIVES TO GOODS

We have now explored three ways of arguing to conclusions concerning moral permissibility: a direct argument concerning goods, an argument from goods to lives, and a direct argument concerning lives. The fourth and final kind of argument to consider is an argument from lives to goods. Suppose it can be shown, along the lines just described, that a particular kind of non-altruistically-directed life is morally permissible, given how much better it is for me than the alternatives. Then it will follow that it is permissible for me to pursue the particular goods that such a life contains. For example, if it can be shown that living the life of a philosophy teacher is morally permissible, then the permissibility of pursuing the particular goods that such a life contains—the delivery of a well-presented lecture, for example—could be derived from that.

It is significant that an argument of this indirect kind—defending goods via the lives that contain them—might succeed in establishing the permissibility of a good even though that good is not itself requirement-grounding. Is my interest in delivering a well-presented lecture something that can ground a *requirement* of beneficence on others? I doubt it. The fact that it is good for me means that others do have a reason of beneficence to help me; but it does not seem to be a reason for which, if you choose not to act on it, you display a *failure* of beneficence. And surely, an argument that relied on claiming that what I have just said is *absurd*—that to deny that this interest grounds requirements of beneficence is to depart radically from our ordinary conception of beneficence—looks very unconvincing. However, the point to notice is that, even if this good is not requirement-grounding, there can still be an argument of the indirect kind for the permissibility of pursuing it. If the life of a philosophy teacher is permissible for me, because of the way in which *living this life* is requirement-grounding, then that supports the permissibility of pursuing the constituent goods it contains, even if those goods are not themselves requirement-grounding.

A Distinction between Goods

To see the broader significance of this final kind of argument—an argument from lives to goods—let me distinguish two general classes of goods.

Intrinsically life-enhancing goods, I have stipulated, are those things that intrinsically make the life of a person who has them better than it otherwise would be.[16] Just what these goods are, and how we should settle such questions, are controversial matters about which I shall say something shortly. But it is not controversial that there are such things: lives can be made better or worse by the goods and evils they contain. We can contrast these with a second class of goods, which we might call 'purely episodic'. This second class contains anything that is genuinely good for a person, but which makes her life overall no better. Suppose I have some minor stroke of good luck: I find a $20 note, say. Many people are inclined to think of this as a purely episodic good: it seems right to them to say that I am benefited—I am better off, by exactly $20—but not that this makes any difference to how good my life is as a whole.[17]

Whether that is right or not is debatable.[18] A view that needs to be considered is that there are no purely episodic goods. Anything that is good for you makes your life better to *some* extent: it is just that it would be pragmatically odd to mention something that makes only a tiny contribution to how good your life is when making a judgement about that life overall. So perhaps, having made the conceptual distinction between life-enhancing and purely episodic goods, we should say that there is nothing that instantiates the concept of a purely episodic good. Actually, it seems to me that this is a possibility that does not ultimately affect any of my conclusions. But at this point, we should notice that this possibility remains open.

Showing that one kind of life is better than the available alternatives—that is, giving an argument of the third form, a direct argument concerning lives—means appealing to the life-enhancing goods, and not the purely episodic goods, that it contains. For the features of a life that make it a better life are life-enhancing goods. So if one life is better than another, there will be a life-enhancing good that it contains in virtue of which it is better. Purely episodic goods, by contrast, are things that it would be good to have but that make no difference to how good my life is overall. So my invoking a purely episodic good to explain the difference between the life that I prefer and the one that I will otherwise have to lead cannot show that the former is any better.

However, having recognized this, it is important to notice a further point. If my life were stripped of all the purely episodic goods it contains, it would certainly be worse. For any particular cup of coffee, pleasant conversation, hour of absorbed reading, or weekend outing with my children, it is plausible to think that my life would have been no worse without it. But if it were shorn of these and every other good with the same purely episodic value, it would certainly be much worse. Thus, containing these purely episodic goods is a life-enhancing good. There is therefore an argument from the permissibility of the lives that contain purely episodic goods to the permissibility of pursuing them. The case for the permissibility of leading a particular non-altruistically-directed life comes from an appeal to life-enhancing goods and not purely episodic goods. But given the permissibility of that life, the pursuit of the purely episodic goods it contains is permissible.[19]

Which Goods Are Life-Enhancing?

Which goods *are* intrinsically life-enhancing? Properly arguing for an answer to this question would require another book, containing arguments independent of the ones given here.[20] So I am not about to defend an answer. Nonetheless, let me state one. It is unlikely to be exactly correct; but it at least offers a plausible first sketch of the kind of account that will need to be supplied in its place, and gives us a concrete view to work with in what follows. It consists of a list of seven different—and apparently mutually irreducible—categories of goods.

The first of these categories is the one I have appealed to most often in giving examples of life-enhancing goods. This is the category of close personal relationships—relationships of friendship and love. These will clearly feature in an account of the goods that make almost any life (perhaps any life whatever) better, and whose absence makes it worse, no matter what a person's circumstances are, rich or poor.[21] Given that our aim is to find requirements to govern the relation between rich and poor that are impartially acceptable, that is important.

I have also often mentioned a second category: this contains achievements in the pursuit of worthwhile personal projects. A widely held view is that achievements that make a genuine contribution to worthwhile projects improve a life (perhaps every life) of which they are a part, and that a life is made worse by the lack of any such achievements. This way of putting the point, of course, leaves open the further large question just which projects are worthwhile. However, it does seem clear that in order for a given achievement to contribute to making a person's life better, it must itself contribute to a worthwhile activity. An achievement, no matter how difficult, that contributes to an activity which is itself worthless will show only that the achiever has been wasting his time.[22] It is sometimes complained that the idea that any life is improved by containing achievements of this kind involves a Westerner's cultural parochialism, and is alien to more traditional outlooks.[23] However, this seems misplaced as an objection to the claim that worthwhile achievements improve a person's life: rather, it points to a good question about which achievements really are worthwhile—whether it is ones that involve success in competition, or contributions to the life of a community. I am not endorsing a shallow, CV-building conception of worthwhile achievement. I am simply making the general point that making a significant contribution to worthwhile activities is one of the things that can help to make lives good. The generality of this point is important. For again, it means that we have a claim about life-enhancing goods that is true of both the affluent and the very poor.

What should be added to these first two categories of life-enhancing goods? Five further kinds of life-enhancing goods which seem to many people to be irreducible to each other and to achievement are these: enjoyment, understanding of oneself and the world, autonomy, involvement in the life of a culture or community, and the freedom to live in accordance with one's fundamental beliefs and commitments.[24] Each of these further categories, like the first two, can plausibly be claimed to supply us with a class of goods that are life-enhancing for rich and poor alike. Clearly, the ability people have to secure these goods does depend crucially, and often tragically, on their material resources. But it is not as if their status *as goods* for a person itself depends on her material wealth. Enjoyment, understanding, autonomy, community participation, and the freedom to live a life of integrity should be invoked to assess how well off someone is, irrespective of her material standard of living. The poor may certainly be deprived of these goods, but that should not lead us to doubt whether these things even qualify as life-enhancing goods for them. On the contrary: if we want to spell out what is bad about poverty, it is deprivations with respect to these goods that we can most plausibly point to.

This gives us a seven-member list of life-enhancing goods. I claim no originality for it:[25] it is simply being offered as an obvious starting point on the road towards a properly defended account. Going further down that road would mean engaging with several further issues. Let me very briefly mention four of the more obvious ones.

The first issue concerns whether the list is too short or too long. There does indeed seem to be a strong case for adding to it the development of one's own talents: the view that this makes a person's life better, irrespective of the achievements she may have been fortunate enough to accomplish, is widely endorsed. But perhaps this can itself be thought of as a kind of achievement. Likewise, there may be a case for adding freedom from suffering to the list. Clearly, this is normally a precondition for the possession of the other goods on the list. But perhaps a life could be made worse by containing extremes of suffering than it would have been without them, even if it remained unchanged in respect of goods belonging to the other categories. Working in the other direction, it might be wondered whether the last two members of the list should be amalgamated. Perhaps any religious or other life-shaping commitment should be thought of as a kind of community-involvement, even when pursued in solitude. And perhaps the values of community-involvement can in turn be assimilated to that of friendship. To settle this, we should need to consider examples in which it is plausible to think that lives are made better by one kind of good without another: persecuted communities (where the absence of freedom to pursue a way of life can be accompanied by strong bonds of community-involvement) would be one obvious case to think about. My own view is that reflection of this sort will bear out the distinctness of the members of the list I have given; but clearly there is scope for an extensive discussion here.

A second issue concerns, not which items belong on our list of life-enhancing goods, but the relationships between those items. In particular, what is the relationship between enjoyment and the others? Take, for example, the question of the connection between enjoyment and personal relationships. There seems little ground for thinking that, once the list includes enjoyment, the mention of personal relationships as well is simply redundant. For friendship would seem to be irreplaceable by other enjoyments: a life full of other enjoyments, but which lacked friendship, would seem in that respect to be worse. However, is a life that includes only painful close personal relationships better than it would have been without them?[26] If not, perhaps enjoyment should be treated as a precondition on a personal relationship's being a life-enhancing good.

The third issue concerns the scope of application of this list. Does the bearing that each item on the list has upon the quality of a person's life vary from one person to another?[27] And if so, might not some items on the list have *no* bearing on how good some lives are? Close personal relationships, it might be thought, make a big difference to the quality of my life, but not to Caesar Augustus'. Given the kind of intense focus some well-lived lives possess, it might be argued that their lacking goods of some kinds makes them no worse.[28]

The only way of giving a thoroughly grounded answer to this third question—and the same goes for the first two—would be to address a deeper issue: In virtue of what does a good qualify as life-enhancing? Can this be derived from facts about human nature or individual motivation? Can it be derived from more fundamental principles of reason? Or should we renounce the attempt to find a normative argument that will derive conclusions about life-enhancing goods from a further set of normatively significant premisses, and aim instead to anchor the justification of an account of life-enhancing goods in an epistemology of value?[29]

This is not the place to attempt to tackle such issues. Resolving them is a large, independent project of its own. The seven-member list offered here is a sensible starting point for a properly defended account. I do not make a larger claim for it than that. However, it will be useful to work with it here, as giving us a plausible if provisional concrete account of the life-enhancing goods that are important to my argument.

9.6 CONCLUSIONS

In this chapter I have taken the argument against the Extreme Demand, and asked how much further an argument of the same general form can be extended. Two conclusions can be drawn from this discussion—a conclusion about lives, and a conclusion about goods.

(1) My living one particular kind of life rather than another violates no requirement of beneficence if either:

> its permissibility is entailed by the permissibility of pursuing a particular good or class of goods, or
>
> it is better than the available alternatives by a requirement-grounding amount.

(2) My pursuing one particular good or class of goods rather than another violates no requirement of beneficence if either:

> its permissibility is entailed by the permissibility of living a kind of life that contains it, or
>
> it is better than the available alternatives by a requirement-grounding amount.

Several corollaries have been drawn from these conclusions. Three of the main ones are these:

> Pursuing commitment goods violates no requirement of beneficence, even when there are alternatives that would be no worse for you.
>
> Living a non-altruistically-directed life violates no requirement of beneficence, even when an altruistically directed life would be no worse for you.
>
> Leading a life that contains purely episodic goods violates no requirement of beneficence.

A question that has been emphasized throughout this discussion is how much worse it would be for you to pursue different goods, or live a different life—whether it would be worse enough to amount to a 'requirement-grounding' loss. In emphasizing this, however, I have not been saying that your reason for pursuing the goods you do, or living in the way you do, is that it is better for you. That is often false, as we saw in Chapter 8.[e] Your friendships are life-enhancing goods—they make your life better than it

[e] Sect. 8.1.

would be without them—but that is not your reason for befriending the people you do. Nor have I suggested otherwise. The claim has not been that your reason for pursuing the goods you do is that they are better for you than the alternatives. Rather, it has been that this is part of the justification that can be given for denying that you are required to forgo these goods in order to help other people who are much worse off than you. For when these goods are substantially better than the alternatives, they can ground requirements of beneficence on others to help you. And when that is true, there is a case for thinking that they are morally permissible.

I began by pointing out that an account of the moral demands of affluence needs an argument for permission, and an argument for requirement. We have now gone a substantial distance towards completing the argument for permission. However, we have not yet finished it. For although we have reached conclusions about the lives it is permissible to live and the goods it is permissible to pursue, we have still to spell out how much it is permissible to spend on those goods, within those lives. On top of this, we also need to supply an argument for requirement. These two tasks need to be tackled next.

10

Requirement

To complete our account of the moral demands of affluence, we need to do two further things. The first is to complete the argument for permission developed so far. We now have an account of the kinds of life it is morally permissible to live, and the goods it is morally permissible to pursue. However, that still leaves open the question how much time and money it is permissible to spend on such goods, within such lives. (Or at least, how much spending within these lives and on these goods violates no requirement of beneficence. As before, my discussion in this chapter is governed by this scope qualification, but I won't keep repeating it.) The first aim of this chapter will be to answer that further question.

Having done that, I will have completed my argument for permission. However, that is only half of what is needed for an account of the moral demands of affluence. An argument for permission establishes an upper limit to those demands. But it is not itself a justification for accepting any such demands. Giving that justification means supplying an argument for requirement. That is the second aim of this chapter.

By the end of the chapter my account of the moral demands of affluence will be complete. The last section discusses the practical implications of this account.

10.1 HOW MUCH SPENDING IS MORALLY PERMISSIBLE?

We have a description of the kinds of life within which, and the kinds of good on which, some spending is morally defensible. To complete our argument for permission, we need to answer one further question. *How much* of one's time and money it is morally defensible to spend within these lives and on these goods? To answer this, I propose that we turn to the by now familiar principle:

> If it is absurd to deny that your pursuing or having *x* can ground requirements on others to help you, then your pursuing or having *x* violates no requirement of beneficence.

When we used this principle to generate conclusions about the lives it is permissible to live and the goods it is permissible to pursue, we noticed that there are two options. One is to apply the principle directly—substituting for x either a kind of life, or a good or class of goods, and drawing conclusions about which ones are morally permissible. The other option is an indirect argument, deriving conclusions about the lives it is permissible to live from the goods it is permissible to pursue, or vice versa. Turning to the question how much spending is permissible within these lives and on these goods, we find that a corresponding pair of options is available. An answer to this question can be produced by applying our principle directly to levels of personal spending.[1] Or we can derive an answer indirectly, inferring the permissibility of a given level of personal spending from the permissibility of living a certain kind of life or pursuing a certain good or class of goods. Let us examine these two options in turn.

Direct Arguments

A direct argument for the permissibility of a given level of personal spending will be one which substitutes that level for x in our principle. If your interest in attaining or retaining a given level of personal spending is requirement-grounding—if it would be absurd to deny that this interest can ground a requirement of beneficence on others to help you—then attaining or retaining that level of personal spending must be permissible.

Talk of 'attaining or retaining a given level of personal spending' is implicitly comparative. Your interest in having a certain level of personal spending is your interest in having this one rather than a lower one.[2] If so, we can phrase the direct application of our principle to levels of personal spending like this:

> If it is absurd to deny that your interest in having the higher of two possible alternative levels of personal spending can ground requirements on others to help you, then your sustaining the higher level of personal spending violates no requirements of beneficence.

Notice that this can be used to address two importantly different questions. There is a question about particular activities, and a question about one's life as a whole. Given a particular activity you are engaged in, you can ask 'How much time and money should I spend on this activity?' You can also ask the different, global question 'How much time and money should I spend, overall, on myself and sources of personal fulfilment, and how much should I spend on helping other people?'

How often do we actually ask ourselves these questions? It seems to me that most reflective people will at some stage ask themselves the second one. And we all often ask ourselves the first kind of question—although I doubt there are many people who ask it very often in the context of wondering how far their pursuit of a personally significant activity is compatible with what they ought to be doing to help other people. The fact that we do not nag ourselves more often with questions of these two kinds seems to me both sane and morally unproblematic, and I shall return to this later in the chapter. However, let us ignore that for the moment. Leaving aside the issue of how often we should actually ask ourselves these questions, let us see how a direct argument answers them.

The questions are different; so are the answers. Start with the first. When you ask how much spending on a particular activity of yours is morally permissible, you need to look at the implications of different possible levels of spending on it. If a restriction in the amount you spend on a given activity will leave you no worse off, then it cannot be requirement-grounding. Requirements of beneficence are requirements to benefit other people: if a lower level of spending would be no worse for you, I confer no benefit on you in helping you to avoid it.

On its own, though, this point does not get us very far. It means that our argument provides no defence of personal spending that is completely wasteful, conferring no benefit on anyone. However, there does not seem to be any upper limit on the spending through which you could benefit yourself. In relation to a wide range of worthwhile personal projects, it seems that there will always be ways of spending money that will help you to achieve more. There are always going to be ways of spending it on tuition, interaction, and assistance from others in the same field, on useful equipment, and on freeing yourself from other demands on your time. Moreover, a similar point would seem even to apply to a good like friendship. As we have seen, not all spending on friends will improve a friendship.[a] But suppose you were intent on finding ways in which, by spending money, you could make some genuine contribution to deepening the mutual concern and engagement between you and your friends: is there not still an unlimited amount you might spend? Of course, it seems likely that a law of diminishing returns will apply as your spending on friendships and achievements increases. But it is hard to see why we should think that these diminishing returns ever dwindle down to zero. There does not appear to be any upper limit to the spending on friendships which has the potential to increase their life-enhancing value.

In applying our principle, however, the question we have to ask is not whether a higher level of spending would or could be better for me, but whether it is better by a large enough amount to make it absurd to deny that it can ground requirements on others to help me. If *that* is true, then there is a direct argument for the permissibility of my retaining the higher level of spending on the activity. But otherwise, there is not. Whenever something would be good for me (and is not directed towards morally objectionable ends), there is a reason for others to help me to get it. But if

[a] Sect. 8.1.

the benefit in question is getting a little bit more of a good I have a lot of already, the case for thinking that this benefit is requirement-grounding will be weak. It will not be absurd to deny that others are morally *required* to help me to get that further small benefit.

The second, different question we can ask is 'What overall level of personal spending is it morally permissible for me to sustain?' This is a question not about spending on a particular activity, but about my life as a whole. A direct argument gives us the following answer. Given any two proposed levels of personal spending, I can ask to what extent my life as a whole would be made worse by restricting myself to the lower one. If it would be a requirement-grounding loss, then there is an argument for the moral permissibility of retaining the higher rather than the lower level.

This gives us a way of answering both questions. We should think of the first as nested within the second. Settling the second question is a matter of determining what overall budget for personal spending it is defensible for me to sustain. Once I have settled that, I can then ask myself how much, within that overall budget, it is defensible for me to spend on any given activity. When I do this, I am moving to the first question.

Later in the chapter I shall offer a practical application of these conclusions. However, it should already be obvious that what I have said is not going to give us a precise specification of the amount of personal spending that is morally defensible on any given activity, or within a life overall. What it suggests instead is that there is a graduated spectrum. The worse it would be for me to restrict my personal spending, the more absurd it is to deny that another person could be required to help me to avoid that restriction, and thus the stronger is the case for thinking that avoiding the restriction is permissible. However, surely the absence of a sharp boundary demarcating the sacrifices that are required is a point in favour of the current view rather than against it.[3] As I said in Chapter 9, I am not ruling out the possibility that there may be some way of providing a further, more definite account of how large a loss must be in order to be requirement-grounding. However, giving that account would be independent of the rest of my argument, and I am not going to attempt it.[b] Without it, we already have clear opinions about the sorts of losses to other people that are and are not large enough to ground requirements on us to help them. It is those opinions that we ought to invoke in assessing how much personal spending is morally permissible—at least until we are given reasons for revising them.

Indirect Arguments

When a restriction in my personal spending would be requirement-grounding, it is morally permissible for me not to make it. As we have just seen, that

[b] Sect. 9.2.

gives us a direct way of arguing for the permissibility of a given level of personal spending. However, there is also another, less direct way. This starts by showing the permissibility of either living a certain kind of life or pursuing a certain good or class of goods, and then infers the permissibility of the forms of personal spending that are necessary to doing those things.

Drawing on the previous chapter, we can identify two arguments of this indirect kind: an argument concerning goods, and an argument concerning lives. First, in the discussion of 'commitment goods'—goods such as friendship and integrity—it was argued that I can permissibly remain committed to the particular friends and convictions I have although other, cheaper ones would be no worse for me.[c] I can permissibly retain the attitudes of commitment that are distinctive of the possession of these goods, and retaining these attitudes is incompatible with discarding my friends or convictions in favour of cheaper ones. If this is right, then it gives us one way in which retaining a higher level of personal spending might be permissible even though a lower one would be no worse for me. If I had cheaper friends and the rest of my life stayed the same, that would be one way in which I could live at a lower level of personal spending without its being any worse for me. There is no direct argument for the permissibility of my refusing to do this, since the lower level of spending would not itself represent a requirement-grounding loss. But if it is permissible to have the attitudes distinctive of commitment goods such as friendship, then there is an indirect argument for the permissibility of the forms of spending through which those commitments are expressed.

The other indirect argument comes from the defence of living a non-altruistically-directed life.[d] I can permissibly live a non-altruistically-directed life, even when an altruistically directed life would be no worse. Again, if that is true, it implies that a higher level of personal spending will be permissible though there is a lower one—the one to which I would be restricting myself if I led an altruistically directed life—that would be no worse for me.

The Argument for Permission: Conclusion

How much personal spending is morally permissible? The answer we have arrived at can be summarized as follows:

> My sustaining a certain level of personal spending violates no requirement of beneficence if either:
>
> (i) its permissibility is entailed by the permissibility of living a particular kind of life or the permissibility of pursuing a particular good or class of goods, or
>
> (ii) restricting it further would be a requirement-grounding loss.

[c] Sect. 9.2, 'Commitment Goods'. [d] Sect. 9.3.

This has the same general structure as the two conclusions defended in Chapter 9, concerning the kind of life it is permissible to live and the goods it is permissible to pursue.[e] As before, the first clause is generated by an indirect argument while the second comes from a direct argument. As we have seen, there are two different questions about personal spending, and this conclusion can be used to answer them both: the global question what overall level of personal spending it is permissible to maintain across one's life as a whole, and the more specific question how much of that overall budget is permissible to spend on a given activity.

The conclusion just set out serves as a succinct statement of the overall conclusion of our argument for permission. But it needs to be read in conjunction with the two conclusions defended in Chapter 9. They tell us how to interpret clause (i), by specifying which lives it is permissible to live and which goods it is permissible to pursue.

It might be wondered whether clause (ii) will ever be satisfied. For it seems that, for any given level of personal spending that you are currently sustaining, there will always be some marginally lower level you could restrict yourself to instead without a requirement-grounding loss. I shall come to this issue later in the chapter.[f] Before I do that, however, we should turn to our next task. We have completed an argument for permission; now we need to supply an argument for requirement.

10.2 THE ARGUMENT FOR REQUIREMENT

Our argument for requirement will need to come from a different source. An argument of the kind used against the Extreme Demand can tell us which forms of personal spending are morally defensible. However, in order to draw conclusions about which sacrifices in personal spending are morally required, we need to be told which forms of personal spending are morally *in*defensible. For that, we need to look elsewhere.

However, we do not need to look far. To see the argument for requirement, we need to appreciate the relationship between the two halves of this book.

Part I set out an argument for thinking that there are extensive moral requirements of beneficence. We should now ask what we have learned about that argument. Which elements of the argument of Part I have been called into question, and which ones stand unchallenged? Recall the starting point of that argument. It began from the assumption that I can be morally required to make some effort to save another person's life directly. And surely, nothing that has been said since has given us a reason to doubt *this*. Our argument for permission has done nothing to undermine it. As has

[e] Sect. 9.6. [f] Sect. 10.3, 'Drawing a Line'.

been pointed out already, there is no credible case for thinking that the requirement to save someone's life at small cost could be rejected from any impartial point of view that is appropriate to thinking about concern for others.[g] But, next, we have been given no grounds to challenge the life-saving analogy, either. The argument against the Extreme Demand has not supplied us with some further case, overlooked in Part I, for thinking that there is after all a morally important difference between helping directly and contributing to helping indirectly. And if not, then the argument of Part I still stands as a justification for thinking that we are morally required to make contributions of time and money to aid agencies.

Part II has not given us any grounds to doubt *these* claims. What it has shown instead is that we should not approach the life-saving analogy by iterating it. Iterating the life-saving analogy means treating each person I could contribute towards helping as though he were the *only* person needing help. But that leads to the Extreme Demand, and we have seen that this must be rejected. Requiring me to go this far in responding to other people's interests is requiring me to live an altruistically focused life; but that is something it does not make sense to require of me in responding to others' interests. We have found nothing wrong with the life-saving analogy itself. But we are justified in rejecting the kind of iterative approach to it that yields the Extreme Demand.

Part I has defended the life-saving analogy, but has shown that an iterative approach to it yields the Extreme Demand. Part II has shown that the Extreme Demand must be rejected. Together, then, they give us an argument for adopting the other possible approach to the life-saving analogy: an aggregative approach. We are justified, that is, in thinking that there is a degree of overall sacrifice beyond which you can defensibly refuse to contribute to giving life-saving help to other people, even though the cost of helping another individual is small. You cannot be required to restrict your personal spending down to the point at which your share of the cost of saving one more person would be great enough to justify you in refusing. You are justified, instead, in appealing to the size of the overall sacrifice you have made, and treating the significance of that overall sacrifice as a ground for being unwilling to do more.

What this means is that the argument for requirement that we are looking for was supplied in Part I. In Part II, the aim has been to identify the point at which the case given in Part I for requiring me to contribute towards helping other people can be met. That case can be met when my overall sacrifice is large enough: this is something I can sensibly appeal to in order to justify an unwillingness to go further. But before my overall sacrifice has become this large, that case remains undefeated. So it generates requirements on me to continue to help.

[g] Sect. 7.4.

Thus, although we should reject the Extreme Demand, we should accept instead the following parallel but different claim:

> I am morally required to keep contributing my time and money to aid agencies (or to some other comparably important cause) until either:
>
> (*a*) there are no longer any lives to be saved (or comparably important goals achieved) by those agencies, or
>
> (*b*) extending further my overall contribution to our collectively saving lives (or achieving something comparably important) would be a large enough sacrifice to excuse my refusing to contribute.

Instead of talking, as the Extreme Demand did, about my share of the cost saving one further life, clause (*b*) now focuses on my *overall* contribution to saving lives. How large must this overall contribution be in order to justify an unwillingness to go further? Part II has answered that question. The past chapter and a half has spelt out the kinds of life, the goods pursued within them, and the amount of spending on those goods, that are morally permissible.

Notice that there is something we still need to explain. Chapter 5 presented an argument for favouring an iterative over an aggregative approach to the life-saving analogy. We have found that the conclusion of that argument is wrong. However, we have yet to identify the fault in the reasoning leading to that conclusion. Spelling out that fault is something I shall leave until the final chapter.

10.3 THE MORAL DEMANDS OF AFFLUENCE

We have arrived at an account of the moral demands of affluence: it tells us which forms of personal spending are morally defensible, and which restrictions are morally required. According to the argument for permission, if certain conditions are satisfied, I violate no requirement of beneficence. The argument for requirement (derived from Part I) adds that if those same conditions are not satisfied, then I *do* violate a requirement of beneficence. Beneficence requires me to contribute towards helping other people who desperately need it, until my overall sacrifice is large enough for me to be able to invoke the argument for permission to justify refusing to go further.

Putting the argument for permission and the argument for requirement together, the conclusion they jointly generate is this:

> I am required to keep contributing my time and money to aid agencies (or to some other comparably important cause), until I reach an overall

level of personal spending for which either:

(i) its permissibility is entailed by the permissibility of living a particular kind of life or the permissibility of pursuing a particular good or class of goods, or

(ii) restricting it further would be a requirement-grounding loss.

To interpret this conclusion, we need to read it in conjunction with Chapter 9. Its implications can be summed up as follows. I can justify refusing to reduce my personal spending any further when, but only when, one of the following is true:

It would deprive me of a non-altruistically-directed life.

It would worsen my life by a requirement-grounding amount.

It would deprive me of a good that is better than the alternatives by a requirement-grounding amount.

It would deprive me of a commitment good.

I can justifiably live a non-altruistically-directed life, and I can justifiably refuse to relinquish commitment goods, even when there are alternatives that would be no worse for me. But otherwise, I am morally required to sustain my overall personal spending at a level for which restricting it further would be a requirement-grounding loss.

Is there Another Argument for Permission?

My overall strategy of argument in the past two chapters has been simple. I have presented an argument for permission, and have then argued that, for those forms of spending that are not defended by any argument for permission, Part I still supplies an argument requiring us to renounce them.

This leaves open a possibility that ought to be acknowledged. In developing an argument for permission, I have used one particular strategy, extending the kind of argument that was used against the Extreme Demand. However, I have not tried to show that this is the only successful strategy of argument for permission. For one thing, I have only maintained that, when a proposed standard of requirement for beneficence can be impartially rejected, that is *sufficient* to justify its rejection; but not that it is *necessary*. Perhaps there is a way of rejecting a proposed standard of requirement for beneficence without showing that it can be impartially rejected. But in addition, I have said nothing to guarantee that the only way to show that a standard of requirement for beneficence can be impartially rejected is by means of the particular kind of argument I have developed here, appealing to 'requirement-grounding' benefits and losses.

This leaves open the possibility that other arguments for permission could establish more robust conclusions, and thus limit further the reach of the argument for requirement presented in Part I. Having said that, though, it is up to someone who thinks that there is a stronger argument for permission to produce it. And in advance of that, while it must be acknowledged that I have not argued against the possibility of producing such an argument, we have no reason for thinking that there actually is one.

Drawing a Line

According to the conclusion we have reached, one of the conditions under which I can justifiably stop restricting my personal spending is when:

(ii) restricting it further would be a requirement-grounding loss.

It might seem that this condition will never be satisfied. Whatever your current level of personal spending, you could always make some further restriction without a requirement-grounding loss. Let me now respond to this apparent problem. It relies either on a misreading of clause (ii), or a fallacy.

First, the misreading. Clause (ii) had better not be read as saying that, in order to justifiably stop restricting my personal spending, I must have reached the point at which any further incremental restriction would *itself* constitute a requirement-grounding loss. For that amounts to an iterative approach to the sacrifices I am required to make to help other people. And we have seen that this must be rejected in favour of an aggregative approach. What I should be asking is whether, if I were to restrict my personal spending further, that would make my *overall* restriction in personal spending large enough to be a requirement-grounding loss.

But this leads to a second worry. Surely there is no sharp boundary between an overall restriction in personal spending that is a requirement-grounding loss and one that is not. If, so far, my overall restriction in personal spending is not large enough to be a requirement-grounding loss, then there will always be *some* further incremental sacrifice I could make without my overall restriction becoming that large. So it still looks as though clause (ii) will never be satisfied.

However, now there is a danger of committing a fallacy. I cannot be required to keep on giving up increments of my time and money until the next increment would itself make the difference between an overall sacrifice that is not requirement-grounding and one that is. For, given the absence of a sharp boundary, my overall sacrifice might be requirement-grounding even though no incremental sacrifice itself has made this difference. And an overall sacrifice that is requirement-grounding is one I can justifiably refuse to make. Of course, there are sorites puzzles about how it can be possible for me to suffer a requirement-grounding loss through making a series of incremental sacrifices none of which makes the difference between not suffering such a loss and suffering it. But this should not make us doubt that I can suffer such a loss through making a series of incremental sacrifices none of which makes this difference. After all, what makes sorites puzzles so puzzling is that this form of reasoning is fallacious.[4]

I am justified, then, in not thinking that I must keep on giving up increments of my time and money until the next increment would itself make the difference between an overall sacrifice that is not requirement-grounding and one that is. Instead, I am justified in asking what line it is reasonable for me to draw between the overall sacrifices that are and are not requirement-grounding.[5] It is reasonable to draw such a line, and reasonable not to cross this line once drawn. Of course, I should not make any bogus pretence of precision when I do so. The absence of a sharp boundary means that there will be no exactly correct answer. I am justified in stopping before my overall sacrifice is excessive. But there is no incremental sacrifice which is the last one I am able to make before my overall sacrifice becomes excessive.[6]

The point I am making can be summed up simply. Clause (ii) should not be read as saying that 'there is no further incremental sacrifice that I could make without my overall restriction becoming large enough to be a requirement-grounding loss'. Instead, it should be read as saying that 'I have come to the line it is reasonable for me to draw between the overall restrictions in personal spending that are not large enough to be a requirement-grounding loss, and those that are'.

This does not mean that wherever I choose to draw this line is right. The question that will arise for any given degree of personal sacrifice is in what ways it leaves me worse off. And this is not settled by my say-so. I might be wrong about this in one of two ways. I might have false views about whether a certain degree of monetary restriction will restrict my ability to perform a certain kind of action. Or I might have false views about whether performing that action is central to pursuing a given life-enhancing good. Clearly, there is scope for debate and disagreement about what is central and what is peripheral to the pursuit of various different life-enhancing goods. Some examples will be discussed shortly. It is in the resolution of these evaluative questions that the defensibility of a person's policy of personal spending ultimately lies.

10.4 WHICH AGGREGATIVE APPROACH DOES THIS GIVE US?

I have defended an aggregative approach to thinking about how far we are morally required to go in helping other people. But there are many different possible aggregative approaches, and they vary greatly from each other. Which of these different aggregative approaches is the one we have arrived at?

What all aggregative approaches have in common is the denial that, to work out the overall sacrifice that can be required to contribute towards helping several people, we should sum the separate sacrifices that could be required to contribute towards helping each individual person if he were the only remaining person needing help. However, as we saw in Chapter 5, this leaves open various possible ways of specifying that overall sacrifice. We noticed four main dimensions of variation.[h] An aggregative view can specify the overall sacrifice required of us in terms of time and money directly, or other goods which they can secure; it can measure this sacrifice in terms of an amount given up, or an amount retained; and it can treat this sacrifice synchronically or diachronically. The fourth dimension of variation concerns the different claims that can be made about the relationship between the size of the sacrifice I am required to make and the number of people I could contribute towards helping. One kind of aggregative view holds that, whatever the number of people who need help, the maximum sacrifice that can be morally required to contribute towards helping them is the same. But other versions deny this, holding that the sacrifice that can be required to contribute towards helping other people varies as a function of the number of people who need help.

We can now spell out the kind of aggregative view that has been supported by the arguments of this book, in relation to these four dimensions of variation.

First, it is clear that the size of the overall sacrifice it requires of us is not to be specified directly in terms of time and money. What is morally significant is the extent to which my commitment to, or pursuit of, intrinsically life-enhancing goods is being compromised, in the various ways spelt out above. Secondly, if sacrifices are being measured in this way, then it is more accurate to say that they are being measured in terms of the amount you are left with than the amount you are required to give up. The question for me to ask about a given level of personal spending is what impact it has on my commitment to, or pursuit of, such goods. And as far as I can see, the answer to *this* question will be unaffected by the amount of personal resources I had to begin with. In Chapter 9 we were unable to find a defence of the pursuit of expensive life-enhancing goods when there are cheaper alternatives that would be no worse for a person. The richer are thus required, on this view, to give up a greater proportion of their wealth than the less rich, in order to arrive at the same degree of restriction in their ability to pursue life-enhancing goods. However, I have not defended the view that the same material amount of personal spending is required of everyone. Given the variation in the life-enhancing goods around which different people's lives are structured, there will be a variation in the amount of time and money they can defensibly spend on themselves.

On the third question—whether sacrifices should be treated synchronically or diachronically—we should say this. I need to ask myself whether sacrifices

[h] Sect. 5.4.

I have made for others in the past affect the extent to which giving something else up now compromises my commitment to, or pursuit of, life-enhancing goods. And the answer may well be that they do. For when my overall sacrifice is assessed, on this aggregative view, what is being assessed is the impact on my life as a whole. This gives us a clear sense in which sacrifices are being calculated diachronically. However, it is not as if I have a kind of moral account extending across my life, into which I can deposit moral credit until I have made the cumulative sacrifice for other people that is required of me, at which point I can stop helping people thereafter. Rather, what is being assessed is whether my overall policy of personal spending involves restricting it in a way that makes it reasonable to think that going further would be a requirement-grounding loss. I *now* ought to be restricting my personal spending in line with this policy; and this makes it hard to see how a policy of ceasing to make any further sacrifices beyond a certain date could be defensible.

The final element of our aggregative view is the relationship it gives us between the amount that can be required of me to contribute towards helping a single person, and the amount that can be required to contribute towards helping several. What is the relationship between these amounts?

First, notice that my account has implications for situations in which help can be given to needy people directly, as well as those in which it involves contributions to a collective action. The aim has been to say how far each of us can be morally required to go in contributing to collective actions of beneficence. But this has been approached by answering a more general question: how far can requirements of beneficence extend overall? And that has implications for how far I could be required to go in helping needy people directly on my own. If there were many people whose lives I could save directly, the argument of Part II of this book would tell me how far I could be morally required to go in that situation too.

The primary concern in this book has been to identify what beneficence requires of us overall, and we now have an account of that. How does this relate to what can be required of me to help, or to contribute to helping, a single person? The short answer is an agnostic one. The account given so far is consistent with either holding or denying that a lesser amount is required in the single-person case. When the question arose earlier of how much a person can be morally required to sacrifice to save someone else's life directly, I simply referred to the broad 'common-sense' view that sacrifices of money and time that are merely inconvenient can be required, but not risking death, permanent injury, or the impairment of your life prospects.[i] This 'common-sense' view is consistent with my account; and a more specific answer is not required by that account.

[i] Sect. 5.1.

Having said this, however, there is a simple argument that suggests itself at this point. I have given an account of the maximum sacrifice that can be required of me in responding to the interests of several other people in my life-saving help. Given this, why should any *less* be required of me in relation to a single needy person? Once I have reached a point at which I can defensibly refuse to impose a requirement-grounding loss on myself, I can explain why requiring me to go further would be asking too much. But what can I say to justify an unwillingness to go that far? Perhaps there is an answer to this question. But I cannot see what it is. And without it, we ought to take the account of what can be morally required of me to save, or contribute to saving, several lives to serve equally as an account of what can be morally required of me to save, or contribute to saving, one. Indeed, the account I have offered does look recognizable as a way of describing the kind of sacrifice we take to be heroic in relation to saving a single life. Once a sacrifice is large enough to have a significant life-impairing impact on me, we start to think of it as heroic rather than morally required. However, whether or not this view agrees with 'common sense', it is the view for which I have offered a justification.[7]

10.5 PRACTICAL IMPLICATIONS

A few pages ago I summed up the implications of my view as follows. I can justify refusing to reduce my personal spending any further when, but only when, one of the following is true:

> It would deprive me of a non-altruistically-directed life.
>
> It would worsen my life by a requirement-grounding amount.
>
> It would deprive me of a good that is better than the alternatives by a requirement-grounding amount.
>
> It would deprive me of a commitment good.

When we apply this as a test for morally permissible personal spending, what does it mean in practice?

I do not think it makes sense to aim for some general description, applicable to everyone, of all the particular forms of spending that are permissible and impermissible according to this test. What passes or fails the test will depend on what is life-enhancing for a person, and this varies according to the circumstances and constituents of a life. Different levels of spending will be defensible, depending on the goods around which different lives are structured. The requirement-grounding goods around which your life is structured may be more expensive than the ones that occupy my life, and if so, my personal spending ought to be lower than yours. In saying this, I am not saying that the mere fact that you happen to be pursuing certain goods legitimizes them: if cheaper ones would not be substantially worse for you, pursuing expensive non-commitment goods cannot be defended. However, the friendships you and I form may require different levels of spending, and our different aptitudes may mean that the fields of achievement that would be most life-enhancing for you may be more expensive than the ones that would be most fulfilling for me.

Moreover, for any given individual, there will not be an exact answer to the question how much personal spending passes this test. Clearly, there are forms of restriction in the amount I spend in connection with my friendships that I can observe without compromising my commitment to my friends (and which are therefore required of me), and forms of restriction which I would be unable to impose without losing the wholeheartedness of my commitment to them—the kind of wholeheartedness that I can be required to support in others. But it is not as if there is an exact point demarcating these forms of restriction from each other. Nor is that an objection to the view I am advocating. What is being defended is an aggregative approach to required personal sacrifice, and we should expect that the line that such an approach justifies us in drawing is one that could with equal justification have been drawn elsewhere.

Having said this, I do think there are some forms of spending that are ruled out, and some that are ruled in, for almost everyone. We shall come to these shortly. But first of all, the whole idea of subjecting forms of personal spending to a test such as the one offered above needs to be defended against a powerful misgiving. As a prescription for the kind of practical deliberation that should preoccupy a morally good agent, this seems forbiddingly unattractive. Am I proposing that whenever someone walks around a supermarket, he should be pestering himself with the question whether forgoing this purchase in favour of a cheaper alternative would make his life substantially worse? If so, it seems plain that the answer to that question would almost always be No. But this seems intolerable. A life consumed by thinking in this niggardly way would be thoroughly repellent: it would involve the kind of 'moral fanaticism' or 'moral totalitarianism' sometimes complained of by critics of utilitarianism.[8]

How to Deliberate about Personal Spending

It is important to see that the repellence of this outlook is precisely why my argument does not entail it. For having this outlook would itself worsen your life enough to justify refusing to adopt it. Earlier, I argued that pursuing purely episodic goods is morally defensible:[j] a similar point shows what

[j] Sect. 9.5, 'A Distinction between Goods'.

is wrong with the idea of constantly evaluating every purchase to decide whether it is dispensable. The problem with allowing this to monopolize your thoughts is that it would threaten to take over your life, interfering with your receptiveness and commitment to genuine goods. Of course, that is a large part of the tragedy of poverty for the many people whom it afflicts. But that only strengthens the case for denying that it can be morally required of anyone. A life would be made substantially worse by being taken over by concerns about spending in this way. There is no bias towards the well-off in saying this: the poor have a clear case for thinking that this is one of the principal evils they suffer. But if so, this deliberative attitude can defensibly be resisted.

My argument does not require a puritanical and continual self-vigilance in relation to money; but if not, what deliberative policy does it require? The alternative is to assess your overall level of spending on yourself at periodic intervals. Doing so annually, for instance, would seem as sensible as any other interval. In doing so, you ought to review the amounts you have spent on yourself and given away over the past year, and ask yourself whether your life is being substantially compromised by your restriction in spending on yourself—interpreting this question in the appropriate way, where 'substantially' means substantially enough to worsen your life in a requirement-grounding way, or to otherwise compromise your ability to lead the kind of life or pursue the kinds of good that can be defended by means of the arguments in Chapter 9. If the answer is Yes—*the* answer, and not just your answer—then there is nothing morally wrong in reducing the amount you give away. If it is No, it would be wrong not to give away more.[9] Once you have deliberated in this way about your overall budget for personal spending, you will be justified in not reopening questions of moral permissibility whenever you spend money.

Having said this, there seems to be nothing wrong with requiring us to think about major outlays by subjecting them directly to the test that has been set out. Requiring us to ask of every purchase we make whether it is right or wrong would be a life-stunting imposition. But asking whether a certain amount is the right amount to spend on a car would not. After all, most of us deliberate a lot about large-scale spending already. Granted, there are few people who make such decisions by asking what is the *morally* right amount to spend. But the view that we ought to conduct such decisions, along with overall budgetary decisions that govern smaller purchases, in the way I am recommending clearly cannot be rejected on the grounds that it is unduly intrusive. It is no more intrusive than the deliberating we already do.

Some Examples

When we do this thinking, what should we conclude? As far as I can see, there are some kinds of personal spending that clearly fail our test for almost everyone, some that clearly pass it for almost everyone, and some for which it all depends on the circumstances of the case. Let me now give some examples.

First, it seems clear that, on the view we have arrived at, expensive purchases that are made purely for the sake of enjoyment are morally indefensible. When we ask whether there is an alternative, cheaper source of enjoyment that would involve no substantially life-diminishing loss to you, the answer will always be Yes. As far as I can see, this means that buying expensive clothes or furniture, a new car (or often, any car at all), or books for a private library is usually morally wrong, as the world now stands. It is not as if there is anything about these objects as such that makes it wrong to spend money on them: for some people it will be right. Buying these things might in some circumstances make a great enough instrumental contribution to other life-enhancing goods to justify them—where a person lacks alternative means of access to transport or books. But if not, there will be cheaper ways of living that make your life no worse.

Let me be clear about this. I am not making the puritanical claim that enjoying the comfort produced by owning expensive goods, or simply enjoying the ownership of them, is in itself bad. On the contrary: as far as I can see, these forms of enjoyment are just as good as any others. However, although these forms of enjoyment are goods, they are not goods that can reasonably be invoked to justify not joining in efforts to help other people. To do that, I should have to be able to defend choosing *these* forms of enjoyment over other, cheaper forms in preference to joining in efforts to help people who have nothing. And it is difficult to see how there could be a convincing case for thinking that. *These* forms of spending cannot sensibly be invoked in the course of explaining to the destitute why, impartially speaking, my spending my resources on commitments of personal significance must be held to be acceptable.

I am not even saying that, as things stand, it is wrong to buy things for the sake of enjoyment. For I have said that there are two kinds of spending decision that need to be subjected to the proposed test of moral acceptability: decisions about your budget for routine spending, and decisions about major, out-of-the-ordinary purchases. Buying a car falls into the latter category. But picking something off the supermarket shelf belongs to the former. There is nothing wrong with making *these* choices for reasons of enjoyment. Why not? Because of the case for making your day-to-day life free from constant self-scrutiny. Your routine spending should be governed by an overall budget that is morally defensible; but, in spending the amount which that budget allows you, there is nothing wrong with doing so from motives of enjoyment.

There are some major forms of spending that, it seems, will usually pass our test. I think this is true of spending on one's own education, including the kind of expensive tertiary education that is available to relatively few people, globally speaking. For it is almost always reasonable to believe that this will substantially advance a person's understanding, achievements, and participation in a culture, throughout her later life. If so, it will be defensible, in virtue of the life-enhancing value of these goods. The same argument would appear to justify spending on private tuition and equipment to develop an outstanding sporting or musical talent. In general, developing your talents will enhance your achievements and understanding.[10] Clearly, the reasonableness of thinking that spending of these kinds will substantially contribute to improving a person's life will depend on the reasonableness of believing in the talent of the recipient. So expensive music lessons (or instruments) for the talentless seem hard to justify. However, up to a point, it seems sensible to see tuition in music, drama, and other arts as making an important contribution to the goods of understanding and participation in a culture, even for the talentless.[11]

For many other forms of personal spending, however, it will not make sense to offer such neat judgements. They will sometimes be defensible, sometimes not, and most commonly they will be partly defensible and partly indefensible, with the circumstances of the case being all-important in determining just what we should say. Let me illustrate this with a single example: holiday travel. If this simply amounts to enjoyable tourism, then (like all of the other goods that have been discussed) it seems hard to deny that it is good for those who do it, and plausible to maintain it makes their lives better. However, like other expensive enjoyments, it is hard to see how it can qualify on these grounds as morally defensible. Expensive enjoyments are replaceable without life-diminishing loss by cheaper ones. However, this is only to say that defending holiday travel simply as a form of enjoyment looks unconvincing. The important further question to pursue will concern what contribution it makes to your personal development, or the growth of life-enhancing personal relationships—or to what extent the relaxation it involves is instrumental to the attainment of other goods. And when we ask this question, the only sensible answer will be that this contribution varies greatly from one case to the next.

Do not make the mistake of thinking that this is a way of letting us all morally off the hook. I am not saying that whether your life would be substantially worse without expensive holidays depends on whether you *think* your life would be stunted without them. The question is whether it *would* be. But whether it makes sense to think this depends on the circumstances of your case—in just what important respects your life would be worse if you spent less.

I will not attempt to give a full survey of all the categories of personal spending covered by my view. That would be a tedious exercise: it would simply mean repeating, in relation to other kinds of spending, the points I have made so far. But before I conclude, I ought briefly to discuss the application of my view to two other prominent objects of personal spending: children and investments.

A parent can, I think, invoke the argument that has been presented here to defend spending on her children. To require her to give this up would be to require her to compromise fundamentally her commitment to her children, and that is something she can permissibly refuse to do, for the reasons I have given. But that is not to say that every form of spending on your children is morally defensible. The important point to bring out here is an analogue of one made about friendship earlier.[k] The defensible forms of spending on children are those without which the full commitment of a parent to her child would be compromised: for it is the value of this commitment-good that is being appealed to in rejecting a more restrictive standard of requirement. But this will not suffice to defend every way in which you might benefit your child. If it is good for my son to get a bike, it looks as though it will be better for him to get a better bike. Perhaps we should even say that his life as a whole will go a little bit better if he gets the better bike and all else is equal. However, it would be very odd to hold that if I refrain from getting him the better bike, that compromises my commitment to my child. It is only benefits that are bound up in this way in the commitment of parent to child that are the ones on which personal spending is defensible.

Finally, there is no obstacle in what has been said here to the permissibility of investing money to increase your wealth. It is what you spend it on after you have invested it that raises the moral questions I have been concerned with. Of course, if you invest it to the exclusion of helping people in dire need, then that plainly leaves you open to criticism. And if you invest it recklessly, then there will be an objection of moral irresponsibility to be levelled against you, and not just one of imprudence. But these possibilities aside, my argument will not lead to the conclusion that personal investments are wrong.[12] Protecting the various life-enhancing commitments that I can defensibly pursue will give me a reason to seek financial security, and if I do not indefensibly spend the money I have invested once I have cashed in the investment, then there is no objection to raise.

Finding the Right Level

I have not attempted to formulate these remarks on the practical consequences of my view as a clear-cut set of universal prescriptions. But I think that what I have said makes it sensible to doubt whether that could be an appropriate aim of this discussion. What I have done is to set out clearly the terms in which, according to the argument presented here, practical

[k] Sect. 8.1.

deliberation about personal spending should be conducted, given the needs of others in the world we currently inhabit. The right policy is to set yourself a budget, and ask yourself whether your life is substantially diminished by adopting the constraints you do. Questions about how well your life is going are not easy, but they are familiar. We all think about these questions anyway: my conclusion is a conclusion about the way in which we should raise them. Thus, there is no special psychological strain involved in the picture of deliberation I am recommending. It may still seem that there is an unpleasantly puritanical-seeming air to it. But this cannot be because it would make us obsessed with not enjoying ourselves. Rather, the principal form of deliberation I have talked about concerns the budget we set ourselves within which to seek fulfilment and enjoyment. If it is genuinely for reasons of a constricted budget that we are lacking these things, then my view tells us to raise it.

The brevity of this discussion may make it sound as though deliberating about the impact that your level of spending on yourself has upon your ability to live a good life is rather simple. On the contrary, these are delicate questions. If I am thinking about the extent to which my monetary sacrifices are impairing my personal relationships, for example, I will need to pursue this by thinking about the particular respects in which this may be the case, and tackling the counterfactual question of how those relationships would genuinely be improved by spending more money. But although these questions are delicate, they are not impossible. Indeed, most of us have plenty of experience in thinking about the course our lives are taking and how they might be improved. And this—at least, given the appropriate conception of life-enhancing goods—is the right issue for us to be thinking about.

My view could be described as a moderately demanding one. It does not yield an extremely demanding moral outlook, in the sense outlined in Chapter 5. It is revisionary, though, in a demanding direction. There are monetary sacrifices that each of us could make without depriving our lives of worthwhile achievement, enjoyment, close personal relationships, community involvement, understanding, integrity, or autonomy to any significant degree—certainly not enough to make our lives substantially worse. I have argued that it is morally wrong for us not to make them.

11

Overview

THE two parts of this book have combined to answer the question raised at the start: the question how much an affluent person ought to be doing for the very poor. In this final chapter we ought to stand back and take an overview of that answer and the argument that has led us to it. What kind of argument has it been, how do its different parts fit together, and how far does its conclusion reach?

Part I gave us an argument that seemed to lead to an extremely demanding conclusion. That conclusion has been rejected in Part II, and a more moderately demanding outlook proposed in its place. It is the more moderately demanding view, I have argued, which should in fact be drawn from the book's opening reflections about the analogy between saving a life directly and contributing to an aid agency. However, while I have attacked and replaced the conclusion of the argument presented in Part I, I have not yet identified exactly what mistake was made in the reasoning that led to it. We do already know broadly where to look. The discussion in Part II, as we have seen, gives us no grounds to fault the life-saving analogy itself. What it does show, I have argued, is that we ought to reject the iterative approach to this analogy in favour of an aggregative one. But a forceful-looking argument was given in Chapter 5 for taking the iterative approach. What remains to be explained is just what was wrong with that argument.

I should also clarify the scope of the conclusion for which I have been arguing. It might seem as though I have been arguing that extreme personal sacrifices cannot be morally demanded of individuals. But I do not think that this blanket claim is true; nor is it supported by the argument presented here. The conclusion I have reached is a more qualified one. I need to spell out exactly what the qualifications are.

Last of all, I shall quickly survey some of the strengths of the argument I have set out. Part I closed with a list of requirements that need to be met by a convincing response to the problem of demandingness generated by the life-saving analogy. I shall explain how the argument of Part II has met them.

11.1 FAULTING THE ARGUMENT OF PART I

In Part I we saw that iterating the life-saving analogy leads to an extremely demanding conclusion. Part II has argued that that conclusion must be wrong: it would require us to compromise impartially acceptable personal commitments in a fundamental way, and that is something we can reasonably refuse to do.

However, it has not yet been explained what was wrong with the argument *for* the iterative approach, presented in Chapter 5.[a] This involved a simple but powerful-looking thought. For each of the individuals whom a beneficent person could help, her reason for helping is *that he needs help*, and not simply that *this action furthers the interests of other people*. But that makes it hard to see how what she has done for others could ever properly be treated as countervailing against her reason for contributing towards helping the next person. If the cost to her of doing this remains small, how can she properly appeal to what she has done for others to justify a refusal to contribute to helping *him*?

It might be complained that Part II gets us no closer to explaining how what I have done for *others* is relevant to what I can be required to do to contribute to helping the next person. Worse, it might even seem to be begging the question. Grant that I can defensibly refuse to undergo a requirement-grounding loss in contributing towards helping others: does this not simply leave open whether to take an aggregative or an iterative approach towards requirement grounding losses? Given a series of incremental sacrifices I could make, there are two very different questions I can ask: 'Does my overall sacrifice amount to a requirement-grounding loss?' versus 'Would the next incremental sacrifice amount to a requirement-grounding loss?' The objection being made against an iterative approach is that taking this approach leads me, *overall*, to undergo a requirement-grounding loss. But proponents of the iterative approach are claiming that a relevant justification for ceasing to contribute towards helping others must be based on the cost of a contribution to helping the next person, not on the overall cost of such contributions.

However, the previous chapters have not begged the question against the iterative approach: they have shown why it must be rejected. The iterative approach requires me to keep on making personal sacrifices until the next incremental sacrifice would itself amount to a requirement-grounding loss. But meeting that standard of requirement would mean compromising my commitment to life-enhancing goods in a way that I can defensibly refuse to do. The argument, therefore, has not begged the question. It has shown why approaching personal life-enhancing goods as

[a] Sect. 5.5, 'Reply: The Case for an Iterative Approach'.

the iterative approach would require is something we can defensibly refuse to do.

How has this shown up a fault in the argument for the iterative approach? What seems right about that argument is that surely it *is* hard to see how I can justify refusing to contribute towards helping one person by appealing to what I have done for others. However, it should now be possible to see that *this* is not the justification proposed by the argument of Part II. Rather, it tells me that I can justify my decision to limit the contributions I make towards helping other people as follows. It is reasonable for me to have a policy of contributing towards helping others that allows me to retain a defensible engagement with my own projects, relationships, and other life-enhancing goods, while recognizing the claims that other people's interests make on me. But having such a policy makes it reasonable for me to stop contributing towards helping other people before I reach the point at which my share of the cost of helping one more person would itself involve a requirement-grounding sacrifice. If I undertook to contribute towards helping every person for whom my share of the cost of helping was small, the effect of this would be to impose a requirement-grounding loss on me. But it is impartially acceptable, and therefore reasonable, for me to refuse to do that. This is not a justification for doing nothing. But it is a justification for making a reasonable judgement about how much I can afford to give away without undergoing a requirement-grounding loss, and refusing to give away more. I am not appealing to what I have done for others to justify an unwillingness to contribute towards helping the next person. I am appealing to the reasonableness of my having a policy of contributing to helping other people that still allows me to retain a defensible engagement with life-enhancing goods.

It does seem right to insist that a beneficent person's reason for helping a needy person is *that he needs help*. And it does seem right that what she has done for others is not itself an appropriately countervailing consideration. But the mistake contained in the argument for the iterative approach is its assumption that there is no *other* countervailing consideration. What Part II has given us is an extended argument for thinking that it is reasonable for a beneficent person to refuse to worsen her life to a requirement-grounding degree in order to help other people, and for treating *this* as an appropriately countervailing consideration in relation to beneficence. What that argument shows is *why* it must be legitimate for me to defend my unwillingness to save the next person by appealing to considerations of overall cost. I can legitimately constrain my willingness to contribute towards helping others by reference to my engagement with defensible life-enhancing goods. But having this engagement is incompatible with an iterative approach to the demands of beneficence.

11.2 BEGGING THE QUESTION?

The argument for permission developed in Part II takes a distinctive form. Its strategy is to tie together the question how far I can be morally required to go in helping others, and the question which of my interests ground requirements on others to help me. What ties these questions together is the principle that my interests in getting what it is wrong to have cannot ground requirements on others to help me. Against the problem of demandingness generated in Part I, this gives us an effective strategy of reply. The starting-point for Part I is that beneficence can obviously require us to save other people's lives. That *is* obvious. But it is no less obvious that beneficence can require us to help people in other important ways. And if so, then the interests that ground those requirements must be interests that it is not wrong to satisfy.

I just discussed the question whether my argument for an aggregative approach begs the question against an iterative approach. There are other ways in which my argument for permission might be thought, in appealing to claims about 'what it is absurd to deny', to beg the question against a more demanding view. I responded to one of these earlier.[b] My argument does not simply reduce to the assertion that it is absurd to deny that the requirements of beneficence are not extreme. Rather, what it is doing is to point out the way in which facts about what beneficence *does* require have implications for what it does not require.

However, there is a further worry about begging the question that should also be addressed. Suppose I can see that your suit is about to be dirtied, and I could easily prevent this. You haven't noticed that it is about to slip off the coathanger you are carrying, and I could point this out without being a busybody or treating you like a child. Then arguably, it would be wrong not to do so: beneficence requires me to do it. And it will only make sense to say that I am required to help you not to dirty your suit if it is morally permissible for you, in these circumstances, to stop your suit from being dirtied. However, what that establishes is limited. Obviously, this does not mean that it is morally permissible for you always and everywhere to do what is required to stop your suit from being dirtied. If saving someone's life directly means dirtying your suit, then you are morally required to dirty your suit. And if I know this, I am obviously *not* required to help you avoid dirtying your suit when it means letting someone die.

The worry, then, is this. It is only obvious what interests I can be required to help you to pursue in a given situation if it is already obvious what interests you are morally entitled to pursue in that situation. So claims about the interests that are 'requirement-grounding' already presuppose claims about

[b] Sect. 9.2, 'What it is Absurd to Deny'.

the interests it is permissible to pursue. Turning back to the kinds of judgement that occupied Chapters 8–10, the problem can be put like this. It may seem obvious that I can be required to help you pursue your musical career when it is easy for me to do so. But this will only seem obvious if we are already presupposing that pursuing your musical career is something it is morally permissible for you to do. It is not an argument for that conclusion. To suggest that it is begs the question against someone with an extremely demanding moral outlook—someone who thinks that musical careers ought not to be pursued while others are starving.

The reply to this objection is that it confuses entailment with priority. My argument does rely on claiming that I can be required to help you get or retain a good only if you are morally entitled to get or retain it. However, that does not mean that we must have some way of independently establishing claims about what people are morally entitled to get or retain, prior to deriving any conclusions about the help we are required to give each other. On the contrary: the example just used in stating the objection shows that that priority-claim itself has to be wrong. When someone's life is at stake, the reason you are not entitled to retain a clean suit is *because* you are required to help him. This is not to say that the priority runs in the other direction: it is not as if claims about the help we are required to give each other can be established prior to and independently of facts about what people are morally entitled to get or retain. Examples of the kind mentioned in Chapter 8, where I am not required to help you because your purposes are bad (you are a gangster with a jammed gun, for example), suffice to show that. Rather, the right thing to say is that facts about what people are morally entitled to get or retain and facts about the help we are required to give each other are interdependent. *This* is what my argument is relying on. An extremely demanding view has radical consequences for the kinds of interests that are requirement-grounding. So if an argument for that demanding view starts from observations about the interests that *are* obviously requirement-grounding, it faces a decisive objection.

My reply is effective against the kind of argument developed in Part I. It would not be effective against a more radical argument that purports to show why our conception of what beneficence requires (what it does require, rather than how those requirements are limited) must be overturned completely. This possibility has to be acknowledged. However, suffice it to say that I cannot see how an argument of that more radical kind could be made to look convincing, and that nothing we have seen here supports it.

11.3 THE SCOPE OF THE ARGUMENT

I have argued that there are limits to what can be morally required of us out of concern for other people's interests. These limits should not be thought of as sharply determinate; but that does not make it any less reasonable to advocate them, and live in accordance with them.

The scope of the conclusion established by this argument is restricted in an important way. It is a claim about the moral requirements of *beneficence*. It tells us what beneficence does morally require of us; and also what it does not. My conclusion is not the general claim that the demands of morality cannot be extreme. In fact, I think that general claim is false. Its falsity is not something I am going to try to establish here. But let me at least give some plausible examples of extremely demanding moral requirements, in order to explain how nothing in my argument stands in their way. The broad lines of the explanation are straightforward enough. I have been concerned to determine how much morality can sensibly demand of us, simply in response to others' interests in our help. The structure of the argument has been that it cannot be wrong for my willingness to respond to the interests of strangers to be constrained by my engagement with the life-enhancing goods that structure my own life. But others' interests in my help are not the only source of morally important reasons. Accordingly, nothing has been said here to resist the idea that the moral demands arising from other sources may still be extreme.

Required Self-Sacrifice

It seems that morality can sometimes demand a lot of us—that there can be cases where great self-sacrifice can be morally required.[c] If caring for your children turns out to be unexpectedly burdensome, you cannot simply dissociate yourself from them on the grounds that that would give you a better life; in wartime it may be wrong for you to refuse to risk your life along with others; if someone has been wrongly convicted of a capital crime that you have committed, it may be wrong to fail to give yourself up. Had I been arguing for the broad conclusion that great self-sacrifice can never be demanded of a person in order to contribute towards helping others, then I should have had to reject these judgements.

On the contrary, though, these examples illustrate three categories of morally required self-sacrifice that are, in fact, compatible with my argument. The first category contains obligations, understood as moral requirements assumed through an explicit act of commitment, and special duties, understood as requirements attaching to roles I occupy in relation to some but not all people.[1] Many requirements of these kinds cannot impartially be rejected, even though meeting them would be extremely demanding. And if not, the argument I have presented cannot stand in their way.

[c] Sect. 6.4, 'Problems'.

Take the example of parental responsibility. I might well prefer to see our current system of responsibility for the upbringing of children, in which that responsibility is borne by their parents, replaced by some alternative—a Spartan system, perhaps, in which child-rearing is entrusted to the state. Moreover, I might argue that this preference is impartially acceptable—it is acceptable from a point of view that does not unduly favour anyone's interests. However, what cannot be impartially acceptable is that, in a society in which the former system already prevails, I should be able to make an exception of myself. I have myself benefited from the prevailing system; no one else, given that this system prevails, can be fairly charged with the burden of looking after my children; and consequently, the costs to my children of being abandoned by me are great. Furthermore, I have the choice whether to assume parenthood and the attendant responsibilities or not. If, abstracting from my own situation, I ask whether this requirement is rejectable from an appropriately impartial point of view, then the answer is clearly No. So our argument—an argument against requirements of beneficence or fairness that are impartially rejectable—offers no resistance to strong requirements of parental responsibility.

If there is a duty to fight in a self-defensive war, it is arguably not a special duty or an obligation, as just defined. Rather, the best way to make the case for this is to characterize the wrongness of refusing to join in as a matter of free riding. Given our collective need for self-defence, it is wrong for me to rely on others' willingness to risk their lives to provide it while being unwilling to do so myself. This style of argument raises some large issues.[2] But if it is right, then there is no difficulty seeing how it can be endorsed alongside the earlier defence of spending on personal commitments. After all, when I ask whether the requirement to risk one's life by contributing to a collective act of self-defence is impartially rejectable, the answer will again be No.

It is easy to see how the third example, in which I have committed a capital crime, invites a similar treatment. Of course, if *I* am going to be the one who stands to lose my life by giving myself up, then I have a powerful incentive not to do so. However, if, from a point of view impartial between my predicament and everyone else's, we consider the demand that those who have committed crimes do not allow others to be punished in their place, it is hard to see how this demand could be rejectable.

I am not offering these brief remarks as complete discussions of these three issues. Rather, I am claiming only that *if* these are (as they appear to be) cases of required self-sacrifice, then the plausible justifications for thinking so are ones which my argument has no difficulty accommodating. I have defended a conclusion about the moral requirements generated by reasons of beneficence. It is compatible with allowing that requirements of great self-sacrifice are generated by other sources. Indeed, as far as I can see, there is no obstacle to accepting that morality may under some circumstances require you to sacrifice everything, by requiring your death.

I have argued this by giving examples of moral requirements that do not seem to be impartially rejectable. However, notice that even if a moral requirement *is* impartially rejectable, that will not suffice to show that my argument opposes it. In Chapter 7 I argued that standards of requirement for beneficence or fairness must not be impartially rejectable. But I gave no argument for thinking that this test applies to moral requirements of other kinds.[d] Nothing has been said here to justify applying a test of impartial acceptability to proposed requirements of loyalty, say, or integrity.

Arguments from Justice

In general, then, my argument is compatible with the existence of moral requirements of great self-sacrifice. Moreover, we should notice that it is even compatible with the idea that great self-sacrifice might, after all, be required of us in contributing to aid agencies. To see why, we need to recall the opening chapter.

At the start of the book I distinguished two common forms of argument for the wrongness of not giving money to aid agencies. The simpler of the two is the argument from beneficence on which I have concentrated—the argument that my relationship to the beneficiaries of aid agencies is morally analogous to my relationship to someone who stands directly in need of my life-saving help. I have been concerned to establish the plausibility, but also the limitations, of this first kind of argument. But that means I have left open what should be said about the second kind of argument. This kind of argument maintains that *justice* generates a collective responsibility on us to help the very poor, and that giving money to aid agencies is required of me in order to discharge my share of that collective responsibility. Arguments of this second form are independent of the first. But that means that nothing I have said here speaks against the thought that the demands *they* generate might turn out to be extreme.

Various different arguments from justice of this general form are possible. Three were identified at the start of Chapter 1: I called them arguments from rectificatory, distributive, and regulative justice.

According to the argument from rectificatory justice, we are collectively responsible for helping the poor, since we bear a collective responsibility for creating and sustaining their poverty. Our responsibility for the evils they suffer gives them a moral claim on our help. What ought I to do individually, in the light of this? The natural way to answer this is to identify what we ought collectively to be doing to rectify the injustice, and to maintain that

[d] Sect. 7.6.

each of us ought to contribute his fair share towards that collective task. And arguably, this is independent of whether others are actually doing their share.

Clearly, this strategy of argument raises several questions. If I am neither a colonialist nor an international financier, in virtue of what can I be said to participate in this collective responsibility? Is this responsibility divisible in such a way that shares of it can be discharged by some individuals independently of the rest? Are donations to voluntary non-government aid agencies an appropriate way to discharge *this* responsibility? And if there is a 'fair share' of the responsibility that could appropriately be discharged in this way, is it indeed right that it can be required from me when others are not complying?

Having distinguished this line of thought from the one I have pursued here, I am not about to open a discussion of these questions. I concentrated in Part I on arguing that even if we are *not* responsible for the destitution that other people suffer, it is wrong for us to do nothing about it. However, the point to bring out now is that it is also true that nothing that was said in Part II, about the limitations on these demands, addresses these thoughts about our collective responsibility for rectifying injustice. A case for the existence of requirements of rectificatory justice will be a case for thinking that those requirements cannot impartially be rejected. Thus, an argument of the form I have given cannot sensibly resist the idea that our personal commitments should be constrained by such requirements.

Would the moral demands generated by an argument from rectificatory justice be extreme? This is an important question, but also an involved one, and I shall have to leave it as beyond the scope of this book. Answering it would mean making an assessment of the overall cost of redressing past and present injustices to the poor, and then defending a method for allocating to each affluent person her fair share of that cost. And that would mean opening up the whole subject of the nature and extent of the injustices that the rich may be held to have done (and to be doing) to the poor. Perhaps the result of this enquiry would be that, given the actual global distribution of wealth, anyone's discharging her share of the claimed collective responsibility would mean making sacrifices which were not great. In fact, I am inclined to think that is right.[e] In that case, nothing would be added to our existing conclusion. But perhaps I am wrong about that, and the demands involved in discharging that responsibility are extreme. I cannot claim to have ruled out this possibility.

Another possibility that remains open is an argument from distributive justice. I have emphasized the difference between my own post-distributive question concerning the impartial evaluation of policies of personal spending,

[e] See Sect. 5.2.

and the different, distributive question that more naturally comes to mind when considering the different conceptions of impartiality I have discussed.[f] However, suppose we were to ask that distributive question: Which principles for collectively regulating the allocation of resources are impartially acceptable? Versions of the Priority View will reply that we must take into account the way in which everyone's interests would be affected by different candidate principles, and give priority to the interests of the worse-off. And if such distributive questions can properly be raised internationally, it is clear that we have not collectively adopted the distributive principles that are supported by many versions of *this* view. Suppose it could be shown that we ought to be, but are not, collectively adopting a set of distributive principles which eliminates destitution, on a global scale. What does this show about what I ought to do individually? Again, one plausible view (although not the only possible one)[3] is that I ought to do my share of what we all ought to be doing, even if others are not doing theirs. We collectively ought to be living according to these distributive principles; therefore I ought to be discharging my share of this collective responsibility, even when others are not.

Again, nothing I have said rules out the possibility that extreme moral demands might be derivable in this way. A lot would have to be done in order to sustain that argument—enough to fill another book, at least. A version of the Priority View would have to be defended as the appropriate conception of distributive impartiality; it would need to be shown that distributive questions can sensibly be raised on a global scale; and it would then have to be argued that it is wrong for me not to contribute unilaterally to my part of the distributive action which we ought collectively to be taking. I have not begun to discuss any of this. But nor has my argument provided any obstacle to thinking it could be done. Beyond this, the question of just how we should assess any affluent individual's fair share of the overall burden of helping the destitute would have to be tackled. But again, nothing has been said here to rule out ways of assessing it that place an extremely uncomfortable requirement on us. On especially strong versions of the Priority View, the collective demands on the affluent to redistribute their resources in favour of the destitute might be very great; some versions of the Fair Share View will require a large share of that redistribution to be taken by people like me.

A third possibility to notice is an argument objecting to the rules that currently govern international trade and financial accountability, on the grounds that they unfairly enforce others' poverty for our advantage. I dubbed this an argument from regulative justice: it raises an objection to the fairness of the rules governing international relations, without deriving this from the claim that the vastly unequal global pattern of goods-distribution

[f] Sect. 7.5, 'Distributive versus Post-Distributive Questions'.

is intrinsically unfair. If the rules are unfair, then it can be argued that we are collectively responsible for reforming them; and again perhaps that I ought to play my part in doing so even when others are not. Again, much more would need to be said to make all of this convincing; but once more, I have done nothing to preclude it.

In short, without having argued against any of this, it is hard to see how I could be entitled to rule out the possibility that arguments such as these will yield stronger moral demands than the ones I have advocated. For all I have shown to the contrary, there might be an argument from rectificatory, distributive, or regulative justice—or an argument of some other kind—showing that I am indeed required to impose substantial life-diminishing losses on myself in order to assist those who are much worse off. What I have argued is that such requirements cannot be generated by an argument from beneficence.

11.4 SAVING LIVES DIRECTLY

I have maintained that there is a line you can reasonably draw in relation to your personal spending, and that it is reasonable for you not to cross that line, even if your share of the cost of helping another desperately needy person is still very small. Suppose, then, you have drawn such a line, and are keeping to it. But suppose you *now* find yourself in an emergency situation in which someone's life needs to be saved directly by you at small cost—a cost as small as your share of the cost of our collectively saving someone's life through an aid agency. Can you now defensibly leave the person in front of you to die? It may seem that it is an implication of my argument that you can. The aggregative approach defended in Part II seems to allow you to ask yourself one question about how far beneficence can require you to go overall in helping or contributing towards helping other people. So if you can defensibly refuse to make another contribution to an aid agency, on the grounds that you have done enough overall, must it not then be equally defensible to say the same about a directly life-saving action? If there is any associated cost—even a very small one—you can say that you have already done enough for needy people overall. But that looks wrong. It is surely hard to accept that this could justify you in leaving someone to die in front of you.[4]

If my argument did have this implication, how serious an objection would that be? I am not sure. This does strike me as counter-intuitive, but that could only begin to be an objection if we were given a properly justified, less counter-intuitive alternative. Anyway, whether this counter-intuitive claim would be problematic or not, it is not an implication of my argument. There are two separate reasons for this.

First of all, as Chapter 4 pointed out, it is arguable that your contribution to an aid agency will not itself make a significant difference to anyone. This does not defeat the case for requiring you to contribute: you can be required to play your part in collective actions of beneficence. However, it does seem important here. For a situation in which you can save someone's life directly is one in which you do make a significant difference to someone. So, as I pointed out earlier, there is a clear reason for thinking that, if I have a choice between saving someone's life myself and contributing, in a way that does not itself make a significant difference, to a collective life-saving action, then I ought to do the former.[g]

If I were facing a situation of the kind just described—if, having already set a reasonable policy of personal spending, I faced an emergency in which someone needed to be rescued—I would indeed be facing just such a choice. Among the options I would then have would be these two. I could save the person's life and then, if this cost me anything, take that into account as part of my overall budget for contributing to saving the lives of strangers; or I could let the person die, and spend the whole of that budget on donations to aid agencies. I can rightly hold that, since spending on my personal commitments is morally defensible, it is defensible for me to nominate an amount of personal spending that I cannot be required to compromise for the sake of helping the needy. But that still leaves me with a choice between, on the one hand, helping now and reducing my future donations by a correspondingly small amount, or, on the other, not helping now and making no reduction. If making the reduction will not itself make a significant difference to anyone, but saving a life certainly will, this will surely be the right thing to do.

This first answer relies on the claim that my contribution to an aid agency will not itself make a significant difference to anyone, which I have said is arguably true. Suppose it is false. There remains a second reason why my argument does not imply that refusing to save a life directly is morally acceptable. To see this, recall the force that was claimed for the life-saving analogy in Chapter 2.[h] Failing to contribute to aid agencies is wrong for the same reason that failing to save lives directly is wrong. But the first kind of failure is not as blameworthy as the second, and perhaps not as wrong either. Failing to save lives directly is more blameworthy than failing to contribute to aid agencies, since the reason on which you ought to be acting—someone else's desperate need—is more vividly inescapable in the direct case. Moreover, my argument leaves it open that failing to save lives directly is not only more blameworthy, but more wrong too. I argued that there are reasons of beneficence that are not affected by the immediacy or directness of your relationship to someone who needs to be helped. However, I have not argued against the idea that relationships of immediacy or directness

[g] Sect. 4.5. [h] Sect. 2.4.

create *further* reasons to help. And if so, there is no obstacle to accepting that, given a choice between the two, you should save the life directly instead of making the contribution towards helping indirectly.

11.5 THE ADVANTAGES OF THIS ARGUMENT

The end of Part I left us with a list of requirements that would need to be met by a convincing reply to the problem of demandingness generated in the first half of the book. As far as I can see, all of those requirements have been met by the argument developed in Part II.

One requirement was that, given the kind of theoretical neutrality involved in generating the problem, a fully effective reply to it should not presuppose a global moral theory either. Now admittedly, the argument of Part II has been more ambitious and extensive than Part I, in various ways. It has made a case for linking the acceptability of a proposed requirement of practical concern for other people's interests to the evaluation of that requirement from an appropriately impartial point of view. And it has sought to argue that, for any plausible conception of appropriate impartiality, certain demanding standards of requirement to aid are impartially rejectable, and then to describe the standard of requirement that is not rejectable in this way. This has involved claims about the preconditions for the value of life, the constitution of goods such as friendship and personal achievement, the moral status of the interests we can be required to help people pursue, and the connection between what we can be required to help others to pursue and what it is morally acceptable to pursue for ourselves. However, none of this has involved drawing on a global moral theory of the kind avoided in Part I. The guiding strategy of argument throughout the book has been to take the considerations that do provide us with good moral reasons, and identify what else we are committed to holding if our recognition of these reasons is to make sense.

Thus, the theoretical neutrality of the problem set out in Part I has been appropriately matched by that of the solution developed in Part II. On top of this, there was a list of various other requirements—seven in all—which had also to be met in order to overcome the various problems identified in Chapter 6. The first of these was to produce an argument justifying an aggregative rather than an iterative approach to considerations of the cost to an agent of helping others. This has been the central thrust of my objection to the Extreme Demand. To take an iterative approach would itself be to compromise your personal commitments in a way that you can defensibly refuse to do. But there is no such argument against an aggregative approach; so, if we recognize requirements of beneficence at all, this is the way we ought to approach them.

The next requirement was to defend more-than-minimal personal spending. Arguments from the presuppositions of beneficence—arguments such as those of Kant and Williams—can provoke a worry about whether they meet this requirement. Supposing they succeed in showing that *some* personal partiality is morally defensible, it is doubtful whether they give us an argument against the Extreme Demand, let alone a defence of higher levels of personal spending. But my argument met this requirement in Chapters 8–10. Extending the argument against the Extreme Demand, it was shown that the conclusion that should be drawn is a moderately demanding rather than an ascetic one.

The third requirement was that of showing what mistake in reasoning is made by the iterative argument, rather than simply justifying a different conclusion. This was met earlier in the present chapter.[i] The iterative argument trades on the thought that, as long as the cost of contributing to helping a further person is small, there is no consideration that countervails against the reason of beneficence for helping. But Part II has shown that this is a mistake. It is reasonable to refuse to impose a requirement-grounding loss on myself in helping others, and this is what provides an appropriately countervailing consideration in relation to beneficence.

Fourthly, there was the requirement to allow for (or provide a convincing argument against) situations in which great self-sacrifice *is* morally required. We saw earlier in this chapter how the restricted scope of my conclusion accommodates this requirement.[j] And notice that it also allows for cases of supererogation (the fifth requirement). I have been asking what standard of practical concern for other people can be morally demanded of us. I have argued that requirement-grounding losses cannot be morally demanded of us in responding to others' interests in our help. But this provides no obstacle to thinking that someone who *does* treat others' interests as a decisive reason beyond that point is especially admirable in respect of beneficence. I have argued that the impartial rejectability of a proposal requiring me to act in a certain way is a good objection to that proposed standard of requirement. But I have certainly not given any reasons for thinking that the impartial rejectability of such a proposal is actually a justification for requiring me *not* to act in that way.

The sixth requirement was that the argument must avoid egoism. My defence of the pursuit of personal goods clearly does not go *that* far: in arguing from the presuppositions of beneficence, it starts by taking it for granted that egoism is false. Moreover, we have seen that it avoids a permissive conclusion, and sensibly makes room for a wide range of moral constraints on personal spending.

The final requirement was that, since the conclusion that the Extreme Demand should be rejected is not itself very controversial, a convincing

[i] Sect. 11.1. [j] Sect. 11.3, 'Required Self-Sacrifice'.

argument for it should not appeal to markedly more controversial claims in supporting it. This was a problem for several of the strategies of argument surveyed in Chapter 6. However, an argument from the presuppositions of beneficence itself avoids that problem too. Of course, the reasoning to my conclusion has been more abstract and involved than most people's reasons for rejecting the Extreme Demand. But the materials from which it works are simply those features of beneficence that are appealed to in attempting to make a case for the Extreme Demand originally. If my argument is controversial, it is not because it assumes a contentious starting point. Perhaps the moves it makes from that starting point—its claims about what is required if others' interests are to provide us with compelling reasons—are dubious. I do not think so; but that is something I have to leave to the reader to judge.

11.6 CONCLUSION

Simply described, the view I have defended has three main components.

The first of them is the life-saving analogy defended in Part I—the analogy between failing to save someone's life directly at little cost and failing to contribute to aid agencies that help the very poor. Given the straightforward grounds for thinking that the failure to help someone in the first of these ways amounts to a failure of beneficence, we can ask why the same should not be said of the second sort of failure as well. This question could be satisfactorily answered if there were some countervailing consideration that reconciled giving nothing to aid agencies with beneficence. But the first four chapters argued against this. The analogy must be accepted, and with it, the judgement that it is wrong for an affluent person to contribute nothing to aid agencies.

Having defended this analogy, I then faced the question how it should be approached: Chapter 5 presented the choice between an iterative and an aggregative approach. My eventual answer to this question supplied the second component of my overall view. It is right to approach the life-saving analogy aggregatively, assessing the overall sacrifice that is required of you to contribute towards helping other people, instead of taking an iterative approach, which specifies a degree of sacrifice that you are required to make for each successive person whom you could contribute to helping.

The third component is the account, defended in Chapters 9 and 10, of *how much* you can be required to sacrifice overall in contributing to helping the poor. I argued that you are required to restrict your personal spending until going further would worsen your life by a requirement-grounding amount, with two exceptions: you can justifiably live a non-altruistically-directed life, and pursue commitment goods within it, even when there are alternatives that would be no worse. Refusing to give up more than this can be defended, I argued, by appealing to the connection between what we are required to do for others and what they are required to do for us. I accepted that this does not produce a sharp boundary between the sacrifices in personal spending that are and are not required. However, rather than constituting an objection to my view, this simply showed us how to formulate its conclusion. In order for your conduct to be defensible, you need not be justified in thinking that the line you have drawn with respect to personal spending is the uniquely reasonable line to draw. As long as it is *a* reasonable line to draw, that will be enough.

The view I have defended has the virtue of explaining what seems absurd about the extremely demanding conclusion. But it does so in a way that preserves the force of the life-saving analogy. This is not to say, however, that it is a comfortable vindication of moral 'common sense', as revealed in the practical attitudes of most affluent people. It claims that most of us ought to change our practice, in a demanding direction. Living up to the conclusion of this book would be uncomfortable, for most of us—but not in the life-constricting or -diminishing way that makes an extremely demanding moral outlook seem so unattractive. It exhorts us to combine a proper recognition of the desperate needs of other people with a full engagement with the goods that provide us with our own interests. This is not easy: I doubt whether we can ever be confident that we are living just as we ought to be. But the ambition of living up to both of these aims is not an unrealistic one. We are left with a serious practical challenge; but not, I think, one that is beyond us.

APPENDIX 1
Poverty and Aid

THIS appendix gives a short digest of some of the main available information about world poverty and aid at the time of writing, together with some relevant sources.

THE WORLD BANK'S INCOME POVERTY LINES

The most widely cited estimate of the scale of world poverty is the one regularly published by the World Bank in its annual *World Development Indicators*. This is based on household surveys produced under its Living Standards Measurement Study. Figures are generated for the number of people 'living on less than $1 a day' and 'living on less than $2 a day'—where what is being calculated is the per capita purchasing power of households, measured currently against the benchmark of the purchasing power of US$1.08 in 1993. (When the World Bank first began publishing these figures in 1990, it calculated the number of people whose daily income had a purchasing power parity of $1 in 1985. The new benchmark has been used, and earlier figures recalculated in line with it, since 2000.) Given the scale of the task involved in collecting these data, there is a lag of several years in their publication. In mid-2003 the latest year for which the World Bank made income-based poverty assessments was 1998. For that year, the figure for the number of people living on less than $1 a day was 1,174.9 million people—23.4 per cent of the global population. The number living on less than $2 a day in 1998 was 2,811.5 million people—56.1 per cent of world population.

The World Bank also calculates what it calls the 'poverty gap ratio' as a measure of the depth of poverty in countries where people are below the $1 a day line. This takes those who are below the $1 a day line, and measures their mean distance below it. There are thirteen countries for which this mean distance is more than 20 cents below the poverty line.

There is a clear and widely discussed trend in these figures. In the eleven years from 1987 the absolute number of people assessed as living under the $1 a day poverty line fell slightly, and the percentage dropped from 28.3 per cent. And although the number living under the $2 a day line rose slightly in this period, the percentage in this group dropped too, from 61 per cent.

Sources

World Bank, PovertyNet, <http://www.worldbank.org/poverty/>.
World Bank, *World Development Indicators 2003*.

SHORTCOMINGS

Just what conclusions we are able to draw from these figures about poverty itself is less clear. The methods used to produce the World Bank's $1 a day and $2 a day poverty lines suffer from several serious shortcomings.

One problem is that a misleading impression of precision may be created by the exactitude of the figures that are supplied. They are actually calculated by taking data from the populations for which survey data are available and then extrapolating from those data on the assumption that unsurveyed populations in the same region of the world follow the same pattern. A second problem is the arbitrariness of the $1 a day and $2 a day lines. What has obvious importance to an assessment of absolute poverty is people's ability to secure the basic necessities of life. But there is no clear correlation between this and the $1 a day threshold, despite its frequent use as a measure of the extent of absolute poverty. A concern expressed by some writers is that many more people may be absolutely poor than the 1.2 billion people below the lower of the World Bank's two lines. Others have argued that incentives to under-report some economic transactions may well mean that many people who are classified on the basis of household surveys as falling below the $1 a day line are not in fact absolutely poor, because they have other, unreported sources of income.

These problems are significant, but they are not themselves obstacles to using the World Bank's international poverty lines to make useful cross-temporal comparisons. People whose reported income gives them a purchasing power of less than $1 per day are obviously materially very badly off, and it is important to know whether global social, economic, and political trends are lessening or increasing the number and proportion of the world's population in this material position. However, there is a serious further problem with the methodology behind the construction of the World Bank's international poverty lines—one which means that it cannot be used to make reliable cross-temporal comparisons of the scale of global poverty. You can pass from one side of the $1 a day line to the other without any change to how badly off you are. And you can pass from being below that line to being above it while you become worse off.

This can be seen by appreciating the two-stage procedure that the World Bank uses to determine whether you fall above or below its $1 a day line. First, it takes your national currency and establishes how much of that currency had purchasing power parity with US$1.08 in 1993. This is done by considering the pattern of international consumption at that time, weighting commodities in proportion to their shares in international consumption, and then determining how much of your currency had purchasing power parity with $1.08 across that weighted range of commodities. Let's call this amount 10 shillings. The second stage is to work out the amount of your currency which *now* has the same amount of purchasing power as 10 shillings had in 1993. And this is simply done by reference to the Consumer Price Index for your national economy. This considers the consumption pattern in your national economy, weights commodities in proportion to their shares in national consumption, and then says how much of your currency now has the purchasing power that 10 shillings had in 1993. Suppose the answer is 15 shillings. Then if your income is now more than 15 shillings a day, you are above the $1 a day line.

The problem with this is that you might have had 9 shillings a day in 1993, have 16 shillings a day now, and be worse off than before. The systemic problem with the World Bank's method is that the consumption patterns that characterize a national or international economy do not match the consumption patterns of the very poor. Thus, suppose that, between 1993 and now, services and high-tech goods have come to occupy an increasing proportion of your national economy, while the price of food has risen faster than the price of those services and goods. The purchasing power of your 16 shillings is being judged in relation to the entire range of goods and services consumed in your national economy. But if you are poor, you may well only be spending it on food. And 16 shillings might buy you less food than 9 shillings bought in 1993, even if, across the weighted range of commodities being bought by everyone, its average purchasing power is greater than that of 9 shillings in 1993.

Unlike some of its critics, I think the World Bank's attempts to calculate the numbers of people with incomes below these two lines remain worthwhile in giving us a vivid idea of the scale of global income poverty. However, given the shortcomings just mentioned, it is hard to see how this exercise can establish conclusions about whether global poverty is rising or falling.

Sources

The most thorough exposition of these problems that I know of is:

Thomas Pogge and Sanjay Reddy, *How Not to Count the Poor*.

For a reply by the Research Manager for Poverty in the World Bank's Development Research Group, see:

Martin Ravallion, *How Not to Count the Poor: A Reply to Reddy and Pogge*.

For a discussion of alternative methods of measuring poverty, see:

Shaohua Chen and Martin Ravallion, 'How Did the World's Poorest Fare in the 1990s?'

Aline Coudouel, Jesko Hentschel, and Quentin Wodon, 'Poverty Measurement and Analysis'.

INCOME INEQUALITY

Global income inequality is widely claimed to be increasing, and on some measures it clearly is. The absolute gap between the incomes of rich and poor is widening, and on some measures, so is the 'relative inequality': the ratio by which the incomes of the rich exceed those of the poor. Calculated in terms of average income, the average income in the richest 20 countries is 37 times greater than the average income in the poorest 20, and this gap has doubled in the last 40 years. The richest 1 per cent of the world's population now receives as much income as the poorest 57 per cent. Fifty-four countries are poorer now than they were in 1990.

A measure of inequality that is more sensitive to differences in the middle of the income distribution is the Gini coefficient. This is calculated by plotting a curve describing the cumulative amounts of income received by a given proportion of the population, and then measuring the degree to which that curve differs from the straight line that would be produced by a perfectly equal income distribution. On a scale on which 0 represents perfect equality and 100 represents a distribution in which one individual has everything, the highest national Gini coefficient is that of Namibia, at 70.7, while the lowest is Hungary, at 24.4. Using individual household survey data, a recent estimate of the world Gini coefficient puts it at 66. There are eight countries in which the share of income of the richest 20 per cent is more than 30 times the share of the poorest 20 per cent.

The question of causality, of course, is more complicated. Several studies appear to show that the effect of trade liberalization and economic growth on relative inequality is neutral, when inter-country comparisons are weighted by population. However, this result is much influenced by the fast-growing economies of India and China. The general picture appears to be this. Arguably, national economic growth tends to result in everyone's income growing at a similar rate. But this sees the absolute gap between rich and poor widening within a country. And the rates of economic growth have been significantly worse in the poorest countries.

Sources

UNDP, Human Development Indicators 2003, <http://www.undp.org/hdr2003/indicator/>.

UNDP, *Human Development Report 2003*.

World Bank, *World Development Report 2004*.

For the global inequality figures, see:

Branko Milanovic, 'True World Income Distribution, 1988 and 1993: First Calculation Based on Household Surveys Alone'.

For different measures of income inequality, see:

World Income Inequality Database, established by the Social Development & Poverty Elimination Division of the UNDP: <http://www.wider.unu.edu/wiid/wiid.htm>.

For an analysis of the theoretical issues in the measurement of economic inequality, see:

Amartya Sen, *On Economic Inequality*.

For trends in inequality, see:

<http://www.worldbank.org/poverty/data/trends/inequal.htm>.

For a clear, non-technical survey of the issues, see:

Martin Ravallion, *The Debate on Globalization, Poverty and Inequality: Why Measurement Matters*.

For a discussion of the importance of inequality within developing countries, see:
Nancy Birdsall, 'Why Inequality Matters: Some Economic Issues'.

HEALTH AND EDUCATION: THE UNDP INDICATORS

The most authoritative source of statistical measures in relation to global standards of health and education is the *Human Development Report*, published annually by the United Nations Development Programme (UNDP), using data collected by UNESCO, UNICEF, and the World Health Organization (WHO).

In 2001 life expectancy at birth was less than 40 years in eight countries and less than 50 in a further 22 countries, all in sub-Saharan Africa. The WHO also publishes figures representing 'healthy life expectancy', in which life expectancy is adjusted downwards to take account of the years expected to be spent in poor health, based on the current distribution of states of health and disease in the surveyed population. On this measure, healthy life expectancy in 2001 was less than 30 years in three countries, less than 40 in a further 22 countries, and less than 50 in a further 27. In some countries these figures are lower now than they were in 1975—this is true of several of the former soviet republics and the AIDS- and war-ravaged countries of central and southern Africa—but otherwise there has been a marked upward trend across the world. Globally, life expectancy has risen from about 46 to 66 in the last 50 years.

The mortality rate between birth and the age of 5 has improved sharply across the world in the last 30 years. In 2001 the global mortality rate was 81 under-fives per 1,000 live births, compared with 147 in 1970. Moreover, the rate has improved during this period in every country in the world—except Zambia. However, in 14 countries it has worsened since 1990. There are 316 deaths before 5 per 1,000 live births in Sierra Leone. The rate is over 200 in a further seven countries in sub-Saharan Africa, and over 100 in a further 37 countries. In Sweden the rate is 3.

The maternal mortality rate has also improved across the world, but in sub-Saharan Africa 1 per cent of live births still result in the mother's death.

In 2001 there were 34 countries in which more than a quarter of children under 5 were underweight for their age (more than two standard deviations below the median weight of the reference population). In 11 of those countries the figure was above 40 per cent, and the global total is 170 million children under 5. Rates for child malnutrition fell across most of the world during the 1990s, but rose in sub-Saharan Africa. According to the figures for undernourished people of all ages in 2000—assessed as the percentage of the population 'whose food intake is chronically insufficient to meet their minimum energy requirements', this runs at 24 per cent of the entire population of South Asia, and 33 per cent of the population of sub-Saharan Africa. In seven countries it is above 50 per cent, and in a further eight countries above 40 per cent.

The UNDP measures literacy as 'the percentage of people aged 15 and above who can, with understanding, both read and write a short, simple statement on their everyday life'. According to its figures for 2001, adult literacy was then below 30 per cent in three countries, below 40 per cent in a further four countries, and below 50 per cent in a further 12 countries. However, this is one of the areas of development in which there has been a consistent global improvement. With the exception of a few countries where high literacy rates have remained constant, every country has recorded an increase in literacy in the period 1990–2001. According to the figures for 2000, there are four countries in which less than half of the population receive five years of primary education, and a further 15 countries in which less than three-quarters do so. 115 million of the 680 million primary-school-age children in the developing world do not attend school. The percentage of the eligible population enrolled for primary education in sub-Saharan Africa was 59 per cent. But again, the trend is upward here, even in the poorest countries.

The UNDP also calculates several summary measures of country-by-country living standards, of which the best known is its Human Development Index (HDI), in which measures of life expectancy, educational standards (a combined measure of adult literacy and educational enrolment), and per capita gross domestic product are equally weighted. (Each of these is calculated as the ratio of a given country's figure to the maximum figure, and a logarithm of income is taken to reflect the diminishing marginal contribution that money makes to well-being.) There is a clear upwards trend in this index across the world since 1975. However, it fell in 21 countries during the 1990s, and the HDI for Zimbabwe, Zambia, and the Congo is lower now than it was in 1975.

Sources

UNDP, Human Development Indicators 2003, <http://www.undp.org/hdr2003/indicator/>.

UNDP, *Human Development Report 2003*.

WHO <http://www.who.int/research/en/>.

Is increased aid spending the way to address these problems? For discussion, see:

ODI Briefing Paper, *Can We Attain the Millennium Development Goals in Education and Health through Public Expenditure and Aid?*

SOME FURTHER FACTS ABOUT HEALTH

UNICEF and the WHO also publish their own annual reports, which provide further data illustrating the stark global disparities in access to health care. According to their estimates, 11 million children currently die each year under the age of 5, 6.6 million of them from malnutrition-associated causes. Of the 130 million children born around the world each year, 30 million receive no vaccination; nearly 3 million children under 5 die from diseases that are preventable with currently available vaccines. (Malaria currently kills 1 million children under 5 annually, measles 500,000, and tuberculosis and other respiratory infections 1.8 million.) About 2 million children under 5 die from acute respiratory infection. An estimated 1.6 million die from diarrhoeal dehydration, which is mainly caused by the absence of safe drinking water and sanitation. In 29 countries less than half of the population have access to improved sanitation facilities (measured according to minimum WHO hygiene standards); in 17, less than half of the population have sustainable access to an improved water source. There has been progress in increasing vaccination coverage during the 1990s, and in preventing deaths from diarrhoeal dehydration (which the WHO estimated at 2.2 million in 1998) but progress in increasing the proportion of the population of Africa and Asia with access to improved water and sanitation has been poor.

For a discussion of the cost of preventing or treating the diseases just mentioned, see Appendix 2.

No health economist would claim that there is a linear correlation between health spending and improved health outcomes. However, there is obviously a connection. In the United States in 2000 the average annual per capita health spending (public and private) was $4,499. In 29 countries it was less than $50, and in five, less than $20. In 27 countries less than half of the population have access to at least 20 of the most essential drugs (as assessed by the WHO Department of Essential Drugs and Medicines Policy) continuously and affordably available within one hour's travel from home. Ten per cent of health research and development spending is currently directed at the health problems of 90 per cent of the world's population.

Sources

UNDP, Human Development Indicators 2003, <http://www.undp.org/hdr2003/indicator/>.

UNICEF, *The State of the World's Children 2003* and *The State of the World's Children 1998*.

WHO, Global Database on Child Growth and Malnutrition, <http://www.who.int/nutgrowthdb/>.

WHO, *World Health Report 2003*.

World Bank, *World Development Report 2004*.

For further data on and discussion of global malnutrition, see:

FAO, *State of Food Insecurity in the World 2003*.

Phillips Foster and Howard D. Leathers, *The World Food Problem: Tackling the Causes of Undernutrition in the Third World*.

For a discussion of attempts to survey other indicators of child deprivation, beyond measures of income, education and health, see:

Howard White, Jennifer Leavy, and Andrew Masters, *Comparative Perspectives on Child Poverty: A Review of Poverty Measures*.

AID: OFFICIAL DEVELOPMENT ASSISTANCE

The Organisation for Economic Co-operation and Development (OECD) publishes its International Development Statistics annually. These set out the aid flows from the 22 member countries belonging to the OECD's Development Assistance Committee (DAC). The figures it supplies for Official Development Assistance (ODA) cover both direct, government-to-government 'bilateral' aid—including both grants and concessional loans extended 'with promotion of economic development and welfare as the main objective'—and 'multilateral' aid provided by donor governments through agencies such as those of the United Nations and European Community and through the 'replenishments' that underwrite the activities of the World Bank.

In 2002 DAC countries supplied $57 billion in ODA—0.23 per cent of their combined gross national income (GNI) (an average of $63 per capita in the DAC countries, in 2000 $US—down from $75 per capita in 1990, again measured in 2000 $US). This figure has declined from a high-water mark of 0.33 per cent in 1992, and is well short of the 0.7 per cent target first proposed by the 1969 Pearson Report on International Development, and endorsed by the UN General Assembly in 1970. (Denmark, Luxembourg, the Netherlands, Norway, and Sweden do currently exceed that target.) Of this, 23 per cent of ODA is given to the countries classified as 'least developed'. This figure is declining as a percentage of ODA: it was 28 per cent in 1990. DAC countries have pledged to increase their aid commitments by $16 billion by 2006. This would represent 0.26 per cent of GNI.

Among recipients, in 2001 there were 10 countries for which ODA receipts amounted to more than 20 per cent of gross national product (GNP), and a further 25 countries for which it amounted to more than 10 per cent of GNP. (In 1990 there were 17 countries for which ODA amounted to more than 20 per cent of GNP.) As a group, the 49 least developed countries were in 2001 receiving ODA at 8.45 per cent of GNP in 2001, compared to 12.92 per cent in 1990. The highest per capita recipient of ODA is Israel.

What should our reaction to these figures be? DAC governments are routinely criticized for failing to meet the UN targets. However, whether that is to be lamented does seem to depend on one's view of the purposes and effects of ODA aid. As most analysts point out, it functions primarily as an instrument of foreign policy and, to varying degrees, of trade promotion and subsidization of donor-country industry. Some of its more forceful critics are discussed in Chapter 3.

Sources

OECD, International Development Statistics Online, <http://www.oecd.org/dataoecd/50/17/5037721.htm>.

UNDP, *Human Development Report 2003*, 290.

For criticism of DAC government miserliness, see:

Tony German and Judith Randel, 'Never Richer, Never Meaner'.

For critical explanations of the structure of ODA aid, see:

Kunibert Raffer and H. W. Singer, *The Foreign Aid Business: Economic Assistance and Development Co-operation.*

David Sogge, *Give and Take: What's the Matter with Foreign Aid?*

For a defence, see:

Robert Cassen and Associates, *Does Aid Work?*

NON-GOVERNMENT AID

Non-government organizations (NGOs) in DAC countries spent a further $7 billion, or 0.03 per cent of GNI, in recipient countries in 2002, excluding funds administered by them through ODA programmes. In two countries, Norway and Ireland, more than 0.1 per cent of GNI is spent through private donations to NGOs. The aggregate figure in 1990 was also 0.03 per cent of GNI. It is estimated that NGOs spend the same amount again in ODA-derived funds. This means that total aid flows through NGOs are equal to about a quarter of the ODA total.

There has been a large increase in the number of international NGOs during the 1990s. Obviously, the number depends on how they are defined; but according to one careful recent attempt to classify and count them, the recorded number increased from 13,000 in 1981 to 47,000 in 2001.

Sources

Development Initiatives, *Global Development Assistance: The Role of Non-Governmental Organisations and Other Charity Flows.*

OECD, International Development Statistics Online, <http://www.oecd.org/dataoecd/50/17/5037721.htm>.

For the number of NGOs, see:

Helmut Anheier and Nuno Themudo, 'Organisational Forms of Global Civil Society', 194.

DEBT AND TRADE

Large amounts of money flow from poor countries to rich. In 1999 the value of debt service payments from developing countries to developed countries was 13 times the value of grant aid to them. Of the DAC countries, only Belgium receives more than 1 per cent of the value of its imports from the countries classified by the OECD as least developed.

In 1996 the International Monetary Fund (IMF) began the Heavily Indebted Poor Countries (HIPC) initiative. Of the 42 countries covered by this initiative, 34 are in sub-Saharan Africa. Debt relief proceeds in two stages, which involve meeting IMF-imposed conditions for economic reform and the implementation of poverty-reduction strategies. At the first stage, reaching the 'decision point' entitles a country to debt service relief. Thereafter, reaching the 'completion point' is the trigger for certain forms of debt stock relief. In early 1993 eight countries had reached their completion points, and another 18 had reached their decision points. For these 26 countries, debt service payments will be about one-third lower in 2001–5 than in 1998–9, and over half of the money saved in this way is being directed towards increased health and education spending.

However, this is not enough to say that the HIPC initiative has been a success. Although eight countries have reached their completion points, that is only eight out of the 19 that had been scheduled to do so. For two of the eight countries, new borrowing has meant falling back into debt traps, with their ratio of net value of debt to exports rising once more above the 150 per cent threshold at which countries qualified for inclusion in the HIPC scheme in the first place.

The current remaining debt burden of the HIPC countries, approximately US$137 billion, is less than the total net worth of the world's six richest individuals.

Sources

Forbes.com, <http://www.forbes.com/2003/02/26/billionaireland.html>.
Jubilee Research, <http://www.jubilee2000uk.org/>.
UNDP, *Human Development Report 2003*.

Are these figures on debt and trade evidence of the exploitation of poor countries? For opposition to that view, see:

P. T. Bauer, *Equality, the Third World and Economic Delusion*, esp. ch. 4: 'Western Guilt and Third World Poverty' and ch. 5: 'Foreign Aid and its Hydra-Headed Rationalization', sect. 4.

Appendix 2
The Cost of Saving a Life

Appendix 1 has given an indication of the numbers of people whose lives are threatened by severe material deprivation. What is the cost of saving one of those lives, or preventing a threat to the life of one of those people? The estimates I have seen range from one dollar to $9 million. But those are not answers to the same question. In order to arrive at a meaningful answer, we need to give some thought to just what is being asked.

LOW-END ESTIMATES

In Chapter 5 I mentioned some answers that are well towards the lower end of the range. These report the costs of actually administering some effective health interventions, which are extremely small. According to the Rehydration Project, $1 is the cost of administering oral rehydration therapy to treat a child for the dehydration caused by diarrhoea. This is estimated to be effective in 90 per cent of cases, for a condition that currently kills 1.6 million children under the age of 5 each year. The World Health Organization estimates that the cost of the drugs required for an effective course of treatment against tuberculosis can be as low as $10. And UNICEF's figure for vaccinating a child to provide protection 'from Vitamin A deficiency and a host of deadly diseases, including diphtheria, pertussis, tetanus, polio, measles, childhood tuberculosis, hepatitis B, and Hib (Haemophilus influenzae type b), which is a major cause of pneumonia and meningitis' is $20–30. In each case, these costs do not merely represent the price of the medicines, but include the staff costs and overheads required to administer them as well.

I also cited figures for emergency disaster relief. The cost of supplying people with food, shelter, sanitation, and basic medical care in emergency relief camps has been estimated by Oxfam at £50–150 for one person for six months (at today's prices), and at the time of writing, the Disasters Emergency Committee estimates that this costs £100 for one family for one month.

A major cause of mortality among the chronically poor is simple malnutrition: this currently kills 6.6 million children under the age of 5 each year. The UN Food and Agriculture Organization (FAO) estimates the cost of feeding the world's 214 million hungriest people at $5.2 billion per year, which is $24 each.

TWO PROBLEMS

It is not uncommon to see figures such as these represented as the cost of saving a person's life: 'Relief groups calculate the cost of saving a life in Afghanistan over the next six to eight months at $50.' However, this is misleading, for several reasons. (They are reasons why the agencies I referred to above do not make this kind of claim.) Let us start by looking at two of the more obvious ones.

The first reason is clearest in relation to vaccination and emergency disaster relief. To say that vaccinating children, or giving families emergency supplies, is saving their lives implies that they would have died without these actions. But of course that is not going to be true of everyone who receives these forms of assistance. This point is clearly acknowledged in many emergency relief operation evaluation reports, in explaining why it is not possible to say how much difference the activities of a given agency have made to overall mortality. The second point is the converse of the first. I cannot claim to have saved your life if I save you from one threat only for you to die from another. So it will be misleading to cite the low cost of treating one cause of child mortality as the cost of saving a life, if it is only the cost of treating one of many such causes.

UNGER'S ESTIMATE

In his book *Living High and Letting Die*, Peter Unger adopts an approach that addresses these two points. Using figures from the World Bank's Population Health and Nutrition Department and UNICEF, he calculates the annual health care costs of treating a 'typically sick' child between the ages of 2 and 6, adds figures to represent the costs of donor- and recipient-country administration, and arrives at a result (in 1996) of $200 per child. Unger's conclusion is that $200 is the cost of taking a 'typically sick' 2-year-old and giving him a greater than 90 per cent chance, at age 6, of living to 21.

TWO MORE PROBLEMS

Unger rightly points out that no amount of spending will *guarantee* that a 2-year-old will reach 21. He might have added that for any 'typically sick' 2-year-old, there is no way to guarantee that that child would not have survived to 21 without the intervention. However, similar points hold in any situation in which a person needs life-saving assistance. So if I know that, by spending $200 on a child with a high chance of dying unaided, I can ensure that he reaches an age at which his chances of reaching 21 are over 90 per cent, then it does seem that I can think of this as the cost of saving his life.

However, there remain two reasons why Unger's calculation will not show this. First, his method is to calculate the cost (based on a figure of $16 per year for local health care expenses) of treating a 'typically sick' 2-year-old each year until the age of 6, at which point his chances of reaching 21 are over 90 per cent. However, this is not the cost of *ensuring* that a 2-year-old reaches the age of 6. It is the cost of successfully treating those 2- to 6-year-olds who are successfully treated. The success rates for those treatments may well be high. But unless they are rates of 100 per cent, Unger's $200 figure will not be the cost of giving a 2-year-old a 90 per cent chance of reaching 21.

Is that a serious problem? Not obviously. If $200 will significantly raise a 2-year-old's chance of reaching adulthood, that still provides a very strong reason for giving $200.

Another problem, though, is more significant. As I read him, Unger is suggesting that if I give $200 to an aid agency then (on average) one child's life will be saved. However, that is false for a separate reason, which affects all of the low-end estimates mentioned so far. To see this clearly, go back to the ORT figure of $1. This is the cost of administering ORT to a dehydrated child in a health clinic. But it is not the case that if I give an extra $1 to UNICEF, one extra child's life will be saved. There is no queue of dehydrated children at health clinics waiting for $1 donations to fund their treatment. The cost of ensuring that children do not die of dehydration is the cost of ensuring that they receive appropriate treatment when they need it. In part, of course, meeting this cost means ensuring that there are staffed health clinics containing rehydration salts. But the much more expensive part of this cost is the cost of ensuring that the most vulnerable children are at those clinics when they need to be. And the cost of ensuring *this* includes the cost of creating extra health facilities, securing the opportunities for the poorest people to use them, and supplying the basic forms of health education that ensure that they are used.

The more general point is this. Given the appropriate statistics, we can work out the average cost of treating those children who do get treated, and this cost may be very low. But what we want to know is the cost of extending treatment to those children who are *not* currently getting it: that is, the marginal cost of treating an extra child. And none of the calculations mentioned so far will help us to do that.

HEALTH ECONOMICS

Our question is, What is the marginal cost of saving an extra life, rather than the average cost of saving lives so far? For answers to this question, we can turn to health economics for help, in its attempts to quantify the correlation between health spending and mortality. However, if we expect neat answers, we will be disappointed. Resolving the substantial questions debated by health economists, and doing so for *all* of the poverty-related diseases that are major causes of global mortality, is a mammoth task.

Two issues make attempts to quantify the correlation between health spending and mortality highly controversial, and explain the wide variation in the figures produced by such attempts. One is the difficulty of answering the question, in relation to any given health intervention, what would have happened without it. That is, what are the other variables we need to control for in order to establish the causal efficacy of a given intervention, and how do we devise a study that controls for them? And the other is the range of further, related assumptions that need to be made, and are made differently by different researchers, about the quality of the data from which they are working, about how to define the costs and assess the coverage of a given intervention, and about how to extrapolate from one set of local conditions to cover others.

The result of this is a striking variation in the figures produced by these studies. To take a representative example, a 1991 survey of studies of the cost-effectiveness of anti-malaria interventions found that estimates of the cost of these interventions per year of life saved varied between $2.10 and $259. When this range of uncertainty is compounded for all the other major poverty-related causes of mortality, the resulting figure for protecting poor people from threats from all of those causes is even less clear. However, one thing that does seem plain is that the cost of saving extra lives will need to be thought of as being considerably higher than the low-end figures mentioned above.

One way to try to estimate a lower boundary for this cost is to take the World Bank-derived figure of $25–30 billion per year which the UNDP cites as the amount of increased aid spending it estimates as the cost of reaching the Millennium Development Goals for health. There are three of these goals: to reduce the under-5 mortality rate by two-thirds, to reduce the maternal mortality rate by three-quarters, and to halt and reverse the spread of HIV–AIDS, malaria, and tuberculosis, between 1990 and 2015. Using their current figures for these causes of mortality, and assuming current projections for the rate of population increase (since these goals concern the mortality *rate*, rather than the absolute incidence), I arrive at an implied figure of $2,500–3,000 per life saved.

However, the method used by the World Bank to arrive at their figure of $25–30 billion is, as before, to estimate the average cost of supplying resources to those already within the system, rather than the incremental cost of bringing those from outside the system into it. And the latter cost is going to be higher. The neediest people—the people who are not being reached by current health spending—are the hardest and most expensive to reach: they are the most physically isolated, the most educationally disadvantaged, and the likeliest to be pre-empted by other people competing for access to the same goods. (This is what poverty *is*: a powerlessness to get access to basic goods.)

What about an upper boundary? One way to try to establish that is to look at some of the sophisticated work that has been done in wealthy countries to estimate the cost of reducing mortality there, using reliable sources of statistical data. But here the figures run into the millions. For example, a recent authoritative study estimates the cost, through increased welfare spending, of reducing child mortality during the depression of the 1930s in the United States at $2.5 million per life saved—although it acknowledges that others' estimates have ranged as high as $9 million. This gives us an upper boundary for thinking about the costs of saving lives. Presumably the cost of lowering the mortality rate in today's poorest countries, where the per capita health spending is less than $20, is lower than the cost of doing that in a country with less poverty.

This does not get us very far. There are many questions to be asked about the figures that supply these upper and lower boundaries, and they still differ from each other by a factor of 1,000. Moreover, they do not give us guidance on how to think about the cost of saving extra lives through humanitarian relief, where relief operation evaluators are reluctant even to attempt to produce such figures. I am not going to attempt to go further here into the questions that would be needed to resolve these issues. To see why, we need to ask ourselves one further question.

DOES THIS MATTER?

Answering these questions matters if you think that the case for requiring me to contribute to aid agencies comes from the fact that my giving money to an aid agency will itself make the difference between life and death for someone. However, in Chapter 4 I argued against that view. There is reason to doubt whether this is the right way to think about giving money to aid agencies; but nonetheless, there remains a strong case for thinking that making such contributions is morally required. If I do so, I am contributing to a collective action of saving lives. We ought collectively to be doing that, and I ought to be joining in.

This leads to two simple observations about the figures I have just been discussing. First, the case for requiring me to contribute comes from the importance of contributing to helping the people who are already being helped, and not from the importance of my performing an action that will lead to an extra person's being helped (desirable though that would obviously be). And even the smallest figures I have been discussing do serve to indicate the average cost of our collectively supplying important forms of help to those who need it. But secondly (as I pointed out in Section 5.3), even if the average cost of our collectively helping one needy person runs into the millions, my own share of that collective cost will still be very small, given the number of people who are contributing towards helping: a fraction of a dollar, rather than a fraction of a cent. And that is enough to show that the Extreme Demand would indeed be extremely demanding, even if the figure that properly represents the cost of saving one poverty-afflicted life is right at the top of the spectrum just discussed.

What does of course matter is whether there are effective things that we can collectively do to help the poor. I argued in Chapter 3 that the answer to this is Yes. And in thinking about the help we can give, we should not concentrate exclusively on threats to people's lives. I acknowledged this at the start of the book; and a major concern in Part II was to emphasize the range of interests apart from interests in life itself that ground requirements of beneficence.

Sources

For the figures on low-cost health interventions:

Rehydration Project, <http://www.rehydrate.org/>.
UNICEF, <http://www.unicef.org/immunization/index_bigpicture.html>.
WHO, <http://www.who.int/mediacentre/factsheets/fs104/en/>.

For the figures on disaster relief:

Disasters Emergency Committee, <http://www.dec.org.uk/index.cfm/asset_id,999/index.html>.

For the FAO figure on feeding the hungry:

UNDP, *Human Development Report 2003*, 90.

For the quoted claim about $50 saving a life in Afghanistan:

Bob Geary, 'Afghanistan Seen through the Eyes of an Aid Worker'.

Unger's calculation:

Peter Unger, *Living High and Letting Die: Our Illusion of Innocence*, 146–8.

For the figures on malaria:

José A. Najera, Bernhard Liese, and Jeffrey S. Hammer, *Health Sector Priorities Review: Malaria.*

On United States child mortality in 1930s:

Price V. Fishback, Michael R. Haines, and Shawn Kantor, *The Welfare of Children during the Great Depression.*

The source of the UNDP's costing of the Millennium Development Goals for health is:

Shantayanan Devarajan, Margaret J. Miller, and Eric V. Swanson, *Goals for Development: History, Prospects and Costs*, 16.

(However, note that these authors point out at p. 21: 'Estimates of the costs of meeting specific human development goals, such as those for education and health, are highly problematic. The relationship between public expenditures and outcomes is complex and empirical evidence from developing countries suggests only a weak link between public spending on education and school enrollments, or between health expenditures and mortality or disease.')

For relief operation evaluation reports, the British Disasters Emergency Committee publishes the independent evaluation reports it has commissioned to evaluate the relief operations of its twelve member agencies, since 1998, against the principles of the Red Cross code:

<http://www.dec.org.uk/index.cfm/asset_id,469/index.html>.

Some further sources on the cost-effectiveness of aid:

Active Learning Network for Accountability and Performance in Humanitarian Action, <www.alnap.org/>.

Centre for Research on the Epidemiology of Disasters, <http://www.cred.be/>.

DAC Network on Development Evaluation, <http://www.oecd.org/department/0,2688,en_2649_34435_1_1_1_1_1,00.html>.

FAO Food Security and Agricultural Projects Analysis Service, <http://www.fao.org/es/ESA/fsecur_FSinf_en.htm>.

Overseas Development Institute, <http://www.odi.org.uk/>.

Notes

INTRODUCTION

1. Cited in David Reiff, *A Bed for the Night*, 22.

CHAPTER 1

1. How many, and how extreme? The simplest answer is to cite the World Bank's figure of 1.2 billion people who currently subsist on less than $1 a day. For further discussion and sources, see App. 1.
2. For this approach to the question, see e.g. Brian Barry, 'Humanity and Justice in Global Perspective', Onora O'Neill, *Faces of Hunger*, Charles Beitz, *Political Theory and International Relations*, Stanley Hoffman, *Duties beyond Borders*, Henry Shue, *Basic Rights*, Peter Brown and Henry Shue (eds.), *Food Policy*, Philip Alston and Katarina Tomasevski (eds.), *The Right to Food*, and James P. Sterba, 'Global Justice'; also the works cited in nn. 8–10.
3. This is currently the weighted average for the countries of the Organisation for Economic Co-operation and Development (OECD) which give 0.23 per cent of gross national income as Official Development Assistance, and whose citizens give another 0.03 per cent privately, according to the OECD's International Development Statistics Online, <http://www.oecd.org/dataoecd/ 50/17/5037721.htm>. For a survey of the current statistics concerning world poverty and aid, see App. 1, where I refer also to the reservations of some analysts about the kinds of 'aid' covered by these figures.
4. And thus recognizing the extent to which the need for our 'aid' results from unjust institutional structures that reinforce the privileged position from which we are able to offer it. Philosophers who have recently made this point include Thomas Nagel, 'Poverty and Food', Barry, 'Humanity and Justice in Global Perspective', 247–50, Onora O'Neill, 'The Great Maxims of Justice and Charity', Thomas W. Pogge, ' "Assisting" the Global Poor', and Irwin Goldstein, 'Review of Peter Unger, *Living High and Letting Die*'. See also Andrew Kuper, 'Global Poverty Relief—More than Charity'. The point is not new. Thus Kant: 'If men were scrupulously just there would be no poor to whom we could give alms and think that we had realized the merit of benevolence. . . . It would be better to see whether the poor man could not be helped in some other way which would not entail his being degraded by accepting alms.' Immanuel Kant, *Lectures on Ethics*, 236. For the antecedents of this line of thought in Grotius, Pufendorf, and Locke, see J. B. Schneewind, 'Philosophical Ideas of Charity: Some Historical Reflections'.

In Ch. 3 I shall have a good deal more to say about the political nature of world poverty, and the limitations of a resource-transfer approach to addressing it.

5. This objection is raised by Paul Gomberg, 'The Fallacy of Philanthropy'. I agree with him that poverty is a political problem, and philanthropy is not going to solve it. However, I am less confident than he is that Marxism offers the right model for a universal political solution.

   For an argument that the political nature of the problem of world poverty means that it is not a moral problem, see Rudiger Bittner, 'Morality and World Hunger'.

6. For aid workers, there is a real and important difference between humanitarian aid and other kinds of action on behalf of the needy, such as the promotion of economic and social development, or the advocacy of rights. These differences have often been reflected in troublingly divergent responses to practical questions. In crisis situations caused by abusive governments, for example, humanitarian agencies have tended to cooperate with those governments to negotiate access to the affected people, while rights advocates have denounced the abuse. Some of the problems with the former policy have led humanitarian agencies increasingly to seek to incorporate rights advocacy into their work. For discussion of these issues, see Mary B. Anderson, *Do No Harm*, Fiona Terry, *Condemned to Repeat?*, and Larry Minear, *The Humanitarian Enterprise*. David Rieff, *A Bed for the Night*, makes an impassioned case for thinking that this change to the ethos of the humanitarian agencies is a retrograde step.

   In Ch. 3 I shall give some attention to the impact of these issues on the question of just which agencies, if any, we are morally required to support.

7. For some further taxonomy of arguments for this conclusion, see Garrett Cullity, 'The Life-Saving Analogy', 51–2.

8. On the moral requirement to right past wrongs, see A. John Simmons, 'Historical Rights and Fair Shares'. For objections to this line of argument, see Christopher Morris, 'Existential Limits to the Rectification of Past Wrongs', and Jeremy Waldron, 'Superseding Historic Injustice'. For a helpful background discussion of the question how to distribute responsibilities for remedying deprivation, see David Miller, 'Distributing Responsibilities'. P. T. Bauer, *Equality, the Third World and Economic Delusion*, argues vigorously against the idea that there are any past wrongs to right—see ch. 4: 'Western Guilt and Third World Poverty', and pp. 120–2.

9. See e.g. the essays collected in Ian Shapiro and Lea Brilmayer (eds.), *Global Justice*; Thomas W. Pogge (ed.), *Global Justice*; and Robin Attfield and Barry Wilkins (eds.), *International Justice and the Third World*; also Peter Jones, 'Global Distributive Justice'. The argument from distributive justice is attacked by P. T. Bauer, 'Foreign Aid and its Hydra-Headed Rationalization', 116–20, and (less stridently) by John Rawls, *The Law of Peoples*, sects. 15 and 16. For a critique of Rawls, see Pogge, 'An Egalitarian Law of Peoples'.

10. The strongest recent advocate of this line of argument is Thomas Pogge: see e.g. his 'Human Rights and Human Responsibilities' and *World Poverty and Human Rights*. See also the other contributions to Pablo De Greiff and Ciaran Cronin (eds.), *Global Justice and Transnational Politics*; and Barry, 'Humanity and Justice in Global Perspective', 227–9, who focuses on the

aspect of regulative justice that he calls 'justice as requital'. (Barry also mentions a fourth argument that could be added to the list in the text: an argument from 'justice as fair play', pp. 229–34.)

Of course, I am not saying that these three arguments from justice are mutually exclusive; only that they are independent of each other.

11. I discuss 'fair share' views of the moral demands of affluence in Sect. 5.2.
12. See e.g. Liam B. Murphy, 'The Demands of Beneficence', and L. Jonathan Cohen, 'Who is Starving Whom?' Interestingly, however, in his book *Moral Demands in Nonideal Theory*, Murphy develops a sustained criticism of attempts to reject a moral outlook on the grounds that it is excessively demanding; and thus forgoes this strategy of argument for his own 'fair share' view.
13. Unless I can assume that someone else will help if I do not, or I am committed to doing something else more important, or there will be further bad consequences of helping, or there is some other countervailing consideration. I shall omit these qualifications in what follows.
14. For the seminal argument of this form, see Peter Singer, 'Famine, Affluence and Morality'. Subsequent, and slightly different, presentations of his argument can be found in his 'Postscript to "Famine, Affluence and Morality" ', 'Reconsidering the Famine Relief Argument', and *Practical Ethics*. For a similar approach, see John M. Whelan, Jr., 'Famine and Charity'. For critical discussions of Singer's argument, see F. M. Kamm, 'Faminine Ethics', Colin McGinn, 'Our Duties to Animals and the Poor', Michael McKinsey, 'Obligations to the Starving', and John Arthur, 'Rights and the Duty to Bring Aid'. In Singer's most recent treatment of this topic, the emphasis is on the collective question I distinguished at the start, rather than the individual one: see *One World*, ch. 5.

    Onora O'Neill, 'Lifeboat Earth', develops a life-saving analogy in a Kantian direction rather than Singer's utilitarian one. James Rachels, 'Killing and Starving to Death', and Peter Unger, *Living High and Letting Die*, invoke the life-saving analogy in support of the stronger claim that not contributing money to aid agencies is as wrong as killing people: Singer also makes this claim in *Practical Ethics*, 222. (However, see Fred Feldman, 'Unger's *Living High and Letting Die*', and Kamm, 'Rescue and Harm', 42–4, for a discussion of the relativism that Unger seems committed to.) For further discussion of this stronger claim, see Jonathan Bennett, 'Morality and Consequences', sect. 2.
15. McKinsey, 'Obligations to the Starving', 309–10, identifies the same analogy, and calls it the 'life-saving model'.
16. I return to this point, and take fuller account of it, in Sect. 4.5, 'A Corollary: Other Evils', and Ch. 8. n.14. It is a point emphasized by Michael Ignatieff, *The Needs of Strangers*—see esp. pp. 15–16. For an interesting historical discussion, see John D. Jones, 'Poverty as *Malum Simpliciter*'.
17. Not everyone finds this as hard as I do: see the works cited in n. 27. Hence the need for the argument of Ch. 2. Someone maintaining the moral significance of the immediacy of my relationship to other people's need will need to be clearer than I have been in the text about how to classify difficult cases. For example, if I know that there are destitute people living in the same large city as me, and occasionally see them, is my relationship to them immediate or not? (On this question, see the distinction between 'real distance' and

'moral distance' in Michael Ignatieff, 'The Stories We Tell: Television and Humanitarian Aid', 290–1.) If my attack in Ch. 2 on the moral significance of immediacy succeeds, it succeeds however we draw this line.

18. I do occasionally encounter this reply when presenting this argument in seminars. And this view seems to be implied by philosophers like Judith Jarvis Thomson, 'A Defense of Abortion', and Jan Narveson, 'Feeding the Hungry', who hold that if a person has no *right* to your assistance then withholding that assistance is not morally wrong.
19. Singer, 'Famine, Affluence and Morality', 231.
20. See e.g. Barry, 'Humanity and Justice in Global Perspective', 220–1, Shelly Kagan, *The Limits of Morality*, 3–4, Unger, *Living High and Letting Die*, 9; Joel Feinberg, 'The Moral and Legal Responsibility of the Bad Samaritan', 192. For critical discussion, see David Schmidtz, 'Islands in a Sea of Obligation'. A web search on the words 'drowning child' suggests that there are a lot of philosophers who use Singer's example in teaching. The example itself (if not the use to which he puts it) pre-dates Singer: 'A number of people who stand round a shallow pond in which a child is drowning, and let it drown without taking the trouble to ascertain the depth of the pond, are, no doubt, shameful cowards, but they can hardly be said to have killed the child': James Fitzjames Stephen, *A History of the Criminal Law of England* (1883), iii. 10.
21. I take the term 'subsumptive' from Jonathan Dancy, *Moral Reasons*, 82.
22. This reconstruction of Singer's argument is closest to the formulation he gives in *Practical Ethics*, 168, which proposes the principle: 'if it is in our power to prevent something very bad happening, without thereby sacrificing anything of comparable moral significance, we ought to do it', and makes fully explicit the claim that this principle *supports* the judgements that instantiate it. Singer's two earlier presentations of the argument formulate this principle slightly differently, and claim also that a weaker principle will equally establish the conclusion that non-contribution to humanitarian aid agencies is wrong: 'if it is in our power to prevent something very bad from happening, without thereby sacrificing anything morally significant, we ought, morally, to do it'. See 'Famine, Affluence and Morality', 231, and 'Reconsidering the Famine Relief Argument', 37.

    For an interesting antecedent to Singer, see Henry Sidgwick, *The Methods of Ethics*, 253.
23. A good point of entry into the debate over the role of moral principles in the justification of moral judgements is Brad Hooker and Margaret Little (eds.), *Moral Particularism*. My own views are set out in Cullity, 'Particularism and Presumptive Reasons'.
24. It might seem tempting to object that this will turn out to be a subsumptive argument too: it is appealing to the principle that failures of beneficence are wrong. However, as we shall see in Ch. 2, this 'principle' would be trivial: what makes something a failure of beneficence (as I shall be using this phrase) is that it is wrong. This is therefore not a candidate for a genuinely subsumptive argument, nor a sensible target for someone attacking the appeal to principles in moral reasoning. Of course, the wrongness of any particular

failure of beneficence is an instance of the more general fact that failures of beneficence are wrong; but that is not to say that the wrongness of the particular failure of beneficence is *justified* by its subsumption under the general principle. (I am aware that, if I were attempting to argue against a subsumptive picture of moral justification here, rather than merely to flag the issue, I would need to say a good deal more about exactly what makes an argument 'genuinely subsumptive'.)

25. My argument also differs from those that ground a moral requirement on us to help the poor in their *right* to our help. For noteworthy arguments of this form, see Shue, *Basic Rights*, Alan Gewirth, 'Starvation and Human Rights', Onora O'Neill, *Faces of Hunger* and 'Lifeboat Earth', and Amartya Sen, 'The Right Not To Be Hungry'. For a discussion of the way in which rights to charity might be grounded differently from rights to justice, see O'Neill, 'The Great Maxims of Justice and Charity'. The non-subsumptive form of my argument distinguishes it also from Unger, *Living High and Letting Die*—as does the fact that I shall not be following his intuition-sifting approach. His aim is to be highly discriminating about the intuitions which correspond to justifying moral principles but, as I read him, his guiding methodology is similar to Singer's, in aiming to use those intuitive judgements as reliable indicators of the justifying principles under which correct moral judgements can be subsumed. For further discussion of Unger's method, see Robert Hanna, 'Must We Be Good Samaritans?'

26. Compare James R. Otteson, 'Limits on Our Obligation to Give', sect. V; Patricia Smith, 'The Duty to Rescue and the Slippery Slope Problem', 24.

27. The most forceful recent advocate of the moral significance of immediacy is F. M. Kamm: see esp. her 'Does Distance Matter Morally to the Duty to Rescue?', 'Faminine Ethics', 'Rescue and Harm', sect. II, and 'Review of Peter Unger, *Living High and Letting Die*'. (However, Kamm's emphasis is primarily on showing that we intuitively see distance as morally significant: her remarks on how this view might be justified are less developed.) The same line is taken by Smith, 'The Duty to Rescue and the Slippery Slope Problem', 28–9; and Jennifer Trusted, 'Rich and Poor', 297. Compare also the different but related point made in Bernard Williams, *Ethics and the Limits of Philosophy*, 186; and see also Judith Lichtenberg, 'National Boundaries and Moral Boundaries', 97; Bennett, 'Morality and Consequences', 88–9, and the contributions to *The Monist*, 86 (2003) issue on 'Moral Distance'. For an argument that what is morally significant is the greater 'moral determinacy' of situations in which someone's need is presented immediately, see Violetta Igneski, 'Distance, Determinacy and the Duty to Aid'.

28. I have in mind here especially the opposition to 'the morality system' expressed in Williams, *Ethics and the Limits of Philosophy*, ch. 10, and *Making Sense of Humanity*, chs. 1, 2, 3, 6, and 21. See also Susan Wolf, 'Morality and Partiality', 257–8.

29. I am not saying that your reason for saving a person's life ought to be that not doing so would be wrong. For my reservations about that claim, see Cullity, 'Sympathy, Discernment, and Reasons'.

CHAPTER 2

1. See e.g. Liam B. Murphy, 'Help and Beneficence' and *Moral Demands in Nonideal Theory*, 3.
2. William K. Frankena, 'Beneficence/Benevolence', 2–3, analyses this 'morally appropriate furthering of other people's interests' as a combination of beneficence, benevolence, and responsibility.
3. In Cullity, 'International Aid and the Scope of Kindness', I called this practical concern 'kindness'. That now seems to me a mistake. 'Kindness' is our name for beneficence when it is on a small and everyday scale, and carries connotations of warmth and friendliness: to call failing to save a person's life 'unkind' sounds too weak. Beneficence is the general quality that is shared by dramatic actions such as saving someone's life and the more ordinary friendly gestures and good turns that are kind. Actions of *humanity*, we might say (following Barry, 'Humanity and Justice in Global Perspective', 219–20), are those beneficent actions directed towards the relief of others' distress. In this chapter I shall be concerned with this subset of beneficent actions. But later it will be important to my argument to consider requirements of beneficence more generally.

   Notice that beneficence, understood in this way, will include acting to safeguard other people's rights, when that is in their interests. It therefore overlaps with the requirements of justice. Someone who recognizes only these requirements of justice still faces a problem about their demandingness: see Martha C. Nussbaum, 'Duties of Justice, Duties of Material Aid', 192–3.
4. A person's needs are a subset of the things it is in her interests to have—a subset that provides especially strong reasons for getting those things and thus for beneficent action. I shall not be providing or appealing to a theory of needs here: the claims I make about needs—such as that people need to be protected against threats to their lives—will be true on any plausible theory. For two notable discussions, see David Braybrooke, *Meeting Needs*, and Ignatieff, *The Needs of Strangers*.
5. I do not think that *every* time we talk about someone's concern, this can be re-expressed by talking about what she regards as good reasons (at least, not if 'regards as' means 'believes to be'). I might have a phobic concern to avoid Fido without believing I have a good reason to avoid Fido. (For the example, see Patricia S. Greenspan, *Emotions and Reasons*, 17–20.)
6. Ordinary speakers do often use a possessive phrase in this way—taking 'her reason' to refer to the consideration which is such that her regarding that consideration (rightly or wrongly) as a good reason for an action explains her performing that action. Some philosophers reserve the possessive phrase for this use—e.g. Stephen L. Darwall, *Impartial Reason*, 32. T. M. Scanlon, *What We Owe to Each Other*, 19, calls this an 'operative reason'. However, many instead follow Donald Davidson, 'Actions, Reasons and Causes', in using 'the agent's reason' to refer to the combination of mental states that explain her action.
7. Not everyone prefers to speak this way. In Sect. 2.5 I explain why this does not affect my argument.

8. I am not claiming that any of these act-descriptions suffices to establish the appropriateness of moral criticism—only that it appears to most of us that there are actions meeting those descriptions that it would be right to criticize.
9. For similar distinctions between the different ways in which one consideration can countervail against the force of another as a reason for acting, see Scanlon, *What We Owe to Each Other*, 50–5, and Walter Sinnott-Armstrong, 'Some Varieties of Particularism', 5.
10. 'Maleficence' is too specific: more commonly, the failure to help others takes the form of not being bothered to do so, rather than actually seeking to do them harm. 'Callousness' covers both malice and indifference, but only with respect to the failure to offer large-scale help; it also carries connotations of lack of compunction, which again makes it too specific.
11. This is accepted by some apparent opponents of my argument. For example, John Kekes, 'Benevolence: A Minor Virtue', 31, accepts that, in the absence of overriding claims on our resources, the need of distant strangers does create obligations on us, but he denies that benevolence has anything to do with discharging it. This does not contradict anything I say here.
12. For discussions that suggest one or the other of these two challenges, see the work cited in Ch. 1 n. 27.
13. This appears to be the strategy of Singer, 'Famine, Affluence and Morality', 231–4; also Unger, *Living High and Letting Die*. Unger seeks to demonstrate the distortional impact on our moral thinking of the separation or grouping of morally significant features of situations. I think he faces a challenge from opponents who hold that the way in which our judgements vary with the separation or grouping of features is evidence of the moral significance of separation and grouping.
14. See Shelly Kagan, 'The Additive Fallacy', for criticism of the assumption that 'the function that determines the overall status of the act given the values of the particular [moral] factors [present in the act] is an additive one' (p. 30).
15. This is often suggested by expositors of Kant. Thus, the sympathetically motivated person helps 'just because he feels like it' (Ralph C. S. Walker, *Kant*, 159); 'because this happens to fit in with [his] inclinations' (H. J. Paton, *The Categorical Imperative*, 54); 'only because he wants to' (Marcia Baron, 'Kantian Ethics', 61); 'only because of [his] inclination' (Henry E. Allison, *Kant's Theory of Freedom*, 111); because he 'responds to suffering *and* takes that response to give him a reason to help' (Barbara Herman, *The Practice of Moral Judgment*, 12).
16. See Cullity, 'Sympathy, Discernment, and Reasons'.
17. Kant's objection to helping from the motive of sympathy is sometimes explained as involving this thought. See the discussion of Kant's views on 'self-love' in Andrews Reath, 'Kant's Theory of Moral Sensibility', sect. III; also Christine M. Korsgaard, 'From Duty and for the Sake of the Noble', 213.
18. I am not offering this as an *analysis* of 'good reason for action': I take the concept of a good reason to be the primitive normative concept. Compare Scanlon, *What We Owe to Each Other*, 17–18, and Joseph Raz, 'Explaining Normativity: On Rationality and the Justification of Reason'. For criticism of this claim, see the Editor's Introduction to Jonathan Dancy (ed.), *Normativity*.

19. For this distinction between the aim of a sympathetic action and the sympathetic agent's reason for it, see Barbara Herman, 'Rules, Motives, and Helping Actions' and *The Practice of Moral Judgment*, ch. 2, sect. I; Allison, *Kant's Theory of Freedom*, 102–3; and Christine M. Korsgaard, 'Kant's Analysis of Obligation', esp. p. 56 ('The pleasure a sympathetic person takes in helping is not an ulterior purpose, but is rather the reason why he makes *helping* his purpose'), and 'From Duty and for the Sake of the Noble'.
20. Sinnott-Armstrong, 'Some Varieties of Particularism', 5, distinguishes 'underminers' from 'reversers'. Notice that my category of underminers is broader than his, not only in including reversers, but also in including considerations that weaken the force of a reason without extinguishing it altogether.
21. For the polarity metaphor, see Jonathan Dancy, 'The Particularist's Progress', 130–2.
22. Actually, I think that in the case where I must choose between two people, it might indeed be wrong to help the less deserving person—but only because there is someone else whom there is more reason to help instead, and not because it is in itself wrong to help the less deserving person.
23. It might seem tempting to reply: 'Of course non-immediately presented interests provide us with weaker reasons to help other people. After all, we *do* respond to immediately presented interests much more readily than non-immediately presented ones.' But this confuses motivating reasons—the reasons explaining why we are motivated to act as we actually do—with the normative reasons that I am discussing: the reasons that really do count in favour of doing things. I do not deny that we are more strongly motivated to respond to immediately presented needs. Moreover, I think this is morally significant: see Sects. 2.4 and 11.4.
24. One might question this distinction. I have defended it elsewhere: see Cullity, 'Particularism and Presumptive Reasons'. However, rejecting it would simplify my argument rather than complicate it: it would allow us to concentrate solely on the earlier question whether immediacy is part of the content of a beneficent person's reason, and leave aside the question whether it can be treated as an underminer.
25. For this objection, see Gomberg, 'The Fallacy of Philanthropy', 35, and Smith, 'The Duty to Rescue and the Slippery Slope Problem', 26–8. For relevant discussion of a similar point, see Stephen L. Darwall, *Philosophical Ethics*, 217.
26. On the significance of identifying individual beneficiaries in motivating beneficent action, see Robert Frank, 'Motivation, Cognition, and Charitable Giving'. On the way in which this encourages television journalism to depoliticize humanitarian disasters, see Ignatieff, 'The Stories We Tell: Television and Humanitarian Aid', 294–5.
27. For some of the *other* factors that seem clearly to be correlated with a greater propensity to help other people, see John Campbell, 'Can Philosophical Accounts of Altruism Accommodate Experimental Data on Helping Behaviour?'
28. For Shelly Kagan's discussion of this point, and its relation to the issue of whether we are capable of acting much more impartially than we do, see *The Limits of Morality*, 291–300.

29. Kant seems to include this as one of the 'natural obstacles' of sensibility, the overcoming of which increases the merit of an action. See Immanuel Kant, *The Metaphysics of Morals*, 19–20 (*Ak.* 6.228).
30. To what extent this has been true in different slaveholding societies is an interesting question. Attempts to justify slavery are often suggestive of the extent to which there was a perception of its morally problematic nature, to which a response was required. On the degree to which this is true of Aristotle, see Giuseppe Cambiano, 'Aristotle and the Anonymous Opponents of Slavery'. On the debate about slavery in the classical world more generally, see Peter Garnsey, *Ideas of Slavery from Aristotle to Augustine*. On the same question in relation to medieval serfdom, see Christopher Dyer, 'Memories of Freedom'. For a discussion of the relationship between religious and racial justifications of New World slavery, see Robin Blackburn, *The Making of New World Slavery*, ch. 1.
31. Talking of 'objective' and 'subjective' wrongness in this way would coincide, as far as I can see, with the distinction made by Derek Parfit, *Reasons and Persons*, 25; but not with the one made by Sidgwick. On Sidgwick's usage, an action is subjectively wrong when the person performing it believes it to be wrong, so the slaveholders' actions would not count as subjectively wrong at all—see *The Methods of Ethics*, III. i. 3.
32. The phrase 'blameless wrongdoing' comes from Parfit, *Reasons and Persons*, 31–5.
33. For support, one might turn to Soran Reader, 'Distance, Relationship, and Moral Obligation'. However, her claim that such relationships are a necessary condition for requirements of beneficence is one I have argued against.
34. What would a complete theory of beneficence look like? One way of thinking of this would be as specifying exactly which considerations, under which circumstances, can properly be regarded as countervailing in relation to the form of concern distinctive of beneficence. A more modest goal (although still a large one) would be simply to specify all those considerations which do under some circumstances countervail in relation to beneficence, without trying to specify those circumstances.
35. Eliminating the ambiguities in this description generates different versions of welfarist consequentialism.
36. For the objection that consequentialists make the mistake of taking beneficence for the whole of morality, see Philippa Foot, 'Utilitarianism and the Virtues'.

    Singer maintains that his own argument for the life-saving analogy is independent of a commitment to consequentialism: see his 'Postscript to "Famine, Affluence and Morality" ', 35–6, and *Practical Ethics*, 168–71. However, this is often disputed: see e.g. Susan James, 'The Duty to Relieve Suffering', 5, 15; Jan Narveson, 'Equality vs Liberty: Advantage, Liberty', 45–6; O'Neill, *Faces of Hunger*, 56–8; Douglas Odegard, 'Charity and Moral Imperatives', 92; Mike W. Martin, *Virtuous Giving*, 65; Cullity, 'International Aid and the Scope of Kindness', 102–4; McGinn, 'Our Duties to Animals and the Poor'. For the same complaint about Unger, see McGinn, 'Saint Elsewhere'.
37. Different sorts of priority-claims are made by different kinds of 'virtue-ethical' approaches. See Cullity, 'Could There Be a Virtue Theory in Ethics?' for an

attempt to distinguish them. I cannot see how the argument presented here commits me to any of these priority-claims.

38. Strictly speaking, my claim is that if an action of helping is wrong, and not helping would *not* be wrong, then helping is not beneficent. If there can be tragic dilemmas in which both helping and not helping are wrong, then I think there might be no failure of discernment in helping, even though it was wrong. Therefore, if beneficence requires proper discernment, that does not rule out actions of beneficence that are wrong in situations where not acting beneficently would be wrong too. The sentence in the text could be tightened up to reflect this by saying that if injustice, dishonesty, or capriciousness makes an action *uniquely* wrong, it cannot count as beneficent—where an action is uniquely wrong when performing it would be wrong and not performing it would not be wrong.

CHAPTER 3

1. Philosophical discussions of the moral demands of affluence have been surprisingly uncritical of the rhetoric of humanitarian fundraisers. A notable exception is Schmidtz, 'Islands in a Sea of Obligation', 684–7. Some others are mentioned in n. 4 below.
2. Graham Hancock was the East Africa correspondent for *The Economist*. Michael Maren is a journalist and former aid worker with the Peace Corps and USAID. Alex de Waal is a human rights activist, currently Director of Justice Africa, and has worked as a consultant to Oxfam. David Sogge is an aid analyst who has worked for private American, Canadian, and Dutch aid agencies.
3. Rieff, *A Bed for the Night*, 56. Compare Sogge, *Give and Take*, 166.
4. See e.g. John Kekes, 'On the Supposed Obligation to Relieve Famine', Goldstein, 'Review of Peter Unger, *Living High and Letting Die*', and Gomberg, 'The Fallacy of Philanthropy'. Concerns with conceiving of the moral issues surrounding poverty as issues of rescue are also reflected in Nagel, 'Poverty and Food', O'Neill, 'The Great Maxims of Justice and Charity', Alan Gewirth, 'Private Philanthropy and Positive Rights', and Pogge, ' "Assisting" the Global Poor'. This objection is also suggested by Martha Nussbaum, 'If Oxfam Ran the World'.
5. Thomas Malthus, *An Essay on the Principle of Population*; for a brief commentary, see David Arnold, *Famine: Social Crisis and Historical Change*, 34–42.
6. See Garrett Hardin, 'Lifeboat Ethics: The Case against Helping the Poor' and 'Living on a Lifeboat'; George R. Lucas, Jr., and Thomas W. Ogletree (eds.), *Lifeboat Ethics*—especially the contributions by Fletcher, Englehardt, and Hardin—Paul Paddock and William Paddock, *Famine—1975!*; Paul Ehrlich, *The Population Bomb*; and Donella H. Meadows *et al.*, *The Limits of Growth*. As is pointed out by O'Neill, *Faces of Hunger*, 15, Malthus himself does not take the further step to advocating the 'triage' policy recommended by these authors.

7. Garrett Hardin, *The Ostrich Factor: Our Population Myopia*; Paul Erlich, *The Population Explosion.*
8. See Amartya Sen, *Development as Freedom*, 205; Phillips Foster and Howard D. Leathers, *The World Food Problem*, 112–15; and Frances Moore Lappé *et al.*, *World Hunger: 12 Myths*, 8. They cite FAO, *FAO Production Yearbook*, xlvi and xlix (1993, 1996). See also Bauer, *Equality, the Third World and Economic Delusion*, ch. 3: 'The Population Explosion: Myths and Realities', for an emphasis on countries in which rapid population increase has been exceeded by the rate of increase in real income.
9. Lappé *et al.*, *World Hunger: 12 Myths*, 10–11.
10. See Amartya Sen, *Poverty and Famines*, 7–8, 39–51, 154–66; Jean Drèze and Amartya Sen, *Hunger and Public Action*, ch. 2; Sen, *Development as Freedom*, ch. 7; S. R. Osmani, 'The Food Problems of Bangladesh'; Foster and Leathers, *The World Food Problem*, pt. 2; and Frances Moore Lappé and Joseph Collins, *Food First*, 40–52. Even in countries where a collapse in food availability has undoubtedly contributed to famine, such as Ethiopia in the latter part of the last century, it is argued that the fuller causal background suggests ways in which starvation was avertible—see B. G. Kumar, 'Ethiopian Famines 1973–1985', 209–13.
11. Sen, *Poverty and Famines*, 58. The 'current supply' of rice was a technical term employed by the official Famine Inquiry Commission reporting on the Bengal famine to denote the sum of the spring and winter crops of the year in question, the winter crop of the preceding year, and net imports.
12. See Sen, *Poverty and Famines*, 137–50; Tony Jackson and Deborah Eade, *Against the Grain*, 15–16; Lappé and Collins, *Food First*, 25–8; Martin Ravallion, *Markets and Famines.*
13. Jean Drèze, 'Famine Prevention in India', 68—for an extended discussion of the Maharashtra drought, see pp. 65–97.
14. Drèze and Sen, *Hunger and Public Action*, 122.
15. The seminal work here is Sen, *Poverty and Famines*. For further applications of this approach, see in particular the authors collected in Jean Drèze and Amartya Sen (eds.), *The Political Economy of Hunger*, vols. i–iii.
16. Sen, *Poverty and Famines*, 3.
17. See Piet Terhal and Indira Hirway, 'Rural Public Works and Food Entitlement Protection'; Drèze and Sen, *Hunger and Public Action*, ch. 8; Drèze, 'Famine Prevention in India', 89–99. For a study of the economic effects of such programmes, and further references, see Martin Ravallion, 'Market Responses to Anti-Hunger Policies', 245–55.
18. Drèze and Sen, *Hunger and Public Action*, 98.
19. e.g. Ravallion, *Markets and Famines* and 'Famines and Economics'; Drèze and Sen, *Hunger and Public Action* and Drèze and Sen (eds.), *The Political Economy of Hunger*; Helen O'Neill and John Toye (eds.), *A World without Famine?*; Joachim von Braun *et al.*, *Famine in Africa: Causes, Reasons, Prevention.*

    For a historical survey, see Lucile F. Newman (ed.), *Hunger in History*. On the role of public health measures in reducing famine-related mortality, see Alex de Waal, *Famines That Kill: Darfur 1984–1985.*

20. See Drèze and Sen, *Hunger and Public Action*, ch. 8 'Experiences and Lessons'—esp. pp. 126, 133, 135, 140, 146, 159.
21. On the latter point, see also Narasimhan Ram, 'An Independent Press and Anti-Hunger Strategies'; and Alex de Waal, *Famine Crimes*, ch. 11.
22. See Sen, *Development as Freedom*, esp. pp. 178–84.
23. See Jackson and Eade, *Against the Grain*, ch. 8; John Cathie, *The Political Economy of Food Aid*, 4, 7, 152–4.
24. Jackson and Eade, *Against the Grain*, 8–9, 89–90.
25. Christopher Stevens, *Food Aid and the Developing World*, 200.
26. Ibid. 200–1; Ravallion, *Markets and Famines*. For other criticisms of food aid, see Stephen Hellinger *et al.*, *Aid for Just Development*; Frank Vibert, *Home Truths for Foreign Aid*; P. T. Bauer, *Reality and Rhetoric*; and Keith Griffin, *World Hunger and the World Economy*. For defences of food aid, see H. Singer *et al.*, *Food Aid*; and Willy Brandt, *Common Crisis North–South*, 130–2.
27. For a collection of work that acknowledges, analyses, and responds to these criticisms of food aid, see Edward Clay and Olav Stokke (eds.), *Food Aid Reconsidered*.
28. Jackson and Eade, *Against the Grain*, ch. 2; Frances Moore Lappé *et al.*, *Aid as Obstacle*, 115–18; de Waal, *Famine Crimes*, chs. 4–10.
29. To take one example, the Sudanese famine of 1984–5 has been attributed to the government's passing on the debt incurred in financing the purchase of agricultural machinery in the form of higher food prices, which became unaffordable when the drought destroyed employment prospects—see Nick Cater, *Sudan: The Roots of Famine*. For another example, see the account of the disastrous Ausaid project in Coast Province, Kenya, between 1976 and 1989 given by Doug Porter *et al.*, *Development in Practice: Paved with Good Intentions*. See also Bauer, 'Foreign Aid and its Hydra-Headed Rationalization'.
30. See Barbara Dinham and Colin Hines, *Agribusiness in Africa*, 41–2, 129–33; Lappé *et al.*, *Aid as Obstacle*; Lappé and Collins, *Food First*; Andrew Pearse, *Seeds of Plenty, Seeds of Want*; Desmond McNeill, *The Contradictions of Foreign Aid*, ch. 5; and Susan George, *Ill Fares the Land*.

    For the case against the Bretton Woods institutions (i.e. the World Bank and the International Monetary Fund), see Kevin Danaher (ed.), *50 Years is Enough*, and Catherine Caufield, *Masters of Illusion*. The case for the defence is mounted by World Bank, *Assessing Aid*, and supported, with qualifications, by Robert Cassen and Associates, *Does Aid Work*?, and Michael Lipton and John Toye, *Does Aid Work in India*?
31. Few people are now willing to argue that technological innovation can solve hunger without structural change. But to what extent is technological innovation *part* of the solution? For an introduction to the literature debating this, see Lappé *et al.*, *World Hunger: 12 Myths*, ch. 5.
32. For this diagnosis of the failure of aid to produce development in Africa (but without the conclusion that aid should be abandoned), see Carol Lancaster, *Aid to Africa*.
33. See Lappé and Collins, *Food First*, ch. 16, for an endorsement of the post-revolutionary land reform policies of China, Cuba, and Vietnam. However, for a more nuanced view, see Lappé *et al.*, *World Hunger: 12 Myths*, e.g. p. 88.

34. Drèze and Sen, *Hunger and Public Action*, ch. 8.
35. Vibert, *Home Truths for Foreign Aid*, 24.
36. This objection is particularly obvious in relation to government-to-government aid: see e.g. Bauer, *Equality, the Third World and Economic Delusion*, 93–5, and Sogge, *Give and Take*, 8. For some recent examples concerning non-government aid, take the way in which the refugee camps set up by Western non-government aid agencies in northern Zaire in 1996–7 were infiltrated and controlled by Hutu militia groups from Rwanda, or the way in which refugee groups were used in Somalia during the dictatorship of Siyyad Barre to control aid and manipulate clan loyalties, as documented by Michael Maren, *The Road to Hell*. See also Terry, *Condemned to Repeat?*, and Peter Uvin, *Aiding Violence: The Development Enterprise in Rwanda*.
37. See Bauer, 'Foreign Aid and its Hydra-Headed Rationalization', sect. 8.
38. See n. 30 above.
39. A claim that is contested by critics of aid on the right: see e.g. Bauer, 'Foreign Aid and its Hydra-Headed Rationalization', sect. 14.
40. See Teresa Hayter, *Aid as Imperialism*.
41. For sustained broadsides in this spirit, see Graham Hancock, *Lords of Poverty*, and Maren, *The Road to Hell*.
42. The 1990s saw a dramatic expansion of the NGO aid sector, fuelled largely by a sharp increase in the proportion of Official Development Assistance channelled through NGOs by Organisation for Economic Co-operation and Development (OECD) governments. For figures, see Michael Edwards and David Hulme (eds.), *Beyond the Magic Bullet*, 3–4, and App. 2 below.

    The label 'NGO' covers a very disparate group of organizations, which have widely varying aims, structures, sizes, and levels of competence. On this, see Kunibert Raffer and H. W. Singer, *The Foreign Aid Business*, ch. 10.
43. Hancock, *Lords of Poverty*, p. xiii. The same point is made by Bauer, *Equality, the Third World and Economic Delusion*, 128–9, 274, and Sogge, *Give and Take*, 160. See also John Madeley, *When Aid is No Help*: ch. 10 makes the case for improving the record of official aid by channelling it through NGOs, something that has been done to a much greater extent since the publication of his book.
44. e.g. Maren, *The Road to Hell*; Terry, *Condemned to Repeat?* See also Jean-Dominique Merchet, 'Humanitarian Organizations Have Become Businesses'—an interview exploring Sylvie Brunel's decision to resign as president of the French NGO Action Contre Faim.
45. For the point that poor people are not helped by being taught to see themselves as victims, see Schmidtz, 'Islands in a Sea of Obligation', 704, 705. This objection is emphasized by both Ralph Waldo Emerson, 'Gifts', and Kant, *Lectures on Ethics*, 'Poverty and Charity'. (Kant is careful to acknowledge that this is an objection to almsgiving, though, rather than to helping.)
46. More than one writer comments on the spectacle of NGOs jostling for media attention in the Zairean camps of 1996–7. On the inability of NGOs to form equitable partnerships with each other, see Alan Fowler, 'Authentic NGDO Partnership in the New Policy Agenda for International Aid'.
47. See Edwards and Hulme (eds.), *Beyond the Magic Bullet*, Introduction; John Farrington *et al.*, *Reluctant Partners?*, 184–5.

48. Maren, *The Road to Hell*, ch. 12.
49. Ibid. 51, 176; Hancock, *Lords of Poverty*, pt. 5.
50. Maren, *The Road to Hell*, ch. 9; Terry, *Condemned to Repeat?*
51. Maren, *The Road to Hell*, 269, concludes that NGOs should be overseen by an independent watchdog. 'What is really required is a truly independent agency—not one like InterAction, which is composed of NGOs—to look after the interests of the targets of development and relief, a.k.a., the needy. The organization should be staffed by professionals who have the time and resources to produce detailed analyses of what these organizations are doing for the poor of the Third World. Those that do effective aid work should be singled out so "customers" know where to spend their money. In the short run, that will stop the wildfire proliferation of NGOs, and eventually reduce them to a manageable number so that relief circuses like Rwanda don't ever happen again.' However, in interviews since his book's publication he has made the much stronger claim that the aid industry should be abolished altogether, and we are making a sentimental mistake if we support it. (See his web site, <http://www.netnomad.com/>.)
52. Two short introductory descriptions of the Grameen Bank are Jessica Matthews, 'Little World Banks', and David Bornstein, 'The Barefoot Bank with Cheek'; for an economist's evaluation, see Atiur Rahman, 'Rural Development from Below'. The Grameen Bank was founded by the Bangladeshi economist Muhammad Yunus, and formally established as a bank in 1983; it provides loans averaging $100 to the least advantaged citizens of rural Bangladesh, primarily women. According to Matthews, the Grameen Bank boasts a 97 per cent loan recovery rate; and 48 per cent of those who have borrowed from it for ten years have crossed the poverty line.
53. On the importance of NGOs' role in advocacy and lobbying, see Raffer and Singer, *The Foreign Aid Business*, ch. 10. For some case studies, see Seamus Cleary, *The Role of NGOs under Authoritarian Political Systems*. See also the work cited in n. 70 below. NGOs playing a watchdog role in critically monitoring official aid include British Overseas NGOs for Development, Bretton Woods Project, and Development Group for Alternative Policies. For the role of human rights NGOs as providers of information on the basis of which pressure for political change can be exerted through government aid programmes, see Mick Moore and Mark Robinson, 'Can Foreign Aid Be Used to Promote Good Government in Developing Countries?', 156. For an evaluation of NGO micro-finance schemes, see Imran Matin *et al.*, 'Finance for the Poor'.

    However, on the limitations and pitfalls of NGO attempts to foster broader political change in poor countries, see Edwards and Hulme (eds.), *Beyond the Magic Bullet*, 5–6, and Alan Fowler, 'NGOs as Agents of Democratisation'.
54. For examples of interaction between NGOs and governments to scale up the effects of successful programmes, see Farrington *et al.*, *Reluctant Partners?*, e.g. at p. 187.
55. This point is accepted by de Waal, *Famine Crimes*, 220: 'It is morally unacceptable to allow people to suffer and die on the grounds that relieving their suffering will support an obnoxious government or army.' But he continues: 'The big question is therefore: Can humanitarian agencies save lives in the absence of any

form of political contract? Can they act in a technically proficient and politically inoffensive way, while others struggle to create political contracts or resolve political crises?'

56. For a sensitive, well-informed, and politically intelligent history of modern humanitarian aid, see Rieff, *A Bed for the Night*. He quotes approvingly Sadako Ogata's remark that 'there are no humanitarian solutions to humanitarian problems' and argues that humanitarianism is losing its way in attempting to go beyond a focus on meeting 'the humanitarian imperative'. For a similar view, expressed fifteen years earlier, see Bruce Nichols, 'Rubberband Humanitarianism'.
57. Most seriously so in situations where that attitude is exploited for military advantage in situations of military conflict. For a telling study of this disturbing pattern of manipulation of the humanitarian aid industry, see Terry, *Condemned to Repeat?*
58. See de Waal, *Famine Crimes* (esp. chs. 1 and 11), and *Who Fights? Who Cares?*, 153; also Sogge, *Give and Take*, 101, 122, 135, 178–85.
59. A point emphasized by Rieff, *A Bed for the Night* (esp. chs 4 and 5, on Bosnia and Rwanda); also Ignatieff, 'The Stories We Tell: Television and Humanitarian Aid', 297–301.
60. *This* is something that NGOs are criticized for too—see e.g. Minear, *The Humanitarian Enterprise*, 182; Terje Tvedt, *Angels of Mercy or Development Diplomats?*, 88–90.
61. See e.g. David Rieff, 'Charity on the Rampage', 136–8; Raymond Bonner, 'Review of Michael Maren, *The Road to Hell*'.
62. Maren, *The Road to Hell*, 214. He cites Steven Hansch *et al.*, *Lives Lost, Lives Saved.*
63. There is a very large literature on this, and I cannot claim to have sampled more than a small part of it. However, the parts I have seen certainly bear out this claim. Three of the more prominent recent large-scale surveys, synthesizing the results of a wide range of evaluation reports on NGO activities, are Roger C. Riddell *et al.*, *Searching for Impact and Methods*, Kees Biekart, *The Politics of Civil Society Building*, and Alan Fowler, *Civil Society, NGDOs and Social Development*. In addition to this, most OECD governments publish evaluation reports on NGO work. For some recent British examples, see C. Cameron and J. Cocking, *The Evaluation of NGO Activities*, and M. A. Surr, *Evaluations of Non Government Organisations (NGOs) Development Projects Synthesis Report*. For an older, much-cited American example, see Judith Tendler, *Turning Private Voluntary Organizations into Development Agencies*.

    For other assessments of the efficacy of NGO development work, see e.g. Roger Riddell and Mark Robinson, *The Impact of NGO Poverty-Alleviation Projects*, Minear, *The Humanitarian Enterprise*, Raffer and Singer, *The Foreign Aid Business*, ch. 10, and David H. Smith, 'Grassroots Associations Are Important: Some Theory and a Review of the Impact Literature'.

    For assessments of the efficacy of NGO relief work, see the studies by Riddell and Cameron cited above; J. Borton *et al.*, *NGOs and Relief Operations*, Philip Johnston, 'Relief and Reality', Ian Smillie, 'Painting Canadian Roses Red', 189, and Larry Minear, *Helping People in an Age of Conflict*.

It should be acknowledged, however, that a common refrain in the literature concerns the difficulty of making reliable assessments of the overall impact of NGO activity, given the many other causally influential factors bearing on relief and development outcomes. See e.g. Edwards and Hulme (eds.), *Beyond the Magic Bullet*, 9–11. NGOs and the governments that fund them have often been criticized for failing to adopt more rigorous and transparent evaluation procedures: for these criticisms, and evidence of what is now being done to address them, see e.g. Smillie, 'Painting Canadian Roses Red'. For a collection of case studies examining current practice, see Adrian Wood *et al.* (eds.), *Evaluating International Humanitarian Action*.

64. One philosopher who has noticed and tellingly emphasized this point is Schmidtz, 'Islands in a Sea of Obligation', 685–8.
65. It is advocated by Karl Borgin and Kathleen Corbett, *The Destruction of a Continent: Africa and International Aid*, ch. 10.
66. See de Waal, *Famine Crimes*, p. xvi, where he quotes approvingly the opinion of Hugo Slim, 'Doing the Right Thing', that political crises are not like forest fires that will burn themselves out by being left alone. Several analysts make the same point about official development assistance: for all of its manifest shortcomings, it is not credible that the poor would be helped by removing it. See e.g. Roger C. Riddell, *Foreign Aid Reconsidered*, 240–1; J. R. Parkinson (ed.), *Poverty and Aid*, 6.
67. See the work cited in n. 63 above. On the question of whether emergency relief aid can be administered in a politically and economically sensitive way, see the case studies discussed by Anderson, *Do No Harm*, and 'You Save My Life Today, but for What Tomorrow?' Some aid agencies (including some of those most heavily criticized in the past) are demonstrably working to publicize and counteract the use of aid in fuelling conflict. See e.g. ICRC, *War, Money and Survival*.

    Many studies on the topic of economically and politically sensitive NGO development project design have been published in journals such as *World Development*: see e.g. Michael Edwards, 'NGO Performance—What Breeds Success? New Evidence from South Asia'; Norman Uphoff, 'Grassroots Organizations and NGOs in Rural Development', esp. sect. 5 and 6; Paul J. Nelson and Ellen Dorsey, 'At the Nexus of Human Rights and Development: New Methods and Strategies of Global NGOs'; and Alnoor Ebrahim, 'Accountability in Practice: Mechanisms for NGOs'.
68. Bribes and 'taxes' are routinely extracted from aid workers as the price of transporting relief supplies to needy people. This is bad, for the reasons de Waal and others give. But often it is right for the aid workers to pay them as the price of getting aid through.
69. Clearly, this changes the life-saving analogy in one important way. We are imagining a situation in which someone's life needs to be saved but it is no longer a situation in which I am morally required to save that life. I return to this issue in Ch. 4.
70. For examples of effective human rights advocacy by NGOs, see Michael Edwards and John Gaventa (eds.), *Global Citizen Action*, Thomas G. Weiss and Leon Gordenker (eds.), *NGOs, the UN and Global Governance*, and Kathryn Sikkink, 'Human Rights Issue-Networks in Latin America'; also Raffer and

Singer, *The Foreign Aid Business*, 144–9. For an evaluation of advocacy work by UK NGOs, see Alan Hudson, 'NGOs' Transnational Advocacy Networks'.

71. I am not claiming that Oxfam's record is perfect. For telling criticisms of some of its activities, see Maren, *The Road to Hell*, 98; de Waal, *Famine Crimes*, 75, 198, 207–8; Rakiya Omar and Alex de Waal, 'Humanitarianism Unbound?'; Terry, *Condemned to Repeat?*; and M. Jennings, ' "Almost an Oxfam in Itself": Oxfam, Ujamaa and Development in Tanzania'. However, I have not seen any serious case mounted for thinking that its activities, taken as a whole, do more harm than good.
72. For the view that advocacy and humanitarian work are not compatible in practice, however, see Nichols, 'Rubberband Humanitarianism', 209, and Rieff, *A Bed for the Night*.
73. For a dissenting voice, though, from a perspective that favours a free market approach to charity, see Nicholas Eberstadt, 'Aid Harms the Hungry'.
74. The same reply applies to the point, forcefully emphasized by Schmidtz, 'Islands in a Sea of Obligation', 685–6, that it is not immediately obvious which relief operations or aid agencies are doing good, and which are doing harm. I draw the same conclusion as him: 'we have to take responsibility for distinguishing between aid that helps beneficiaries resume meaningful lives and aid that turns people into seekers of aid' (p. 705).
75. Michael Maren is someone who has obviously done this.
76. I am using 'blameworthy' and 'wrong' in the same way as Sect. 2.4. The wrongness of an action reflects the force and kind of reasons against doing it. Its blameworthiness reflects the extent to which blame attaches to your failure to act on those reasons.
77. See e.g. Schmidtz, 'Islands in a Sea of Obligation', 690; McKinsey, 'Obligations to the Starving', 314.
78. For each of the considerations that can be met by this third sort of reply, the first will apply as well. The deeper objection to these proposals is that they do nothing to explain how not responding to the dire need of others involves no failure of beneficence. Since they do nothing to show this for direct responses to immediately presented emergencies, they can do nothing to show this for contributions to aid agencies.
79. This was Sidgwick's objection: see *The Methods of Ethics*, 436.
80. See Gewirth, 'Private Philanthropy and Positive Rights', 73–7.
81. See Trusted, 'Rich and Poor', 299–300.
82. See Arthur, 'Rights and the Duty to Bring Aid'; and Thomas Young, 'Analogical Reasoning and Easy Rescue Cases'.

CHAPTER 4

1. Conversations with John Broome have helped me to see this. I am grateful also to Howard Sobel for correspondence on this issue.
2. One reader worried here that if this is true of everyone, then there is no chance that the decision will ever be made; but such decisions *are* made; so this cannot be true. However, I think that is a mistake. If this is true of everyone, what

follows is that there is no chance the decision will ever by triggered by the donation of any one person. But that still leaves it open that it can be triggered by the donations of several of us.

3. For a brief description of how Oxfam assigns funds to emergency relief, see <http://www.oxfam.org.uk/what_we_do/emergencies/how_we_work/factfile/fundraising.htm>. It maintains a reserve, called the 'Catastrophe Fund', on which it draws to address a new emergency while it waits for fundraising efforts to take effect.

   A more detailed account of relief agencies' responses to humanitarian emergencies is contained in the independent evaluation reports made public by the Disasters Emergency Committee (DEC, an umbrella group coordinating relief appeals from UK charities). In the report on DEC members' response to the Sudan crisis of 1998, it is made clear that total DEC expenditure exceeded the appeal funds that had been released, 'indicating other sources for largely DEC funded projects'. (See the report *Disasters Emergency Committee: Sudan Crisis Appeal*, 49, <http://www.dec.org.uk/uploads/documents/sudan.pdf>.)

4. For versions of this objection, see Whelan, 'Famine and Charity', 158–61, and Robert E. Goodin, *Protecting the Vulnerable*, 162–3. Whelan thinks the objection shows that no individual purchase of mine can be faulted for being a failure to give to charity, but endorses a version of the life-saving analogy in support of the conclusion that it is wrong not (in general) to contribute to charity. According to Goodin, the objection shows that our responsibility towards the starving is a collective rather than an individual one, but he adds that it is wrong for any individual not to contribute to the fulfilment of that collective responsibility. However, while neither draws from the objection the conclusion that contributing nothing to aid agencies is morally acceptable, it is not clear what entitles them to resist it. Why should non-contribution be wrong if it makes no difference whether or not I contribute?

5. See Brian Barry, *Political Argument*, 328–30; Jonathan Glover, 'It Makes No Difference Whether or Not I Do It'; M. J. Scott-Taggart, 'Collective and Individual Responsibility'; Donald H. Regan, *Utilitarianism and Co-operation*, 56–65; Parfit, *Reasons and Persons*, ch. 3; Bart Gruzalski, 'Parfit's Impact on Utilitarianism', 777–82, and Parfit, 'Comments', 846–9; Michael Otsuka, 'The Paradox of Group Beneficence'; and the contributions to Michael J. Almeida (ed.), *Imperceptible Harms*.

6. Thus Glover, 'It Makes No Difference Whether or Not I Do It', 174–5, gives the example of a hundred bandits each stealing one bean from each of the hundred-bean lunches of a hundred villagers; Parfit, *Reasons and Persons*, 76, gives the example of failing to add a pint of water to a thousand-pint tank which will be taken to a thousand severely thirsty men.

7. Parfit, *Reasons and Persons*, ch. 3, argues that this does not require the existence of imperceptible harms and benefits; Otsuka, 'The Paradox of Group Beneficence', argues that it does. For further discussion, see Cullity, 'Pooled Beneficence', sect. II.

8. For this use of 'non-rival', see e.g. Michael Taylor, *The Possibility of Cooperation*, 7. It is similar but not identical to the definitions given in David W. Pearce (ed.), *The Macmillan Dictionary of Modern Economics*, 352, and Donald Rutherford, *Dictionary of Economics*, 375.

9. This account of what is wrong with free riding might seem to invite an objection. Public goods can be produced by a group that ought not to be producing them. Perhaps the benefit is not worth the cost, or there is a moral objection to the means by which it is produced. But even in these circumstances, taking a benefit without paying can be free riding. If a group is producing a good when it ought not to, taking the good without paying the announced price might still be wrong. If you have an objection to the production of the good, you ought not to take it. So it seems that you can be free riding even when the collective activity on which you are free riding is not the meeting of a collective imperative.

   Two options are possible in reply to this. One is to qualify the claim about free riding: this involves failing to contribute to what we ought to be doing, *relative to our shared aims*. Perhaps what I ought to be doing, all things considered, is to renounce the aim, rather than contribute to our collectively meeting it. But if I do share that aim, and I help myself to its fulfilment, relying on others to contribute to meeting it without doing so myself, then I am still acting unfairly. The second option is to retain the claim that, even in this case, I am failing to contribute to a collective imperative. I am violating the convention that taking goods to which a publicly understood price attaches binds one to pay that price; and this convention is something that we ought collectively to sustain. It confers a benefit on all of us: the second-order benefit of having the opportunity to enjoy first-order goods if one wishes. This benefit is produced by imposing a cost—namely, adhering to the conditional requirement that if you accept those first-order goods, you must pay the publicly understood price. Thus, it might still be maintained that the free rider is, even here, relying on others to do what we ought collectively to be doing, without contributing himself.
10. 'In the purest case.' An interesting question is to what extent any real-world public good is worth its cost to *every* member of a group that is called upon to contribute to producing it. Very often, justifications for imposing costs on members of a community towards producing a public good will need to appeal either to the fact that the good belongs to a *range* of goods which together are worth their cost to everyone; or to a moral justification for requiring some people to contribute towards producing benefits for others.
11. I am not saying that we can never be morally required to act unilaterally towards fulfilling a collective imperative; only that, when we are, the reason is different.
12. It is a corollary of this point that we might fail to do what we collectively ought to be doing without any individual's acting unfairly. Often, a preparedness to cooperate will not be *sufficient* for achieving a collective goal. That will also require leadership from someone in initiating and coordinating a plan for us to work around. We might fail to do what we ought for various reasons: a failure of cooperative spirit is one; a failure of leadership another. Only the first is a failure of *fairness*.
13. See Ch. 1 n. 12, and Sect. 5.2. (at n. 11).
14. Notice also that I am not saying that, in individual actions, saving lives always takes precedence over preventing threats. If I could either save one person's life or directly myself prevent future threats to two, I should probably prevent the threats.

CHAPTER 5

1. I have in mind especially Peter Singer, Peter Unger, and James Fishkin. However, not all of the elements of what follows are explicit in Singer's presentation of the life-saving analogy, and Unger's presentation definitely diverges from what is said here in one central respect. Unger's argument does not proceed by iterating the life-saving analogy for each needy person who could be helped at a distance. (For this (mis)reading of his argument, see David Lewis, 'Illusory Innocence?', 35.) Rather, he argues that, since we can be required to make very great financial sacrifices to save *one* person's life directly, the sacrifices we can be required to make are no smaller when there are many lives we could save at a distance. See Unger, *Living High and Letting Die*, ch. 6. (However, for the objection that Unger *should* then iterate his own argument, see Schmidtz, 'Islands in a Sea of Obligation', 692.) For Singer's various discussions of the life-saving analogy, see Ch.1 n. 14. The problem raised by this iterative argument is the subject of James S. Fishkin, *The Limits of Obligation*—see esp. pp. 3–7. See also Martin, *Virtuous Giving*, 64–5.
2. Those who hold severely demanding moral views often follow Sidgwick, *The Methods of Ethics*, 220–1, 490–3, in distinguishing between what you should believe and what you should advocate. See Peter Singer, 'Reconsidering the Famine Relief Argument', 48–9, and *Practical Ethics*, 180–1; Jonathan Glover, *Causing Death and Saving Lives*, 109–11; and Unger, *Living High and Letting Die*, 156–7. See also Parfit, *Reasons and Persons*, 41.
3. These figures come from various pieces of fundraising literature produced by Oxfam in the 1990s. In early 2004 the Disasters Emergency Committee was quoting £100 as the cost of feeding a family for one month, and providing other survival supplies (blankets, water purification tablets, and other household items). Source: <http://www.dec.org.uk/index.cfm/asset_id,999/-index.html>.
4. The quoted sentence and accompanying figures are from the website of the Rehydration Project, <http://www.rehydrate.org/>, in early 2004.
5. World Health Organization, <http://www.who.int/mediacentre/factsheets/fs104/en/>. For Peter Unger's derivation of $200 as the cost of health spending which would give a 'typically sick' 2-year-old in a poor country a greater than 90 per cent chance of reaching 21, see *Living High and Letting Die*, 146–9. I comment on this and the other figures given in the text in App. 2.
6. <http://www.unicef.org/immunization/index_bigpicture.html>. Again, see App. 2 for further discussion.
7. Unger, *Living High and Letting Die*, 136. Liam B. Murphy, *Moral Demands in Nonideal Theory*, 127, discusses a similar example which he attributes to Shelly Kagan.
8. Moreover, giving a £150 contribution in one lump sum is not my only option. If giving a total of £150 to an aid agency is a life-saving contribution, and spreading this over the course of my life would not be a sacrifice comparable to a long-term injury, then the Severe Demand requires it. Spread over thirty years, that could be done by giving £5 per year. And I would have to be *very* poor before *this* could sensibly be compared to a long-term injury. This wouldn't quite require me to reduce myself to a level of basic subsistence myself: for

someone at that level, an extra £5 per year to spend on himself would be terrifically valuable. (This is about 2.5 per cent of the annual income of those on the lowest of the World Bank's poverty lines.) But it would mean bringing myself close to it.

9. Aid agencies are rightly reluctant to claim that these amounts represent the average cost of saving a life; nor even to attempt the kind of analysis that could try to justify such claims. So are their evaluators: see e.g. the evaluation reports on Disasters Emergency Committee (DEC) relief operations, available at <http://www.dec.org.uk/index.cfm/asset_id,469/index.html>, which routinely make the point about the impossibility of screening out all the other causal factors in order to quantify the number of lives saved by DEC work. For further discussion, see App. 2.

10. Notice that a Fair Share View need not involve the claim that requiring me to do more than my share to make up for others' failure to pull their weight is *unfair*. It might seem simply analytic to hold that it is unfair to demand of me that I do more than my fair share; and the view is usually formulated this way. (See Cohen, 'Who is Starving Whom?', and Dan W. Brock, 'Defending Moral Options', 912, who calls this the 'Why me?' objection to the extremely demanding moral outlook of Kagan, *The Limits of Morality*. See Kagan, 'Replies to My Critics', 924–5, for a reply to Brock.) However, on reflection, we need to be more careful about this. What 'my fair share' refers to is the proportion of the total cost that it would be fair to allocate to me, if everyone were pulling their weight. Suppose you claim that, when others are *not* pulling their weight, I am required to do more. You should not restrict the claim to me alone: you can claim that this applies to everyone else as well. In particular, you should apply it to each person who is not pulling his weight. You should say that anyone who is not pulling his weight is required to do so, and, given that not everyone else is doing so, each of us is required to pull more than his weight. Given that not everyone is complying, you are applying the requirement to do more than one's fair share to *each* of us. But if it applies to each of us, not requiring more from me than anyone else, that is a ground for denying that the requirement is *unfair*. Is that ground decisive? That would need further discussion. Suffice it to say that a Fair Share View can be more cautiously formulated. It can be expressed as the claim that it is *unreasonable* to require anyone to do more than his fair share, to make up for the fact that others are doing less. For the more cautious view, see Murphy, 'The Demands of Beneficence', 283.

11. See App. 1. There does remain an important question how far above those poverty lines a person would need to be raised in order no longer to be subject to the kind of deprivation that grounds requirements of beneficence.

12. Murphy, *Moral Demands in Nonideal Theory*—see also Murphy, 'The Demands of Beneficence'.

13. Murphy, *Moral Demands in Nonideal Theory*, 74–80.

14. For the primary application of 'agent-relative' and 'agent-neutral' to distinguish types of reasons, see Thomas Nagel, *The View from Nowhere*, 152–3, and Parfit, *Reasons and Persons*, 143. (Nagel first expressed this as the distinction between 'subjective' and 'objective' reasons in *The Possibility of Altruism*, 90.) For Parfit's use of 'agent-relative' and 'agent-neutral' to distinguish types of

moral theories, see Parfit, *Reasons and Persons*, 27. For further discussion of the distinction, and its relation to the definition of consequentialism, see David McNaughton and Piers Rawling, 'Value and Agent-Relative Reasons', John Skorupski, 'Agent-Neutrality, Consequentialism, Utilitarianism', and John Broome, 'Skorupski on Agent-Neutrality'.

15. This objection has often been made against Fair Share Views. See e.g. Joel Feinberg, *Doing and Deserving*, 244; Singer, 'Famine, Affluence and Morality', 232–4; Bennett, 'Morality and Consequences', 84; Fishkin, *The Limits of Obligation*, ch. 10; Barry, 'Humanity and Justice in Global Perspective', 222; Goodin, *Protecting the Vulnerable*, 134–44; Schmidtz, 'Islands in a Sea of Obligation', 700; and Tim Mulgan, *The Demands of Consequentialism*, 117–20, 216–18.

    For Murphy's reply, see Murphy, *Moral Demands in Nonideal Theory*, 127–33. (An earlier, different response is given in Murphy, 'The Demands of Beneficence', 291–3.)

16. For empirical work suggesting that the probability of someone's receiving help is reduced as the number of bystanders increases, see John M. Darley and Bibb Latane, *The Unresponsive Bystander: Why Doesn't He Help?*

17. He makes a reply of the same type against the other main objection that has been raised against his view. This is that it makes what I am required to do for the poor implausibly dependent on contingent numbers: it depends on how many needy people there are, how many better-off people there are, and how badly and well off the two groups happen to be. But why should what it is reasonable to require from *me* depend on any of this? According to his Fair Share View, if the scale of global deprivation were great enough in relation to the scale of global affluence, then the requirement that applied to me *would* be extremely demanding after all. Worse, he seems committed to the converse conclusion: if a tiny amount of my resources were capable of saving billions of lives, there would be nothing wrong with refusing, provided other people were failing to give the same help. For this objection, see Tim Mulgan, 'Two Conceptions of Benevolence', 76; the reply is in Liam B. Murphy, 'A Relatively Plausible Principle of Beneficence'. (Mulgan responds in *The Demands of Consequentialism*, ch. 4.)

18. For further discussion, see App. 2.

19. For a philosopher's discussion of Schweitzer's own views about the moral demands of affluence, see Mike W. Martin, 'Good Fortune Obligates'. According to Schweitzer, requirements of beneficence are grounded in requirements of gratitude.

20. For this line of argument, see James Griffin, 'Review of Shelly Kagan, *The Limits of Morality*', 129–31, and *Value Judgement*, 87–92; also John Cottingham, 'The Ethics of Self-Concern', 801, 816; J. L. Mackie, *Ethics*, 131–4; and Owen Flanagan, *Varieties of Moral Personality*, ch. 2. Kagan discusses a similar argument as the 'negative argument' for a moderate position on the demands of morality in *The Limits of Morality*, ch. 8. (For a reply, see Michael Bratman, 'Kagan on "The Appeal to Cost"'.) For a defence of consequentialism against the same objection of motivational impossibility, see Danny Scoccia, 'Utilitarianism, Sociobiology, and the Limits of Benevolence'.

I discuss some related objections to the Extreme Demand in Ch. 6, esp. Sect. 6.5.

21. See Singer, 'Famine, Affluence and Morality', 238, and *Practical Ethics*, 163; also Unger, *Living High and Letting Die*, 150–2.
22. Compare the 'personal conversion' envisaged by Nagel, *The View from Nowhere*, 206. Notice, however, that the Extreme Demand does not require of us the complete impartiality that Nagel is concerned with. Compare also Kagan, *The Limits of Morality*, 393; and Flanagan, *Varieties of Moral Personality*, chs. 3 and 4.
23. Apparently, this effect can be reliably induced by subjecting a person to severe and prolonged feelings of guilt, accompanied by physiological stresses, which furnish a background against which effective indoctrination can take place. There is no evident reason why the inducement of guilt in relation to world poverty could not furnish the material for the use of similar techniques. See e.g. William Sargant, *Battle for the Mind*; James A. C. Brown, *Techniques of Persuasion*; and Edgar H. Schein, *Coercive Persuasion*. (The quotation—from Apuleius' *The Golden Ass*—is cited by Sargant, 145.) According to Sargant (pp. 65–71), the only sorts of people who do not eventually succumb to the prolonged application of these techniques are obsessional neurotics and outright psychotics; but even in these cases, surgical leucotomy can often produce similar results. Such techniques have apparently been used commercially for some time, reportedly producing greater devotion to commercial goals and a corresponding lessening of personal attachments. For an early example, see Mark Brewer, 'We're Gonna Tear You Down and Put You Back Together'.

    Admittedly, it seems that the internalization of norms of extreme self-sacrifice does standardly require group reinforcement: this might not be something you can induce in isolation. However, the group need not be large.
24. Two relevant studies are Samuel Oliner and Pearl Oliner, *The Altruistic Personality*, and Kristen Renwick Monroe, *The Heart of Altruism*. See also Flanagan, *Varieties of Moral Personality*, chs. 1–4, which helpfully emphasizes the cultural determinants of our psychological traits.
25. Compare Kagan, *The Limits of Morality*, 361–2, 399.
26. Compare Scanlon, *What We Owe to Each Other*, 224. Notice that this aggregative approach solves the problem discussed in Fishkin, *The Limits of Obligation*: the problem of how to reconcile the acceptance of a 'principle of minimal altruism' (which requires us to make small sacrifices when it will help other people greatly) with a 'cutoff for heroism' (pp. 3–9). The two can be reconciled by reading the principle of minimal altruism as requiring small *aggregate* sacrifices.
27. As we have just seen, aggregative views can allow that this maximum aggregate sacrifice is relative to the number of people you could help at that time.
28. It would be possible to claim that the overall sacrifice that can be required of me to contribute towards helping several people is *greater* than the sum of the separate sacrifices that could be required of me to help them one after the other; but it is hard to see what could make this look plausible.
29. This scenario is discussed by McGinn, 'Saint Elsewhere'; also Schmidtz, 'Islands in a Sea of Obligation', 693; and McKinsey, 'Obligations to the Starving', 312.

30. People react to it very differently. Smith, 'The Duty to Rescue and the Slippery Slope Problem', 27, maintains that 'the general view' is that I am not required to help anyone in a large-scale catastrophe of this kind, in contrast with a case in which a single person needs to be rescued. Several people who have discussed this with me have taken the opposite view, maintaining that in this case I would be required to devote my entire life to helping other people.
31. For this challenge, compare Fishkin, *The Limits of Obligation*, 163–6. It is sometimes asserted that what I have done for others clearly *does* justify declining to help someone: see e.g. Smith, 'The Duty to Rescue and the Slippery Slope Problem', 23. In this book, I am looking for an argument that will either support that claim, or provide an alternative reply to the challenge.
32. Compare Lewis, 'Illusory Innocence?', 36, on Unger: 'even if we cannot diagnose the flaw, it is more credible that the argument has a flaw than that its most extreme conclusion is true'.
33. For this line of argument, see McGinn, 'Saint Elsewhere'; Lewis, 'Illusory Innocence?', 36; and Schmidtz, 'Islands in a Sea of Obligation', 686. One response to this is given by Barry, 'Humanity and Justice in Global Perspective', 222. This book is another.
34. Let me acknowledge that, until I have done that, I cannot claim to have provided a good objection to a Fair Share View such as Murphy's. For his claim is to provide a relatively plausible view of the demands of beneficence: one that is more plausible than the alternatives. (See Murphy, 'A Relatively Plausible Principle of Beneficence' and *Moral Demands in Nonideal Theory*, 133–4.) If the alternative to a Fair Share View is the Extreme Demand, then there would be a strong case for holding that Fair Share Views, for all their faults, are less implausible. My aim in what follows is to vindicate a view that is more plausible than either.

CHAPTER 6

1. Compare the fourfold taxonomy of responses to extremely demanding moral outlooks in Samuel Scheffler, *Human Morality*, 17. He divides the first of the alternatives I give here into two.
2. I mean this to span two possibilities: that I have most reason to disregard morality; and that there is a disunity within practical reason, so that we cannot move beyond judgements about what is morally right and what is personally best to an overall verdict about what there is most reason to do. For further discussion and references, see Sect. 6.5 and nn. 31 and 32 below.
3. This third response to 'the problem of demandingness' has been embraced by Singer, 'Famine, Affluence and Morality' and *Practical Ethics*, ch. 8; Glover, *Causing Death and Saving Lives*, 108; Rachels, 'Killing and Starving to Death'; Kagan, *The Limits of Morality*, 403; and Unger, *Living High and Letting Die*.
4. This line of thought can be traced back at least as far as Francis Hutcheson, *An Inquiry into the Original of Our Ideas of Beauty and Virtue* (1725); and, for the extremely demanding conclusion, William Godwin, *An Enquiry concerning Political Justice* (1798), II. ii. The thought that this is absurdly

demanding is just as old: see e.g. Richard Price, *A Review of the Principal Questions and Difficulties in Morals* (1758), ch. 7.

5. See Ch. 5 n. 14. 'Evaluator-neutral' might be more accurate here.
6. See e.g. Samuel Scheffler, *The Rejection of Consequentialism*, 1, and *Consequentialism and its Critics*, Introduction, 1. However, contrast Bernard Williams, 'A Critique of Utilitarianism', Foot, 'Utilitarianism and the Virtues', 196, and Philip Pettit, 'Consequentialism', 230–3, whose weaker definition includes only the first of these assumptions—thereby allowing versions of egoism to count as consequentialist. For further discussion, see the articles cited at the end of Ch. 5 n. 14.

   Notice also that the first assumption seems to exclude indirect consequentialism, according to which the rightness of a particular action is determined by the value not of its own outcome but of the outcome of actions of the same kind. (Different versions of indirect consequentialism identify different categories of act-kind as relevant.) For this reason, Scheffler makes the two assumptions definitive of *act*-consequentialism.
7. Thomas Nagel is the most prominent contemporary advocate of this second line of thought, which he develops in *The Possibility of Altruism*, 'The Limits of Objectivity', and *The View from Nowhere*, chs. 8–10. According to Nagel, each of us is capable of reflecting on the world both from her own personal point of view, and from a point of view that abstracts from this, considering objectively her own point of view itself, as one subjective point of view in a world containing many others. I can recognize a range of commitments, projects, and relationships as having special importance for me, and thus as sources of fulfilment; but I can equally recognize the different ranges of goods that have importance for others. Abstracting from all of these subjective normative points of view, I can recognize that, objectively speaking, no one person's fulfilment is more important than anyone else's. His concern with the resulting problem of demandingness is discussed in *The View from Nowhere*, ch. 10.

   Nagel's treatment of the demands of morality is modified in *Equality and Partiality*. There, his direct concern is with the question what political solution we ought collectively to institute in response to the problem of enormous global disparities of wealth and opportunities, rather than the moral question what I ought individually to be doing for the poor. However, in answering the political question, he claims that an extremely demanding redistributive standard can reasonably be rejected by the affluent, given that each affluent person has his own life to lead. And this at least strongly suggests (although it does not strictly entail) the view that it is not unreasonable, and hence not wrong, for an affluent individual to refuse to meet an extremely demanding standard of personal requirement.
8. Fishkin, *The Limits of Obligation*, emphasizes this point: see e.g. pp. 71–2.
9. See e.g. Peter Railton, 'Alienation, Consequentialism and the Demands of Morality'; Wolf, 'Morality and Partiality'; also Kekes, 'Benevolence: A Minor Virtue', 28, who emphasizes that personal relationships are *moral* relationships.
10. See e.g. Bernard Williams, 'Persons, Character and Morality', sect. II; Martin, *Virtuous Giving*, 65–6; Cottingham, 'The Ethics of Self-Concern', 800.

11. See John O'Connor, 'Philanthropy and Selfishness'.
12. See John Cottingham, 'Partiality, Favouritism and Morality', 364–5.
13. See David Heyd, *Supererogation*, 172–8.
14. See e.g. Gewirth, 'Private Philanthropy and Positive Rights', 70–1; and Martin, *Virtuous Giving*, 68.
15. See Susan Wolf, 'Moral Saints' and 'Morality and Partiality'; also Cottingham, 'The Ethics of Self-Concern', 813–14.
16. Scanlon, *What We Owe to Each Other*, ch. 3: 'Well-Being'. In Scanlon's terminology, well-being is an 'inclusive good' (pp. 127, 142).

    Compare the contrast between 'plural-interest' and 'deliberative-field' models of practical deliberation drawn by Barbara Herman, 'Agency, Attachment, and Difference', 191–7.
17. Schmidtz, 'Islands in a Sea of Obligation', 701–3; Gewirth, 'Private Philanthropy and Positive Rights', 77.
18. In Part II, I develop an objection to the Extreme Demand which has this basic form. However, I shall not be attempting to formulate a general test for when a moral outlook is over-demanding. For the difficulties with such a test, see Murphy, *Moral Demands in Nonideal Theory*, ch. 3. A general claim of the form 'Morality cannot demand that we sustain losses of magnitude L' prompts the question 'Losses with respect to what baseline?'; and a general claim of the form 'Morality cannot demand that we restrict ourselves below level of well-being W' prompts the question 'What if we are already below it, and can only rise above it by attacking other people?'
19. For this claim on behalf of a Kantian view, see e.g. Baron, 'Kantian Ethics', 20, and Herman, 'Agency, Attachment, and Difference'; for the same claim on behalf of act-consequentialism, see Philip Pettit, 'The Consequentialist Perspective', 163–9, and Frank Jackson, 'Decision-Theoretic Consequentialism and the Nearest and Dearest Objection'; for rule-consequentialism, see Brad Hooker, 'Rule-Consequentialism and Demandingness' and *Ideal Code, Real World*; on behalf of an Aristotelian view, see Cottingham, 'The Ethics of Self-Concern'; for contractualism, see Scanlon, *What We Owe to Each Other*, 224–5. The same claim is suggested on behalf of different virtue theories by Rosalind Hursthouse, *On Virtue Ethics*, 226, J. D. Wallace, *Virtues and Vices*, 146–9, and Alasdair MacIntyre, *After Virtue*, 221. For a survey of medieval Christian treatments of the duties of charity and almsgiving, and their limits, see Scott Davis, 'Giving', and Suzanne Roberts, 'Giving'. Alan Gewirth makes the same claim on behalf of his theory of rights as protections of agency: see his 'Private Philanthropy and Positive Rights'.
20. The classic sources of this view are Plato's *Protagoras*, Hobbes's *Leviathan*, and Hume's *Second Enquiry*. For more recent formulations, see Mackie, *Ethics*, ch. 5, and G. J. Warnock, *The Object of Morality*.
21. Compare Wallace, *Virtues and Vices*, 146–9.
22. Mackie, *Ethics*.
23. Ibid. 129–34. Compare William K. Frankena, *Ethics*, 116: 'Morality is made for man, not man for morality.'
24. Compare Richard Taylor, 'Ancient Wisdom and Modern Folly'; Cottingham, 'The Ethics of Self-Concern', 812–13; and F. H. Bradley, 'The Limits of

Individual and National Self-Sacrifice'. For discussion of how this Aristotelian view avoids egoism, see Sarah Broadie, *Ethics with Aristotle*, 110–18; and compare Thomas Hurka, *Perfectionism*, 62–8.

25. See Scheffler, *Human Morality*, esp. p. 122; and compare Scheffler, *The Rejection of Consequentialism*, ch. 3, on 'the natural independence of the personal point of view'. For a more radical rejection of the idea that rational agents face a problem of reconciling a personal and an impersonal point of view, see Susan Wolf, 'Morality and the View from Here'.
26. Jackson, 'Decision-Theoretic Consequentialism and the Nearest and Dearest Objection'.
27. Braybrooke, *Meeting Needs*, 283; Mackie, *Ethics*, 131–4. See also Ch. 5 n. 2 above.
28. See e.g. Schmidtz, 'Islands in a Sea of Obligation', 687–8, 701–3; and Jennifer Trusted, 'The Problem of Absolute Poverty: What Are Our Moral Obligations to the Destitute?', 17–19.
29. For this reply, see Singer, 'Famine, Affluence and Morality', 233–4. The other reply is that, given how badly off some people are, it would not be worse for *everyone* if everyone were required to comply with an extremely demanding moral standard.
30. Compare Murphy, *Moral Demands in Nonideal Theory*, 35–9, 61–2.
31. A leading example of this view is Catherine Wilson, 'On Some Alleged Limitations to Moral Endeavor'. On my reading, Nagel, *The View from Nowhere*, chs. 8–10, presents a version of this view as well. Wolf, 'Moral Saints', is read by Wilson as offering this first view, but is often interpreted as arguing for the second instead. (See also Wolf, 'Morality and Partiality', esp. pp. 253–6.)
32. Another possible claim is the one made by Bratman, 'Kagan on "The Appeal to Cost" ', 330–1: although I do not have most reason to do what is best for me, if I rank this goal highest then pursuing it will be the most rational thing to do, and hence (he argues) morally permissible.
33. Compare the authors cited in n. 24. Of course, an argument of this form had better not simply be trading on an equivocation on 'a life that is bad for me', sliding from 'a life that is detrimental to my interests' to 'a life which, if lived by me, would be bad'. The challenge for a proponent of this argument is to defend an inference from the first to the second.
34. The argument in Sect. 5.3, 'Motivational Limits', invoking the limits on our motivational capacity to meet the Extreme Demand, can be seen as a more modest argument of the same general kind.
35. This requirement is widely accepted, but its interpretation is contested. Christine M. Korsgaard, 'Skepticism about Practical Reason', argues that the Humean use of it begs the question against the view that there are considerations which rationality requires any person to be motivated by, independently of facts about her own motivational nature. Derek Parfit, 'Reasons and Motivation', 101, makes a similar point by distinguishing between readings of the internalism requirement as a claim about 'substantive' or 'procedural' rationality. For someone who rejects the internalism requirement, see John McDowell, 'Might there Be External Reasons?'

36. For a version of this argument, see Scheffler, *Human Morality*, 74. I think the remarks of Williams, *Ethics and the Limits of Philosophy*, 186, and Simon Blackburn, *Ruling Passions*, 211–12, on distinguishing cases of immediate rescue from situations of more distant need, should be read in the context of their more general 'Humeanism' about practical reason. (For further discussion of Williams, see Cullity, 'Practical Theory'.)

    For a related but different argument, which is concerned to emphasize that we could not properly hold a person morally accountable for failing to live the disintegrated life, see R. Jay Wallace, 'Reason and Responsibility', sect. 4.
37. For an explanation of Kant's own version of this strategy, see Onora O'Neill, 'Vindicating Reason'. It has affinities with a further strategy: that of deriving conclusions about practical reasons from an account of the constitutive aim of action, paralleling the way in which it can be claimed that conclusions about theoretical reasons can be derived from the constitutive aim of belief (the truth). For further discussion of the three-pole picture of theories of practical reason presented in the text, and more on this further alternative, see Garrett Cullity and Berys Gaut (eds.), *Ethics and Practical Reason*, Introduction.
38. See Herman, 'Agency, Attachment, and Difference', for this argument within a Kantian framework; Gilbert Harman, 'Practical Reasoning', offers a Humean picture of practical reason which emphasizes the coherence-securing role of practical reason in relation to the ends given to us by our desires.
39. See Scanlon, *What We Owe to Each Other*, 224–5. For Scanlon's explanation of the way in which his treatment of the limits of the moral requirement to give aid involves arguing 'upward' from intuitive judgements about reasonableness, see p. 242. Scanlon explains judgements of reasonableness as judgements about what there is reason to think given a presupposed aim, body of information, and range of relevant reasons: see pp. 32–3, 191–7. For an argument that he still confronts a problem of demandingness, see Elizabeth Ashford, 'The Demandingness of Scanlon's Contractualism'.
40. See Kagan, *The Limits of Morality*, for a sustained account of the difficulties in defending the view that self-sacrifice to promote what is impartially best is not morally required, while seeking to allow that it can be morally permissible.
41. In Kagan's terminology, the problem is how to oppose the 'extremist' view that you are morally required to promote what is impartially best, without committing yourself to the 'minimalist' view that helping other people is never morally required. See *The Limits of Morality*, 1–6, 386–93.
42. See especially *Ak.* 6.393, 6.450–1. For discussion, see Barbara Herman, 'Mutual Aid and Respect for Persons'; and the reply of Stephen Engstrom, 'Herman on Mutual Aid'; also Thomas E. Hill, 'Servility and Self-Respect', and Patricia M. McGoldrick, 'Saints and Heroes', 526–7.
43. The first half of 'The Doctrine of Virtue' is occupied in arguing for this claim.
44. *Ak.* 6.393. It is interesting to find the same form of argument echoed by as un-Kantian a figure as D. H. Lawrence: 'Why should I care for my neighbour's property, or my neighbour's life, if I do not care for my own?' *The Letters of D. H. Lawrence*, 357.

45. The fact that Williams's argument belongs to this kind shows how broad that usage is.
46. Williams, 'Persons, Character and Morality', 12.
47. Ibid. 18—he echoes Ludwig Wittgenstein, *Tractatus Logico-Philosophicus*, sect. 2.0211.
48. For a slightly different reconstruction of Williams's argument, see Flanagan, *Varieties of Moral Personality*, ch. 3.
49. See Williams, 'Persons, Character and Morality', 1–5, for his emphasis that the target of the argument is broader than consequentialism, covering other impartialist conceptions of morality as well.
50. Compare Flanagan, *Varieties of Moral Personality*, 70.
51. I shall use phrases such as 'personal spending' and 'spending on yourself' to refer to spending on all sources of personal fulfilment, and not just selfish ones: they are intended to include spending on non-selfish projects of your own (projects of understanding, say, or creation), or on your family and friends, in circumstances in which greater benefit might have been derived by others had you spent the same amount on them.
52. For one example, Wallace's argument in 'Reason and Responsibility' concerning standards for moral accountability, which has affinities with the arguments I describe in Sect. 6.5, perhaps needs to be placed in a separate category of its own.

CHAPTER 7

1. For advocates of this response, see Ch. 6 n. 3.
2. Compare Thomas Nagel, *Equality and Partiality*, ch. 15; Scanlon, *What We Owe to Each Other*, ch. 5; and Wolf, 'Morality and Partiality', esp. pp. 246, 252.
3. Compare Nagel, *Equality and Partiality*, 15–17 and ch. 5, where the question how much personal partiality is impartially acceptable is characterized as a Kantian one, for reasons elaborated in Barbara Herman, 'Integrity and Impartiality', and Marcia Baron, 'Impartiality and Friendship'. See also Scanlon, *What We Owe to Each Other*, 225; Wolf, 'Morality and Partiality', 246–8; and Marilyn Friedman, 'The Practice of Partiality', 833.
4. Another would be to argue that partiality is best for everyone: the gains to those who stand to benefit from others' impartiality would be outweighed by the costs to everyone of being impartial. If so, it might make sense from a point of view that favoured no one to judge that the overall costs of observing a requirement of impartiality in our dealings with each other would outweigh the benefits. For some doubts about that line of argument, see Friedman, 'The Practice of Partiality', 827–31.
5. See the discussion of 'pure impartiality' in John Cottingham, 'Impartiality', 716; and Bernard Gert, 'Impartiality', 600. Simon Blackburn, *The Oxford Dictionary of Philosophy*, 188, offers a more restrictive definition, taking impartial distributions of burdens and benefits to be those governed only by considerations of desert—with different accounts of desert generating different

conceptions of impartiality. But again, some accounts of desert will generate conceptions of impartiality for which the impartial acceptability of conduct will be no defence against an accusation of selfishness.

I do think it is too weak to say (with Herman, 'Agency, Attachment, and Difference', 185) that impartiality need only amount to 'the requirement that like cases be treated alike'.

6. Compare Nagel, *Equality and Partiality*, ch. 5.
7. Sometimes, it seems tempting to say that the action of distributing the good can be fair even though the resulting distribution is unfair. Thus, sometimes the fair way to distribute a valuable but indivisible good will be by a lottery. But that results in a distribution in which one person has the good and every other equally deserving person lacks it. The procedure will be fair if equally deserving people have an equal chance to get the good, but the distribution itself is not. (Of course, if you simply understand 'fair distribution' to mean 'distribution resulting from a fair act of distributing', then you will not make this distinction.) See the discussion of distributions produced by gambling in John Rawls, *A Theory of Justice*, 86.
8. Contrast this with the simpler suggestion that a fair distribution *satisfies* each claim in proportion to its strength—see John Broome, 'Fairness'. Situations in which it is fair to use a lottery to distribute a good to which everyone has an equal claim seem to me better handled by the account I give in the text.

   I am taking your *claim* to a good to be a consideration which, if undefeated, amounts to your claim-*right* to that good, the correlative of which is a duty (of the agent(s) against whom you have the claim-right) to give you the good.
9. Contrast A. John Simmons, 'Fairness'.
10. Of course, it is natural to speak of a judge as dispensing the good of justice; but it is not as if she is assessing different people's claims to this good, and then deciding how much of it each person is to get. Everyone should be treated with *complete* justice.

    I am not claiming that distributive and procedural unfairness are mutually exclusive, however: the breach of established rules for the distribution of a good might involve both.
11. Notice that this formulation spans two importantly different kinds of case. One is where the thing that ought to be done is a collective action, the performance of which requires an appropriate form of impartiality from individual contributors. However, there are other requirements of fairness in which I ought to do something, and doing it requires a form of impartiality, but this is not a contribution to some collective action that ought to be performed. (For an example, consider a case in which I have a fiduciary responsibility to distribute a good fairly.)

    Moreover, notice that the thing that ought to be done need not be something that ought *morally* to be done. Cases of free riding are typically cases in which we ought to be producing a public good, but only because of the benefit we derive from it. However, producing that good requires a form of impartiality from contributors, and the free rider's failure to display this form of impartiality is unfair. I discuss this further in 'Public Goods and Fairness'.

12. Remember, I am using 'beneficence' to refer to the *properly discriminating* practical concern for others' interests that we should aspire to have.
13. Of course, it has often been held that you should give concern for others priority over your own material welfare. But most of the ascetic religious outlooks that make this claim involve the view that material sacrifices are actually good for you, all things (including posthumous benefits) considered. I am discussing a proposal that really is telling you to choose what is *bad* for you, all things considered, to confer lesser benefits on others.
14. The Proceduralist View should not itself be identified with libertarianism, which is a political doctrine about the limits of legitimate state coercion over individual freedoms. It seems coherent (if implausible) to hold that impartiality should be no concern of the state's, and thus to reconcile a non-Proceduralist account of impartiality, according to which a certain social arrangement is impartially unacceptable, with the libertarian claim that it would be wrong to use state power to resist it. However, it is usual to find libertarians anchoring their political views in Proceduralist claims about impartiality and fairness—as in Robert Nozick, *Anarchy, State, and Utopia*, chs. 7 and 8.
15. I think that, on the best way to read Proceduralists like Nozick, they are not denying this. They do not deny that there are requirements of beneficence on us to have a practical concern for how well off other people are; but they do deny that distributive justice should have any direct concern with how well off people are.
16. Many versions of consequentialism give variants of the Equal Weighting View; Rawls is presenting another variant in *A Theory of Justice*.
17. See Nagel, *Equality and Partiality*, esp. pp. 12, 65–74; and, for discussion, Derek Parfit, 'Equality or Priority?'; Scanlon, *What We Owe to Each Other*, 223–9; and David Brink, 'The Separateness of Persons, Distributive Norms, and Moral Theory'.
18. See John C. Harsanyi, *Essays in Ethics, Social Behaviour, and Scientific Explanation*, and 'Morality and the Theory of Rational Behaviour'.
19. See Rawls, *A Theory of Justice*.
20. For surveys of these possibilities, see Parfit, *Reasons and Persons*, app. I, James Griffin, *Well-Being*, chs. 1–4, and Scanlon, *What We Owe to Each Other*, ch. 3.
21. For the clearest expression of this view, see Friedrich Nietzsche, *Schopenhauer as Educator*, 60: 'How does your individual life receive the highest value and deepest significance? How is it least wasted? To be sure, only by living for the benefit of the rarest and most valuable specimens.' The same view is suggested by Jan Narveson, 'Aesthetics, Charity, Utility, and Distributive Justice', 551: 'the importance of the kind of life we have set out to live is greater than the amount of suffering preventable by depriving ourselves of the means to live it'. For discussion, see Hurka, *Perfectionism*, 75–9.
22. For this debate, see e.g. the symposium in *Ethics*, 101 (July 1991); Griffin, *Well-Being*, ch. 9; Lawrence Blum, 'Friendship, Beneficence, and Impartiality'; and Wolf, 'Morality and Partiality'. For an attempt to argue the other way—that the more impartial areas of moral concern are to be justified by reference to basic forms of partial attachment—see Andrew Oldenquist, 'Loyalties'.

CHAPTER 8

1. I do not claim that this is the *only* kind of answer that can be given to this question. For perhaps a life may be in itself good for its possessor. See Sect. 8.3 for a further acknowledgement of this possibility.
2. Compare Scanlon, *What We Owe to Each Other*, 128–9, 219.
3. Good starting points for the literature on friendship are Neera Kapur Badhwar (ed.), *Friendship* for contemporary essays, and Michael Pakaluk (ed.), *Other Selves*, for the classic discussions. Another interesting collection is George Graham and Hugh LaFollette (eds.), *Person to Person*. See also Lawrence Blum, *Friendship, Altruism and Morality*, esp. chs. 3 and 4.
4. This point has often been made about friendship. See e.g. Scanlon, *What We Owe to Each Other*, 88–90, 123–4; Lawrence Blum, 'Vocation, Friendship, and Community', 106, 112, 118, and 'Friendship as a Moral Phenomenon', 75; Wolf, 'Morality and the View from Here', 207–12.
5. For that claim, see e.g. Cottingham, 'Partiality, Favouritism and Morality', 369. For its rejection, see Blum, 'Friendship, Beneficence, and Impartiality', 49–50, 55–7.
6. Compare Emerson, 'Gifts'.
7. Sometimes friendship does involve satisfying the interests of my friends instead of others' interests in receiving the same good. If a friend and a stranger need to be rescued, it may be an expression of friendship to rescue the friend. But it seems hard to make sense even of these cases in terms of simply giving a priority-weighting to the interests of my friends. If a stranger is injured more seriously than a friend, shouldn't I ask my friend to wait while I tend to the stranger?
8. Compare Scanlon, *What We Owe to Each Other*, ch. 3, esp. sect. 4.
9. Of course, this is not to say that *all* friendships and close personal relationships are good. On the different moral qualities of such relationships, see Friedman, 'The Practice of Partiality'.
10. The phrase 'bearably and usefully' here allows for the point that it may be difficult to eradicate my personal partiality, and it may be counter-productive to try too hard to do so. See Peter Singer, *One World*, 170–83, and Sect. 5.3 above.
11. Compare Blum, 'Friendship, Beneficence, and Impartiality', esp. p. 57.
12. Elizabeth Telfer makes the point that it seems a necessary condition of friendship that it involves various kinds of shared activity, and not merely mutually appreciated benevolence: see Telfer, 'Friendship', 223–4. (In doing so, she seems to advance beyond Aristotle's definition at *Nicomachean Ethics* $1155^{b}28–56^{a}5$.) My point is that nothing prevents this shared activity from having a thoroughly altruistic focus. Also instructive here is Kagan, *The Limits of Morality*, 367–9: I agree with him completely that what has been said so far does not yet amount to a good objection to an extremely demanding moral outlook.
13. Compare David S. Oderberg, *Moral Theory*, ch. 4; also the different view of Richard Norman, *Ethics, Killing and War*, 55–62. For the rejection of the second answer, see e.g. R. G. Frey, 'Moral Standing, the Value of Lives, and Speciesism', 142–3, and 'Morals and Medicine', 473–4.

14. For an extended discussion of this point, see the work of Amartya Sen and Martha Nussbaum on the way in which material deprivation attacks the 'capabilities' of poor people: esp. Sen, *Commodities and Capabilities* and 'Capability and Well-Being'; and Nussbaum, *Women and Human Development: The Capabilities Approach*. For a detailed empirical study of the range of deprivations associated with material poverty by a philosophically informed economist, see Partha Dasgupta, *An Inquiry into Well-Being and Destitution*.
15. Actually, I think the lives of most of the world's poorest people count as non-altruistically-focused too, and that the Extreme Demand carries the implication that even *they* are acting wrongly. For most of the very poor, periods of life-threatening crisis are episodic. Most people who suffer the evils of starvation and other poverty-related threats to life do not do so continuously throughout their lives, and the Extreme Demand will apply to anyone with some spare time left over after coping with necessities. Almost anyone who has some time to spare, during some period of her life, from keeping herself and her dependants healthy will be violating the Extreme Demand, provided *some* of that spare time could have been spent relieving others' suffering without crippling demoralization.

    However, I shall not attempt to argue this through fully, as my argument does not rely on this strong claim.
16. Compare Scanlon's 'Principle of Helpfulness' in *What We Owe to Each Other*, 224–5.
17. Compare Dancy, *Moral Reasons*, 60–2; David McNaughton, *Moral Vision*, 192–4.
18. This point has often been made by Kantian moral philosophers. See e.g. Barbara Herman, 'On the Value of Acting from the Motive of Duty' and *The Practice of Moral Judgment*, chs. 1 and 2; Baron, 'Kantian Ethics', 56–64, and *Kantian Ethics almost without Apology*, pt. II; Korsgaard, 'From Duty and for the Sake of the Noble'; Allison, *Kant's Theory of Freedom*, ch. 6, esp. pp. 111–13; Paul Benson, 'Moral Worth'; Paton, *The Categorical Imperative*, 54. In Cullity, 'Sympathy, Discernment, and Reasons', I argue that this point should not take us in the direction in which these philosophers take it. For another non-Kantian acknowledgement of the point, see Lawrence Blum, *Moral Perception and Particularity*, ch. 8, 'Compassion'.

CHAPTER 9

1. I dealt with misgivings about the language of 'requirement' and 'permission' at the end of Ch. 1.
2. The claimed absurdity is denying that the interests in question *can* ground requirements of beneficence—not denying that they always do. If you have made an important promise that it would now be very costly to keep, it is not absurd to deny that I am required to help you break the promise.
3. The text presents these cases in which benefits are conferred. However, perhaps we ought to distinguish between conferring a benefit and averting a loss. For psychological research that illustrates the different values that people typically

place on what they think of as gains and losses, see Amos Tversky and Daniel Kahneman, 'The Framing of Decisions and the Psychology of Choice'.

4. P. F. Strawson, 'Social Morality and Individual Ideal', 26. I owe the reference to Brad Hooker.
5. Does this rely on the fact that what is being destroyed has an aesthetic value independent of the benefit to its owner? I don't think so. If I know that the money you hoard under your bed is about to be eaten by rats, then failing to tell you could be a failure of beneficence too.
6. There may also be a difference between helping you to retain a good and helping you to gain it. We certainly seem to act as though there is a significant difference between losing something and not gaining it: see n. 3 above.
7. An implication of the view spelled out here is, however, that it could be defensible to continue pursuing activities that it was indefensible to have embarked on. Presumably, for *all* of us there were alternative, cheaper ways of structuring our lives that would have been no worse for us had we chosen them when we were younger. But although it would not have been substantially worse for us to have chosen a different path in the past, it may be substantially worse for us to do so now. Again, this seems more significant in relation to achievements than enjoyments.
8. Compare Blum, 'Vocation, Friendship, and Community', 118.
9. This point should not be overstated. I am not saying that true friendships are irrevocable, nor that they cannot be constrained by other commitments and interests: there are circumstances in which it makes sense to abandon them. And I am not staking anything significant on a merely definitional claim about 'friendship'. I have no objection to calling a relationship that one is willing to abandon in favour of a cheaper one a friendship. The point is just that a willingness to replace my relationship to a person with another relationship that is just as good for me would deprive me of a dimension of commitment that is characteristic of the kinds of personal relationship that supply us with a distinctive sort of life-enhancing good.
10. The good of community involvement invites a similar conclusion, but for a different, more straightforward reason. Here it will also often not be sensible to raise the question of whether my commitment to this community might be replaceable by commitment to another one which would be no worse. But where this is true, it will usually be because my involvement in this community *is* better for me. If it is not better for me, then it is indeed hard to see why I cannot be morally required to link myself to another community where an equal degree of involvement leaves me with more resources to help other people.
11. Compare Blum, 'Vocation, Friendship, and Community', for a discussion of careers that amount to *vocations*.
12. For a parallel discussion of these goods, see Wolf, 'Morality and the View from Here', 207–14.
13. Of course, you might be less *likely* to sustain your commitment to a project that generates goods of achievement if you were more prepared than you are to abandon it in favour of a cheaper alternative. But the claim about friendship is the stronger one that a willingness to abandon it would itself amount

to lacking an attitude that is *constitutive* of a certain distinctive and important kind of life-enhancing good.

14. Someone who says No to this is Unger, *Living High and Letting Die*, 150–2.
15. It might seem tempting to object to this: 'But why isn't pursuing a career as a philosophy teacher when others are starving an immoral end?' This objection is discussed in Sect. 11.2.
16. If it is intrinsically good for you to be alive, then not everything that is intrinsically good for you makes you better off than you otherwise would be. See Parfit, *Reasons and Persons*, app. G.
17. Notice that being 'purely episodic' in this sense is not a matter of being datable, but only of not impinging on the quality of one's life as a whole. Thus, the common view is that, if we consider the set of all the datable enjoyments that your life contains, your life's containing that set of enjoyments is not a purely episodic good—your life would be worse without them. Moreover, this would seem the right thing to say even if each particular enjoyment *is* purely episodic.
18. For relevant discussion, see the discussion of the 'Principle of Temporal Good' in John Broome, *Weighing Goods*, ch. 11.
19. This can be true even if, for each purely episodic good, there is no justification for thinking that that good in particular is one that it must be permissible for me to pursue. Even so, we could still have a justification of the pursuit of purely episodic goods in general, although none in particular. We might think of the resulting view as involving an 'imperfect permission' to pursue purely episodic goods, by analogy with the kinds of 'imperfect duties' defended by Kant and Mill—duties to perform a kind of action that do not entail duties to perform any given instance of that kind. See Kant, *The Metaphysics of Morals*, *Ak.* 6.390–1, and John Stuart Mill, *Utilitarianism*, ch. 5, para. 15.

    Are there any purely episodic goods that are themselves directly requirement-grounding? I am not sure. It is clear enough, I think, that we have morally compelling reasons to help other people to retain purely episodic goods: I gave some examples at the start of Sect. 9.2. What is less clear is whether we are ever required by beneficence to help a person to pursue one purely episodic good in preference to another alternative one.
20. A book such as Griffin, *Well-Being*.
21. I am not claiming that all close personal relationships are good. For a reminder of the implausibility of *that* claim, see Friedman, 'The Practice of Partiality', 820–5. Nor do I want to underestimate the cultural variability of such relationships: on this point, see Flanagan, *Varieties of Moral Personality*, 95–7.
22. See Griffin, *Well-Being*, 65. This is not to deny that an assiduous worker in a worthless enterprise may still have a better life than she would have had if she were idle. But if this is true, it will be true in one of two ways. First, her work may bring with it other goods—such as enjoyment. But secondly, we might want to say that achieving the self-command necessary to reaching a difficult goal is itself a worthwhile achievement: that is, even if the goal in question is worthless, the achievement of self-command is not.
23. See e.g. Flanagan, *Varieties of Moral Personality*, 44.

24. In each case, I think we should add the same qualification as I made concerning achievements and friendships: it is not as though a life is made better by containing just *any* enjoyment or belonging to just *any* community or culture, but only those worth having or belonging to.
25. It is a slightly expanded version of the list given by Griffin, *Well-Being*, 67—adding some further goods emphasized in T. M. Scanlon, 'The Moral Basis of Interpersonal Comparisons'. See also Scanlon, 'Value, Desire, and Quality of Life', for an endorsement of this starting point and a discussion of how to advance beyond it. Scanlon develops his views further in *What We Owe to Each Other*, ch. 3. For other relevant discussions, see L. W. Sumner, 'Something in Between', and Andrew Moore, 'Objective Human Goods'.
26. And if so, is it better in virtue of the good of friendship? One might, for example, think that the painful relationships do have value, but that this is a matter of their contribution to the good of understanding. This would mean denying that enjoyment is a precondition on a friendship's being valuable for me; but it might still be claimed that in order to be valuable for me *as a friendship*—that is, to have a value that is not reducible to any of the other categories of goods—a friendship must be enjoyable.
27. I agree with Griffin, *Well-Being*, 58–9, that the answer to this certainly seems to be Yes.
28. For scepticism about this claim, see ibid. 70–1.
29. See W. D. Ross, *The Right and the Good*, ch. 5. The method endorsed by Griffin, *Well-Being*, 65–6, suggests a version of this last approach.

CHAPTER 10

1. Remember: 'personal spending' is being understood here to include the expenditure of time and money not only on oneself, but also on partiality-involving commitments to other things that have personal significance. (See Ch. 6 n. 51.)
2. In Sect. 9.2, 'Choices between Goods', a distinction was made between helping you to retain or gain a good, and helping you to pursue one good instead of a possible alternative. There is a clear difference between these: a difference between, say, helping you to avoid spilling your drink on the floor and helping you to get one drink rather than another. However, there is no corresponding distinction to be made in relation to levels of personal spending. To miss out on one level of personal spending is to have a different one.
3. Compare, in a different context, C. D. Broad, 'On the Function of False Hypotheses in Ethics', 389–90: 'it is no objection to say that it is totally impossible to determine exactly where this point comes in any particular case. This is quite true, but it is too common a difficulty in ethics to worry us, and we know that we are lucky in ethical questions if we can state upper and lower limits that are not too ridiculously far apart.'
4. Of course, explaining *how* it is fallacious is a matter of controversy among logicians. But what sets up their problem is the obviousness of the claim that this reasoning *is* fallacious. And that is the only claim upon which I am relying here.

5. These claims are paralleled in many other areas of our practical thought. Consider one of them: my judgements about how much sleep I need each night. It would only be if I were getting practically no sleep at all that I could sensibly say that five minutes less would by itself significantly impair my work the next day. But clearly, if I started off with more than enough sleep and then reduced the amount I was getting by five minutes every night, my work would certainly be significantly impaired well before I reached the unhappy level at which five minutes itself made a difference. And if my work would be significantly impaired by doing this, that is a good reason not to do it. At which point would my work begin to be significantly impaired by lack of sleep? It does not seem to make sense to seek to answer this exactly. However, I can certainly take a reasonable view on how much sleep I need each night, without any claims to precision. It can be reasonable for me to settle on a policy, even though getting five minutes' less sleep would make a negligible difference. For treating it as important whether getting five minutes' less sleep would make a significant difference is something there is good reason for me not to do.
6. I talk of 'drawing a line': perhaps a better metaphor, given the graduated strengths of the reasons involved, is Susan Wolf's 'shading an area'—see 'Morality and Partiality', 252.
7. In Sect. 5.1 I mentioned Peter Unger's example of Bob, who can only save a life directly by destroying the uninsured Bugatti in which he has invested his life savings. Unger thinks Bob is morally required to destroy the car, and I am inclined to agree that, in many circumstances, that would be true. In Ch. 4 we saw that, arguably, contributions to aid agencies—perhaps even Bugatti-sized contributions—do not save lives. However, there might still seem to be a problem here for the view I am defending. For if my argument works to limit the requirements of beneficence in relation to contributions to aid agencies, it will work equally to limit the requirements of beneficence on Bob. And that seems to leave me with two alternatives. Either losing your life savings is not requirement-grounding, in which case we are all required by beneficence to give away our life savings immediately; or it is, and Bob can permissibly let someone die to save his car.

   The reply to this, though, is to draw attention to the way in which Bob's situation has been presented to us as a one-off case. It is natural to assume that, once Bob destroys his car, he is not prevented from taking steps to improve his material situation afterwards. I think that dropping that assumption makes an important difference. It would be different if we were requiring Bob to commit himself to reducing permanently the amount he spends on the goods his life contains. If he could only save a life by making a permanent monetary sacrifice that would worsen his life overall genuinely and substantially, then my view is that now he violates no requirement of beneficence in refusing. This is not wrong, in the same way that it is not wrong for him to refuse to suffer a permanent, life-impairing injury to save a life. I do not expect everyone's intuitive judgements to agree with this. However, I do claim to have given an argument to support these views.

   A further objection needs a reply. What if, having reduced my personal spending just short of a requirement-grounding loss, I *then* encounter someone whose life needs to be saved directly? This is discussed in Sect. 11.4.

8. For the first phrase, see Marcus G. Singer, *Generalization in Ethics*, 61; for the second, see Anthony Quinton, *Utilitarian Ethics*, 47.
9. If it made sense to think of an exact borderline between substantial and insubstantial sacrifices, then there would be a possibility that the No answer resulted from your having spent exactly the amount required of you and no more. But that could never be a reasonable thing to believe. It would always be more reasonable for you to reduce your spending for the following year, and then to assess whether this made your life any worse.
10. Moreover, as I remarked in Sect. 9.5, 'Which Goods are Life-Enhancing?', there may be a plausible case for thinking that the development of one's talents is itself an intrinsically life-enhancing good that should be added to our list.
11. 'Why can I not appeal to the good of participating in a materialistic culture as a justification for spending a lot on myself?' A full answer to this would be lengthy. But in summary, I think we must distinguish between participation in the life of a community or culture, and simply doing the same sorts of thing as the people around me. And while patterns of high consumption might be necessary for the latter, they are usually not going to be necessary for the former. If not, there are less materialistic alternatives that could give you a life that is no worse.
12. Obviously, there are *other* questions that can be raised, independently of the argument of this book, about the morality of investing your money in enterprises that have an adverse impact on other people.

CHAPTER 11

1. This is one standard way of using the terms 'duty' and 'obligation'—see e.g. E. J. Lemmon, 'Moral Dilemmas', 140–3—but by no means the only one. Notice that it does not seem to make the two mutually exclusive.
2. One of the main ones is whether I can properly be accused of free riding in respect of a benefit which I have not gone out of my way to take. My own views on this are set out in Cullity, 'Moral Free Riding'.
3. It is rejected by G. A. Cohen, *If You're an Egalitarian, How Come You're so Rich?*, ch. 10, and Thomas Nagel, 'Libertarianism without Foundations', 145–6.
4. For this problem, see Unger, *Living High and Letting Die*, 59–61. For the possibility of using this problem to support an iterative over an aggregative approach (and a reply), see Brad Hooker, 'Sacrificing for the Good of Strangers—Repeatedly', 181. (However, for my non-iterative reading of Unger, see Ch. 5 n. 1.)

References

AIKEN, WILLIAM, AND HUGH LAFOLLETTE (eds.), *World Hunger and Moral Obligation*, 1st edn. (Englewood Cliffs, NJ: Prentice-Hall, 1977).

—— (eds.), *World Hunger and Morality*, 2nd edn. (Englewood Cliffs, NJ: Prentice-Hall, 1996).

ALLISON, HENRY E., *Kant's Theory of Freedom* (Cambridge: Cambridge University Press, 1990).

ALMEIDA, MICHAEL J. (ed.), *Imperceptible Harms* (Dordrecht: Kluwer, 2000).

ALSTON, PHILIP, AND KATARINA TOMASEVSKI (eds.), *The Right to Food* (Dordrecht: Nijhoff, 1984).

ANDERSON, MARY B., '"You Save My Life Today, but for What Tomorrow?" Some Moral Dilemmas of Humanitarian Aid', in Jonathan Moore (ed.), *Hard Choices: Moral Dilemmas in Humanitarian Intervention* (Lanham, Md.: Rowman & Littlefield, 1998), 137–56.

—— *Do No Harm: How Aid Can Support Peace—or War* (Boulder, Colo.: Lynne Rienner, 1999).

ANHEIER, HELMUT, AND NUNO THEMUDO, 'Organisational Forms of Global Civil Society: Implications of Going Global', in Marlies Glasius, Mary Kaldor, and Helmut Anheier (eds.), *Global Civil Society 2002* (Oxford: Oxford University Press, 2002), 191–216; <http://www.lse.ac.uk/Depts/global/Yearbook/outline 2002. htm>.

ARISTOTLE, *Nicomachean Ethics*, trans. Roger Crisp (Cambridge: Cambridge University Press, 2000).

ARNOLD, DAVID, *Famine: Social Crisis and Historical Change* (Oxford: Blackwell, 1988).

ARTHUR, JOHN, 'Rights and the Duty to Bring Aid', in William Aiken and Hugh LaFollette (eds.), *World Hunger and Moral Obligation*, 1st edn. (Englewood Cliffs, NJ: Prentice-Hall, 1977), 37–48.

ASHFORD, ELIZABETH, 'The Demandingness of Scanlon's Contractualism', *Ethics*, 113 (2003), 273–304.

ATTFIELD, ROBIN, AND BARRY WILKINS (eds.), *International Justice and the Third World* (New York: Routledge, 1992).

BADHWAR, NEERA KAPUR (ed.), *Friendship: A Philosophical Reader* (Ithaca, NY: Cornell University Press, 1993).

BARON, MARCIA, 'Impartiality and Friendship', *Ethics*, 101 (1991), 836–57.

—— *Kantian Ethics almost without Apology* (Ithaca, NY: Cornell University Press, 1995).

—— 'Kantian Ethics', in Marcia W. Baron, Philip Pettit, and Michael Slote (eds.), *Three Methods of Ethics* (Oxford: Blackwell, 1997), 3–91.

—— PHILIP PETTIT, AND MICHAEL SLOTE, *Three Methods of Ethics: A Debate* (Oxford: Blackwell, 1997).

BARRY, BRIAN, *Political Argument* (London: Routledge & Kegan Paul, 1965).

—— 'Humanity and Justice in Global Perspective', *Nomos*, 24 (1982), 219–52.

BAUER, P. T., *Equality, the Third World and Economic Delusion* (London: Weidenfeld & Nicolson, 1981).

—— 'Foreign Aid and its Hydra-Headed Rationalization', in his *Equality, the Third World and Economic Delusion*, ch. 5.

—— *Reality and Rhetoric: Studies in the Economics of Development* (London: Weidenfeld & Nicolson, 1984).

BEITZ, CHARLES, *Political Theory and International Relations* (Princeton: Princeton University Press, 1979).

BENNETT, JONATHAN, 'Morality and Consequences', in Sterling M. McMurrin (ed.), *The Tanner Lectures on Human Values*, ii (Cambridge: Cambridge University Press, 1981), 45–116.

BENSON, PAUL, 'Moral Worth', *Philosophical Studies*, 51 (1987), 365–82.

BIEKART, KEES, *The Politics of Civil Society Building: European Private Aid Agencies and Democratic Transitions in Central America* (Utrecht: International Books, 1998).

BIRDSALL, NANCY, 'Why Inequality Matters: Some Economic Issues', *Ethics and International Affairs*, 15 (2001), 3–28.

BITTNER, RUDIGER, 'Morality and World Hunger', in Thomas W. Pogge (ed.), *Global Justice* (Oxford: Blackwell, 2001), 24–31.

BLACKBURN, ROBIN, *The Making of New World Slavery: From the Baroque to the Modern 1492–1800* (London: Verso, 1997).

BLACKBURN, SIMON, *The Oxford Dictionary of Philosophy* (Oxford: Oxford University Press, 1994).

—— *Ruling Passions* (Oxford: Clarendon Press, 1998).

BLUM, LAWRENCE, *Friendship, Altruism and Morality* (London: Routledge & Kegan Paul, 1980).

—— 'Friendship as a Moral Phenomenon', in his *Friendship, Altruism and Morality*, 67–83.

—— 'Friendship, Beneficence, and Impartiality', in his *Friendship, Altruism and Morality*, 43–66.

—— *Moral Perception and Particularity* (Cambridge: Cambridge University Press, 1994).

—— 'Vocation, Friendship, and Community: Limitations of the Personal-Impersonal Framework', in his *Moral Perception and Particularity*, 98–123.

BONNER, RAYMOND, 'Review of Michael Maren, *The Road to Hell*', *New York Times Book Review*, 23 Mar. 1997, 23.

BORGIN, KARL, AND KATHLEEN CORBETT, *The Destruction of a Continent: Africa and International Aid* (San Diego: Harcourt Brace Jovanovich, 1982).

BORNSTEIN, DAVID, 'The Barefoot Bank with Cheek', *Atlantic Monthly*, (Dec. 1995), 40–7.

BORTON, J., N. NICHOLDS, C. BENSON, AND S. DHIRI, *NGOs and Relief Operations: Trends and Policy Implications*, ODI Briefing Paper (London: Overseas Development Institute, 1994).

BRADLEY, F. H., 'The Limits of Individual and National Self-Sacrifice', in his *Collected Essays*, i (Oxford: Clarendon Press, 1935).

BRANDT, WILLY, *Common Crisis North–South: Cooperation for World Recovery* (London: Pan Books, 1983).

BRATMAN, MICHAEL, 'Kagan on "The Appeal to Cost" ', *Ethics*, 101 (1994), 325–32.

BRAYBROOKE, DAVID, *Meeting Needs* (Princeton: Princeton University Press, 1987).

BREWER, MARK, 'We're Gonna Tear You Down and Put You back Together', *Psychology Today*, 9/3 (1975), 35–40, 82–9.

BRINK, DAVID, 'The Separateness of Persons, Distributive Norms, and Moral Theory', in R. G. Frey and Christopher W. Morris (eds.), *Value, Welfare, and Morality* (Cambridge: Cambridge University Press, 1993), 252–89.

BROAD, C. D., 'On the Function of False Hypotheses in Ethics', *International Journal of Ethics*, 26 (1916), 377–97.

BROADIE, SARAH, *Ethics with Aristotle* (New York: Oxford University Press, 1991).

BROCK, DAN W., 'Defending Moral Options', *Philosophy and Phenomenological Research*, 51 (1991), 909–13.

BROOME, JOHN, 'Fairness', *Proceedings of the Aristotelian Society*, 91 (1990), 87–101.

—— 'Skorupski on Agent-Neutrality', *Utilitas*, 7 (1995), 315–17.

—— *Weighing Goods: Equality, Uncertainty and Time* (Oxford: Blackwell, 1991).

BROWN, JAMES A. C., *Techniques of Persuasion: From Propaganda to Brainwashing* (Harmondsworth: Penguin, 1963).

BROWN, PETER G., 'Food as National Property', in Peter G. Brown and Henry Shue (eds.), *Food Policy*, 65–78.

—— AND HENRY SHUE (eds.), *Food Policy: The Responsibility of the United States in Life and Death Choices* (New York: Free Press, 1977).

CAMBIANO, GIUSEPPE, 'Aristotle and the Anonymous Opponents of Slavery', in M. I. Finley (ed.), *Classical Slavery* (London: Frank Cass, 1987), 21–41.

CAMERON, C., AND J. COCKING, *The Evaluation of NGO Activities: Organisation, Methodology and Results* (London: Overseas Development Administration, 1993).

CAMPBELL, JOHN, 'Can Philosophical Accounts of Altruism Accommodate Experimental Data on Helping Behaviour?', *Australasian Journal of Philosophy*, 77 (1999), 26–45.

CARR, BRIAN, 'Pity and Compassion as Social Virtues', *Philosophy*, 74 (1999), 411–29.

CASSEN, ROBERT, AND ASSOCIATES, *Does Aid Work? Report to an Intergovernmental Task Force*, 2nd edn. (Oxford: Clarendon Press, 1994).

CATER, NICK, *Sudan: The Roots of Famine* (Oxford: Oxfam Publications, 1986).

CATHIE, JOHN, *The Political Economy of Food Aid* (Aldershot: Gower, 1982).

CAUFIELD, CATHERINE, *Masters of Illusion: The World Bank and the Poverty of Nations* (New York: Henry Holt, 1996).

CHATTERJEE, DEEN K. (ed.), *The Ethics of Assistance: Morality and the Distant Needy* (Cambridge: Cambridge University Press, 2004).

CHEN, SHAOHUA, AND MARTIN RAVALLION, 'How Did the World's Poorest Fare in the 1990s?', *Review of Income and Wealth*, 47 (2001), 283–300; <http://www.worldbank.org/research/povmonitor/pdfs/methodology.pdf>.

CLARK, JOHN, *Democratizing Development: The Role of Voluntary Organizations* (West Hartford, Conn.: Kumarian Press, 1991).

CLAY, EDWARD, AND OLAV STOKKE (eds.), *Food Aid Reconsidered: Assessing the Impact on Third World Countries* (London: Frank Cass, 1991).

CLEARY, SEAMUS, *The Role of NGOs under Authoritarian Political Systems* (London: Macmillan, 1997).

COHEN, G. A., *If You're an Egalitarian, How Come You're so Rich?* (Cambridge, Mass.: Harvard University Press, 2000).

COHEN, L. JONATHAN, 'Who is Starving Whom?', *Theoria*, 47 (1981), 65–81.

COTTINGHAM, JOHN, 'Partiality, Favouritism and Morality', *Philosophical Quarterly*, 36 (1986), 357–73.

—— 'The Ethics of Self-Concern', *Ethics*, 101 (1991), 798–817.

—— 'Impartiality', in Edward Craig (ed.), *The Routledge Encyclopedia of Philosophy*, iv (London: Routledge, 1998), 714–17.

COUDOUEL, ALINE, JESKO HENTSCHEL, AND QUENTIN WODON, 'Poverty Measurement and Analysis', in Jeni Klugman (ed.), *Sourcebook for Poverty Reduction Strategies*, 2 vols. (Washington: World Bank, 2002), vol. i, ch. i; <http://www.worldbank.org/poverty/strategies/sourctoc.htm>.

CULLITY, GARRETT, 'International Aid and the Scope of Kindness', *Ethics*, 105 (1994), 99–127.

—— 'Moral Free Riding', *Philosophy and Public Affairs*, 24 (1995), 3–34.

—— 'The Life-Saving Analogy', in William Aiken and Hugh LaFollette (eds.), *World Hunger and Morality*, 2nd edn. (Englewood Cliffs, NJ: Prentice-Hall, 1996), 51–69.

—— 'Practical Theory', in Garrett Cullity and Berys Gaut (eds.), *Ethics and Practical Reason* (Oxford: Clarendon Press, 1997), 101–24.

—— 'Could there be a Virtue Theory in Ethics?,' *Ethical Theory and Moral Practice*, 2 (1999), 277–94.

—— 'Pooled Beneficence', in Michael J. Almeida (ed.), *Imperceptible Harms* (Dordrecht: Kluwer, 2000), 9–42.

—— 'Particularism and Presumptive Reasons', *Proceedings of the Aristotelian Society*, Suppl. vol. 76 (2002), 169–90.

—— 'Sympathy, Discernment, and Reasons', *Philosophy and Phenomenological Research*, 68 (2004), 37–62.

—— 'Public Goods and Fairness', unpub.

—— AND BERYS GAUT (eds.), *Ethics and Practical Reason* (Oxford: Clarendon Press, 1997).

DANAHER, KEVIN (ed.), *50 Years is Enough: The Case against the World Bank and the International Monetary Fund* (Boston: South End Press, 1994).

DANCY, JONATHAN, *Moral Reasons* (Oxford: Blackwell, 1993).

—— 'The Particularist's Progress', in Brad Hooker and Margaret Little (eds.), *Moral Particularism* (Oxford: Oxford University Press, 2000), 130–56.

—— (ed.), *Normativity* (Oxford: Blackwell, 2000).

Darley, John M., and Bibb Latane, *The Unresponsive Bystander: Why Doesn't he Help?* (New York: Basic Books, 1970).

Darwall, Stephen L., *Impartial Reason* (Ithaca, NY: Cornell University Press, 1983).

—— *Philosophical Ethics* (Boulder, Colo.: Westview Press, 1998).

Dasgupta, Partha, *An Inquiry into Well-Being and Destitution* (Oxford: Clarendon Press, 1993).

Davidson, Donald, 'Actions, Reasons and Causes', *Journal of Philosophy*, 60 (1963), 685–700.

Davis, Scott, 'Philanthropy as a Virtue in Late Antiquity and the Middle Ages', in J. B. Schneewind (ed.), *Giving: Western Ideas of Philanthropy* (Bloomington: Indiana University Press, 1996), 1–23.

De Greiff, Pablo, and Ciaran Cronin (eds.), *Global Justice and Transnational Politics: Essays on the Moral and Political Challenges of Globalization* (Cambridge, Mass.: MIT Press, 2002).

de Waal, Alex, *Famines that Kill: Darfur 1984–1985* (Oxford: Clarendon Press, 1989).

—— *Famine Crimes: Politics and the Disaster Relief Industry in Africa* (London: African Rights and the International African Institute, 1997).

—— *Who Fights? Who Cares?* (Trenton, NJ: Africa World Press, 2000).

Devarajan, Shantayanan, Margaret J. Miller, and Eric V. Swanson, *Goals for Development: History, Propects and Costs*, Working Paper 2819 (Washington, World Bank, Apr. 2002); <http://econ.worldbank.org/files/13269_wps2819.pdf>.

Development Initiatives, *Global Development Assistance: The Role of Non-Governmental Organisations and Other Charity Flows* (Evercreech: Development Initiatives, 2000).

Dinham, Barbara, and Colin Hines, *Agribusiness in Africa* (London: Earth Resources Research, 1983).

Drèze, Jean, 'Famine Prevention in India', in Jean Drèze and Amartya Sen (eds.), *The Political Economy of Hunger*, ii: *Famine Prevention* (Oxford: Clarendon Press, 1990), 13–122.

—— and Amartya Sen, *Hunger and Public Action* (Oxford: Clarendon Press, 1989).

—— —— (eds.), *The Political Economy of Hunger*, i: *Entitlement and Well-Being* (Oxford: Clarendon Press, 1990).

—— —— (eds.) *The Political Economy of Hunger*, ii: *Famine Prevention* (Oxford: Clarendon Press, 1990).

—— —— (eds.) *The Political Economy of Hunger*, iii: *Endemic Hunger* (Oxford: Clarendon Press, 1991).

Dyer, Christopher, 'Memories of Freedom: Attitudes towards Serfdom in England, 1200–1350', in M. L. Bush (ed.), *Serfdom and Slavery: Studies in Legal Bondage* (London: Longman, 1996), 199–224.

Eberstadt, 'Aid Harms the Hungry', *Weekly Standard* (Washington), 17 Mar. 1997; <http://www.aei.org/news/newsID.16573/news_detail.asp>.

Ebrahim, Alnoor, 'Accountability in Practice: Mechanisms for NGOs', *World Development*, 31 (2003), 813–29.

Edwards, Michael, 'NGO Performance—What Breeds Success? New Evidence from South Asia', *World Development*, 27 (1999), 361–74.

—— and John Gaventa (eds.), *Global Citizen Action* (Boulder, Colo.: Lynne Rienner, 2001).

—— and David Hulme (eds.), *Beyond the Magic Bullet: NGO Performance and Accountability* (West Hartford, Conn.: Kumarian Press, 1996).

Ehrlich, Paul, *The Population Bomb* (New York: Ballantine Books, 1971).

Emerson, Ralph Waldo, 'Gifts', in *The Complete Works of Ralph Waldo Emerson*, iii (Cambridge, Mass.: Harvard University Press, 1983), 91–6.

Engstrom, Stephen, 'Herman on Mutual Aid', *Ethics*, 96 (1986), 346–9.

Erlich, Paul, *The Population Explosion* (New York: Simon & Schuster, 1990).

FAO (Food and Agriculture Organization of the United Nations), *FAO Production Yearbook*, xlvi (Rome: FAO, 1993).

—— *FAO Trade Yearbook* (Rome: FAO, 1994).

—— *FAO Production Yearbook*, xlix (Rome: FAO, 1996).

—— *State of Food Insecurity in the World 2003* (Rome: FAO, 2003).

Farrington, John, Anthony Bebbington, with Kate Wellard, and David J. Lewis, *Reluctant Partners? Non-Governmental Organizations, the State and Sustainable Agricultural Development* (London: Routledge, 1993).

Feinberg, Joel, *Doing and Deserving* (Princeton: Princeton University Press, 1970).

—— 'The Moral and Legal Responsibility of the Bad Samaritan', in his *Freedom and Fulfillment* (Princeton: Princeton University Press, 1992).

Feldman, Fred, 'Unger's *Living High and Letting Die*', *Nous*, 32 (1998), 138–47.

Fishback, Price V., Michael R. Haines, and Shawn Kantor, *The Welfare of Children During the Great Depression*, National Bureau of Economic Research Working Paper No. W8902 (Cambridge, Mass.: National Bureau of Economic Research, Apr. 2002); <http://nber.org/papers/w8902.pdf>.

Fishkin, James S., *The Limits of Obligation* (New Haven: Yale University Press, 1982).

Flanagan, Owen, *Varieties of Moral Personality: Ethics and Psychological Realism* (Cambridge, Mass.: Harvard University Press, 1991).

Foot, Philippa, 'Utilitarianism and the Virtues', *Mind*, 94 (1985), 196–209.

Foster, Phillips, and Howard D. Leathers, *The World Food Problem: Tackling the Causes of Undernutrition in the Third World*, 2nd edn. (Boulder, Colo.: Lynne Rienner, 1999).

Fowler, Alan, 'NGOs as Agents of Democratisation: An African Perspective', *Journal of International Development*, 5 (1993), 325–39.

—— 'Authentic NGDO Partnership in the New Policy Agenda for International Aid: Dead End or Light Ahead?', *Development and Change*, 29 (1998), 137–59.

—— *Civil Society, NGDOs and Social Development: Changing the Rules of the Game*, Geneva 2000, Occasional Paper 1 (Geneva: UNRISD, 1999).

Frank, Robert, 'Motivation, Cognition, and Charitable Giving', in J. B. Schneewind (ed.), *Giving: Western Ideas of Philanthropy* (Bloomington: Indiana University Press, 1996), 130–52.

Frankena, William K., *Ethics*, 2nd edn. (Englewood Cliffs, NJ: Prentice-Hall, 1973).

—— 'Beneficence/Benevolence', *Social Philosophy and Policy*, 4 (1987), 1–20.

FREY, R. G., 'Moral Standing, the Value of Lives, and Speciesism', in Hugh LaFollette (ed.), *Ethics in Practice: An Anthology* (Oxford: Blackwell, 1997).

—— 'Morals and Medicine', in Helga Kuhse and Peter Singer (eds.), *Bioethics: An Anthology* (Oxford: Blackwell, 1999).

FRIEDMAN, MARILYN, 'The Practice of Partiality', *Ethics*, 101 (1991), 818–35.

GARNSEY, PETER, *Ideas of Slavery from Aristotle to Augustine* (Cambridge: Cambridge University Press, 1996).

GEARY, BOB, 'Afghanistan Seen through the Eyes of an Aid Worker', *Independent Weekly*, 29 Nov. 2001; <http://www.alternet.org/story.html?StoryID=11985>.

GEORGE, SUSAN, *Ill Fares the Land: Essays on Food, Hunger and Power* (Washington: Institute for Policy Studies, 1984).

GERMAN, TONY, AND JUDITH RANDEL, 'Never Richer, Never Meaner', in Tony German, Judith Randel, and Deborah Ewing (eds.), *Reality of Aid 2002* (Manila: Ibon Books, 2002), 145–57; <http://www.devinit.org/ktrends.pdf>.

GERT, BERNARD, 'Impartiality', in Lawrence C. Becker and Charlotte B. Becker (eds.), *Encyclopedia of Ethics*, 1st edn., i (Chicago: St James Press, 1992).

GEWIRTH, ALAN, 'Starvation and Human Rights', in his *Human Rights: Essays on Justification and Applications* (Chicago: University of Chicago Press, 1982), 197–217.

—— 'Private Philanthropy and Positive Rights', *Social Philosophy and Policy*, 4 (1987), 55–78.

GLOVER, JONATHAN, 'It Makes No Difference Whether or Not I Do It', *Proceedings of the Aristotelian Society*, Suppl. vol. 49 (1975), 171–90.

—— *Causing Death and Saving Lives* (Harmondsworth: Penguin, 1977).

GODWIN, WILLIAM, *An Enquiry concerning Political Justice*, 3rd edn. (1798), ed. F. E. L. Priestley (Toronto: University of Toronto Press, 1946).

GOLDSTEIN, IRWIN, 'Review of Peter Unger, *Living High and Letting Die*', *Philosophia*, 28 (2001), 557–61.

GOMBERG, PAUL, 'The Fallacy of Philanthropy', *Canadian Journal of Philosophy*, 32 (2002), 29–66.

GOODIN, ROBERT E., *Protecting the Vulnerable: A Reanalysis of Our Social Responsibilities* (Chicago: University of Chicago Press, 1985).

GRAHAM, GEORGE, AND HUGH LAFOLLETTE (eds.), *Person to Person* (Philadelphia: Temple University Press, 1989).

GREENSPAN, PATRICIA S., *Emotions and Reasons: An Inquiry into Emotional Justification* (New York: Routledge, 1988).

GRIFFIN, JAMES, *Well-Being: Its Meaning, Measurement and Moral Importance* (Oxford: Clarendon Press, 1986).

—— 'Review of Shelly Kagan, *The Limits of Morality*', *Mind*, 99 (1990), 128–31.

—— *Value Judgement* (Oxford: Clarendon Press, 1996).

GRIFFIN, KEITH, *World Hunger and the World Economy* (London: Macmillan, 1987).

GRUZALSKI, BART, 'Parfit's Impact on Utilitarianism', *Ethics*, 96 (1986), 760–83.

HANCOCK, GRAHAM, *Lords of Poverty* (London: Mandarin, 1991).

HANNA, ROBERT, 'Must We Be Good Samaritans?', *Canadian Journal of Philosophy*, 28 (1998), 453–70.

HANSCH, STEVEN, SCOTT LILLIBRIDGE, GRACE EGELAND, CHARLES TELLER, AND MICHAEL TOOLE, *Lives Lost, Lives Saved: Excess Mortality and the Impact of Health Interventions in the Somalia Emergency* (Washington: Refugee Policy Group, 1994).

HARDIN, GARRETT, 'Lifeboat Ethics: The Case against Helping the Poor', *Psychology Today*, 8/4 (1974), 38–43, 123–6.

—— 'Living on a Lifeboat', in Jan Narveson (ed.), *Moral Issues* (Toronto: Oxford University Press, 1983), 166–78.

—— *The Ostrich Factor: Our Population Myopia* (New York: Oxford University Press, 1999).

HARMAN, GILBERT, 'Practical Reasoning', *Review of Metaphysics*, 29 (1976), 431–63.

HARSANYI, JOHN C., *Essays in Ethics, Social Behaviour, and Scientific Explanation* (Dordrecht: Reidel, 1976).

—— 'Morality and the Theory of Rational Behaviour', *Social Research*, 44 (1977), 623–56; repr. in Amartya Sen and Bernard Williams (eds.), *Utilitarianism and Beyond* (Cambridge: Cambridge University Press, 1982), 39–62.

HAYTER, TERESA, *Aid as Imperialism* (Harmondsworth: Penguin, 1971).

HELLINGER, STEPHEN, DOUGLAS HELLINGER, AND FRED M. O'REGAN, *Aid for Just Development: Report on the Future of Foreign Assistance* (Boulder, Colo.: Lynne Rienner, 1988).

HERMAN, BARBARA, 'On the Value of Acting from the Motive of Duty', *Philosophical Review*, 90 (1981), 359–82.

—— 'Mutual Aid and Respect for Persons', *Ethics*, 94 (1984), 577–602.

—— 'Rules, Motives, and Helping Actions', *Philosophical Studies*, 45 (1984), 369–77.

—— 'Agency, Attachment, and Difference', in her *The Practice of Moral Judgment*, 184–207.

—— 'Integrity and Impartiality', in her *The Practice of Moral Judgment*, 23–44.

—— *The Practice of Moral Judgment* (Cambridge, Mass.: Harvard University Press, 1993).

HEYD, DAVID, *Supererogation: Its Status in Ethical Theory* (Cambridge: Cambridge University Press, 1982).

HILL, THOMAS E., 'Servility and Self-Respect', *The Monist*, 57 (1973), 84–104.

HOBBES, THOMAS, *Leviathan* (1651), ed. Richard Tuck (Cambridge: Cambridge University Press, 1996).

HOFFMAN, STANLEY, *Duties beyond Borders: On the Limits and Possibilities of Ethical International Politics* (Syracuse, NY: Syracuse University Press, 1981).

HOOKER, BRAD, 'Rule-Consequentialism and Demandingness: A Reply to Carson', *Mind*, 100 (1991), 270–6.

—— 'Sacrificing for the Good of Strangers—Repeatedly', *Philosophy and Phenomenological Research*, 59 (1999), 177–81.

—— *Ideal Code, Real World: A Rule-Consequentialist Theory of Morality* (Oxford: Clarendon Press, 2000).

—— and Margaret Little (eds.), *Moral Particularism* (Oxford: Oxford University Press, 2000).

Hudson, Alan, 'NGOs' Transnational Advocacy Networks: From "Legitimacy" to "Political Responsibility"?', *Global Networks: A Journal of Transnational Affairs*, 1 (2001), 331–52.

Hume, David, *An Enquiry concerning the Principles of Morals* (1751), ed. L. A. Selby-Bigge, rev. P. H. Nidditch, 3rd edn. (Oxford: Clarendon Press, 1975).

Hurka, Thomas, *Perfectionism* (New York: Oxford University Press, 1993).

Hursthouse, Rosalind, 'Normative Virtue Ethics', in Roger Crisp (ed.), *How should One Live?* (Oxford: Clarendon Press, 1996).

—— *On Virtue Ethics* (Oxford: Oxford University Press, 1999).

Hutcheson, Francis, *An Inquiry into the Original of Our Ideas of Beauty and Virtue* (1725), in *Collected Works of Francis Hutcheson*, i, ed. Bernhard Fabian (Hildesheim: Georg Olms Verlag, 1990).

ICRC (International Committee of the Red Cross), *War, Money and Survival* (Geneva: ICRC, 2000).

Ignatieff, Michael, *The Needs of Strangers* (London: Vintage, 1984).

—— 'The Stories We Tell: Television and Humanitarian Aid', in Jonathan Moore (ed.), *Hard Choices: Moral Dilemmas in Humanitarian Intervention* (Lanham, Md.: Rowman & Littlefield, 1998), 287–302.

Igneski, Violetta, 'Distance, Determinacy and the Duty to Aid: A Reply to Kamm', *Law and Philosophy*, 20 (2001), 605–16.

Jackson, Frank, 'Decision-Theoretic Consequentialism and the Nearest and Dearest Objection', *Ethics*, 101 (1991), 461–82.

Jackson, Tony, and Deborah Eade, *Against the Grain: The Dilemma of Project Food Aid* (Oxford: Oxfam Publications, 1982).

James, Susan, 'The Duty to Relieve Suffering', *Ethics*, 93 (1982), 4–21.

Jennings, M., ' "Almost an Oxfam in Itself": Oxfam, Ujamaa and Development in Tanzania', *African Affairs*, 101 (2002), 509–31.

Johnston, Philip, 'Relief and Reality', in Kevin Cahill (ed.), *A Framework for Survival: Health, Human Rights, and Humanitarian Assistance in Conflicts and Disasters* (New York: Basic Books, 1993).

Jones, John D., 'Poverty as *Malum Simpliciter*: A Reading of Aquinas's *Summa contra gentiles* 3.133', *Philosophy and Theology*, 13 (2001), 213–39.

Jones, Peter, 'Global Distributive Justice', in Andrew Valls (ed.), *Ethics in International Affairs: Theories and Cases* (Lanham, Md.: Rowman & Littlefield, 2000).

Kagan, Shelly, 'The Additive Fallacy', *Ethics*, 99 (1988), 5–31.

—— *The Limits of Morality* (Oxford: Clarendon Press, 1989).

—— 'Replies to My Critics', *Philosophy and Phenomenological Research*, 51 (1991), 919–28.

Kamm, F. M., 'Faminine Ethics: The Problem of Distance in Morality and Singer's Ethical Theory', in Dale Jamieson (ed.), *Singer and His Critics* (Oxford: Blackwell, 1999), 163–208.

—— 'Rescue and Harm: Discussion of Peter Unger's *Living High and Letting Die*', *Legal Theory*, 5 (1999), 1–44.

KAMM, F. M., 'Review of Peter Unger, *Living High and Letting Die*', *Philosophical Review*, 108 (1999), 300–5.

—— 'Does Distance Matter Morally to the Duty to Rescue?', *Law and Philosophy*, 19 (2000), 655–81.

KANT, IMMANUEL, *Lectures on Ethics* (1781), trans. Louis Infield (London: Methuen, 1930).

—— *The Metaphysics of Morals* (1797), trans. Mary Gregor (Cambridge: Cambridge University Press, 1996). Page references are to the Prussian Academy (*Ak.*) pagination, given in the margins of this edition.

KEKES, JOHN, 'Benevolence: A Minor Virtue', *Social Philosophy and Policy*, 4 (1987), 21–36.

—— 'On the Supposed Obligation to Relieve Famine', *Philosophy*, 77 (2002), 503–17.

KORSGAARD, CHRISTINE M., 'Skepticism about Practical Reason', *Journal of Philosophy*, 83 (1986), 5–25.

—— 'From Duty and for the Sake of the Noble: Kant and Aristotle on Morally Good Action', in Stephen Engstrom and Jennifer Whiting (eds.), *Aristotle, Kant and the Stoics: Rethinking Happiness and Duty* (Cambridge: Cambridge University Press, 1996), 203–36.

—— 'Kant's Analysis of Obligation: The Argument of *Groundwork I*', in her *Creating the Kingdom of Ends* (Cambridge: Cambridge University Press, 1996), 43–76.

KUMAR, B. G., 'Ethiopian Famines 1973–1985: A Case Study', in Jean Drèze and Amartya Sen (eds.), *The Political Economy of Hunger*, ii: *Famine Prevention* (Oxford: Clarendon Press, 1990), 173–213.

KUPER, ANDREW, 'Global Poverty Relief—More than Charity: Cosmopolitan Alternatives to the "Singer Solution"', *Ethics and International Affairs*, 16 (2002), 107–20.

LANCASTER, CAROL, *Aid to Africa: So Much to Do, So Little Done* (Chicago: University of Chicago Press, 1999).

LAPPÉ, FRANCES MOORE, AND JOSEPH COLLINS, *Food First* (London: Sphere Books, 1982).

—— —— AND DAVID KINLEY, *Aid as Obstacle: Twenty Questions about Our Foreign Aid and the Hungry* (San Francisco: Institute for Food and Development Policy, 1980).

—— —— AND PETER ROSSET, WITH LUIS ESPARZA, *World Hunger: 12 Myths*, 2nd edn. (New York: Grove Press, 1998).

LAWRENCE, D. H., *The Letters of D. H. Lawrence*, ed. Aldous Huxley (London: William Heinemann, 1934).

LEMMON, E. J., 'Moral Dilemmas', *Philosophical Review*, 71 (1962), 139–58.

LEWIS, DAVID, 'Illusory Innocence?', *Eureka Street*, 6 (1996), 35–6.

LICHTENBERG, JUDITH, 'National Boundaries and Moral Boundaries', in Peter G. Brown and Henry Shue (eds.), *Boundaries: National Autonomy and its Limits* (Totowa, NJ: Rowman & Littlefield, 1981), 79–100.

LIPTON, MICHAEL, AND JOHN TOYE, *Does Aid Work in India? A Country Study of the Impact of Official Development Assistance* (London: Routledge, 1990).

LUCAS, GEORGE R., Jr., AND THOMAS W. OGLETREE (eds.), *Lifeboat Ethics: The Moral Dilemmas of World Hunger* (New York: Harper & Row, 1976).

MCDOWELL, JOHN, 'Might There Be External Reasons?', in J. E. J. Altham and Ross Harrison (eds.), *World, Mind and Ethics: Essays on the Ethical Philosophy of Bernard Williams* (Cambridge: Cambridge University Press, 1995), 68–85.

MCGINN, COLIN, 'Saint Elsewhere', *New Republic*, 14 Oct. 1996, 54–7.

—— 'Our Duties to Animals and the Poor', in Dale Jamieson (ed.), *Singer and His Critics* (Oxford: Blackwell, 1999), 150–61.

MCGOLDRICK, PATRICIA M., 'Saints and Heroes: A Plea for the Supererogatory', *Philosophy*, 59 (1984), 523–8.

MACINTYRE, ALASDAIR, *After Virtue*, 2nd edn. (London: Duckworth, 1985).

MACKIE, J. L., *Ethics: Inventing Right and Wrong* (Harmondsworth: Penguin, 1977).

MCKINSEY, MICHAEL, 'Obligations to the Starving', *Nous*, 15 (1981), 309–24.

MCNAUGHTON, DAVID, *Moral Vision: An Introduction to Ethics* (Oxford: Blackwell, 1988).

—— AND PIERS RAWLING, 'Value and Agent-Relative Reasons', *Utilitas*, 7 (1995), 31–47.

MCNEILL, DESMOND, *The Contradictions of Foreign Aid* (London: Croom Helm, 1981).

MADELEY, JOHN, *When Aid is No Help: How Projects Fail, and How They Could Succeed* (London: Intermediate Technology Publications, 1991).

MALTHUS, THOMAS, *An Essay on the Principle of Population* (1798), ed. Patricia James (Cambridge: Cambridge University Press, 1989).

MAREN, MICHAEL, *The Road to Hell: The Ravaging Effects of Foreign Aid and International Charity* (New York: Free Press, 1997).

MARTIN, MIKE W., *Virtuous Giving: Philanthropy, Voluntary Service, and Caring* (Bloomington: Indiana University Press, 1994).

—— 'Good Fortune Obligates: Gratitude, Philanthropy, and Colonialism', *Southern Journal of Philosophy*, 31 (1999), 57–75.

MATIN, IMRAN, DAVID HULME, AND STUART RUTHERFORD, 'Finance for the Poor: From Microcredit to Microfinancial Services', *Journal of International Development*, 14 (2000), 273–94.

MATTHEWS, JESSICA, 'Little World Banks', in Kevin Danaher (ed.), *50 Years is Enough: The Case Against the World Bank and the International Monetary Fund* (Boston: South End Press, 1994), 183–5.

MEADOWS, DONELLA H., DENNIS L. MEADOWS, JORGEN RANDERS, AND WILLIAM W. BEHRENS, III, *The Limits of Growth: A Report for the Club of Rome's Project on the Predicament of Mankind* (London: Pan Books, 1972).

MEIER, GERALD M., *Emerging from Poverty* (New York: Oxford University Press, 1984).

MERCHET, JEAN-DOMINIQUE, 'Humanitarian Organizations Have Become Businesses', *Libération*, 7 Mar. 2002; trans. at <http://www.globalpolicy.org/ngos/role/globdem/credib/2002/0307bus.htm>.

MILANOVIC, BRANKO, 'True World Income Distribution, 1988 and 1993: First Calculation Based on Household Surveys Alone', *Economic Journal*, 112 (2002), 51–92.

MILL, JOHN STUART, *Utilitarianism* (1863), ed. Roger Crisp (Oxford: Oxford University Press, 1998).

MILLER, DAVID, 'Distributing Responsibilities', *Journal of Political Philosophy*, 9 (2001), 453–71.

MINEAR, LARRY, *Helping People in an Age of Conflict: Professionalism in US Voluntary Humanitarian Assistance* (New York: InterAction, 1988).

—— *The Humanitarian Enterprise: Dilemmas and Discoveries* (Bloomfield, Conn.: Kumarian Press, 2002).

MONROE, KRISTEN RENWICK, *The Heart of Altruism: Perceptions of a Common Humanity* (Princeton: Princeton University Press, 1996).

MOORE, ANDREW, 'Objective Human Goods', in Roger Crisp (ed.), *Well Being and Morality: Essays in Honour of James Griffin* (Oxford: Clarendon Oxford Press, 2000), 75–89.

MOORE, MICK, AND MARK ROBINSON, 'Can Foreign Aid Be Used to Promote Good Government in Developing Countries?', *Ethics and International Affairs*, 8 (1994), 141–58.

MORRIS, CHRISTOPHER, 'Existential Limits to the Rectification of Past Wrongs', *American Philosophical Quarterly*, 21 (1984), 175–82.

MULGAN, TIM, 'Two Conceptions of Benevolence', *Philosophy and Public Affairs*, 26 (1997), 62–79.

—— *The Demands of Consequentialism* (Oxford: Clarendon Press, 2001).

MURPHY, LIAM B., 'The Demands of Beneficence', *Philosophy and Public Affairs*, 22 (1993), 266–92.

—— 'A Relatively Plausible Principle of Beneficence: Reply to Mulgan', *Philosophy and Public Affairs*, 26 (1997), 80–6.

—— 'Help and Beneficence', in Edward Craig (ed.), *Routledge Encyclopedia of Philosophy*, iv (London: Routledge, 1998), 342–4.

—— *Moral Demands in Nonideal Theory* (New York: Oxford University Press, 2000).

NAGEL, THOMAS, *The Possibility of Altruism* (Oxford: Clarendon Press, 1970).

—— 'Libertarianism without Foundations', *Yale Law Journal*, 85 (1975), 136–49.

—— 'Poverty and Food: Why Charity is Not Enough', in Peter Brown and Henry Shue (eds.), *Food Policy: The Responsibility of the United States in Life and Death Choices* (New York: Free Press, 1977), 54–62.

—— 'The Limits of Objectivity', in Sterling M. McMurrin (ed.), *The Tanner Lectures on Human Values,* i (Salt Lake City: University of Utah Press, 1980), 75–139.

—— *The View from Nowhere* (New York: Oxford University Press, 1986).

—— *Equality and Partiality* (New York: Oxford University Press, 1991).

NAJERA, JOSÉ A., BERNHARD LIESE, AND JEFFREY S. HAMMER, *Health Sector Priorities Review: Malaria*, World Bank Offset Document HSPR-25 (Washington: Population, Health and Nutrition Division, World Bank, 1991).

Narveson, Jan, 'Aesthetics, Charity, Utility, and Distributive Justice', *Monist*, 56 (1972), 527–51.

—— 'Equality vs Liberty: Advantage, Liberty', *Social Philosophy and Policy*, 2 (1984), 33–60.

—— 'Feeding the Hungry', in James Rachels (ed.), *The Right Thing to Do: Basic Readings in Moral Philosophy*, 3rd edn. (New York: McGraw-Hill, 2003), 162–74.

Nelson, Paul J., and Ellen Dorsey, 'At the Nexus of Human Rights and Development: New Methods and Strategies of Global NGOs', *World Development*, 31 (2003), 2013–26.

Newman, Lucile F. (ed.), *Hunger in History: Food Shortage, Poverty, and Deprivation* (Oxford: Blackwell, 1990).

Nichols, Bruce, 'Rubberband Humanitarianism', *Ethics and International Affairs*, 1 (1987), 191–210.

Nietzsche, Friedrich, *Schopenhauer as Educator* (1878), trans. James W. Hillesheim and Malcolm R. Simpson (South Bend, Ind.: Gateway Editions, 1965).

—— *On the Genealogy of Morals* (1887), trans. Douglas Smith (Oxford: Oxford University Press, 1996).

Norman, Richard, *Ethics, Killing and War* (Cambridge: Cambridge University Press, 1995).

Nozick, Robert, *Anarchy, State, and Utopia* (New York: Basic Books, 1974).

Nussbaum, Martha, 'Compassion: The Basic Social Emotion', *Social Philosophy and Policy*, 13 (1996), 27–58.

—— 'If Oxfam Ran the World', *London Review of Books*, 4 Sept. 1997, 18–19.

—— 'Duties of Justice, Duties of Material Aid: Cicero's Problematic Legacy', *Journal of Political Philosophy*, 8 (2000), 176–206.

—— *Women and Human Development: The Capabilities Approach* (Cambridge: Cambridge University Press, 2000).

O'Connor, John, 'Philanthropy and Selfishness', *Social Philosophy and Policy*, 4 (1987), 113–27.

Odegard, Douglas, 'Charity and Moral Imperatives', *Theoria*, 55 (1989), 81–94.

Oderberg, David S., *Moral Theory: A Non-Consequentialist Approach* (Oxford: Blackwell, 2000).

ODI, *Can We Attain the Millennium Development Goals in Education and Health through Public Expenditure and Aid?*, ODI Briefing Paper (London: Overseas Development Institute, Apr. 2003); <http://www.odi.org.uk>.

OECD (Organisation for Economic Co-operation and Development), *1992 Report: Development Co-operation* (Paris: OECD, 1992).

Oldenquist, Andrew, 'Loyalties'. *Journal of Philosophy*, 79 (1982), 173–93.

Oliner, Samuel, and Pearl Oliner, *The Altruistic Personality: Rescuers of Jews in Nazi Europe* (New York: Free Press, 1988).

Omar, Rakiya, and Alex de Waal, *Humanitarianism Unbound? Current Dilemmas Facing Multi-Mandate Relief Operations in Political Emergencies*, Discussion Paper No. 5 (London: African Rights, 1994).

O'Neill, Helen, and John Toye (eds.), *A World without Famine? New Approaches to Aid and Development* (London: Macmillan, 1998).

O'Neill, Onora, 'Lifeboat Earth', *Philosophy and Public Affairs*, 4 (1975), 273–92.

—— *Faces of Hunger: An Essay on Poverty, Justice and Development* (London: Allen & Unwin, 1986).

—— 'The Great Maxims of Justice and Charity', in her *Constructions of Reason* (Cambridge: Cambridge University Press, 1989), 219–33.

—— 'Vindicating Reason', in Paul Guyer (ed.), *The Cambridge Companion to Kant* (Cambridge: Cambridge University Press, 1992), 280–308.

Osmani, S. R., 'The Food Problems of Bangladesh', in Jean Drèze and Amartya Sen (eds.), *The Political Economy of Hunger*, iii: *Endemic Hunger* (Oxford: Clarendon Press, 1991), 307–46.

Otsuka, Michael, 'The Paradox of Group Beneficence', *Philosophy and Public Affairs*, 20 (1991), 132–49.

Otteson, James R., 'Limits on Our Obligation to Give', *Public Affairs Quarterly*, 14 (2000), 183–203.

Paddock, Paul, and William Paddock, *Famine—1975!* (Boston: Little, Brown, 1967).

Pakaluk, Michael (ed.), *Other Selves: Philosophers on Friendship* (Indianapolis: Hackett, 1991).

Parfit, Derek, *Reasons and Persons* (Oxford: Clarendon Press, 1984).

—— 'Comments', *Ethics*, 96 (1986), 823–73.

—— 'Equality or Priority?', *The Lindley Lecture* (Lawrence: University of Kansas Press, 1995); repr. in Matthew Clayton and Andrew Williams (eds.), *The Ideal of Equality* (London: Macmillan, 2000), 81–125.

—— 'Reasons and Motivation', *Proceedings of the Aristotelian Society*, Suppl. vol. 71 (1997), 99–130.

Parkinson, J. R. (ed.), *Poverty and Aid* (Oxford: Blackwell, 1983).

Paton, H. J., *The Categorical Imperative: A Study in Kant's Moral Philosophy*, 4th edn. (London: Hutchinson, 1963).

Pearce, David W. (ed.), *The Macmillan Dictionary of Modern Economics* (London: Macmillan, 1981).

Pearse, Andrew, *Seeds of Plenty, Seeds of Want: Social and Economic Implications of the Green Revolution* (Oxford: Clarendon Press, 1980).

Pettit, Philip, 'Consequentialism', in Peter Singer (ed.), *A Companion to Ethics* (Oxford: Blackwell, 1991), 230–40.

—— 'The Consequentialist Perspective', in Marcia W. Baron, Philip Pettit, and Michael Slote, *Three Methods of Ethics* (Oxford: Blackwell, 1997), 92–174.

Plato, *Protagoras*, trans. C. C. W. Taylor (Oxford: Clarendon Press, 1991).

Pogge, Thomas W., 'An Egalitarian Law of Peoples', *Philosophy and Public Affairs*, 23 (1994), 195–224.

—— 'Human Rights and Human Responsibilities', in Pablo De Greiff and Ciaran Cronin (eds.), *Global Justice and Transnational Politics* (Cambridge, Mass.: MIT Press, 2002), 151–95.

—— *World Poverty and Human Rights: Cosmopolitan Responsibilities and Reforms* (Cambridge: Polity Press, 2002).

—— '"Assisting" the Global Poor', in Deen K. Chatterjee (ed.), *The Ethics of Assistance: Morality and the Distant Needy* (Cambridge: Cambridge University Press, 2004).

—— (ed.), *Global Justice* (Oxford: Blackwell, 2001).

—— and Sanjay Reddy, *How Not to Count the Poor*, Working Paper, <http://www.columbia.edu/~sr793/count. pdf>.

Poppendieck, Janet E., 'Dilemmas of Emergency Food: A Guide for the Perplexed', *Agriculture and Human Values*, 11 (1994), 69–76.

Porter, Doug, Bryant Allen, and Gaye Thompson, *Development in Practice: Paved with Good Intentions* (London: Routledge, 1991).

Price, Richard, *A Review of the Principal Questions and Difficulties in Morals* (1758), ed. D. D. Raphael (Oxford: Clarendon Press, 1974).

Quinton, Anthony, *Utilitarian Ethics* (London: Macmillan, 1973).

Rachels, James, 'Killing and Starving to Death', *Philosophy*, 54 (1979), 154–66.

Raffer, Kunibert, and H. W. Singer, *The Foreign Aid Business: Economic Assistance and Development Co-operation* (Cheltenham: Edward Elgar, 1996).

Rahman, Atiur, 'Rural Development from Below: Lessons Learned from Grameen Bank Experience in Bangladesh', *Journal of Socio-Economics*, 25 (1996), 189–226.

Railton, Peter, 'Alienation, Consequentialism and the Demands of Morality', *Philosophy and Public Affairs*, 13 (1984), 134–71.

Ram, Narasimhan, 'An Independent Press and Anti-Hunger Strategies: The Indian Experience', in Jean Drèze and Amartya Sen (eds.), *The Political Economy of Hunger*, i: *Entitlement and Well-Being* (Oxford: Clarendon Press, 1990), 146–90.

Ravallion, Martin, *Markets and Famines* (Oxford: Clarendon Press, 1987).

—— 'Market Responses to Anti-Hunger Policies: Effects on Wages, Prices and Employment', in Jean Drèze and Amartya Sen (eds.), *The Political Economy of Hunger*, ii: *Famine Prevention* (Oxford: Clarendon Press, 1990), 241–78.

—— 'Famines and Economics', *Journal of Economic Literature*, 35 (1997), 1205–42.

—— *The Debate on Globalization, Poverty and Inequality: Why Measurement Matters*, World Bank Policy Research Working Paper 3038 (Apr. 2003); <http://econ.worldbank.org/files/26010_wps3038.pdf>.

—— *How Not to Count the Poor: A Reply to Reddy and Pogge*, Working Paper, <http://www.columbia.edu/~sr793/wbreply.pdf>.

Rawls, John, *A Theory of Justice* (Cambridge, Mass.: Harvard University Press, 1971).

—— *The Law of Peoples* (Cambridge, Mass.: Harvard University Press, 1999).

Raz, Joseph, 'Explaining Normativity: On Rationality and the Justification of Reason', in Jonathan Dancy (ed.), *Normativity* (Oxford: Blackwell, 2000), 34–59.

Reader, Soran, 'Distance, Relationship, and Moral Obligation', *The Monist*, 86 (2003), 367–81.

Reath, Andrews, 'Kant's Theory of Moral Sensibility: Respect for the Moral Law and the Influence of Inclination', *Kant-Studien*, 80 (1989), 284–302.

Regan, Donald H., *Utilitarianism and Co-operation* (Oxford: Clarendon Press, 1980).

Riddell, Roger C., *Foreign Aid Reconsidered* (Baltimore: Johns Hopkins University Press, 1987).

RIDDELL, ROGER C., AND MARK ROBINSON, *The Impact of NGO Poverty-Alleviation Projects: Results of the Case-Study Evaluations*, ODI Working Paper 68 (London: Overseas Developmental Institute, 1992).

—— S.-K. KRUSE, T. KYLLONEN, S. OJANPERA, AND J.-L. VIELAJUS, *Searching for Impact and Methods: NGO Evaluation Synthesis Study for OECD/DAC* (Helsinki: Ministry of Foreign Affairs, 1997).

RIEFF, DAVID, 'Charity on the Rampage: The Business of Foreign Aid', *Foreign Affairs*, 76 (1997), 132–8.

—— *A Bed for the Night: Humanitarianism in Crisis* (New York: Simon & Schuster, 2002).

ROBERTS, SUZANNE, 'Contexts of Charity in the Middle Ages: Religious, Social, and Civic', in J. B. Schneewind (ed.), *Giving: Western Ideas of Philanthropy* (Bloomington: Indiana University Press, 1996), 24–53.

ROSS, W. D., *The Right and the Good* (Oxford: Clarendon Press, 1930).

RUTHERFORD, DONALD, *Dictionary of Economics* (London: Routledge, 1992).

SARGANT, WILLIAM, *Battle for the Mind: A Physiology of Conversion and Brain-Washing* (London: Heinemann, 1957).

SCANLON, T. M., 'Contractualism and Utilitarianism', in Amartya Sen and Bernard Williams (eds.), *Utilitarianism and Beyond* (Cambridge: Cambridge University Press, 1982), 103–28.

—— 'The Moral Basis of Interpersonal Comparisons', in Jon Elster and John E. Roemer (eds.), *Interpersonal Comparisons of Well-Being* (Cambridge: Cambridge University Press, 1991), 17–44.

—— 'Value, Desire, and Quality of Life', in Martha Nussbaum and Amartya Sen (eds.), *The Quality of Life* (Oxford: Clarendon Press, 1993).

—— *What We Owe to Each Other* (Cambridge, Mass.: Harvard University Press, 1998).

SCHEFFLER, SAMUEL (ed.), *Consequentialism and its Critics* (Oxford: Oxford University Press, 1988).

—— *Human Morality* (New York: Oxford University Press, 1992).

—— *The Rejection of Consequentialism: A Philosophical Investigation of the Considerations Underlying Rival Moral Conceptions*, 2nd edn. (Oxford: Clarendon Press, 1994).

SCHEIN, EDGAR H., *Coercive Persuasion: A Socio-Psychological Analysis of the 'Brainwashing' of American Civilian Prisoners by the Chinese Communists* (New York: W. W. Norton, 1961).

SCHMIDTZ, DAVID, 'Islands in a Sea of Obligation: Limits of the Duty to Rescue', *Law and Philosophy*, 19 (2000), 683–705.

SCHNEEWIND, J. B., 'Philosophical Ideas of Charity: Some Historical Reflections', in J. B. Schneewind (ed.), *Giving: Western Ideas of Philanthropy* (Bloomington: Indiana University Press, 1996), 54–75.

SCOCCIA, DANNY, 'Utilitarianism, Sociobiology, and the Limits of Benevolence', *Journal of Philosophy*, 87 (1990), 329–45.

SCOTT-TAGGART, M. J., 'Collective and Individual Responsibility', *Proceedings of the Aristotelian Society*, Suppl. vol. 49 (1975), 191–209.

SEN, AMARTYA, *Poverty and Famines: An Essay on Entitlement and Deprivation* (Oxford: Clarendon Press, 1981).

—— 'The Right Not To Be Hungry', in P. Alston and K. Tomasevski (eds.), *The Right to Food* (Dordrecht: Martinus Nijhoff, 1984), 69–81.

—— *Commodities and Capabilities* (New York: North-Holland, 1985).

—— 'Capability and Well-Being', in Martha Nussbaum and Amartya Sen (eds.), *Quality of Life* (Oxford: Clarendon Press, 1993), 30–54.

—— *On Economic Inequality*, 2nd edn. (Oxford: Clarendon Press, 1997).

—— *Development as Freedom* (New York: Alfred A. Knopf, 1999).

SHAPIRO, IAN, AND LEA BRILMAYER (eds.), *Global Justice: Nomos XLI* (New York: New York University Press, 1999).

SHUE, HENRY, *Basic Rights: Subsistence, Affluence and US Foreign Policy* (Princeton: Princeton University Press, 1980).

SIDGWICK, HENRY, *The Methods of Ethics*, 7th edn. (London: Macmillan, 1907; Indianapolis: Hackett, 1981).

SIKKINK, KATHRYN, 'Human Rights Issue-Networks in Latin America', *International Organization*, 47 (1993), 411–42.

SIMMONS, A. JOHN, 'Fairness', in Charlotte B. Becker and Lawrence C. Becker (eds.), *Encyclopedia of Ethics*, 1st edn., i (Chicago: St James Press, 1992).

—— 'Historical Rights and Fair Shares', *Law and Philosophy*, 14 (1995), 149–84.

SINGER, H., J. WOOD, AND T. JENNINGS, *Food Aid: The Challenge and the Opportunity* (Oxford: Clarendon Press, 1987).

SINGER, MARCUS G., *Generalization in Ethics* (New York: Atheneum, 1971).

SINGER, PETER, 'Famine, Affluence and Morality', *Philosophy and Public Affairs*, 1 (1972), 229–43.

—— 'Postscript to "Famine, Affluence and Morality" ', in William Aiken and Hugh LaFollette (eds.), *World Hunger and Moral Obligation*, 1st edn. (Englewood Cliffs, NJ: Prentice-Hall, 1977), 33–6.

—— 'Reconsidering the Famine Relief Argument', in Peter G. Brown and Henry Shue (eds.), *Food Policy: The Responsibility of the United States in the Life and Death Choices* (New York: Free Press, 1977), 36–53.

—— *Practical Ethics* (Cambridge: Cambridge University Press, 1979).

—— *One World: The Ethics of Globalisation* (Melbourne: Text Publishing, 2002).

SINNOTT-ARMSTRONG, WALTER, 'Some Varieties of Particularism', *Metaphilosophy*, 30 (1999), 1–12.

SKORUPSKI, JOHN, 'Agent-Neutrality, Consequentialism, Utilitarianism . . . A Terminological Note', *Utilitas*, 7 (1995), 49–54.

SLIM, HUGO, 'Doing the Right Thing: Relief Agencies, Moral Dilemmas, and Moral Responsibility in Political Emergencies and War', *Disasters*, 21 (1997), 244–57.

SMILLIE, IAN, 'Painting Canadian Roses Red', in Michael Edwards and David Hulme (eds.), *Beyond the Magic Bullet: NGO Performance and Accountability* (West Hartford, Conn.: Kumarian Press, 1996), 187–97.

SMITH, DAVID H., 'Grassroots Associations are Important: Some Theory and a Review of the Impact Literature', *Nonprofit and Voluntary Sector Quarterly*, 26 (1997), 269–306.

SMITH, PATRICIA, 'The Duty to Rescue and the Slippery Slope Problem', *Social Theory and Practice*, 16 (1990), 19–41.

SOBEL, JORDAN HOWARD, 'Garrett Cullity's Response to an Imperceptibility Challenge', in Michael J. Almeida (ed.), *Imperceptible Harms and Benefits* (Dordrecht: Kluwer, 2000), 25–48.

SOGGE, DAVID, *Give and Take: What's the Matter with Foreign Aid?* (London: Zed Books, 2002).

STEPHEN, JAMES FITZJAMES, *A History of the Criminal Law of England* (London: Macmillan, 1883).

STERBA, JAMES P., 'Global Justice', in William Aiken and Hugh LaFollette (eds.), *World Hunger and Morality*, 2nd edn. (Upper Saddle River, NJ: Prentice-Hall, 1996), 133–52.

STEVENS, CHRISTOPHER, *Food Aid and the Developing World: Four African Case Studies* (London: Croom Helm, 1979).

STRAWSON, P. F., 'Social Morality and Individual Ideal', in his *Freedom and Resentment and Other Essays* (London: Methuen, 1974), 26–44.

SUMNER, L. W., 'Something in Between', in Roger Crisp and Brad Hooker (eds.), *Well-Being and Morality: Essays in Honour of James Griffin* (Oxford: Clarendon Press, 2000), 1–19.

SURR, M. A., *Evaluations of Non Government Organisations (NGOs) Development Projects Synthesis Report*, Evaluation Report EV 554 (London: Overseas Development Administration, 1995).

TAYLOR, MICHAEL, *The Possibility of Cooperation* (New York: Cambridge University Press, 1987).

TAYLOR, RICHARD, 'Ancient Wisdom and Modern Folly', *Midwest Studies in Philosophy*, 13 (1988), 54–63.

TELFER, ELIZABETH, 'Friendship', *Proceedings of the Aristotelian Society*, 71 (1971), 223–41.

TENDLER, JUDITH, *Turning Private Voluntary Organizations into Development Agencies: Questions for Evaluation*, Program Evaluation Paper No. 2 (Washington: US Agency for International Development, 1982).

TERHAL, PIET, AND INDIRA HIRWAY, 'Rural Public Works and Food Entitlement Protection: Towards a Strategy for Preventing Hunger', in Helen O'Neill and John Toye (eds.), *A World without Famine? New Approaches to Aid and Development* (London: Macmillan, 1998), 373–403.

TERRY, FIONA, *Condemned to Repeat? The Paradox of Humanitarian Action* (Ithaca, NY: Cornell University Press, 2002).

THOMSON, JUDITH JARVIS, 'A Defense of Abortion', *Philosophy and Public Affairs*, 1 (1971), 47–66.

TRUSTED, JENNIFER, 'The Problem of Absolute Poverty: What Are Our Moral Obligations to the Destitute?', in David E. Cooper (ed.), *The Environment in Question: Ethics and Global Issues* (New York: Routledge, 1992), 13–27.

—— 'Rich and Poor', in Brenda Almond (ed.), *Introducing Applied Ethics* (Oxford: Blackwell, 1995), 289–304.

TVEDT, TERJE, *Angels of Mercy or Development Diplomats? NGOs and Foreign Aid* (Trenton, NJ: Africa World Press, 1998).

Tversky, Amos, and Daniel Kahneman, 'The Framing of Decisions and the Psychology of Choice', *Science*, 211 (1981), 453–8.

UNDP (United Nations Development Programme), *Human Development Report 2003* (New York: Oxford University Press, 2003); <http://www.undp.org/hdr2003/>.

Unger, Peter, *Living High and Letting Die: Our Illusion of Innocence* (New York: Oxford University Press, 1996).

UNICEF, *The State of the World's Children 1998: Focus on Nutrition* (New York: Oxford University Press, 1997); <http://www.unicef.org/sowc98/>.

—— *The State of the World's Children 2003: Child Participation* (New York: UNICEF, 2002); <http://www.unicef.org/sowc03/>.

Uphoff, Norman, 'Grassroots Organizations and NGOs in Rural Development: Opportunities with Diminishing States and Expanding Markets', *World Development*, 21 (1993), 607–22.

Uvin, Peter, *Aiding Violence: The Development Enterprise in Rwanda* (West Hartford, Conn.: Kumarian Press, 1998).

Vibert, Frank, *Home Truths for Foreign Aid: How to Encourage Enterprise Abroad* (London: Centre for Policy Studies, 1988).

von Braun, Joachim, Tesfaye Teklu, and Patricia Webb, *Famine in Africa: Causes, Reasons, Prevention* (Baltimore: Johns Hopkins University Press, 1999).

Waldron, Jeremy, 'Superseding Historic Injustice', *Ethics*, 103 (1992), 4–28.

Walker, Ralph C. S., *Kant* (London: Routledge & Kegan Paul, 1978).

Wallace, J. D., *Virtues and Vices* (Ithaca, NY: Cornell University Press, 1978).

Wallace, R. Jay, 'Reason and Responsibility', in Garrett Cullity and Berys Gaut (eds.), *Ethics and Practical Reason* (Oxford: Clarendon Press, 1997), 321–43.

Warnock, G. J., *The Object of Morality* (London: Methuen, 1971).

Weiss, Thomas G., and Leon Gordenker (eds.), *NGOs, the UN and Global Governance* (Boulder, Colo.: Lynne Rienner, 1996).

Whelan, John M., Jr., 'Famine and Charity', *Southern Journal of Philosophy*, 29 (1991), 149–66.

White, Howard, Jennifer Leavy, and Andrew Masters, *Comparative Perspectives on Child Poverty: A Review of Poverty Measures*, Young Lives Working Paper No. 1 (London: Save the Children Fund UK, 2003); <http://www.younglives.org.uk/data/publications/workingpapers.htm>.

WHO, *World Health Report 2003* (Geneva: World Health Organization, 2003); <http://www.who.int/whr/2002/>.

Williams, Bernard, 'A Critique of Utilitarianism', in J. J. C. Smart and Bernard Williams (eds.), *Utilitarianism: For and Against* (Cambridge: Cambridge University Press, 1973), 77–150.

—— 'Persons, Character and Morality', in his *Moral Luck* (Cambridge: Cambridge University Press, 1981), 1–19.

—— *Ethics and the Limits of Philosophy* (London: Collins, 1985).

—— *Making Sense of Humanity and Other Philosophical Papers 1982–1993* (Cambridge: Cambridge University Press, 1995).

Wilson, Catherine, 'On Some Alleged Limitations to Moral Endeavor', *Journal of Philosophy*, 90 (1993), 275–89.

WITTGENSTEIN, LUDWIG, *Tractatus Logico-Philosophicus* (London: Routledge & Kegan Paul, 1922).

WOLF, SUSAN, 'Moral Saints', *Journal of Philosophy*, 79 (1982), 419–39.

—— 'Morality and Partiality', *Philosophical Perspectives*, 6 (1992), 243–59.

—— 'Morality and the View from Here', *Journal of Ethics*, 3 (1999), 203–23.

WOOD, ADRIAN, RAYMOND APTHORPE, AND JOHN BORTON (eds.), *Evaluating International Humanitarian Action: Reflections from Practitioners* (London: Zed Books, 2001).

WORLD BANK, *World Development Report 1990: Poverty* (New York: Oxford University Press, 1990).

—— *World Development Report 1991: The Challenge of Development* (New York: Oxford University Press, 1991).

—— *Assessing Aid: What Works, What Doesn't and Why* (Oxford: Oxford University Press, 1998).

—— *World Development Report 2003: Sustainable Development in a Dynamic World* (New York: Oxford University Press, 2002).

—— *World Development Indicators 2003* (Washington: World Bank, 2003); <http://www.worldbank.org/data/wdi2003/>; <http://www.worldbank.org.poverty/>.

—— *World Development Report 2004: Making Services Work for Poor People* (Washington: World Bank, 2003); <http://econ.worldbank.org/wdr/wdr2004/>.

YOUNG, THOMAS, 'Analogical Reasoning and Easy Rescue Cases', *Journal of Philosophical Research*, 18 (1993), 327–39.

Index

achievements 131, 156, 162–3
agent-neutrality vs -relativity 74–5, 92
aggregative approaches to life-saving analogy 82–6, 173–4, 176–80
  argument for 173
  four dimensions of variation among 83–4, 177–80
  intuitive case for 85–6
aid
  counter-productivity of 35–48
  and economics 37–40, 42–7
  evaluations of 234–7 nn. 53, 63, 67, 70, 71
  humanitarian vs other 43–4, 47–8, 68, 222 n. 6
  and justice 221 n. 4
  and NGOs 41–8, 213
  Official Development Assistance 41, 211–12
  and politics 38–41, 42–8, 222 n. 5
  pooling of 58–65
  and population 36–9
  relief vs development 55–8, 66–7
Allison, Henry 227 n. 15, 228 n. 19, 253 n. 18
altruism, psychology of 228 n. 27, 242, n. 16, 243 nn. 23, 24
altruistically directed lives 158
altruistically focused lives 133–4
Anderson, Mary 222 n. 6, 235 n. 67
Anheier, Helmut 213
appropriate impartiality, *see* impartiality
argument for permission, *see* permission, argument for
argument for requirement 147, 172–4
Aristotelian arguments against extreme moral demands 96–7, 100–1
Aristotle 252 n. 12
Arnold, David 230 n. 5
Arthur, John 223 n. 14, 237 n. 82
ascetic view, rejection of 157–8
Ashford, Elizabeth 247 n. 39

Baron, Marcia 227 n. 15, 246 n. 19, 249 n. 3, 253 n. 18
Barry, Brian 221 nn. 2, 4, 222–3 n. 10, 224 n. 20, 226 n. 3, 238 n. 5, 242 n. 15, 244 n. 33
Bauer, P. T. 214, 222 nn. 8, 9, 231 n. 8, 232 nn. 26, 29, 233 nn. 36, 37, 39, 43
begging the question 151–2, 190–3
belief that aid is counter-productive 49–50
beneficence 16–18
  collective requirements of 60–1, 66–7, 74–6
  content of reasons of 16, 21–3, 134–7
  failures of 18–19, 119–21, 150, 230 n. 38
  and impartiality 118–22
  internal approach to requirements of 119–21
  and justice 221 n. 4, 226 n. 3, 251 n. 15
  and life-saving analogy 13
  and particularity 26–7
  presuppositions of 102–6
  theory of 30, 229 n. 34
  and virtue theory 31
benevolence 103, 227 n. 11
Bennett, Jonathan 223 n. 14, 225 n. 27, 242 n. 15
Benson, Paul 253 n. 18
Biekart, Kees 235 n. 63
Birdsall, Nancy 209
Bittner, Rudiger 222 n. 5
Blackburn, Robin 229 n. 30
Blackburn, Simon 247 n. 36, 249–50 n. 5

blameworthiness
  and ignorance 49–50
  vs wrongness 28–9, 50, 200–1, 237 n. 76
Blum, Lawrence 251 n. 22, 252 nn. 3–5, 11, 253 n. 18, 254 nn. 8, 11
Bonner, Raymond 235 n. 61
Borgin, Karl 235 n. 65
Bornstein, David 234 n. 52
Borton, John 235 n. 63
Bradley, F. H. 246–7 n. 24
Brandt, Willy 232 n. 26
Bratman, Michael 242 n. 20, 247 n. 32
Braybrooke, David 226 n. 4, 247 n. 27
Brewer, Mark 243 n. 23
Brink, David 251 n. 17
Broad, C. D. 256 n. 3
Broadie, Sarah 247 n. 24
Brock, Dan 241 n. 10
Broome, John 237 n. 1, 242 n. 14, 250 n. 8, 255 n. 18
Brown, James A. C. 243 n. 23

Cambiano, Giuseppe 229 n. 30
Cameron, Catherine 235 n. 63
Campbell, John 228 n. 27
Cassen, Robert 232 n. 30
Cater, Nick 232 n. 29
Cathie, John 232 n. 23
Caufield, Catherine 232 n. 30
Chen, Shaohua 207
choices between goods 153–4, 256 n. 2
choices between lives 159–60
claims 116
Cleary, Seamus 234 n. 53
Cocking, Jane 235 n. 63
Cohen, G. A. 258 n. 3
Cohen, L. Jonathan 223 n. 12, 241 n. 10
collective moral requirements 7–8, 60–1
  derivation of individual requirements from 62–5, 74–6
  and Fair Share Views 9–10, 73–7, 244 n. 34
  generation of new 76–7
collectively vs individually based arguments 8–9, 10, 65
Collins, Joseph 231 nn. 10, 12, 232 nn. 30, 33
commitment goods 155–6, 171, 180–1
concern 16, 226 n. 5
conclusion concerning moral demands of affluence 174–5
  practical implications of 180–6
consequentialism 92
  and life-saving analogy 30–1
  welfarist 30–1, 67
contribution, effect of my 58–65
Corbett, Kathleen 235 n. 65
cost
  of meeting Extreme Demand 79–82, 132–4
  of meeting extreme moral demands 93–5, 132–4
  of saving a life 71–3, 215–20
Cottingham, John 242 n. 20, 245 n. 10, 246 nn. 12, 15, 246 nn. 19, 24, 249 n. 5, 252 n. 5
Coudouel, Aline 207
countervailing considerations in relation to beneficence 17–18
  non-immediacy and 23–6
  further candidates for 52–3, 191

Dancy, Jonathan 224 n. 21, 227–8 nn. 18, 21, 253 n. 17
Darley, John 242 n. 16
Darwall, Stephen 226 n. 6, 228 n. 25
Dasgupta, Partha 253 n. 14
Davidson, Donald 226 n. 6
Davis, Scott 246 n. 19
demandingness, problems of 90–107
  theoretical sources of 91–3
  three kinds of 90–1
Devarajan, Shantayanan 220
de Waal, Alex, 34, 44, 45–6, 230 n. 2, 231 n. 19, 232 nn. 21, 28, 234 n. 55, 235 nn. 58, 66, 237 n. 71
Dinham, Barbara 232 n. 30
distributive justice 9, 115–16, 124–5, 197–8
disunity of practical reason 100, 244 n. 2

donation, effect of single 58–65
Dorsey, Ellen 235 n. 67
drawing a line 176–7, 258 n. 9
  and saving lives directly 199–201
Drèze, Jean 231–2 nn. 13, 14, 15, 17–20, 233 n. 34
duties
  and claims 250 n. 8
  imperfect 103, 255 n. 19
  vs obligations 194
Dyer, Christopher 229 n. 30

Eade, Deborah 231 n. 12, 232 nn. 23, 24, 28
Eberstadt, Nicholas 237 n. 73
Ebrahim, Alnoor 235 n. 67
economic objections to aid 37–40, 42–7
Edwards, Michael 235 n. 67
Ehrlich, Paul 230 n. 6, 231 n. 7
Emerson, Ralph Waldo 233 n. 45, 252 n. 6
Engstrom, Stephen 247 n. 42
Equal Weighting View of impartiality 123–4
expensive goods 152–6, 183–4
Extreme Demand 78–9
  application to the poor 253 n. 15
  cost of meeting 79–82, 132–4
  rejection of 128–46
  replacement of 174
extreme moral demands 70
  advocacy of 90, 111, 244–5 nn. 3, 4
  cost of meeting 93–5, 132–4
  survey of arguments against 93–106

Fair Share Views 9–10, 73–7, 244 n. 34
fairness
  and collective imperatives 62–5, 250 n. 11
  and impartiality 115–18
  varieties of 115–17
Farrington, John 233 n. 47, 234 n. 54
Feinberg, Joel 224 n. 20, 242 n. 15
Feldman, Fred 223 n. 14
Fishback, Price 220
Fishkin, James 240 n. 1, 242 n. 15, 243 n. 26, 244 n. 31, 245 n. 8
Flanagan, Owen 242 n. 20, 243 nn. 22, 24, 249 n. 50, 255 nn. 21, 23
Foot, Philippa 229 n. 36, 245 n. 6
Foster, Phillips 211, 231 nn. 8, 10
Fowler, Alan 233 n. 46, 234 n. 53, 235 n. 63
Frank, Robert 228 n. 26
Frankena, William 226 n. 2, 246 n. 23
free riding 63–5, 193
Frey, R. G. 252 n. 13
Friedman, Marilyn 249 nn. 3, 4, 252 n. 9, 255 n. 21
friendship 130–3, 155–6, 162, 164, 169

Garnsey, Peter 229 n. 30
Geary, Bob 220
George, Susan 232 n. 30
German, Tony 212
Gert, Bernard 249 n. 5
Gewirth, Alan 225 n. 25, 230 n. 4, 237 n. 80, 246 nn. 14, 17, 19
Glover, Jonathan 238 nn. 5, 6, 240 n. 2, 244 n. 3
Godwin, William 244–5 n. 4
Goldstein, Irwin 221 n. 4, 230 n. 4
Gomberg, Paul 222 n. 5, 228 n. 25, 230 n. 4
Goodin, Robert 238 n. 4, 242 n. 15
goods
  choices between 153–4, 256 n. 2
  commitment 155–6, 171, 180–1
  vs harms 253–4 n. 3
  life-enhancing, *see* life-enhancing goods
  of partiality 129–31
  purely episodic 161–2
  requirement-grounding 150–1
  see also permission, arguments for
Greenspan, Patricia 226 n. 5
Griffin, James 242 n. 20, 251 nn. 20, 22, 255 nn. 20, 22, 256 nn. 25, 27, 29
Griffin, Keith 232 n. 26
Grotius, Hugo 221 n. 4
Gruzalski, Bart 238 n. 5

Haines, Michael 220
Hammer, Jeffrey 220

Hancock, Graham, 34, 41, 230 n. 2, 233 nn. 41, 43, 234 n. 49
Hanna, Robert 225 n. 25
Hansch, Steven 235 n. 62
Hardin, Garrett 230 n. 6, 231 n. 7
Harman, Gilbert 247 n. 38
Harsanyi, John 251 n. 18
Hayter, Teresa 233 n. 40
Hellinger, Stephen 232 n. 26
Hentschel, Jesko 207
Herman, Barbara 227 n. 15, 228 n. 19, 246 nn. 16, 19, 247 nn. 38, 42, 249 n. 3, 250 n. 5, 253 n. 18
Heyd, David 246 n. 13
Hill, Thomas 247 n. 42
Hines, Colin 232 n. 30
Hirway, Indira 231 n. 17
Hobbes, Thomas 246 n. 20
Hobbesian arguments against extreme moral demands 96
Hoffman, Stanley 221 n. 2
Hooker, Brad 246 n. 19, 258 n. 4
Hudson, Alan 236–7 n. 70
Hume, David 246 n. 20
Humean arguments against extreme moral demands 101
Hurka, Thomas 247 n. 24, 251 n. 21
Hursthouse, Rosalind 246 n. 19
Hutcheson, Francis 244 n. 4

Ignatieff, Michael 223 n. 16, 224 n. 17, 226 n. 4, 228 n. 26, 235 n. 59
Igneski, Violetta 225 n. 27
ignorance 49–50
immediacy 14, 223–4 n. 17
  and content of beneficent person's reason 21–3
  moral significance of 27–9
  non-immediacy as countervailing consideration 23–6
immoral ends 17–18, 24, 159–60
impartiality 114
  appropriate 112, 114, 118, 121–4
  and beneficence 118–22
  and fairness 115–18
  and morality 91–3, 97, 126–7
  and rejection of Extreme Demand 113–15
individually vs collectively based arguments 8–9, 10, 65
integrity 156
interests
  malicious 17–18, 24, 159–60
  as providing reasons 134–6, 141–3
  in what it is wrong to have 137–41, 143–5, 192–3
iterative approach to life-saving analogy 70–1, 78
  case for 86–8
  fault in case for 190–1

Jackson, Frank 246 n. 19, 247 n. 26
Jackson, Tony 231 n. 12, 232 nn. 23, 24, 28
James, Susan 229 n. 36
Jennings, Michael 237 n. 71
Johnston, Philip 235 n. 63
Jones, John D. 223 n. 16
Jones, Peter 222 n. 9
justice
  arguments from 8–9, 196–9
  and beneficence 221 n. 4, 226 n. 3, 251 n. 15
  distributive 9, 115–16, 124–5, 197–8
  rectificatory 8–9, 196–7
  regulative 9, 198–9

Kagan, Shelly 224 n. 20, 227 n. 14, 228 n. 28, 240 n. 7, 241 n. 10, 242 n. 20, 243 nn. 22, 25, 244 n. 3, 248 nn. 40, 41, 252 n. 12
Kahneman, Daniel 254 n. 3
Kamm, F. M. 223 n. 14, 225 n. 27
Kant, Immanuel 103, 105, 221 n. 4, 227 nn. 15, 17, 229 n. 29, 233 n. 45, 247 nn. 37, 42–4, 255 n. 19
Kantian arguments against extreme moral demands 96, 101, 103–4, 105
Kantor, Shawn 220
Kekes, John 227 n. 11, 230 n. 4, 245 n. 9

kindness 18, 226 n. 3
Korsgaard, Christine 227 n. 17, 228 n. 19, 247 n. 35, 253 n. 18
Kumar, B. G. 231 n. 10
Kuper, Andrew 221 n. 4

Lancaster, Carol 232 n. 32
Lappé, Frances 231 nn. 8, 9, 10, 12, 232 nn. 28, 30, 31, 33
Latane, Bibb 242 n. 16
Lawrence, D. H. 247 n. 44
Leathers, Howard 211, 231 nn. 8, 10
Leavy, Jennifer 211
Lemmon, E. J. 258 n. 1
Lewis, David 240 n. 1, 244 nn. 32, 33
libertarianism 251 n. 14
Lichtenberg, Judith 225 n. 27
Liese, Bernhard 220
life, value of 129, 134–5, 255 n. 16
life-enhancing goods, intrinsically 129
  provisional list of 162–5
  vs purely episodic goods 161–2
life-saving analogy 10–15, 19–20, 173
  aid agencies' use of 34–5
  methodological challenge to 13–15, 20–1, 32
  vs threat-preventing analogy 54, 55–6, 66–7
  see also aggregative approaches to life-saving analogy; iterative approach to life-saving analogy
Lipton, Michael 232 n. 30
lives, choices between 159–60
Locke, John 221 n. 4
loss, requirement-grounding, *see* requirement-grounding goods/losses
luxuries 152–6, 183–4

McDowell, John 247 n. 35
McGinn, Colin 223 n. 14, 229 n. 36, 243 n. 29, 244 n. 33
McGoldrick, Patricia 247 n. 42
MacIntyre, Alasdair 246 n. 19
Mackie, J. L. 96, 242 n. 20, 246 nn. 20, 22, 247 n. 27
McKinsey, Michael 223 nn. 14, 15, 237 n. 77, 243 n. 29
McNaughton, David 242 n. 14, 253 n. 17
McNeill, Desmond 232 n. 30
Madeley, John 233 n. 43
malicious interests 17–18, 24, 159–60
Malthus, Thomas, 36–7, 230 nn. 5, 6
Maren, Michael 34, 41–2, 44, 45, 230 n. 2, 233 nn. 36, 41, 44, 234 nn. 48–51, 235 n. 62, 237 nn. 71, 75
Martin, Mike W. 229 n. 36, 240 n. 1, 242 n. 19, 245 n. 10, 246 n. 14
Masters, Andrew 211
Matin, Imran 234 n. 53
Matthews, Jessica 234 n. 52
Meadows, Donella 230 n. 6
Merchet, Jean-Dominique 233 n. 44
meta-ethical arguments against extreme moral demands 96
methodological challenge to life-saving analogy 13–15, 20–1, 32
Milanovic, Branko 208
Mill, John Stuart 255 n. 19
Miller, David 222 n. 8
Miller, Margaret 220
Minear, Larry 222 n. 6, 235 nn. 60, 63
Monroe, Kristen Renwick 243 n. 24
Moore, Andrew 256 n. 25
Moore, Mick 234 n. 53
moral theory, *see* theories of morality, normative
morally compelling reasons 135
  absurd denial of 141–3, 151–2, 192–3
Morris, Christopher 222 n. 8
motivational limits 81–2
Mulgan, Tim 242 nn. 15, 17
Murphy, Liam 74–6, 223 n. 12, 226 n. 1, 240 n. 7, 241 nn. 10, 12, 13, 242 nn. 15, 17, 244 n. 34, 246 n. 18, 247 n. 30

Nagel, Thomas 221 n. 4, 230 n. 4, 241–2 n. 14, 243 n. 22, 247 n. 31, 249 nn. 2, 3, 250 n. 6, 251 n. 17, 258 n. 3
  on demands of morality 245 n. 7
Najera, José 220

Narveson, Jan 224 n. 18, 229 n. 36, 251 n. 21
needs 226 n. 4
Nelson, Paul 235 n. 67
Newman, Lucile 231 n. 19
Nichols, Bruce 235 n. 56, 237 n. 72
Nietzsche, Friedrich 251 n. 21
non-altruistically-directed lives 158, 171
non-altruistically-focused lives 136
  and Extreme Demand 137–43
non-government organizations (NGOs) 41–8, 213
non-immediacy, *see* immediacy
Norman, Richard 252 n. 13
Nozick, Robert 251 nn. 14–15
Nussbaum, Martha 226 n. 3, 230 n. 4, 253 n. 14

obligations vs duties 194
O'Connor, John 245 n. 11
Odegard, Douglas 229 n. 36
Oderberg, David 252 n. 13
Oldenquist, Andrew 251 n. 22
Oliner, Samuel 243 n. 24
Oliner, Pearl 243 n. 24
Omar, Rakiya 237 n. 71
O'Neill, Onora 221 nn. 2, 4, 223 n. 14, 225 n. 25, 229 n. 36, 230 nn. 4, 6, 247 n. 37
Osmani, S. R. 231 n. 8
Otsuka, Michael 238 nn. 5, 7
Otteson, James 225 n. 26
overpopulation 36–9
Oxfam 48, 72, 237 n. 71, 240 n. 3

Paddock, Paul 230 n. 6
Paddock, William 230 n. 6
Parfit, Derek 229 nn. 31, 32, 238 nn. 5–7, 240 n. 2, 241–2 n. 14, 247 n. 35, 251 nn. 17, 20, 255 n. 16
partial compliance, requirements under conditions of 73–7, 99, 126
partiality, personal 130–1
  goods constituted by 129–31
  impartial defensibility of 114
particularity and beneficence 26–7
Paton, H. J. 227 n. 15
Pearse, Andrew 232 n. 30
Perfectionist View of impartiality 124
permission, argument for 147–50, 171–2
  and arguments from goods to lives 157–8
  and arguments from lives to goods 160–2
  and direct arguments concerning goods 150–6
  and direct arguments concerning lives 158–60
  and personal spending 167–71
  principle invoked by 149
permissive conclusion, rejection of 152–6
personal partiality, *see* partiality, personal
personal projects 131, 134, 156, 162–3
personal spending 249 n. 51
  permissible level of 167–71
Pettit, Philip 245 n. 6, 246 n. 19
Plato 246 n. 20
Pogge, Thomas 207, 221 n. 4, 222 nn. 9, 10, 230 n. 4
political objections to aid 38–41, 42–8, 222 n. 5
pooling of aid 58–65
Porter, Doug 232 n. 29
poverty
  badness of 10–11, 68, 135
  facts about 205–14
practical reason
  and arguments against extreme moral demands 100–2, 104
  disunity of 100, 244 n. 2
presuppositions of beneficence 102–6
preventing threats vs saving lives 55–8, 66–7
Price, Richard 245 n. 4
Priority View of impartiality 123, 196
problems of demandingness, *see* demandingness, problems of
Proceduralist View of impartiality 122–3
projects, personal 131, 134, 156, 162–3

Pufendorf, Samuel von 221 n. 4
purely episodic goods 161–2

Quinton, Anthony 258 n. 8

Rachels, James 223 n. 14, 244 n. 3
Raffer, Kunibert 212, 233 n. 42, 234 n. 53, 235 n. 63, 236–7 n. 70
Rahman, Atiur 234 n. 52
Railton, Peter 245 n. 9
Ram, Narasimhan 232 n. 21
Randel, Judith 212
Ravallion, Martin 207, 208, 231 nn. 12, 17, 19, 232 n. 26
Rawling, Piers 242 n. 14
Rawls, John 222 n. 9, 250 n. 7, 251 n. 19
Raz, Joseph 227 n. 18
Reader, Soran 229 n. 33
reasonableness of rejecting Extreme Demand 101, 111–12
reasons 22, 24, 226 n. 6, 227 n. 18
  for helping people 16, 21–3, 134–7
  motivating vs normative 228 n. 23
  see also morally compelling reasons; practical reason
Reath, Andrews 227 n. 17
rectificatory justice 8–9, 196–7
Reddy, Sanjay 207
Regan, Donald 238 n. 5
regulative justice 9, 198–9
required self-sacrifice 102, 194–6
requirement, argument for 147, 172–4
requirement-grounding goods/losses 150–1
  and begging the question 151–2, 192–3
requirement-grounding lives 159
requirements, moral 9
  and legalistic conception of morality 15
rescue, *see* saving lives
Riddell, Roger 235 n. 63, 236 n. 66
Rieff, David 35, 221 n. 1, 222 n. 6, 230 n. 3, 235 nn. 56, 59, 61, 237 n. 72
right to be helped 225 n. 25, 226 n. 3
Roberts, Suzanne 246 n. 19
Robinson, Mark 234 n. 53, 235 n. 63
Ross, W. D. 256 n. 29
Rutherford, Donald 238 n. 8

sacrifice, *see* cost; self-sacrifice
salience 27–8
Sargant, William 243 n. 23
saving lives
  cost of 71–3, 215–20
  directly, implications of my argument for 179–80, 199–201
  vs preventing threats 55–8, 66–7
  reasons for 134–5
Scanlon, T. M. 243 n. 26, 246 n. 19, 249 nn. 2, 3, 251 nn. 17, 20, 252 nn. 2, 4, 8
  on reasonable requirements of assistance 248 n. 39, 253 n. 16
  on reasons 226 n. 6, 227 nn. 9, 18
  on well-being 94, 246 n. 16, 256 n. 25
Scheffler, Samuel 244 n. 1, 245 n. 6, 247 n. 25, 248 n. 36
Schein, Edgar 243 n. 23
Schmidtz, David 224 n. 20, 230 n. 1, 233 n. 45, 235 n. 64, 237 nn. 74, 77, 240 n. 1, 242 n. 15, 243 n. 29, 244 n. 33, 246 n. 17, 247 n. 28
Schneewind, J. B. 221 n. 4
Schweitzer, Albert 80, 242 n. 19
Scoccia, Danny 242 n. 20
Scott-Taggart, M. J. 238 n. 5
self-abnegation 119, 120
self-sacrifice, required 99, 194–6
selfishness 22, 113–14
Sen, Amartya 37–9, 208, 225 n. 25, 231–2 nn. 8, 10–12, 14–20, 22, 233 n. 34, 253 n. 14
Severe Demand 70–3
Shue, Henry 221 n. 2, 225 n. 25
Sidgwick, Henry 224 n. 22, 229 n. 31, 237 n. 79, 240 n. 2
Sikkink, Kathryn 235 n. 70
Simmons, A. John 222 n. 8, 250 n. 9
Singer, H. W. 212, 232 n. 26, 233 n. 42, 234 n. 53, 235 n. 63, 236–7 n. 70

Singer, Marcus G. 258 n. 8
Singer, Peter 227 n. 13, 240 nn. 1, 2, 242 n. 15, 243 n. 21, 244 n. 3, 247 n. 29, 252 n. 10
  consequentialist commitments of 229 n. 36
  his life-saving analogy 2, 12, 223 n. 14, 224 nn. 19, 20, 22
Sinnott-Armstrong, Walter 227 n. 9, 228 n. 20
Skorupski, John 242 n. 14
slavery 28
Slim, Hugo 235 n. 66
Smillie, Ian 235–6 n. 63
Smith, David 235 n. 63
Smith, Patricia 225 nn. 26, 27, 228 n. 25, 244 nn. 30, 31
Sobel, Howard 237 n. 1
Sogge, David 34, 212, 230 nn. 2, 3, 233 nn. 36, 43, 235 n. 58
spending, personal, *see* personal spending
Stephen, James Fitzjames 224 n. 20
Sterba, James 221 n. 2
Stevens, Christopher 232 nn. 25, 26
Strawson, P. F. 254 n. 4
subsumptive picture of moral justification 12–13
Sumner, L. W. 256 n. 25
supererogation 102, 180, 202
Surr, M. A. 235 n. 63
Swanson, Eric 220
sympathy 22, 138

Taylor, Michael 238 n. 8
Taylor, Richard 246 n. 24
Telfer, Elizabeth 252 n. 12
Tendler, Judith 235 n. 63
Terhal, Piet 231 n. 17
Terry, Fiona 222 n. 6, 233 nn. 36, 44, 234 n. 50, 235 n. 57
Themudo, Nuno 213
theories of morality, normative 30
  and arguments against extreme moral demands 95–6, 201
Thomson, Judith Jarvis 224 n. 18
threats, prevention of 55–8, 66–7
Toye, John 232 n. 30
Trusted, Jennifer 225 n. 27, 237 n. 81, 247 n. 28
Tvedt, Terje 235 n. 60
Tversky, Amos 254 n. 3

Unger, Peter 223 n. 14, 224 n. 20, 229 n. 36, 240 nn. 2, 5, 7, 243 n. 21, 244 n. 3, 255 n. 14, 258 n. 4
  Bob's Bugatti example 72, 257 n. 7
  on cost of saving a life 216–17, 220
  and iterative approach to life-saving analogy 240 n. 1
  methodology of 225 n. 25, 227 n. 13
Uphoff, Norman 235 n. 67
Uvin, Peter 233 n. 36

Vibert, Frank 232 n. 26, 233 n. 35
virtue theory 31
von Braun, Joachim 231 n. 19

Waldron, Jeremy 222 n. 8
Walker, Ralph 227 n. 15
Wallace, J. D. 246 nn. 19, 21
Wallace, R. Jay 247 n. 36, 249 n. 52
Warnock, G. J. 246 n. 20
welfarist consequentialism 30–1, 67
Whelan, John 223 n. 14, 238 n. 4
White, Howard 211
Williams, Bernard 104–5, 225 nn. 27, 28, 245 nn. 6, 10, 247 n. 36, 249 nn. 46–9
Wilson, Catherine 247 n. 31
Wittgenstein, Ludwig 249 n. 47
Wodon, Quentin 207
Wolf, Susan 225 n. 28, 245 n. 9, 246 n. 15, 247 nn. 25, 31, 249 nn. 2, 3, 251 n. 22, 252 n. 4, 254 n. 12, 257 n. 6
World Bank 41, 205–7, 221 n. 1, 232 n. 30
wrongness
  vs blameworthiness 28–9, 50, 200–1, 237 n. 76

Young, Thomas 237 n. 82